Journal of Biblical Literature

Volume 137
2018

GENERAL EDITOR
ADELE REINHARTZ
University of Ottawa
Ottawa, ON K1N 6N5

A Quarterly Published by
SBL Press

EDITORIAL BOARD

ELIZABETH BOASE, Flinders University
HELEN BOND, University of Edinburgh
JO-ANN A. BRANT, Goshen College
TONY BURKE, York University
DAVID M. CARR, Union Theological Seminary
RICHARD J. CLIFFORD, Boston College
KELLEY COBLENTZ BAUTCH, St. Edwards University
COLLEEN CONWAY, Seton Hall University
TOAN DO, Australian Catholic University
KATHY EHRENSPERGER, University of Potsdam
GEORG FISCHER, Leopold-Franzens-Universität Innsbruck
PAULA FREDRIKSEN, Hebrew University of Jerusalem
WIL GAFNEY, Brite Divinity School
FRANCES TAYLOR GENCH, Union Presbyterian Seminary
SHIMON GESUNDHEIT, Hebrew University of Jerusalem
MARK GOODACRE, Duke University
MARTIEN A. HALVORSON-TAYLOR, University of Virginia (Charlottesville)
RACHEL HAVRELOCK, University of Illinois at Chicago
ELSE K. HOLT, Aarhus Universitet
DAVID G. HORRELL, University of Exeter
CAROLINE E. JOHNSON HODGE, College of the Holy Cross
JONATHAN KLAWANS, Boston University
JENNIFER KNUST, Boston University
BRUCE W. LONGENECKER, Baylor University
MICHAEL A. LYONS, Simpson University
DANIEL MACHIELA, McMaster University
JOHN W. MARSHALL, University of Toronto
NAPHTALI MESHEL, Hebrew University of Jerusalem
CHRISTINE MITCHELL, St. Andrew's College, University of Saskatchewan
KENNETH NGWA, Drew University
KEN M. PENNER, St. Francis Xavier University
PIERLUIGI PIOVANELLI, University of Ottawa
MARK REASONER, Marian University
THOMAS RÖMER, Collège de France and University of Lausanne
DALIT ROM-SHILONI, Tel Aviv University
JEAN-PIERRE RUIZ, St. John's University (New York)
SETH L. SANDERS, University of California, Davis
KONRAD SCHMID, University of Zurich
WILLIAM M. SCHNIEDEWIND, University of California, Los Angeles
ABRAHAM SMITH, Perkins School of Theology, Southern Methodist University
JOHANNA STIEBERT, University of Leeds
JOHN T. STRONG, Missouri State University
D. ANDREW TEETER, Harvard Divinity School
MATTHEW THIESSEN, McMaster University
STEVEN TUELL, Pittsburgh Theological Seminary
CECILIA WASSEN, Uppsala University
EMMA WASSERMAN, Rutgers University
LAWRENCE M. WILLS, Episcopal Divinity School

Managing Editor: Jonathan M. Potter, Society of Biblical Literature
Editorial Assistant: Caitlin J. Montgomery, Society of Biblical Literature

EDITORIAL MATTERS OF THE *JBL*

1. Prospective contributors should first review the *JBL* submission guidelines available at https://submissions.scholasticahq.com/sites/journal-of-biblical-literature/for-authors. If a manuscript is submitted in a form that departs in major ways from these instructions, it may be returned to the author for revision prior to being considered for publication.
2. Manuscripts may be submitted using our online platform at https://submissions.scholasticahq.com/sites/journal-of-biblical-literature.
3. Communications regarding the *Journal* should be addressed to Adele Reinhartz at jbleditor@gmail.com.
5. Permission to quote more than 500 words may be requested from the Rights and Permissions Department, Society of Biblical Literature, 825 Houston Mill Road, Suite 350, Atlanta, GA 30329, USA (E-mail: sblpressp@sbl-site.org). Please specify volume, year, and inclusive page numbers.

BUSINESS MATTERS OF THE SBL
(not handled by the editors of the *Journal*)

1. All correspondence regarding membership in the Society, subscriptions to the *Journal*, change of address, renewals, missing or defective issues of the *Journal*, and inquiries about other publications of the Society should be addressed to Society of Biblical Literature, Customer Service Department, 825 Houston Mill Road, Atlanta, GA 30329. Phone: 866-727-9955 (toll-free) or 404-727-9498. E-mail: sblservices@sbl-site.org.
2. All correspondence concerning the research and publications programs, the Annual Meeting of the Society, and other business should be addressed to the Executive Director, Society of Biblical Literature, The Luce Center, 825 Houston Mill Road, Atlanta, GA 30329. (E-mail: sblexec@sbl-site.org)
3. Second Class postage paid at Atlanta, Georgia, and at additional mailing offices.

Presidential Address
by
MICHAEL V. FOX

President of the Society of Biblical Literature 2017
Annual Meeting of the Society of Biblical Literature
18 November 2017
Boston, Massachusetts

Introduction given by Brian K. Blount
Vice President, Society of Biblical Literature
doi: http://dx.doi.org/10.15699/jbl.1371.2017.1371

Perhaps a good place to begin an introduction of Michael Fox is the word that opens the Festschrift honoring him: "How do you offer a tribute for someone who would just as soon quietly take his place among the academy's cadre of senior scholars? This problem has been largely solved by the 30 scholars whose articles published here attest Michael's influence and standing in academe. Their quick acceptance of invitations to write essays for this volume is itself a tribute to Michael."[1]

I was particularly fascinated when reading this introduction because of the energy the authors placed in describing Michael's dedication to his students. Clearly, one cannot speak about the work of Michael V. Fox without speaking to his "careful reading of Hebrew texts, his mastery of secondary sources, and his control of English prose."[2] And while the authors further noted Michael's research agenda in wisdom literature, it was not on this topic that their focus lingered. They lingered instead on his dedication and devotion to being the best mentor and instructor he could possibly be for those who studied with him. They went on to note that, while Job did feature prominently in his teaching, the topic of wisdom literature itself did not loom large in his classes generally. They noted that "his main purpose ... has been to give students exposure to the breadth of our discipline."[3]

I learned directly from Michael's former students that he was a rigorous teacher who expected a great deal from his students. He was also a humble colearner who expected to

---

[1] Ronald L. Troxel, Kelvin G. Friebel, and Dennis R. Magary, in *Seeking Out the Wisdom of the Ancients: Essays Offered to Honor Michael V. Fox on the Occasion of His Sixty-Fifth Birthday*, ed. Ronald L. Troxel, Kelvin G. Friebel, and Dennis R. Magary (Winona Lake, IN: Eisenbrauns, 2005), ix.
[2] Ibid., ix.
[3] Ibid., x.

discover new insights through his interactions with them. Allow me to share a selection of representative comments:

> I have said many times that Prof. Fox taught me how to read. It always feels a bit trite when I say that, but it's true. The way he would look at a given verse or passage from multiple angles; the way he would ask "why this word and not that word?"; the way he would think about what a text says and what it does not say; the way he would explore the depths of a metaphor; the way he would wrestle with a passage's ethical or social vision; the way he read the whole in relation to the part and the part in relation to the whole. He left no stone unturned. Delightfully, this is precisely the type of reading he displays in his publications.

From another:

> I first met Michael as his student in the graduate program of the Department of Hebrew and Semitic Studies at the UW–Madison. My initial response to him was fear. He was a demanding teacher, with little tolerance for lack of preparation or slovenly effort. Although those were characteristics I would come to appreciate for the drive they instilled in me, all of us students had a clear sense of his expectations and the seriousness with which he held them.… Over time, fear was replaced by profound respect, not merely for his response to students' concerns, but more so for his desire to learn from his students.

From another:

> I'm happy to wax positive about Michael. He's a great and prolific scholar. Working with him on his HBCE [The Hebrew Bible: Critical Edition] edition of Proverbs was a sheer delight. His intelligence, erudition, and sound judgment were always on display as we worked together to refine his edition and to think through various problems about how to produce an eclectic edition with a full text-critical commentary. His HBCE Proverbs is a magisterial achievement.

And finally:

> When I think of Prof. Fox's work, the words careful, conscientious, and soulful come to mind. His text-critical work is impeccably thoughtful and sensible. His works on Proverbs, Qohelet, Esther, and Job are downright edifying. I'm not certain he would like the words "soulful" or "edifying," but that's how I experience them. His commentaries, in particular, are so in touch with the texts on one hand, and so in touch with human experience on the other, that one reads what he says and thinks "of course it's that way." It's almost like he puts words to what people feel. There's a poetry to his writing. I remember Prof. Fox encouraging his students to write for art: figure out what you want to say, and then take it to the next level by making it artistic.

Given the described dedication to excellence in both his own work and that of his students, it is no wonder that one of his former students included a summative comment that well expresses the views of all of his students with whom I spoke: "Michael," he concluded, "has always personified my idea of the 'ideal scholar.'"

Michael V. Fox is the Jay C. and Ruth Halls-Bascom Professor of Hebrew Emeritus of the University of Wisconsin–Madison, having retired in 2010 after a brilliant scholarly career. Professor Fox received his BA and MA from the University of Michigan in Near Eastern Studies. Rabbinical ordination followed from Hebrew Union College. In 1972, he received the PhD in Hebrew Bible and the Ancient Near East from the Hebrew University of Jerusalem. He followed his graduate work with postdoctoral study in Egyptology at Liverpool University. He also holds an honorary Doctorate of Hebrew Letters from Hebrew Union College.

Professor Fox has served as an instructor and lecturer in Bible at Haifa University and the University of the Negev and as a lecturer in Bible and Egyptology at the Hebrew University. He has also been an affiliate professor at the University of Haifa. He arrived at the University of Wisconsin-Madison in 1977 as an assistant professor and remained until his retirement in 2010 as Professor and Chair of the Hebrew Department.

Professor Fox has served as an editor for *Hebrew Studies* and the SBL Dissertation Series and as a fellow of the American Academy of Jewish Research. He has also served as president of the National Association of Professors of Hebrew, SBL Midwest region, and, of course, as Vice President and President of the Society of Biblical Literature.

While his articles and book chapters are too numerous to list in our context, it is important to note some of the major book projects that he has accomplished during the course of his career.

> 1985: *The Song of Songs and the Ancient Egyptian Love Songs* [Hebrew: *Shire dodim mi-Mitsrayim ha-ʿatiḳah*]. This work was reprinted by the University of Wisconsin Press in 1989, 1999, and 2005.
>
> 1986: Popular commentaries on *Qohelet* and *Song of Songs*
>
> 1987: *Character and Ideology in the Book of Esther*, Studies on Personalities of the Old Testament (Columbia: University of South Carolina Press). A second edition was published in 2001, and the book was reprinted in 2010.
>
> 1999: *A Time to Tear Down and A Time to Build Up: A Rereading of Ecclesiastes* (Grand Rapids: Eerdmans).
>
> 2000, 2009: *Proverbs: A New Translation with Introduction and Commentary*, 2 vols., AB 18A, AYB 18B (New York: Doubleday [vol. 1]; New Haven: Yale University Press [vol. 2]).
>
> 2004: *Ecclesiastes: The Traditional Hebrew Text with the New JPS Translation*, JPS Bible Commentary (Philadelphia: Jewish Publication Society).
>
> 2015: *Proverbs: An Eclectic Edition with Introduction and Textual Commentary*, The Hebrew Bible: A Critical Edition 1 (Atlanta: SBL Press).

He is currently at work on *Job: A Commentary* in the Old Testament Library for Westminster John Knox Press and *From the Pharaohs to the Rabbis: An Intellectual History of Wisdom Literature* for Brill.

Clearly, as his own research and writing attest and as the comments from his students confirm, Professor Fox continues a wonderful career of extraordinary scholarship and mentoring. Along with the authors of his Festschrift, I can think of no better way to give thanks for his career than to appeal to the words they chose from Ben Sira 39:1–3 (NRSV):

> He seeks out the wisdom of all the ancients,
> And is concerned with prophecies;
> He preserves the sayings of the famous
> And penetrates the subtleties of parables;
> He seeks out the hidden meanings of proverbs
> And is at home with the obscurities of parables.

Colleagues, join me in welcoming Society of Biblical Literature president, Michael V. Fox.

The Meanings of the Book of Job

MICHAEL V. FOX
mvfox@wisc.edu
University of Wisconsin–Madison, Madison, WI 53706

The currently dominant readings of the book of Job agree on one essential point: the book refutes the retributory theology assumed to be Jewish orthodoxy, whereby God punishes the wicked and rewards the righteous. God is amoral. When expectations of divine justice are abandoned, divine injustice ceases to be a problem. Important points in the argument of this essay are that the narrative framework in the prologue and epilogue provides the premises of the book and is to be taken seriously, not dismissed as ironic or naïve. Further, God's speech in the theophany does not terrify Job into submission. This means that the book presupposes God's basic concern for justice. God offers Job verbal debate and in no way threatens him. God's rhetoric is directed not so much at emphasizing Job's ignorance as at making him call to mind how much he does know about God's wisdom, power, and providence. The present essay argues, first, that the book of Job teaches that God does punish and recompense, but incompletely. Justice is immensely important to God, but other principles and concerns may override it. Second, God wants human loyalty, even when justice fails. Third, God needs human help to run the world according to the divine will. God's need for humanity gives humans a place of high honor and perhaps some comfort in the midst of inexplicable suffering.

I. The Task

In the 1960s, when I was a rabbinical student at Hebrew Union College, I had the privilege of studying the book of Job with Professor Matitiahu Tsevat. The point of the book of Job, as he explained it, is that justice is *not* at work in the universe, not part of a divine design, not a characteristic of God. God is, in Tsevat's term, *amoral*. God neither rewards good deeds nor punishes bad ones. Without expectations of retributory justice, theodicy—the attempt to justify the unjust actions of a

---

I am grateful to my wife, Jane, for her thoughtful editing of my manuscript and her perceptive comments.

just God—ceases to be a problem, for God is morally neutral. The expectation of divine reward and punishment causes frustration and unhappiness. "Where justice is possible, injustice is too." This interpretation became Tsevat's 1966 article, "The Meaning of the Book of Job," which set a new path for Job interpretation.[1]

As a student, I accepted Tsevat's reading not only because of its innovation and acuity but also because I found it attractive personally, because it was closer to my developing views. For many years I taught Job by this approach, but I eventually abandoned it. One reason for the change was that Tsevat's interpretation of the theophany, which is to say, God's reply in chapters 38–41, came to seem forced, for reasons I will explain. The other reason was that, by Tsevat's theory, the book started to seem *too* comfortable, too easily harmonized with my own deepening skepticism. I needed to view the book from a distance, with *objectivity*, as scholars used to say. It is not my purpose to critique Tsevat's article, and I will not address all its contentions. Rather, I will use his idea as my framework for thinking about this issue.

I have written several articles on Job, some of which I draw upon and synthesize in this essay.[2] Here are the principles taught by the book, in my understanding: First, God does reward and punish and compensate, but incompletely. Justice—the invariable and appropriate reward or punishment for all deeds—is immensely important to God, but it may be overridden by other principles. Second, the book teaches readers to recognize God's beneficence and to remain loyal to him, even in affliction, even in the awareness that God can be unjust; in other words, it teaches the reader to maintain *faith*, a trust in God not based on knowledge. In this regard I move back toward the traditional interpretation, although it is based on a theology that I personally do not hold. Third, the book inculcates the disturbing yet elevating belief that God, for all his wisdom and power, needs human help if he is to rule the world the way he wants.

II. The Prologue

The prologue, Job chapters 1–2, provides the premises of the book and must be taken seriously, and I will use these chapters in describing the book's view of divine justice. There is, however, an alternate view, currently prominent. This holds

---

[1] Matitiahu Tsevat, "The Meaning of the Book of Job," *HUCA* 37 (1966): 75–106, here 97.

[2] Michael V. Fox, "Job 38 and God's Rhetoric," *Semeia* 18 (1981): 53–61; "Job the Pious," *ZAW* 117 (2005): 351–66; "Reading the Tale of Job (Job 1:1–2:13 + 42:7–17)," in *A Critical Engagement: Essays on the Hebrew Bible in Honour of J. Cheryl Exum*, ed. David J. A. Clines and Ellen J. van Wolde, HBM 38 (Sheffield: Sheffield Phoenix, 2010) 162–79; "Behemoth and Leviathan," *Bib* 93 (2012): 261–67; "God's Answer and Job's Response," *Bib* 94 (2013): 1–23; "The Speaker in Job 28," in *"When the Morning Stars Sang": Essays in Honor of Choon Leong Seow on the Occasion of His Sixty-Fifth Birthday*, ed. Scott C. Jones and Christine Roy Yoder, BZAW 500 (Berlin: de Gruyter, 2017), 21–38.

that the prologue is intended to cushion the blow of the book for the pious readers by showing them an anthropomorphic God who sits in his heavenly court and rewards and punishes justly. Sophisticated readers are supposed to recognize the prologue's naiveté by several features that are unbelievable or folkloric. But, in fact, everything in the prologue is consonant with and needed for what follows. Job's superlative righteousness, said to be unbelievable, is required for the development of the story. Without it the friends are right in insisting that Job has done something deserving of punishment. The scene of God in his court is said to be naïve, but this is only by modern standards. Premodern Jews, however sophisticated, believed in God's heavenly court as a physical reality. In any case, this scene is no more naïve than God's speaking from the whirlwind, which no one thinks disproves the credibility of the theophany. Moreover, the switch from prose to poetry at the end of the prologue is not a signal of a shift to a more credible genre, any more than the move from the prose account of the crossing of the sea to the poetic telling makes Exod 15 more credible than Exod 14.[3]

The prologue and the epilogue, whether composed by the main author or borrowed and adapted from a folktale, are integral to the book and its fictional reality. The prologue is a thought experiment, a narrative constructed to help us think through the problems and potentials of our own reality.

But if the prologue is not to be discredited, it does affirm reward and punishment as forces in the working of the world. It implies that, in the usual course of events, God does reward the righteous. Job is introduced in verse 1 as "innocent and honest, fearing God and avoiding evil," and verses 2–4 report on his prospering. I find it impossible to read this sequence as other than causal: Job prospered *because* he was righteous. The concurrence cannot be coincidental, as if implying that Job was righteous and just happened to be fortunate (a reading Alan Cooper prefers[4]), since readers who assumed that virtue brings rewards are assuming causal connection, and the book was written for them, not modern skeptics. In addition, the satan, too, assumes that God *wants* people to be just and that he *wants* to reward the righteous, because he must persuade God to make Job an exception.

But retribution is not an invariable, mechanical process. In the prologue, where Job is still holding to his piety, he declares, "The Lord gives; the Lord takes away. Blessed be the name of the Lord" (1:21b). As Rick Moore observes, Job does not assume that God's behavior can always be explained by the principle of retribution.[5] Job recognizes that good and bad fortune come and go according to God's

---

[3] There are some additional motifs that are proposed to be hints to the prologue's naiveté or irony. They are discussed in Fox, "Reading the Tale of Job." I argue that in no case do they indicate that the prologue is to be discounted in favor of the dialogue and theophany.

[4] Alan Cooper, "Reading and Misreading the Prologue to Job," *JSOT* 46 (1990): 67–79, here 67.

[5] Rick Moore, "The Integrity of Job," *CBQ* 45 (1983): 17–31, here 19–20. But I disagree with Moore's claim that this is an "admission of capricious rule" (20). God has his reasons.

unpredictable will and not only as clearly motivated reward and punishment. Job expresses no regret or penitence, for he sees no insinuation of guilt in his suffering. Soon, however, he will regard his suffering as an accusation of sin, albeit an unjust one.

By the premises of the prologue, this God is not amoral, not indifferent to the standards of justice. He basically wishes to do justice, but he sometimes finds it necessary, for reasons beyond human comprehension, to violate it. Here is my basic answer to Tsevat: In the book there is divine justice, but it is incomplete. It must be so, if human righteousness is to be pure. As the satan points out (1:9–11), if Job is invariably and fully rewarded for his virtues, his motivation might be the expectation of a payoff rather than unselfish, uncalculating love and fear of God. The purity of human loyalty is more important to God than the consistency of his own justice.

III. The Dialogue

When Job's friends arrive from afar, he sits with them in silence for seven days, then bursts into an angry lament. This is the same man as the patient Job of the prologue but at a different stage of grieving. His friends' silent presence has allowed the dams to break and the bitterness to pour forth.

In chapter 3, Job curses the day of his birth and, with it, the world into which he was born. This chapter is, as Leo Perdue says, an "assault on creation."[6] In so many words Job says: life is bad, and death is the only good. Subsequently Job will try to demonstrate this by particular examples.

In the dialogue, Job's view of God is fractured. To Job, God is, on the one hand, unremittingly hostile and unfair; on the other, the final source of hope and justice. As Job sees it, God is directing a violent attack against him, ludicrously sending archers to surround this broken creature as if he were a great enemy (6:4), a Yam or Tannin (7:12). God torments Job at all hours, even pursuing him into his dreams. He both hides his face from Job (13:24) and breathes down his neck, searching out the slightest flaws (7:17, 10:6, 13:27). Not only does God treat Job as his enemy (7:17–29, 19:11, 27:7, etc.), but his hostility embraces all humanity. God created a dreary world for creatures that would be better off dead. Or so it seems to Job.

If Job were really guilty of wrongdoing, he could find some comfort in knowing that he and God at least shared the same ethical standards, and he could try to live up to them. But, Job says, God afflicts Job—and others—with little attention to guilt or innocence. "If I am wicked, woe to me, and if I am righteous, I cannot raise my head. I am sated with disgrace and drunk with my misery" (10:14–15). Not only

---

[6] Leo G. Perdue, "Job's Assault on Creation," *HAR* 10 (1986): 295–315, passim. See also Fredrik Lindström, *Suffering and Sin: Interpretation of Illness in the Individual Complaint Psalms*, ConBOT 37 (Stockholm: Almqvist & Wiksell, 1994), 443.

does God fail to punish the wicked (21:7–33), but he savors the pain of his victims, even the innocent ones: God, as Job asserts in 9:13, "mocks the tribulation of the innocent."

Still, Job wants his day in court, because his complaint, however bitter, is founded on trust. This the belief, expressed often in the complaint of the individual psalms, that the divine listener "works within the same frame of reference and will concede the basis for our complaint."[7] Job's trust in God is expressed most powerfully when he demands a hearing, expecting—though not consistently—a fair one. God, Job says, "will be a salvation for me, because a fraud cannot come before him. I know I will be justified" (13:18). Job is confident of vindication: "For," he says, "[God] knows how I act [lit., 'my way']. If he assays me, I will come forth like gold" (23:10). Job persists in trusting in God's fairness, even though he sees no evidence for it. In chapters 29–31, his peroration, Job speaks almost like a typical complaint psalmist, bewailing his afflictions and alienation from God and insisting on his innocence, reinforcing his claims with a formal oath of innocence (31:1–40). Job is a complainant, not a rebel.

Job sometimes thinks of God as basically just and good but more often speaks of him as bad and unjust. Job tries out various metaphors to explain his dilemma. Is he being hounded by God or attacked full on? Is he the accuser or the accused, the judge or the judged? Will Job's divine assailant give him a fair hearing, which is what Job wants above all else? He knows he is innocent and that he was wronged—but little else.

IV. The Theophany

Job accused God of injustice, inconsistency, and hostility. He accused God of creating a grim world and treating the humans in it cruelly. The theophany, chapters 38–41, is God's response to these accusations, in particular to Job's assertion in chapter 3 that God has perverted creation. But the theophany does not address Job's accusation of personal abuse, which, as God must realize, cannot be denied. Instead, God tries to introduce Job to an alternate worldview, one that may ease his pain.

When God appears, he does not, contrary to what Job feared (9:17–18), terrify him into submission. He does challenge Job to gird his loins. This is, to be sure, a martial image, an act of preparation for battle, but God uses it as a metaphor for a verbal debate, as he says, "I will ask you and you inform me!" (38:3). He does not accuse Job of wrongdoing or of cursing him. He in no way threatens to harm Job, and in fact Job is already tormented beyond the reach of further harm. God grants Job his longed-for hearing and twice pauses to allow him to have his say. For a king to debate with an outraged subject is an expression of respect.

---

[7] Lindström, *Suffering and Sin*, 443.

God's speech is not spoken in anger and arrogance. It is not an attempt to terrify and humiliate the human wretch. He speaks in a tone of didactic persuasiveness and paints a picture of a well-tended world.

God begins both of his speeches by asking, "Who is this who obscures the design [עֵצָה] by words without knowledge?" (38:2, 40:1). This scolding assumes that there is a design in the world that Job could have known and that he does know on some level; otherwise, he would not be rebuked for obscuring it. Since Job has obscured the world's design, God will now clarify it, and the following speeches are to be understood as doing just that. God will offer instruction, teaching Job to recognize the design by pointing him to phenomena that exhibit it.

God's instruction makes extensive use of rhetorical questions. Their tone is not ridicule but persuasion, though, as is typical in pedagogy, they are not devoid of rebuke.[8] Most of the questions have obvious answers and remind Job that he knows much about God's wisdom and power, while also reminding him that much remains unknown. The questions that are beyond Job's grasp, such as "What is the gestation period of the gazelle?" (39:1), have the purpose of reminding him that God has the wisdom necessary for creating and maintaining the world. Job has the very significant wisdom needed to consider the expanses of the universe and recognize God's orderly, benevolent rule, even when many of the particulars remain beyond him. Perhaps his misery prevented him from doing so.

God asks, "Where were you when I founded the earth?" (38:4). If Job were to answer aloud and in full, he could say only, "Nowhere. I had nothing to do with the creation of the world. You did it alone." Job can hardly feel shamed by this fact. God further asks, "Who laid down its measurements—for you know—or who stretched a line upon it?" (38:5). No difficulty here. The parenthetical "for you know" is not facetious; Job knows quite well who the creator is. God's question is meant to evoke awe, not humiliation. And further, "Upon what are its [sc., the world's] sockets sunk?" (38:6a). Job knows the answer and has given it already in 26:7: "upon nothingness." This amazing fact can only evoke awe. The following circumstantial clause, "when the morning stars cried out and all the gods shouted" (38:7), helps paint a glorious and joyful scene, one reminiscent of a temple dedication. Note that this clause assumes Job's knowledge of the angelic rejoicing. God pays Job the compliment of assuming that Job—and, by implication, all humans—can understand much about God's skill as creator, his power as ruler, and the vast breadth of his concerns. In the very process of eliciting a teaching from Job's knowledge, God also reminds him of his inevitable ignorance of vast realms of facts and processes. To be aware of this ignorance is wisdom, too.

After setting the earth's platform in place, God brings the sea under control. In biblical mythology, YHWH fights and defeats Yam.[9] Earlier Job saw himself as

---

[8] Rhetorical questions can create a special intimacy of communication, even while maintaining a degree of facetiousness. I discuss this in "Job 38 and God's Rhetoric," 58–60.

[9] YHWH defeats Yam along with other sea monsters in Pss 74:13–14, 89:9–10, and Isa 51:9–10.

being attacked as Yam was attacked (7:21). Here, God has converted Yam from a monster into an unruly child, with God as his solicitous father (38:8-11). God encloses the infant sea in double doors, clothes him in clouds, and swaddles him in fog. Swaddling is a soothing practice that apparently makes a baby feel secure and quiets it down. But the sea is not, and never will be, entirely pacified, so God shuts him behind a boundary, which is the seashore, and says, with parental sternness, "Thus far and no farther! And here I stop the surging of your waves" (38:11).[10] The sea is still unruly, but not an antagonist. It would be a mistake to impose the sea's qualities as known from elsewhere onto the sea as envisioned in this passage. The author is creating a new vision of the sea, and he will do the like with Leviathan and other creatures.

God cares for his creatures. To the question "Do you hunt food for the lion?," Job's implied answer is "Of course not, but you do" (38:39-40). The lion, of course, does the actual hunting, but this striking question suggests that God, unseen, guides the hunt. God, not Job, prepares food for hungry raven chicks when they "cry out to God" (38:41). God, unseen, is their provider. Predation kills some animals even as it feeds others. This has been brought as evidence of the cruelty of the world God created.[11] But, as Maimonides observes, divine providence protects the species, not the individual.[12]

But does God care for the human species too? He never says he does, but the silence can be tactical. As evidence of divine indifference toward humans, and thus of the lack of justice in the world, Tsevat says that the rain God brings on the desert is "wasted on land uninhabited and uninhabitable" (38:26), an act that is useless and thus lacks moral purpose.[13] But מדבר is the steppe, which includes grazing land. When it receives rain, it blossoms with herbage, and herders bring their animals there to pasture, exactly the process described in Ps 107:33-38 as a blessing to humans.

Some animals were created in a way that preserves them from human exploitation—the wild ox, for example, which cannot be yoked, and the wild ass, which runs free in the desert. Perhaps God has done this to remind humans of their limitations. But he has also created plenty of animals that serve human needs.

The horse (39:19-25) is a special case. When God asks, "Do you give the horse his might" (39:19c), the unspoken answer must be, "No, but you do." But there is

---

[10] Read ופה אשבית גאון גליך. Other meaningful emendations, also using MT's consonants, are possible; see S. R. Driver and George Buchanan Gray, *A Critical and Exegetical Commentary on the Book of Job*, ICC (Edinburgh: T&T Clark, 1921), 300-301.

[11] Edward L. Greenstein, "The Problem of Evil in the Book of Job," in *Mishneh Todah: Studies in Deuteronomy and Its Cultural Environment in Honor of Jeffrey H. Tigay*, ed. Nili Sacher Fox, David A. Glatt-Gilad, and Michael J. Williams (Winona Lake, IN: Eisenbrauns, 2009), 333-62, here 355.

[12] Maimonides, *The Guide of the Perplexed* (Chicago: University of Chicago Press, 1963), Guide III.

[13] Tsevat, "Meaning of the Book of Job," 100.

more to be said. Far from demeaning human wisdom, God chooses an example that exalts it, for it is human wisdom and skill (and much is required) that shapes an unruly beast into a disciplined and fearsome war machine. The horse testifies to God's skills as craftsman, but human participation finishes the task.

The theophany concludes with two great monsters, Leviathan and Behemoth. For the author, both are meant to be real beasts, because the notion of mythical beast is anachronistic, despite the fact that their description includes features we know to be imaginary and based on myth. Leviathan was traditionally described as a fearsome dragon, the embodiment of evil, as in Job's words in 3:8. There has been a deliberate change in the theophany. Here Leviathan is, I have argued, based mainly on the whale, as known from seafarers' reports (see Ps 107:23–24).[14] He lives in the depths of the sea, shoots a spout, and leaves a wake. He also maintains some features of the serpentine dragon. In Ps 104:26, Behemoth, not known by this name elsewhere, fits the description of a hippopotamus for the most part, perhaps as reported by a traveler.[15] He is massively strong, but his strength seems to be for defense.

Many commentators emphasize the evil and violence of these two creatures and assume that their mere existence transmits these qualities to the world. In Job's theophany, however, neither beast actually does anything evil or aggressive. Both are just magnificent and undefeatable, except, of course by YHWH. Since they are under YHWH's control, they present no cause for fear, except for a human foolish enough to attack them. YHWH's defeat of Leviathan is the primeval and continuing act of justice. These creatures do not radiate evil to the world of the theophany, any more than the creation of great sea monsters in Gen 1:21 prevents God from concluding that all his work is "very good." As Carol Newsom says of these two beasts, "Although God's ability to overcome them is taken for granted, there is little or no reference to enmity or hostility between God and these creatures. Instead God describes them with evident admiration."[16]

The theophany reminds Job that God is a skilled creator, a generous and reliable provider for species, and a marvelous artisan and builder. God does not mention humanity, but, in a didactically sound way, he describes his care for animal species and leaves it to Job to draw the analogy with human life. The analogy is an easy one. Like animals, humans eat, reproduce, and feed their young, and God can hardly be absent from the process.

God does not directly respond to Job's questions about his suffering and the world's injustices but speaks about the natural world and its nonhuman creatures. According to David Clines, "the absence of a response is a most telling response, effectively, implicitly. The world that God has created, if its 'Design' (38:2) is

---

[14] Fox, "Behemoth and Leviathan," 261–64.

[15] Ibid., 261–62.

[16] Carol A. Newsom, *The Book of Job: A Contest of Moral Imaginations* (New York: Oxford University Press, 2003), 249.

properly understood, does not contain a principle of retribution."[17] Clines's conclusion is an unjustified inference from silence. God does not always answer questions, and he may sometimes answer them only obliquely. The psalmist in the complaints of the individual asks questions like "Why have you abandoned me?" and "How long, O Lord?," but no answer comes. God does not mention retribution here because that is not what the theophany is about. God has set aside the question of justice in the sense of retribution, which is not to say that there is none but rather that this is not what he chooses to describe. Job is not going to have the rightness of his suffering explained, because that would not help other sufferers. Job can learn in this revelation only what others could deduce without a revelation, by wisdom. Job is shown a world that is just but not perfect. Lions can eat gazelles, raiders can kill people, and gods can torment humans for unknown reasons.

Let me repeat the important restriction on the scope of God's teaching: God cannot tell Job why he is suffering or the book would become irrelevant to sufferers who do not get a personal revelation. (We can learn this as readers, for as such we stand above the world that Job—and God—live in.) For this reason, God changes the subject, from justice to wisdom. This wisdom holds that God has created and governs a world that is good, as in Gen 1. Life, contrary to Job's opening lament, is better than death, but it is still flawed. It has to be, or human fidelity would be inevitably suspect. The satan—that most acute of theologians—taught us this at the start of the book.

V. Job's Response

In 42:2–6, after YHWH's second speech, Job offers a confession that interweaves God's words into his own. God can do everything, Job says, while he, Job himself, is ignorant. His statement in verse 6, על כן אמאס ונחמתי על עפר ואפר, has ambiguities in almost every word.[18] Still, I think the traditional translation is sound philologically and fits the context: "Therefore I feel disgust and I repent on dirt and ashes." The verb מאס, like many verbs of feeling and perception, can be both transitive and intransitive (as this verb is also in 9:2, 32:5); and, as often, נחם means "regret," "repent," "retract." "On dust and ashes" is Job's current location and is also an objective correlative of his status and feelings, which Job epitomized earlier as קלתי, "I am trivial" (40:4).

But even if one accepts this translation or the like, the problem of tone and intention is still unresolved. One can simply say that Job is speaking ironically, as James Williams asserts, which is to say that Job is not sincere in his confession but

---

[17] David J. A. Clines, *Job 38–42*, WBC 18B (Nashville: Nelson, 2011), 1092.
[18] On my parsing of this verse and a survey of its interpretations, see the appendix to "Job the Pious," 364–65.

is trying to placate God by saying what God wants to hear.[19] (Tsevat, translating מאס as "retract," reads 42:6 as Job's repudiation of his erroneous belief in God's justice).[20] I think that Job *is* repenting—not for sins that may have brought on and justified the calamities but for having obscured God's design with ignorant words, which is what God accuses him of doing in 38:2 and 40:3 The author means this confession to be sincere. But whether it is sincere or evasive, which is to say merely giving the appearance of regret while concealing resentment from God's awareness, what is most important to the progression of the drama is that Job *express* regret before his God in the presence of his friends.

Job had offended God's honor by accusations and insults and must now make amends. Doing so requires a ritual to demonstrate subservience and honor, and the confession in 42:2–6, along with Job's expression of humility in 40:4, serves that role. This is a status ritual, to use the term of the sociologist Erving Goffman, or, in this case, a subordination ritual.[21] It is a conventional action whose performance reestablishes and affirms hierarchy, quite apart from the feelings actually held. Like a salute in the military or prostration in a royal court, performance is crucial. In the scene in Job, others are watching: the friends, probably the satan and other angels, and, most important, the reader. This ritual strengthens Job's stature before the sovereign and in no way detracts from his dignity, as an evasive confession would do. Perhaps Job is speaking "like a prince" after all, for a prince, too, must know and display his proper place before the king (Prov 25:6–7, Qoh 8:2, Sir 11:1). As for Job's interior life, that is his business.

VI. The Epilogue

The epilogue, often considered an extraneous happy ending, merely a sop to the pious, is in fact an integral extension of the plot. Immediately after Job's words of repentance, God says to Eliphaz and his two friends, "You have not spoken what is correct about me." Yes, there is more to this sentence, but let us first note that it is directed primarily at Eliphaz and the other two friends, with Job brought in only for comparison: "as has my servant Job" (42:7). The friends will face God's wrath unless they can get Job to intercede for them. Intercession would not be necessary if their mistake lay merely in having maintained a misguided but universally held theological tenet, namely, that God is uniformly just. What angers God is that they have hurt Job. They have been disloyal to their friend.

---

[19] James G. Williams, "'You Have Not Spoken Truth of Me': Mystery and Irony in Job," *ZAW* 83 (1977) 231–55, here 246–47.

[20] Tsevat, "Meaning of the Book of Job," 91.

[21] Erving Goffman, *Interaction Ritual: Essays in Face-to-Face Behavior* (Chicago: Aldine, 1967), 56–57.

The friends erred in insisting that Job's suffering was punishment for some sin. Now the friends must correct their error not by repenting but by appeasing Job. They will thereby have to recognize that Job has a special closeness to God and is not a sinner.

This verse, 42:7, is commonly understood to validate everything Job has said —paradoxically so—since Job spoke many things that were manifestly wrong and God has said that Job spoke in ignorance (38:2, 40:3). Job was right, however, in insisting on his innocence throughout the dialogue. In context, this is what God is affirming as correct. When the friends recognize and acknowledge Job's innocence by asking for his intercession, Job intercedes and God grants his request.

God restores Job's fortunes, but only after he has interceded on behalf of his friends (42:10). Job must do his part to heal the breach with his friends, who, unlike his relations and fair-weather friends (42:11; see 6:1), have stuck by him all along and have done their clumsy best to help him. The restoration of Job's fortune is not a reward (for Job has done nothing calling for one) or a gift of free grace (for this God is not gracious) but a payment of reparation (hence the verb שׁב, "give back," equivalent to the *hiphil* השיב). God's failure to respond directly to Job's lengthy and largely accurate accusations is virtually a plea of nolo contendere, and God, knowing himself to be guilty of having harmed Job הנם, "without warrant" (2:3), must make reparation. He pays double: one part being recompense, the other a penalty. His honor demands it—as does his justice.

VII. THE BOOK AS A WHOLE

The theophany is God's self-defense, not against all charges of injustice but against Job's opening complaint in chapter 3 that God created a miserable world in which life is worse than death. God cannot rebut Job's charge of having caused him unjustified suffering, because God has; and Job can receive no further explanation of his case, because the experiment requires that Job's ignorance continue even now and forever, so as to make it relevant to other sufferers. So what can Job learn that will help him?

God's first teaching to Job, and the author's message to the readers, is *faith*: to trust in God's goodness, even when knowledge fails and goodness is not visible. I state this as the author's message, not my own. It is explicit in the prologue, when God accepts the satan's rigorous view that one must fear God without expectation of reward. But reward may come, and so may misfortune, and so may some reparation. Or maybe not.

This faith is not a comfortable feeling, a confidence that God will do good for you whatever may be, but rather a rugged fidelity to a just but unpredictable ruler, one whose sovereignty requires unpredictability yet whose goodness allows an expectation of fairness and of aid—or at least of openness to human claims: God listens. Job's faith is, as William Brown says, "a defiant trust, that God will ultimately hear him out" (see 23:6–7).[22] For Job to maintain his faith when justice fails and suffering makes no sense is precisely the challenge the satan presented.

Did Job pass the test? Like so much else in the book, this remains unresolved, with commentators on both sides. We will never know the answer to this question, because God pays no further attention to the satan's destructive and unreasonable challenge. Instead, he moves on to the affirmative teachings of the theophany. God has grown by this experience.

Another teaching is equally important but usually neglected: that sufferers and their suffering are important to God. The relationship requires faith in two directions. There is a divine–human partnership.

Job never learns why he suffered, but he does learn that God considers him important, for he appears to Job in a prophetic vision, takes the trouble to persuade him of something, publicly affirms his virtue in the epilogue, and pays him reparations, necessarily incomplete, for the damage he caused. We the readers have already learned of Job's importance, for we know that God has chosen to rely on Job as his test case to prove the possibility of true human loyalty, and proving this is necessary to God's own honor.

Eliphaz asks, facetiously, "Can a man benefit God, or an intelligent person give him a benefit? Is it a delight if you are righteous, or a profit if you make your ways innocent?" (22:2–3). The answer, as both Eliphaz and Job would be surprised to learn, is yes, and this is why Job was so wrong when he said "I am trivial" (40:4).

Job was needy, and he yearned for divine fellowship. When God appeared in the whirlwind, he brought his fellowship. God too is needy, as Carl Jung recognized. God, Jung says, "needs Job's loyalty, and it means so much to him that he shrinks at nothing in carrying out his test. This attitude bestows an almost divine importance on humans, for what else is there in the whole world that could mean anything to one who has everything?"[23] To answer Jung's rhetorical question: God needs honor, the honor that comes from freely granted human loyalty, without considerations of reward or punishment. To prove that this is possible, God experiments on Job, though doing so causes undeniable and unjustified wrong to him, his family, and, as no one seems to notice, his slaves. God must really need Job. The hosannas of quiring angels could not match the honor that one lone, fragile man holds in his hands to offer.

---

[22] William P. Brown, *Wisdom's Wonder: Character, Creation, and Crisis in the Bible's Wisdom Literature* (Grand Rapids: Eerdmans, 2014), 134.

[23] C. G. Jung, "Antwort auf Hiob," in *Menschenbild und Gottesbild*, vol. 4 of *Grundwerk* (Olten: Walter, 1984), 224 (my translation).

The Impact of Siege Warfare on Biblical Conceptualizations of YHWH

ELIZABETH BLOCH-SMITH
e.bloch-smith@ptsem.edu
Princeton Theological Seminary, Princeton, NJ 08542

The physical devastation wrought by the campaigns of Tiglath-pileser III through Nebuchadnezzar with their concomitant death and suffering raises the question of YHWH's role in the unfolding events. In response to increasingly effective foreign siege technology, YHWH's portrayals in prophetic and Deuteronomistic texts evolve from the once-mighty warrior to a supreme commander employing Assyrian and Babylonian tactics in charge of Israelite and enemy forces alike.

One contribution of archaeology to biblical studies is to raise questions prompted by material remains. In this context, the physical devastation wrought by the campaigns of Tiglath-pileser III through Nebuchadnezzar with their concomitant death and suffering raises the question of YHWH's role in the unfolding events. Both biblical texts and archaeological evidence attest to successful assaults on settlements in Israel and Judah beginning in the late eighth century.[1] No match for the Assyrian and Babylonian armies, Israelites retreated from offensive to defensive strategies. This tactical shift occasioned a reconceptualization of the national deity, the warrior god YHWH. Eighth- to sixth-century prophetic and Deuteronomistic references to siege warfare and the deity's response increasingly portray YHWH as a warrior in a new guise, transitioning from field marshal to "situation-room" supreme military commander in charge of all forces—Israelite and enemy alike.

I. Archaeological Evidence of Seige Warfare in the Ninth- to Sixth-Century BCE Southern Levant

The new and improved, more-mobile battering rams of the ninth century, as depicted on Assyrian stone-carved reliefs, enhanced Assyrian fighting capabilities.

---

[1] All years and centuries cited are BCE, and all named sites refer to the ancient settlement, so tel/tell and ḥorvat/khirbet are omitted.

The six-wheeled ram of Assurnasirpal II (first half of the ninth century) covered in shields with a domed tower to accommodate soldiers was still heavy and clunky. Shalmaneser II's more sleek and svelte model pared down in size and weight, while an improvement, proved unwieldy over long distances. By the time of Tiglath-pileser III in the third quarter of the eighth century, the lightweight and maneuverable ram covered in skins and running on four wheels proved highly effective.[2] While the overpowering combination of siege ramps and battering rams is known from second-millennium Ebla documents and Old Babylonian inscriptions from Mari and Boğazköy, the pairing is not attested in southern Levantine contexts before the eighth century.[3]

Archaeological excavations reveal the devastation wrought by the Assyrian invasions. In general, the armies followed major lowland routes destroying strategic sites, especially at road junctions. To reach capital or other target cities, army contingents likely deployed into the highlands, as described in the Rabshakeh account in 2 Kgs 18:17. The extent of settlement destruction varied tremendously. Some important administrative or garrison towns were devastated, while other sites evidence only partial destruction focused on the city gate, in some cases with proximate public or elite structures. Sites to be refitted as Assyrian administrative centers sustained minimal damage.[4]

Major settlements of the northern kingdom were largely destroyed and depopulated by Tiglath-pileser III, Shalmaneser V, and Sargon II. Sennacherib devastated or compromised most of the urban centers and strategic sites of the south. Death, displacement, and disruption affected everyone by the end of the eighth century. Mass graves excavated at Ashdod and Lachish containing the remains of besieged and conquered victims vividly illustrate the profound human toll of siege warfare. Most of the more than fifteen hundred individuals from Lachish, including large numbers of women and children, died with no obvious injuries and so likely succumbed to dehydration, starvation, or illness. These unfortunate individuals, along with those decapitated and fatally injured, display the horrors of long-term siege and capitulation.[5] Cesspool and latrine contents from the 586 destruction of

---

[2] Peter Dubovský, "Tiglath-Pileser III's Campaigns in 734–32 B.C.: Historical Background of Isa 7, 2 Kgs 15–16 and 2 Chr 27–28," *Bib* 87 (2006): 153–70, here 153; Fabrice De Backer, *L'art du siège néo-assyrien*, CHANE 61 (Leiden: Brill, 2013), 11–88.

[3] Michael G. Hasel, *Military Practice and Polemic: Israel's Laws of Warfare in Near Eastern Perspective* (Berrien Springs, MI: Andrews University Press, 2005), 107. This assertion assumes that the Joab attribution in 2 Sam 20:15 is anachronistic (see below).

[4] For further details and references, see Elizabeth Bloch-Smith, "Assyrians Abet Israelite Cultic Reforms: Sennacherib and the Centralization of the Israelite Cult," in *Exploring the Longue Durée: Essays in Honor of Lawrence E. Stager*, ed. J. David Schloen (Winona Lake, IN: Eisenbrauns, 2009), 35–44.

[5] Lachish Tombs 107, 108, 116, and 120 (Olga Tufnell, *The Iron Age*, vol. 3 of *Lachish [Tell ed-Duweir]*, 2 vols. [Oxford: Oxford University Press, 1953], 1:187–96); N. Haas, "Anthropological Observations on the Skeletal Remains Found in Area D (1962–3)," in *Ashdod II–III: The Second*

Jerusalem evidence the increasingly restricted and unhealthy diet during the siege. Household garden plants from the mustard family (cabbage, mustard, radish, and turnip), types of lettuce, and artichokes replaced the standard fare of lentils, peas, wheat, and barley. Unsanitary conditions due to restricted water supplies, human excrement employed as fertilizer, and undercooked meat perhaps due to insufficient fuel would have caused the attested human intestinal parasites—tapeworm and whipworm.[6] Where was Israel's god?

II. Biblical Attestations of Siege Warfare

Biblical references to siege warfare employ a limited vocabulary of generalized terms with more technical terminology introduced in the Babylonian context. In Biblical Hebrew, most siege terminology derives from the root צרר, meaning "to bind/tie up," and its byform צור, used of battle with the meaning "to encircle" or "besiege." Forms of the root בצר, meaning "enclosed" and "made inaccessible," as of a walled town, are synonymous with derivatives of the root צרר. Terms formed from the roots *בקע and *פרץ convey the breaching of defensive fortifications. Even though inscriptions and archaeological remains demonstrate Assyrian use of siege ramps, siege engines, and battering rams, the specialized terms occur primarily in the context of Babylonian warfare and cluster in Ezekiel: *סללה ("to raise/lift up") designates a siege ramp or siege mound; כר and קבל refer to a battering ram or perhaps a siege engine; and דיק denotes a siege tower or a surrounding element such as a circumvallation wall.

According to Deuteronomy and the Deuteronomistic History, the conquest generation, David, and kings of the north (Israel) blockaded enemy towns (*צרר/צור). To conquer the promised land, YHWH commanded Israel to cordon off distant towns in order to defeat hostile forces (Deut 20:12, 19). David's army commander, Joab, successfully besieged Ammon (2 Sam 11:1) and allegedly erected a siege mound around Abel Beth-maacah far to the north (2 Sam 20:15). Among Israelites, only Joab erected a siege mound; all other references pertain to Assyria (once in 2 Kgs 19:32 = Isa 37:33; possibly Jer 6:6) and overwhelmingly to Babylonia.[7] For this reason, Joab's siege mound may be anachronistic. Thereafter, late tenth- to late eighth-century kings of Israel (but not Judah) blockaded enemy

---

and *Third Seasons of Excavations, 1963, 1965, Soundings in 1967*, 2 vols., Atiqot English Series 9–10 (Jerusalem: Department of Antiquities and Museums in the Ministry of Education and Culture, 1971), 1:212–14; Israel Eph'al, *The City Besieged: Siege and Its Manifestations in the Ancient Near East*, CHANE 36 (Leiden: Brill, 2009), 31–34.

[6] Eric H. Cline, *Jerusalem Besieged: From Ancient Canaan to Modern Israel* (Ann Arbor: University of Michigan Press, 2007), 60–61.

[7] Jer 32:24, 33:4, and possibly 6:6; Ezek 4:2, 17:17, 21:27, 26:8–9.

towns. Nadab, Baasha, Omri, and Pekah besieged Philistine Gibbethon, Judahite Ramah, Tirzah, and Jerusalem, respectively (1 Kgs 15:17, 27; 16:17; 2 Kgs 16:5).

Arameans from the time of Ben-hadad blockaded Israelite settlements, including the capital city of Samaria. Describing Ben-hadad's siege technique, Zakkur, king of Hamath, wrote, "They put up a rampart [*š/sr] higher than the wall of Hadrach, and dug a trench [*ḥrṣ] deeper than its moat" (*KAI* 202, line 10).[8] Ahab thwarted the Aramean offensive with the help of the provincial governor's squires, as advised by YHWH through an unnamed prophet (1 Kgs 20:1–21). In a possible second rendition of Ben-hadad's siege of Samaria, the prophet, here identified as Elisha, prophesied relief from the ensuing famine through miraculous divine intervention. YHWH caused the Arameans to hear the din of an approaching army—the heavenly host—prompting a retreat (2 Kgs 7:6). Rather than delineate two versions of the same siege, Wayne Pitard assigns the first battle to Ben-hadad I and the second to the early eighth-century Ben-hadad II to accord with the geopolitical circumstances of the reigns of Joash (2 Kgs 13:14–25) and the Jehu dynasty.[9] Prophetic stories also note marauding bands of Arameans blockading small towns. In pursuit of Elisha, a band encircled the town of Dothan, but the prophet miraculously resolved the conflict (2 Kgs 6:12–23). Each account in which Elijah or Elisha participated entailed miraculous divine intervention without battle, which leaves lingering questions about Israel's successful maneuvers but not necessarily about Aram's besieging Israelite towns.

In further instances of victorious foreign sieges of Israelite cities acknowledged in the Bible, Shalmaneser conquered Samaria (2 Kgs 17:5, 18:9) and Nebuchadnezzar destroyed Jerusalem (2 Kgs 24:10–11, 25:4, Jer 32:2, 37:5, 39:1, Ezek 4:3, Dan 1:1). Each notice employs the root צור/צרר* without mention of siege ramps or battering rams.

III. Israel's God Besieged

Excavated material remains, as well as biblical, Assyrian, and Babylonian references, attest to increased foreign breaching of Israel's defenses. How does this development—the relegation of Israel from offense to defense and from oppressor to vanquished—affect the conceptualization of the deity in the context of Israel's narrated linear history? How does the once-unassailable warrior god YHWH respond to the increasingly effective fighting forces conquering Israelite territory and subjugating the population?

From Joshua through 2 Kings, YHWH's role shifted from victorious battlefield

---

[8] John C. L. Gibson, *Aramaic Inscriptions, Including Inscriptions in the Dialect of Zenjirli*, vol. 2 of *Textbook of Syrian Semitic Inscriptions* (Oxford: Clarendon, 1975), 8–9.

[9] Wayne Pitard, "Ben-Hadad," *ABD* 1:663–65, here 664.

marshal to distant supreme commander of all military forces. In the beginning, to secure the promised land and establish the Davidic dynasty, YHWH and his host fought alongside Joshua, the judges Deborah and Gideon, Judah, and David.[10] As YHWH instructed David, "When you hear the sound of marching in the tops of the balsam trees, then go into action, for the LORD will be going in front of you to attack the Philistine forces" (2 Sam 5:24). This deity commanded a heavenly host of natural elements: hailstones; the sun, moon, and stars; torrential waters (Josh 10:11–13, Judg 5:20–21); and the quaking earth, fire, smoke, wind, thunder, rain, and lightning (1 Sam 12:18, 2 Sam 22:8–18). In this respect, YHWH resembles Ugaritic Baal, who armed himself with the forces of the storm—clouds, winds, lightning bolts, and rains (*KTU* 1.5 V.6–8).[11] YHWH fought on Israel's behalf with heavenly and earthly troops through the time of David. Some of these references to YHWH the warrior occur in old poetic texts celebrating Israelite victories of former times: Exod 15; Deut 32:41–42; 33:26–29; Judg 5; 2 Sam 22:7–18 = Ps 18:7–18; the core of Ps 68; and the Gibeon battle, noted to have been earlier recorded in the Book of Jashar (Josh 10:6–14a).[12] Patrick D. Miller adds old prose traditions of a divine commander and his troops: Josh 5:13–14, Gen 32:2–3, and 2 Sam 5:22–25.[13]

Already from the time of the judges, YHWH was occasionally absent from the battlefield. On those occasions, YHWH devised winning battle plans and deputized "judges" and commanders to lead the troops: an ambush against Ai (Josh 8:18), Barak's charge down Mount Tabor (Judg 4:6–8), Judah leading the battle against Benjamin (Judg 20:18–48), and David defeating the Philistines at Keilah and in the Valley of Rephaim (1 Sam 23:1–13, 2 Sam 5:23–24). In other instances, YHWH miraculously sowed chaos or panic among enemy forces, as in the battles at Gibeon, Mount Tabor, and Mizpah (Josh 10:10, Judg 4:15, 1 Sam 7:10).

After David and Solomon secured the kingdom, formerly victorious Israel was largely reduced to defensive tactics against superior armies. YHWH, who had mustered forces of nature to establish the Davidic kingdom, now donned no weapon, either natural or forged. From his "situation room," Israel's patron god determined military outcomes but did not enter the fray. When the Arameans attacked Jehoram's Israel, YHWH resorted to miraculous defensive actions such as blinding Aramean troops with bright light (2 Kgs 6:18) and causing them to hear the din of the approaching heavenly host (2 Kgs 7:6). Even in Jehoram's campaign against Mesha

---

[10] E.g., Josh 23:9–10, Judg 1:2–4, 5:23, 7:22; see Mark S. Smith, *The Early History of God: Yahweh and the Other Deities in Ancient Israel*, 2nd ed., Biblical Resource Series (Grand Rapids: Eerdmans, 2002), 80–86; Patrick D. Miller Jr., *The Divine Warrior in Early Israel*, HSM 5 (Cambridge: Harvard University Press, 1973; repr., Atlanta: Society of Biblical Literature, 2006), 156.

[11] Debra Scoggins Ballentine, *The Conflict Myth and the Biblical Tradition* (Oxford: Oxford University Press, 2015), 73–108.

[12] Miller also adds Hab 3:3–15 (*Divine Warrior*, 74–128).

[13] Ibid., 128–32.

of Moab, the once-mighty warrior god resorted to inducing visions rather than battle bravura (2 Kgs 3:17–22). Miraculous interventions raise red flags regarding the actual course of battle and its outcome. For these mid-ninth-century battles in the northern kingdom of Israel, YHWH neither led victorious Israelite troops into battle nor commandeered foreign forces. YHWH's sending a "savior/deliverer" to defeat Ben-hadad of Aram recalls the "judges" who led Israel to victory against oppressors, though in this case the anguished king rather than the people beseeched YHWH for help (2 Kgs 13:3–5). In the final divine intervention, in 701, YHWH sent an angel to slay the Assyrian soldiers amassed against Hezekiah's Jerusalem (2 Kgs 19:35).

According to the books of Samuel and Kings, YHWH did not raise a hand or brandish a sword in response to Israelite infidelity. Through the time of David, YHWH punished Israel for other offenses and always with forces of nature rather than the sword (1 Sam 12:18 [demanding a king], 2 Sam 21:1–2 [bloodguilt of Saul and his house], 24:1–16 [David's census]). When the Philistines attacked Israel, the stated reasons were political rather than religious (1 Sam 13, 17, 23). Beginning with the fall of Samaria to the Assyrians, however, YHWH mustered foreign armies to punish Israel for religious sins (2 Kgs 17:6–23; 18:9, 12).[14] Instances in Kings juxtapose a king's cultic abominations with an account of foreign invasion, such as Pharaoh Shishak's campaign during Rehoboam's reign (1 Kgs 14:22–25) and Jehu's losses to Aram (2 Kgs 10:31–33), but no explicit connection is made. Elsewhere, truly abhorrent royal behavior such as that of Manasseh would seem to warrant punishment, but the text's silence likely reflects a lack of foreign invasions during his reign (2 Kgs 21:1–18). Instead, the sinful scions Jehoiakim, Jehoiachin, and Zedekiah suffered Babylonian invasions and sieges for both Manasseh's and their own sins (2 Kgs 23:36–24:4; 24:8–10, 18–19). With the preordained, disastrous denouement rapidly approaching, Dtr summarily inserted "he did what was displeasing to the LORD" for each monarch in order to justify the end (2 Kgs 23:32, 37; 24:9, 19).

How might this development from field marshal to commander-in-chief be understood? From the perspective of a territorial state ruled by the Davidic dynasty, the nation must explain how it initially acquired the territory when beset by formidable past and present indigenous and neighboring foes. Surely, YHWH led the Israelites to victory in accordance with the traditional Levantine and Israelite conception of YHWH the warrior (Exod 15:3, Judg 5:23). Israel likely preserved old accounts of conquest and crafted stories of acquisition celebrating divine assistance in the distant past to claim the territory allegedly promised to Abraham, Jacob, and David (Gen 12:7, 17:8, 28:13–14, 2 Sam 7:10). The narrative shifts in the mid-ninth century when Israel begins losing territory to Aram and Moab. Those military

---

[14] Solomon loses half his kingdom for religious infidelity but to an Israelite, not a foreigner (1 Kgs 11:9–11).

conflicts in which Israel prevailed or survived a siege were attributed to miraculous divine intervention. From the later eighth through the early sixth century, however, superior forces fielded by the Assyrians and Babylonians bested Israel and Judah. For Dtr, YHWH commissioned these foreign forces to exact retribution for the kings' sinful behavior.

The prophetic books of Micah, Isaiah, Jeremiah, and Ezekiel conceptualized YHWH differently than did Dtr in response to Israelite losses to foreign besiegers. Each prophet retained the older notion of god the warrior, but YHWH did not fight on Israel's behalf; YHWH turned against Israel and mustered foreign armies. In spite of the prophetic books' composite character, the explicit identification of the enemy in conjunction with the adoption of siege terminology demonstrates a development from late eighth- through the early sixth-century writings.[15] Neither Amos nor Hosea invokes siege warfare, and for both of these prophets YHWH alone punishes obstinate Israel. Uses of siege terminology plus YHWH's commanding foreign forces to punish Israel begin in the later eighth century with the prophetic books of Micah and Isaiah.

The book of Micah speaks of divine retribution against YHWH's own people at the time of the devastating Assyrian campaigns, "Disaster from the LORD descended on the gate of Jerusalem" (1:12). This oracle overturned the traditional notion of the deity defending the gates, as voiced in a Ugaritic prayer: "When a strong foe attacks your gate, a warrior your walls, you shall lift your eyes to Baal [and say]: 'O Baal, if you drive the strong one from our gate, the warrior from our walls, a bull, O Baal, we shall sanctify'" (*KTU* 1.119.26–36).[16] In "anger and wrath" YHWH will wreak vengeance (5:14), but neither natural forces nor conventional weapons are invoked. Not blind to the political realities, the prophet acknowledged the threat from Assyria (5:4) and Babylonia (4:10) but did not present their armies as YHWH's conscripts and even foretold Israelite subjugation of Assyria and Nimrod, should Assyria attack (5:4–5).

The god depicted in Isaiah disciplined Israel through forces of nature (Isa 3:1, 5:25, 10:17) and an outstretched arm (5:25) but also, for the first time, with designated foreign armies—Arameans, Philistines, and especially the Assyrians (8:7, 9:10–11, 10:5–6).[17] Metaphorical YHWH manifested as fire, "The light of Israel will be fire and its Holy One flame" (10:17), as well as the storm, "like a storm of hail, a destroying tempest, like a storm of mighty overflowing waters" (28:2). The metaphorical punishing force was attributed to Assyria as well. YHWH raged as surging waters, and Assyria devastated in the form of floodwaters, "Assuredly the LORD will bring up against them the mighty, massive waters of the Euphrates, the king of

---

[15] Zephaniah, Nahum, and Habakkuk speak of divine punishment but do not use the language of siege warfare.

[16] See Dennis Pardee, *Ritual and Cult at Ugarit*, WAW 10 (Atlanta: Society of Biblical Literature, 2002), 149–50.

[17] This excludes verses that explicitly pertain to Babylon (e.g., Isa 13).

Assyria and all his multitude. It shall rise above all its channels and flow over all its beds and swirl through Judah like a flash flood reaching up to the neck" (8:7).

Ominously, YHWH appropriated Assyrian (and Babylonian) military tactics—staging a blockade causing famine and dehydration (Isa 5:13, 29:3), erecting siege ramps and siegeworks (29:3, 7) and battering gates (24:12). Isaiah 29:3, in particular, envisioned God laying siege to Ariel (Jerusalem), "I will camp against you ... lay siege to you with a mound/towers, and I will set up siegeworks against you." Escalation in siege warfare prompted a reconceptualization of God as the divine warrior in Mesopotamian guise employing Assyrian battle tactics. In addition, just as YHWH was once metaphorically palpable in overflowing waters, the deity is now manifested in the Assyrian army raging like floodwaters.

The date of Isa 29:1–8 impacts discussion of the "Assyrianization" of Israel's deity. Not surprisingly, attribution and dating remain a desideratum. Peter Machinist, Hermann Spieckermann, and Mark Smith represent scholars who defer Assyrianizing divine traits until the seventh century or later. Their arguments draw on diverse evidence: the reworking of Assyrian propaganda, adopted elements of vassal treaties, and the promotion of a monotheistic conceptualization.[18] Isaiah 29:1–8, however, suggests that Sennacherib's campaign at the end of the eighth century may have fostered Assyrianization of YHWH. The Jerusalem envisioned in Isa 29:1–8, besieged but saved, has been variously dated from the time of Sennacherib through the early sixth century. For example, John Watts considers Isa 29 to reflect the period of the Assyrian and Babylonian campaigns in the seventh and early sixth centuries, but this post-701 context fails to account for Jerusalem's alleged divine salvation in verse 6.[19] Christopher Seitz and Joseph Blenkinsopp date the passage in accordance with known historical events. They regard Isa 29:1–5a as an oracle of destruction in anticipation of Sennacherib's 701 campaign, with the update in verses 5b–8 adding the positive outcome.[20] Depending on the dating of this oracle,

---

[18] Peter Machinist, "Assyria and Its Image in the First Isaiah," *JAOS* 103 (1983): 719–37; Hermann Spieckermann, "Historiography, 'Rod of my Anger,' and Covenant: The Impact of Asshur on the Old Testament," in *Uomini e profeti: Scritti in onore di Horatio Simian-Yofre, SJ*, ed. Elżbieta M. Obara and Paolo D. Succu, AnBib 202 (Rome: Gregorian & Biblical Press, 2013), 319–42, here 322; Mark S. Smith, *God in Translation: Deities in Cross-Cultural Discourse in the Biblical World*, FAT 57 (Tübingen: Mohr Siebeck, 2008), 149–63.

[19] John Watts, *Isaiah 1–33*, rev. ed., WBC 24 (Nashville: Nelson, 2005), xcix–ci, 418–19.

[20] Christopher R. Seitz, *Isaiah 1–39*, IBC (Louisville: John Knox, 1993), 212; Joseph Blenkinsopp, *Isaiah 1–39: A New Translation with Introduction and Commentary*, AB 19 (New York: Doubleday, 2000), 402; but see Otto Kaiser, *Isaiah 13–39: A Commentary*, trans. Robert A. Wilson, OTL (Philadelphia: Westminster, 1974) 265–66. Both Ronald Clements (*Isaiah 1–39*, NCBC [Grand Rapids: Eerdmans, 1980]), following Hermann Barth (*Die Jesaja-Worte in der Josiazeit: Israel und Assur als Thema einer produktiven Neuinterpretation der Jesajaüberlieferung*, WMANT 48 [Neukirchen-Vluyn: Neukirchener Verlag, 1977]), and Willem A. M. Beuken (*Isaiah Chapters 28–39*, HCOT [Leuven: Peeters, 2000], 3–4) attribute the "woe" cries of Israel including

YHWH's besieging Jerusalem may evidence an Assyrianizing of the deity by the end of the eighth century.

Jeremiah's prophetic career, according to the book's introduction, spanned the reign of Josiah to Jerusalem's capitulation to the Babylonians (Jer 1:2–3). Despite repeated references to Josiah (1:2, 3:6, 36:2), most scholars consider the invocation a late addition and date the prophecies no earlier than the late seventh century in the context of Babylonian campaigns.[21] Comparable to the deity depicted in Isaiah, the god of Jeremiah punished the people with forces of nature (Jer 4:6, 23–28; 21:6) but also with an outstretched arm (21:5), conventional weapons (21:4), and an enemy from the north, explicitly identified as Babylon only in chapter 21 (1:15; 4:6–7; 10:22; 13:20; 21:4, 7). At YHWH's command, hostile forces blockade Jerusalem (1:15, 21:9) and erect siege mounds to breach and topple the walls (6:6, 32:24). Jeremiah is the first prophetic book to use the term סללה repeatedly as referring to a siege ramp, perhaps in reference to Assyria (Jer 6:6; see also 2 Kgs 19:32 = Isa 37:33) but certainly to Babylonia (Jer 32:24).

God as portrayed in Ezekiel, like the God depicted in Amos and Jeremiah, brandished the sword (Ezek 21:8–10) and commanded the traditional weapons of nature (13:11–13, 14:21). But Babylon was the primary agent of destruction, the actualization of YHWH's wrath (21:24–27, 23:22–25), "I will direct my passion against you, and they [Babylon] shall deal with you in fury" (23:25). As punishment for its infidelity, Jerusalem would be ravaged by the Babylonians in a divinely ordained assault with siege ramp (סללה), siege tower (דיק), battering ram (קר), and circumvallation wall (4:1–3, 21:27). Use of the specialized terminology for siege assault suggests the striking impact of this military tactic on Israel.

Prophetic works spanning the later eighth to the early sixth century drew on the older notion of the warrior god to relate YHWH's role in past and impending subjugations of Israelites. In the prophetic books discussed here, except Micah, YHWH mustered the powers of nature and the sword but employed them solely to fight against, rather than to support, Israel. Comparable to the Dtr presentation of YHWH, in the prophets YHWH also conscripted foreign armies to punish Israel. Oracles in the books of Amos and Hosea allude to an unnamed foreign enemy, though the "east wind" provides a clue. Oracles in Isaiah explicitly identify Assyria as the oppressor, while those in Jeremiah and Ezekiel name Babylonia as the

---

Isa 29:1–14 to a Josianic redaction, which allows for but does not necessitate an eighth-century date or context of origin.

[21] See, e.g., Robert P. Carroll, *Jeremiah: A Commentary*, OTL (Philadelphia: Westminster, 1986); Jack R. Lundbom, *Jeremiah 1-20: A New Translation with Introduction and Commentary*, AB 21A (New York: Doubleday, 1999), 100–101; Louis Stulman, *Jeremiah*, AOTC (Nashville: Abingdon, 2005), 6–7; Christoph Levin, *The Old Testament: A Brief Introduction*, trans. Margaret Kohl (Princeton: Princeton University Press, 2005), 79–80; Levin, "Noch einmal: Die Anfänge des Propheten Jeremia," *VT* 31 (1981): 428–40; Konrad Schmid, *The Old Testament: A Literary History*, trans. Linda Maloney (Minneapolis: Fortress, 2012), 126.

punitive agent. Isaianic prophecy departs from the others in the portrayal of YHWH as adopting Assyrian tactics and in depicting the Assyrians as a metaphorical, divinely sent, punishing force of nature.

IV. Summary

This marriage of archaeology and textual studies begins from a materialist perspective to consider the changing conception of Israel's patron god in response to ruthless and increasingly devastating Assyrian and Babylonian invasions with mounting territorial losses and human toll. It has been argued that improved Assyrian siege technology forced Israel to move from offense to defense. Already in the mid-ninth century, Arameans besieged Israelite sites with mixed success. By the end of the eighth century, however, enhanced siege tactics with battering rams and siege ramps ensured Assyrian and subsequently Babylonian victory.

Prophetic and Deuteronomistic texts responded differently to Israel's escalating suffering and inexorable defeat. Amos and Hosea, surely cognizant of earlier Aramean sieges, neither employ siege terminology nor name YHWH's mercenary forces. By the later eighth century, Isaiah's and Micah's oracles introduce a belligerent rather than a supportive patron god, siege terminology, and foreign armies conscripted by YHWH to punish Israel. Depending on the dating of contested passages, Isaiah may introduce YHWH the warrior adopting Assyrian tactics in the context of Sennacherib's campaign at the end of the eighth century. Through the late seventh and early sixth centuries, Jeremiah and Ezekiel foster this divine conceptualization in the context of Babylonian campaigns.

In the Deuteronomistic books, YHWH the warrior fights on Israel's behalf to secure the promised territory (Joshua, Judges, 1 and 2 Samuel). With the rise of Aram in the mid-ninth century, YHWH on occasion miraculously brings Israelite victory but also allows the Arameans to punish Israel (2 Kgs 13). With the advent of Assyrian and Babylonian superior siege technology, Israel's god adopts a new role. As advocated by the prophets, YHWH commissions enemy forces to destroy and defeat the sinful kingdoms (2 Kgs 17–25), but, in contrast and perhaps in response to the prophets, YHWH himself abstains from battling against Israel. The conceptual shift from field marshal to commander-in-chief may have begun as early as the mid-ninth century as the tide turned against Israel, but the deluge of the later eighth century surely necessitated a theological response.

Double Trouble: Counting the Cost of Jephthah

ROBIN BAKER
robin.baker@winchester.ac.uk
University of Winchester, Winchester SO22 4NR, UK

The list in Judg 10:6 of the gods of the surrounding nations to which Israel adhered in preference to YHWH is unprecedented in its detail. Moreover, it forms the literal center of the book of Judges according to the masoretic verse count. In the composition's rhetorical plan, similarly, it constitutes the fulcrum in the account of the relations between YHWH and his people. The worship of these deities and the syncretistic application of aspects of their cults to normative Yahwism provoke the response from Israel's god that he will deliver them no more and that they should "appeal to the gods you have chosen" for deliverance. This rupture in the relationship sets the scene for Jephthah's rise. The Gileadites, in extremis, take the initiative to engineer a human solution to a divine problem by approaching Jephthah, a social outcast with proven leadership and combat skills. This article analyzes the place and role of Jephthah in Judges; the repercussions of his brief ascendancy; his relationship with the minor judges, as well as with Ehud and Abimelech; and the meaning of the shibboleth incident. The conclusions challenge the widely held scholarly view, originally proposed by Martin Noth, that Jephthah is the common denominator between the judge-deliverer figures and the minor judges. In addition, it advances a new interpretation of the significance of the choice of the noun *shibboleth* as the password at the Jordan fords.

I. 40 X 2

In a paper published in 1980, J. Alberto Soggin lamented, "Despite forty years of research by leading exegetes, the problem of what the minor judges represent remains unsolved."[1] Today, nigh on forty years later, the reality is substantially the

[1] J. Alberto Soggin, "Das Amt der 'kleinen Richter' in Israel," *VT* 30 (1980): 245–48, here 246.

same. In those eight decades, consideration of the question has been shaped largely by the perspectives of Albrecht Alt and his student Martin Noth. Alt found in the minor judges an authenticity of historical record that he considered to be lacking in the accounts of the major judges. The chief basis for his conclusion was that their respective periods of office are given not in rounded figures, as in the case of the major judges, but in numbers that possess a "completely unartificial appearance."[2] Noth developed Alt's arguments to claim that the key to understanding the role of the minor judges in settlement-era Israel and their relationship with the major judges is furnished in the portrayal of Jephthah, who combines features of both. Alone among the charismatic military leaders, he was also a minor judge.[3] Given the influence that Noth's conclusions have exercised on successive generations of scholars,[4] it is worth quoting his supporting arguments:

> It is very conspicuous that Dtr. finishes his account of Jephthah not as he usually does, by saying that there were 40 years of "rest" after the victory of the hero concerned, but with details which follow the system used in the list of "(minor) judges": a statement concerning his six-year period of office, then the report of his death and place of burial. To this Dtr. attaches statements about three other "judges" who succeeded one another without a break and came immediately after Jephthah. Given Jephthah's presence in both traditions, it is easy to account for the arrangement of material in Judges. The "minor judges" come immediately before and after the Jephthah story: Judges 10–12 is obviously based on the stories of minor judges as Dtr. knew it.[5]

Noth states that the Jephthah narrative would resemble the descriptions of the minor judges more closely had it not been "excessively swelled" by the material dealing with his heroic feats or, as Hartmut Rösel puts it more graphically, if this material had not "ripped apart" the minor judge sequence.[6] Several commentators do not accept the sharp dichotomy that Noth perceived between the major and minor judges. Nevertheless, there has been broad support for his thesis that Jephthah provides the single common denominator between the heroic figures and the standardized list of individuals found in Judg 10:1–5, 12:8–15 and, therefore, uniquely elucidates the role of the judge, major and minor, in the book.[7] This

---

[2] Albrecht Alt, "The Origins of Israelite Law," in *Essays on Old Testament History and Religion*, trans. R. A. Wilson (Oxford: Blackwell, 1966), 79–132, here 102.

[3] Martin Noth, *The History of Israel*, 2nd ed. (London: SCM, 1960), 101–2.

[4] E. Theodore Mullen Jr., "The 'Minor Judges': Some Literary and Historical Considerations," *CBQ* 44 (1982): 185–201, here 186.

[5] Martin Noth, *The Deuteronomistic History*, 2nd ed., JSOTSup 15 (Sheffield: JSOT Press, 1991), 43.

[6] Hartmut Rösel, "Jephtah und das Problem der Richter," *Bib* 61 (1980): 251–55, here 251–52.

[7] See, e.g., E. Jenni, "Jephthah," *BHH* 2:810–11; Wolfgang Richter, "Die Überlieferungen um Jephtah: Ri 10,17–12,6," *Bib* 47 (1966): 485–556, here 555; Hans Wilhelm Hertzberg, *Die Bücher*

assessment, however, is overoptimistic; despite the extensive record of Jephthah's background, attitudes, and behavior supplied in the composition, in reality his story leaves us scarcely the wiser regarding the concrete role of "judge."

In summary, Noth's arguments for Jephthah's membership in the group of minor judges are that the formula "forty years of rest" is absent, the period of his tenure as judge is stated, and his death and place of burial are recorded. All these points, however, apply also to Samson, Jephthah's successor as a judge-deliverer. Moreover, although Jephthah's place of burial is unspecified, in contrast to those of the minor judges ("he was buried in the cities of Gilead" [12:7]), the writer makes a point of being precise in Samson's obituary: "they buried him between Zorah and Eshtaol in the tomb of Manoah his father; and he had judged Israel for twenty years" (16:31). According to Noth's criteria, what distinguishes Samson from the minor judges is that the number of years during which he judged Israel appears to be rounded. Yet there is no reason why twenty should not express as precise a period as the twenty-three years of Tola or, for that matter, the six of Jephthah. But even if one accepts that Samson's period of judging may be a rounded figure, a formidable difficulty besets the Alt-Noth view of the verisimilitudinous quality of the five minor judges' year attributions: taken as a group, they total seventy, one of the most symbolically loaded numbers in the Bible and hardly "unartificial."[8] Jephthah's exclusion from the list of minor judges on the grounds that the writer has deliberately compiled a group of judges who served for seventy years plainly presents a challenge to the prevailing view.[9]

Noth's final argument for Jephthah as a minor judge is that his pericope is lodged within the sequence of minor judges. On this basis, a case can be made, as Lillian Klein proposes, for Samson's membership in the group, since his story

---

Josua, Richter, Ruth, 4th ed., ATD 9 (Göttingen: Vandenhoeck & Ruprecht, 1969), 209, 218; Alan J. Hauser, "The 'Minor Judges': A Re-evaluation," *JBL* 94 (1975): 190–200, here 190 n. 4, 193, 200, https://doi.org/10.2307/3265729; Roland de Vaux, *The Early History of Israel*, 2 vols., trans. David Smith (London: Darton, Longman & Todd, 1978), 2:760–61; J. Alberto Soggin, *Introduction to the Old Testament: From Its Origins to the Closing of the Alexandrian Canon*, 2nd rev. ed., trans. John Bowden (London: SCM, 1980), 176; Soggin, *Judges: A Commentary*, trans. John Bowden, OTL (London: SCM, 1981), 207, but note 196–98; Soggin, "Das Amt der 'kleinen Richter,'" 245; Mullen, "'Minor Judges,'" 199, 201; John Gray, *Joshua, Judges, Ruth*, NCBC (Basingstoke: Marshall Morgan & Scott, 1986), 192–93; Barry G. Webb, *The Book of Judges: An Integrated Reading*, JSOTSup 46 (Sheffield: JSOT Press, 1987), 176 (hereafter *Judges: An Integrated Reading*); Timothy M. Willis, "The Nature of Jephthah's Authority," *CBQ* 59 (1997): 33–44, here 33; Daniel I. Block, *Judges, Ruth*, NAC 6 (Nashville: Broadman & Holman, 1999), 338, 342; K. Lawson Younger Jr., *Judges and Ruth*, NIV Application Commentary (Grand Rapids: Zondervan, 2002), 43.

[8] Robin Baker, *Hollow Men, Strange Women: Riddles, Codes, and Otherness in the Book of Judges*, BibInt 143 (Leiden: Brill, 2016), 151.

[9] In addition, the disparity between the volume of information that the writer provides on Jephthah, who spent less time as judge than any of the minor judges, and the sketchy résumés of the minor judges highlights the incongruity of his membership in their group. Compare Mullen, "'Minor Judges,'" 186 n. 5.

concludes the series.¹⁰ Samson is not introduced, however, with the formula "and after X," which is a unifying trait of the five minor judges—but then neither is Jephthah. Jephthah's story, nevertheless, does end with the formula "And after [Jephthah], Ibzan of Bethlehem judged Israel" (12:8).¹¹ This evidence is not as conclusive as it may first appear: if Samson was the final judge, no one could be said to come after him. No less troubling for the thesis is the existence of similar phraseology following the record of the book's second hero figure, Ehud: "and after him was Shamgar" (3:31).

Although comparative analysis reveals the weakness of each of Noth's points, there is no escaping the fact that the number associated with Jephthah in the role—six—does not conform to the numbers associated with the other major judges.¹² This prompts the questions: If Jephthah's number is not to be interpreted in terms of the minor judge set, how is it to be understood, and what might this reveal about the author's attitude toward him?

In order to answer these questions, it is necessary to consider the meaning of the numbers connected with the judge-heroes. Only with Jephthah and Samson do the year counts relate to periods of judging. Indeed, the book makes no mention of Ehud or Gideon actually "judging."¹³ The years associated with Othniel, Ehud, Deborah, and Gideon refer to the intervals of peace that the land enjoyed resulting from their divinely inspired victories, namely, forty, eighty, forty, and forty years respectively.¹⁴ Perhaps the opposition that is more important than rounded versus unrounded periods is years spent judging versus years spent enjoying the fruits of divine intervention. If the hero achieved something positive and long-lasting, this determines the year record; if she or he did not, the years spent in the role are given. The writer underscores this opposition by means of his characteristic wordplay:¹⁵ the predicate "be at peace, rest" is שקט, while שפט is the predicate "judge." The former is a motif in the first half of the composition, thanks to the achievements of the divinely appointed leaders. It is absent in the second half, in which Jephthah, who was in any case not divinely appointed (11:11, 29), and Samson, who was raised up by YHWH but who profaned his sacred vocation, secure miraculous victories but to no lasting effect.¹⁶ In its place שפט, the word that, in Judges,

---

¹⁰ Lillian R. Klein, *The Triumph of Irony in the Book of Judges*, JSOTSup 68 (Sheffield: Almond, 1988), 83.

¹¹ Compare Hertzberg, *Die Bücher Josua, Richter, Ruth*, 209; Hauser, "'Minor Judges,'" 193.

¹² On Jephthah's six-year term, see Willis, "Nature of Jephthah's Authority," 43–44.

¹³ J. Cheryl Exum, "The Centre Cannot Hold: Thematic and Textual Instabilities in Judges," *CBQ* 52 (1990): 410–31, here 412 n. 6.

¹⁴ Only in the instance of Gideon does the land's peace explicitly not outlive the champion (8:28), contra Susanne Gillmayr-Bucher, "Framework and Discourse in the Book of Judges," *JBL* 128 (2009): 687–702, here 693, https://doi.org/10.2307/25610214.

¹⁵ Compare Scott B. Noegel, "Paronomasia," in *Encyclopedia of Hebrew Language and Linguistics*, ed. Geoffrey Khan, 4 vols. (Leiden: Brill, 2013), 3:24–29, here 24.

¹⁶ Gillmayr-Bucher, "Framework and Discourse," 602; Alt, "The Formation of the Israelite State in Palestine," in *Essays on Old Testament History*, 171–237, here 178 n. 14; Block, *Judges*,

possesses an opaque signification, is used. Moreover, to underline the contrast, Jephthah's six-year שפט tenure represents but one-third of the length of time during which his adversaries, the sons of Ammon, "shattered and crushed" Jephthah's people (10:8).[17] The שקט–שפט opposition elegantly intimates both Israel's growing alienation from their god and the concomitant distortion of the judge-deliverer model that provide the book's main theme.

The wordplay between these two key terms through the book's central section (3:7–16:31) invites us to consider our strategy for reading the work. Noth's thesis regarding Jephthah's role in the composition is predicated on linearity: the fact that his story follows two figures who have features in common and is, in turn, followed by three further such figures is a major plank of his case for Jephthah's membership in this group, although Jephthah shares little of substance with them as a group. Such an approach does not give appropriate weight to the use of ring structures, *inclusio*s, intratextual parallelism, and cross-referencing, which, many scholars recognize, are rhetorical techniques employed widely in Judges.[18] The example of שקט–שפט demonstrates that in this book, as in other ancient narrative works, a text needs to be evaluated contextually, not merely in terms of its immediately contiguous neighbors but in terms of the entire composition.[19] Mary Douglas remarks, concerning the book of Numbers, that "it is rewarding to read Numbers … paying attention to the links connecting the parts to the whole structure instead of going from point to point in the linear sequence required in Western prose readings."[20]

One of the rhetorical devices used copiously in Judges is doubling, which occurs both intra- and interepisodically.[21] This observation is apposite for the

---

Ruth, 385. First Samuel shows that Jephthah and Samson failed to eradicate the military threat to Israel posed by their respective enemies, the Ammonites and the Philistines. This contrasts with the achievement of their predecessors.

[17] Alliterative wordplay characterizes this predicate pair also: וירעצו, וירצצו.

[18] David W. Gooding, "The Composition of the Book of Judges," in *Harry M. Orlinsky Volume*, ed. Baruch A. Levine and Abraham Malamat, ErIsr 16 (Jerusalem: Israel Exploration Society, 1982), 70–79; Younger, *Judges and Ruth*, 138–57, 219–32; Block, *Judges, Ruth*, 262 n. 531, 288, 354; Marc Zvi Brettler, *The Book of Judges*, OTR (London: Routledge, 2002), 81; David M. Gunn, "Joshua and Judges," in *The Literary Guide to the Bible*, ed. Robert Alter and Frank Kermode (Cambridge: Harvard University Press, 1987), 102–21, here 117; J. Cheryl Exum, "Promise and Fulfillment: Narrative Art in Judges 13," *JBL* 99 (1980): 43–59, https://doi.org/10.2307/3265699; Baker, *Hollow Men*, 121–56.

[19] Compare J. Gordon McConville, "1 Kings VIII 46–53 and the Deuteronomic Hope," *VT* 42 (1992): 67–79, here 78; Jan P. Fokkelman, *Reading Biblical Narrative: An Introductory Guide*, trans. Ineke Smit, Tools for Biblical Study 1 (Leiderdorp: Deo, 1999), 116–17.

[20] Mary Douglas, *In the Wilderness: The Doctrine of Defilement in the Book of Numbers*, rev. ed. (Oxford: Oxford University Press, 2001), 101.

[21] Yairah Amit, *The Book of Judges: The Art of Editing*, trans. Jonathan Chipman, BibInt 38 (Leiden: Brill, 1999), 54–55. For a discussion of the symbolism and rhetorical purpose of doubling in Judges, see Baker, *Hollow Men*, 58–59, 60, 77–83.

Jephthah cycle.²² I offer a few examples here, with others provided below in the discussion of Jephthah's dealings with the king of Ammon. The cycle begins and ends with references to Ephraimite territory (10:9, 12:1–6). Its hero is juxtaposed between two women whose relationship forms a chiasmus: his harlot mother and virgin daughter.²³ The word פליטי ("fugitives [of])" occurs twice in Judges in successive verses in the Jephthah section (12:4, 5).²⁴ Interepisodically, features and figures in the episode are paralleled elsewhere, enabling one event to be viewed and interpreted through the lens of another.²⁵ Thus, the verb תנה ("remember"), a word unique to Judges, appears twice with subtly different meanings. In its first occurrence, in the Song of Deborah (5:11), it denotes celebration. In its second, in the account of the annual festival to commemorate Jephthah's sacrificed daughter, it signifies "lament, mourn."²⁶ The four-day period of commemoration for her is reprised in the four days that the Levite spends in his father-in-law's house in Bethlehem, the prelude to the next act of violence against an Israelite woman recounted in the book (19:8–29).

While Jephthah shares specific traits with individual minor judges—he is a Gileadite like Jair; he and Ibzan alone among the judges are noted as having a daughter—the greatest number of correspondences between his story and those of other characters in the work is found in the accounts of Ehud and Abimelech, respectively.²⁷ Alone among the narratives treating the book's major figures, these three end with the statement "and after him." Parallels between Jephthah and Ehud are largely antithetic; with Abimelech, on the other hand, they are primarily synthetic. Theodore Mullen observes that the Abimelech section "effects a complete change in the movement of the narrative. After each of the figures preceding Abimelech (excluding Shamgar), the land enjoyed a period of rest from one to two generations in length. After Abimelech, no periods of peace are noted."²⁸

II. Perturbing Alignments

Both Ehud and Jephthah massacre thousands of their enemies at the Jordan fords.²⁹ With Ehud, the victims are Israel's adversaries fleeing east. With Jephthah,

---

²²Compare Younger, *Judges and Ruth*, 39–40.
²³Klein, *Triumph of Irony*, 99.
²⁴Younger, *Judges and Ruth*, 273.
²⁵Douglas, *In the Wilderness*, 39.
²⁶Compare Alice Logan, "Rehabilitating Jephthah," *JBL* 124 (2009): 665–85, here 675, https://doi.org/10.2307/25610213.
²⁷Barry G. Webb, *The Book of Judges*, NICOT (Grand Rapids: Eerdmans, 2012), 298–99, 343–45 (hereafter *Book of Judges*). On the parallels between Ehud and Jephthah, see Gooding, "Composition of the Book of Judges," 73.
²⁸Mullen, "'Minor Judges,'" 194.
²⁹Robert Polzin notes the analogous wordplay on the meanings "pass over" and "transgress" for עבר in the Ehud and Jephthah sections (*Deuteronomy, Joshua, Judges*, part 1 of *Moses and the*

they are his compatriots, fleeing west (3:28, 12:5–6). Ehud confronts a Moabite oppressor; the Philistines are the next enemy to arise against Israel (3:30–31). Jephthah battles an Ammonite oppressor; Israel's next foe is the Philistines (11:32–33, 13:1). The Moabites ruling Israel in Ehud's time were allied with the Ammonites (3:13). In both stories the period of oppression exercised by the respective "sons of Lot" is identical: eighteen years (3:14, 10:8).[30] Ehud goes twice to the king of Moab, on the second occasion twice promising "a message"; Jephthah sends messages twice to the king of Ammon. These embassies end in the defeat of Moab and Ammon, respectively. The word דבר ("word, message"; 3:19–20, 11:26) is pregnant for both stories. Ehud and Jephthah make spectacular use of language as a means of trapping their adversaries, though, in a chiasmus, the latter is also himself trapped by it.[31] The alternation between Moab and Ammon is central to Jephthah's discourse on Israelite history. He confuses the head of the Ammonite pantheon (Milkom) with his Moabite counterpart, Kemosh.[32] He compares the Ammonite king with whom he is parleying with the Moabite king whom Moses faced (11:24–25). Moreover, a king of Moab is recorded in the Bible sacrificing his child as a holocaust (2 Kgs 3:26–27),[33] a cultic practice Jephthah performed.

Standing in ironic counterpoint to Jephthah's deed, the description of Ehud's assassination of the king of Moab, Eglon, the "calf," is redolent of an act of sacrifice.[34] The term for the homemade blade with which Ehud kills Eglon—להב—is homonymous with the word for "flame."[35] We are, thus, offered a vivid contrast between Ehud's annihilation of the enemy as a divinely empowered action and Jephthah's shedding of the blood of Israelite kin in a cultic practice associated with the peoples whom the Israelites were expected to drive from the land (Lev 18:21, 27–28).[36]

Deuteronomist, A Literary Study of the Deuteronomic History 1 [New York: Seabury, 1980], 180–81); compare Francesca Stavrakopoulou, *King Manasseh and Child Sacrifice: Biblical Distortions of Historical Realities*, BZAW 338 (Berlin: de Gruyter, 2004), 194–95.

[30] Compare C. F. Burney, *The Book of Judges with Introduction and Notes*, 2nd ed. (London: Rivingtons, 1920), 295; Trent C. Butler, *Judges*, WBC 8 (Nashville: Nelson, 2009), 263.

[31] Dennis T. Olson, "The Book of Judges," NIB 2:721–888, here 821. Jephthah's fateful entrapment of himself, his family, and his legacy through utterance is foreshadowed in his name יפתח ("he will open," i.e., his mouth) (J. Cheryl Exum, *Tragedy and Biblical Narrative: Arrows of the Almighty* [Cambridge: Cambridge University Press, 1992], 48–49).

[32] Marc Zvi Brettler, "The Book of Judges: Literature as Politics," JBL 108 (1989): 395–418, here 406, https://doi.org/10.2307/3267111; Yuriah Kim, "Postcolonial Criticism: Who Is the Other in the Book of Judges?," in *Judges and Method: New Approaches in Biblical Studies*, ed. Gale A. Yee, 2nd ed. (Minneapolis: Fortress, 2007), 161–82, here 176.

[33] See Richter, "Die Überlieferungen um Jephtah," 513; Logan, "Rehabilitating Jephthah," 669–70.

[34] Webb, *Book of Judges*, 165–66; Brettler, *Book of Judges*, 29–33; contra Lawson G. Stone, "Eglon's Belly and Ehud's Blade: A Reconsideration," JBL 128 (2009): 649–63, here 649, 655 n. 23, https://doi.org/10.2307/25610212.

[35] Note the alliteration between להב and החלב ("fat") in 3:22, which reinforces the sacrificial allusion. In 13:20, להב denotes the flame rising from a sacrifice.

[36] On dating this text, see Jan Joosten, *People and Land in the Holiness Code: An Exegetical*

Jephthah's slaying of the Ephraimites at the Jordan fords is expressed using the technical term for the sacrificial slaughter of animals, שחט, which occurs only here in Judges. It offers an artful variant on the שקט–שפט parasonance, which defines the essential contrast between Jephthah and Ehud's respective legacies in Israel.

As regards the parallels between Jephthah and Abimelech, the first feature of both characters to confront the reader is their unconventional relationship with their fathers (8:31, 11:1–2). Jephthah is the son of a prostitute and was disowned by his father's family. Abimelech is the son of his father's Shechemite concubine, and he, too, appears to have been disowned by his father's family. Certainly, he disowns them.[37] Neither, however, escapes association with the paternal bloodline, and this leads, in different ways, to their elevation and thence to their most egregious actions.[38] K. Lawson Younger lists further synthetic parallels between Abimelech and Jephthah:

> Both recruit morally empty and reckless men to make up their armed gang (9:4; 11:3). Both are opportunists who negotiate their way into powerful leadership positions (9:1–6; 11:4–11). Both seal the agreement with their subjects in a formal ceremony at a sacred tree (9:6; 11:11). Both turn out to be brutal rulers, slaughtering their own relatives (9:5; 11:34–40) and engaging their own countrymen in battle (9:26–57; 12:1–6). Both end up as tragic figures without a future (9:50–57; 11:34–35).[39]

III. Double Trouble

It is evident, then, that the Judges writer is concerned to establish a connection for Jephthah, the penultimate in the hero series, with Ehud, the second in that company, and also with Abimelech, his immediate predecessor among the book's main characters. Unlike his Benjaminite counterpart, Jephthah did not provide peace for Israel. Indeed, like Abimelech, who brought about Israel's first civil war,[40] Jephthah is instrumental in the eruption of a second, even bloodier one. In contrast to Ehud, both men performed some kind of recognized function in the community: Abimelech "ruled [וישר] over Israel for three years"; Jephthah "judged" Israel for six (9:22, 12:7). In the light of the foregoing discussion, we return to the questions posed earlier: If Jephthah's number is not to be interpreted in terms of the minor judges, how is it to be understood, and what might this reveal about the

---

Study of the Ideational Framework of the Law in Leviticus 17–26, VTSup 67 (Leiden: Brill, 1996), 9 n. 30.

[37] On the implications of fatherlessness in ancient Israel, see Klein, *Triumph of Irony*, 98–99.
[38] Ibid., 77.
[39] Younger, *Judges and Ruth*, 42; also Klein, *Triumph of Irony*, 83–84; Butler, *Judges*, 281, 295.
[40] Webb, *Book of Judges*, 283; Naftali Kraus, *Bírák és próféták: A zsidó nép őstörténete* (Budapest: Wesley János Kiadó, 2006), 58.

author's attitude to him? Jephthah's year attribution is twice Abimelech's, exactly as the years associated with Ehud are, surprisingly, twice Othniel's (3:11, 30), the model of the judge-hero,[41] not to mention Deborah's and Gideon's. These facts are, I suggest, related and enable us to answer the first question. Jephthah's six years need to be understood as twice Abimelech's three. They are only tangentially related to the tenure periods of the minor judges, whose brief notices act to frame and thereby focalize the Jephthah cycle in the book. By the same token, Ehud's achievement is presented as twice Othniel's in the benefit it brought to the land.

In the Hebrew Bible, doubling functions in the legal code as a principle of inheritance for the firstborn son (Deut 21:15–17)[42] and of restitution for a crime (Exod 22:3, 6, 8 [Eng. 4, 7, 9]). On a spiritual plane, it is an expression of divine confirmation, blessing, and punishment (Gen 41:32, Zech 9:12, Isa 40:2, 61:7, Jer 17:18). Jeremiah proclaims the principle with searing clarity: "I will first recompense those who have defiled my land double for their iniquity and their sin" (16:18a).

Thus, the rendering of double in Yahwistic belief possesses emphatic, confirmatory, and retributive/reward aspects. Turning to Judges, in the writer's schema, the lavish use of pairings in the book provides a clue that doubling is significant in the interpretation of his composition. This ubiquitous feature, however, can only *allude* to the hermeneutical function of doubling. The author makes it explicit in a typically artful way by employing his characteristic cross-referencing technique,[43] and he does this in the opening verses of the book's central section, which contains all the year counts. The first foreign enemy to oppress YHWH's people in the promised land was Cushan-rishathaim, Cushan "the doubly wicked," or, as Susan Niditch translates it, "evil times two," king of Aram-naharaim, "Syria of the Double Rivers."[44] The author draws attention to the grammatical dual form of the oppressor's name by repeating it in the name of his kingdom, thus furnishing a rare instance of a rhyming couplet in Judges, which, again, serves to stress its importance.[45] The kingdom is translated "Mesopotamia" in the LXX, and this identification is accepted by many commentators, ancient and modern.[46] Although C. F. Burney averred that Cushan-rishathaim is "a name which can scarcely be the product of mere

---

[41] Robert H. O'Connell, *The Rhetoric of the Book of Judges*, VTSup 63 (Leiden: Brill, 1996), 83–84; Brettler, *Book of Judges*, 4.

[42] See C. F. Burney, *Notes on the Hebrew Text of the Books of Kings with an Introduction and Appendix* (Oxford: Clarendon, 1903), 265.

[43] Gunn, "Joshua and Judges," 105–7; Baker, *Hollow Men*, 81, 114.

[44] Susan Niditch, *Judges: A Commentary*, OTL (Louisville: Westminster John Knox, 2008), 56. Butler remarks, "Thus God gave Israel to Double Trouble" (*Judges*, 68); Block, *Judges, Ruth*, 153.

[45] Brettler, *Book of Judges*, 27; Noegel, "Paronomasia," 27.

[46] Block, *Judges, Ruth*, 152; Butler, *Judges*, 64–65. Josephus describes Cushan-rishathaim as "king of the Assyrians" (*Ant.* 5.3.2 §180). Younger, too, locates the kingdom in northern Mesopotamia (*Judges and Ruth*, 104–5).

invention," and Abraham Malamat endeavored to establish historical bona fides for him, nothing convincing has come of his and others' attempts.[47] To emphasize further the doubling that Cushan-rishathaim represents, his name is repeated twice before Othniel is mentioned in this section and twice after. Furthermore, this name occurs precisely twice as many times as Othniel's, ostensibly the episode's lead character.[48] In addition, with the name Cushan-rishathaim, the author introduces the subject of Mesopotamia, which will feature explicitly (18:30), and play an essential role implicitly, later in the book.

IV. Twice as Good, Twice as Bad

In a theology posited on the idea of peace and prosperity as the corollary of spiritual faithfulness to YHWH and observance of his laws, what was it about Ehud's leadership that resulted in doubling the period of quietness delivered by his model predecessor or by the judge-cum-prophetess who followed him? The narrative tells us: Ehud succeeds in uniting Israel by inspiring Israelites to participate in the work of God. The two verses in which Ehud makes his call to arms to his countrymen show them as one in following his leadership: "And when he came, he blew a shofar on Mount Ephraim, and the sons of Israel came down with him from the mountain and he went in front of them. And he said to them 'Follow (after) me, for YHWH has given your enemies, Moab, into your hand!' And they went down after him" (3:27–28).

This account is strikingly different from the report of the campaigns of Othniel and Deborah. Although both Othniel and Ehud are said to have been "raised up by YHWH to deliver Israel," and, moreover, "the Spirit of God was upon" Othniel (3:9–10, 15), his story gives no indication that he united the people behind his leadership. The account of Othniel's battle more closely resembles the narratives of Shamgar and Samson in its unswerving focus on a single hero. The victory is won by Othniel operating under the power of God's spirit: "he went out to fight, and YHWH delivered Cushan-rishathaim ... into his hand, and his hand prevailed against Cushan" (3:10). Compare this unbroken recital of singular forms with the plural used in the corresponding Ehud portion: "'into your [pl.] hand ... they descended ... they seized the fords ... they did not let ... they killed" (3:28–29). Ehud's call is based on Moab's being "your enemies" to be vanquished by "your hand." Once the Israelites obey his call, it is no longer Ehud plus Israel, let alone Ehud operating solo; the mission becomes Israel's mission, and God's appointed deliverer himself becomes simply a part of the united, conquering people of God.

---

[47] Burney, *Book of Judges*, 64–65; Malamat, "Cushan Rishathaim and the Decline of the Near East around 1200 BC," *JNES* 13 (1954): 231–42. For a digest of the research, see Younger, *Judges and Ruth*, 106–7. He describes the name as "a hebraized pejorative wordplay."

[48] Younger, *Judges and Ruth*, 102–3.

The Deborah cycle differs from the Othniel episode. Like Ehud, Deborah seeks to muster the Israelites, or at least the northern tribes. But she encounters opposition from some quarters (5:23), and half the tribes she summons prefer to be passive bystanders in the conflict (5:15–17).[49] Moreover, even from her own prophetically nominated commander, Barak, she faces equivocation (4:8–9). Gideon achieved unity in Israel only after the conflict with Midian, but he used it to subvert Yahwism by promoting a syncretized version (8:22–27). This initiative gained him great personal popularity during his lifetime but with the ultimate result that the peace in the land was violently shattered on his death and his memory disdained (8:28–9:5).

The message of Judges is that the unity of God's people, participating to achieve his purpose, was the determinant in doubling the period of peace following Ehud's victory. Such unity is witnessed already in the book's opening verse (Judg 1:1). Similarly, the story of the tower of Babel, in which YHWH states, "The people are one … they have one vernacular; … and now they are able to do everything that they purpose without restraint" (Gen 11:6), is a reminder that, according to this theology, human unity represents the most potent force on earth. Ehud's distinction lies in melding that unity with the celestial purpose and power, which gives the meaning to the eighty-year peace.

The double appearance of אחרי ("after") in 3:28, articulated first in Ehud's command and then in the Israelites' obedience to that command, links the narrative to the other two major figures with whom, as we have seen, the word is identified, Abimelech and Jephthah. It is to them we now turn.

Wolfgang Bluedorn suggests that the manner in which Abimelech's three-year rule is introduced bears more resemblance to the periods of oppression ascribed to Israel's foreign enemies than to its leaders. His argument is that, whereas the periods of the latter come at the ends of their sections, those relating to the former appear at the beginnings. Although he overstates the case—Abimelech is first mentioned in 8:31 and arrives in Shechem in 9:1, and his year count is supplied only in 9:22—Bluedorn's point holds and is buttressed by his second observation, namely, that the period is conspicuous by being the shortest of any in Judges.[50] To my knowledge, no commentators, irrespective of whether they perceive Judges to contain a pro- or antimonarchy ideology, have suggested that Abimelech's three-year rule brought benefit to the land and its people.[51] Before his rule, with the exception of the victims of Gideon's retributive action at Penuel and Succoth, which began the pattern of vindictive oppression by Israelite leaders of their own people, no

---

[49] Gregory T. K. Wong, "The Song of Deborah as Polemic," *Bib* 88 (2007): 1–22.

[50] Wolfgang Bluedorn, *Yahweh versus Baalism: A Theological Reading of the Gideon-Abimelech Narrative*, JSOTSup 329 (London: Sheffield Academic, 2001), 231–32. See also Block, *Judges, Ruth*, 322.

[51] Robert G. Boling, *Judges: A New Translation with Introduction and Commentary*, AB 6A (Garden City, NY: Doubleday, 1975), 170.

Israelite blood is reported to have been shed by a compatriot in the era of the judges. Abimelech changed this. His period began with the murder of seventy apparently innocent men and the dishonoring of his father; it ended with a civil war and the destruction of Israel's main city in the settlement era, Shechem. The narrative is exceptionally outspoken in assigning guilt to him and his Shechemite allies and in describing the consequent divine retribution on them both.[52] Beyond the formal markers, therefore, the evidence agrees with Bluedorn that Abimelech's three-year spell as ruler more closely resembles the periods of foreign oppression than the intervals associated with the leadership of Othniel, Ehud, Deborah, and Gideon.[53]

In contrast to his father, Abimelech displayed scant regard for cult. His most egregious iniquities were dishonoring his father (and, ultimately, his mother) and the blood pollution of the promised land. The gravity of this offense cannot be overstated. The law considers the spilling of Israelite blood without cause a heinous transgression against YHWH and a gross desecration of the land itself; consequently, it is injurious to the sanctity of the people: "You shall not pollute the land where you are going, for it is blood that pollutes the land, and the land cannot be cleansed of the blood that is shed in it except by the blood of him who shed it. Do not defile the land therefore that you will inhabit, in the midst of which I dwell, for I am YHWH who dwells in the midst of the sons of Israel" (Num 35:33–34).

This sin, therefore, rendered the land unfit for the habitation of a holy God[54] and posed a threat to the entire divine plan surrounding the settlement. The plan was for the Israelites to dwell in the land, which was divinely promised to their forefathers, in the presence and worship of YHWH and to enjoy his blessings. The legal code, by establishing cities of refuge (one of which was Shechem), aimed to prevent this sin (Deut 9:1–13, Josh 20).[55] Its expiation required the capital punishment of the perpetrator. God brings about the violent deaths of Abimelech and his erstwhile accomplices (9:56–57), thus cleansing the land. Abimelech, then, achieved the opposite of Ehud: he fractured the nation, beginning with his own family,[56] and, in the process, defiled the land.

---

[52] Polzin, *Deuteronomy, Joshua, Judges*, 174–75; Block, *Judges, Ruth*, 355; Webb, *Book of Judges*, 268; Thomas A. Boogaart, "Stone for Stone: Retribution in the Story of Abimelech and Shechem," *JSOT* 32 (1985): 45–56, here 49.

[53] Samson presents an anomaly for this assessment because not only did the foreign power continue to oppress Israel during his insurgency but his year attribution, like Abimelech's, is stated (first) midway through his story (15:20, 16:31).

[54] William Robertson Smith, *Lectures on the Religion of the Semites: The Fundamental Institutions*, 3rd rev. ed. (New York: Macmillan, 1927), 428–29, 446; compare Mary Douglas, *Leviticus as Literature* (Oxford: Oxford University Press, 1999), 131.

[55] So grave a transgression was blood pollution that, on the charge sheet against King Manasseh explaining YHWH's decision to "abandon what remains of my inheritance [Judah] and give them into the hand of their foes as booty and spoil," was the crime that the king had flooded Jerusalem with innocent blood (2 Kgs 21:14–16).

[56] On the debate concerning the degree to which Shechem had a Canaanite population, see

The proposition I am advancing is that the sins committed, the desecration effected, and the damage done to Israel's sanctity and cohesion by Jephthah were qualitatively and quantitatively worse than those perpetrated by Abimelech. Jephthah was "doubly wicked," and this is signaled by his year attribution being twice Abimelech's. Exceptional among all the year counts given in Judges for Israel's leaders, these two men did not attain seven years. The implications of this are considerable, since the seventh year was the time when the achievement of rest for the land (Lev 25:2–7, 20–21) and its people (Jer 12:12–22), as well as YHWH's ownership of the land, was celebrated.[57] The symbolic import of the tenure periods of Abimelech and Jephthah is that they provided no rest and no peace for either land or people.

Jephthah is principally remembered in literature, both exegetical and creative, for his vow resulting in the sacrifice of his daughter. Although the commentaries generally condemn the vow and sacrifice,[58] there have been many attempts to exonerate Jephthah, mainly by suggesting that the killing of his daughter did not literally occur[59] or that Jephthah did immolate her but out of foolishness, not degeneracy.[60] Certainly, his apparent abjectness on recognizing that it is she whom he must sacrifice in order to fulfill his vow to YHWH suggests that it sprang from the former, not the latter. As Cheryl Exum observes, however, it is noteworthy that he does not consider an alternative.[61] Besides, this argument goes, is not YHWH equally culpable because he permitted or, perhaps, engineered the series of events that culminated in the daughter's holocaust and did not provide an alternative, as he did with Abraham?[62] Exum states, "Jephthah is the worst of the lot [of judges], but not merely through a fault of his own."[63] Some scholars have argued that, in certain circumstances, the sacrifice of one's child in the context of religious practice in Syro-Palestine was an acceptable expression of Yahwistic belief and may have been a characteristic of popular Yahwism in the mid-first millennium BCE.[64] The muted

---

Brettler, "Book of Judges: Literature," 406. O'Connell maintains that Abimelech's mother was Canaanite (*Rhetoric of the Book of Judges*, 155).

[57] Biblical evidence indicates that the Sabbatical Year was observed in preexilic Israel (B. Z. Wacholder, "Sabbatical Year," *IDBSup*, 762–63).

[58] David M. Gunn, *Judges*, Blackwell Bible Commentaries (Malden, MA: Blackwell, 2005), 134–69.

[59] Ibid., 140–42, 147–53.

[60] See Logan, "Rehabilitating Jephthah," 665–66; Tony W. Cartledge, *Vows in the Hebrew Bible and the Ancient Near East*, JSOTSup 147 (Sheffield: JSOT Press, 1992), 177–85.

[61] Exum, "Centre Cannot Hold," 422; Exum, *Tragedy and Biblical Narrative*, 50.

[62] Jon D. Levenson, *The Death and Resurrection of the Beloved Son: The Transformation of Child Sacrifice in Judaism and Christianity* (New Haven: Yale University Press, 1993), 16–17. The question is perceptively explored in Block, *Judges, Ruth*, 370–79.

[63] Exum, "Centre Cannot Hold," 421 n. 22; see also Exum, *Tragedy and Biblical Narrative*, 48, 60.

[64] Stavrakopoulou, *King Manasseh*, 194–46; Stavrakopoulou, "The Jerusalem Tophet:

nature of the description of Jephthah's child sacrifice is thus to be understood as the narrator's tacit endorsement of Jephthah's deed.[65] The account perhaps intimates that the vow and its fulfillment were even animated by Yahweh's spirit, which had come upon the warrior.[66]

Discussion of the claim that child sacrifice was native to, and a feature of, preexilic Yahwism lies outside this essay's scope. My interest here is in what the author of Judges believed about this practice[67] and, specifically, how that belief is conveyed through the Jephthah story. In fact, Judges offers no approbation of cultic practices associated with the surrounding peoples, such as "passing children through the fire," a rite repeatedly condemned in the Bible.[68] The writer reveals his attitude to paedicide by the rhetorical framing he uses to set the Jephthah episode, namely, the description of the religious mores prevailing in Israel and YHWH's condemnation of them in the section that introduces the Jephthah cycle (10:6–18). Jephthah's willingness to make the vow, in the knowledge that the holocaust of his daughter was at least a potential outcome, and to carry it out to the letter, as well as his daughter's acceptance of her fate as a reasonable expression of piety, exemplifies how thoroughly by Jephthah's time the rites and rituals associated with the gods of, *inter alia*, Sidon (i.e., Phoenicia), Moab, and Ammon (10:6) had been absorbed into the Israelite cult.[69] In recounting Jephthah's actions, as in his treatment of Gideon and Samson[70] and Micah and Jonathan, the writer does not burden his composition with moralizing commentary. Rather, he allows the narrative to speak for itself, through the context it supplies and the aftermath it describes. His views, where intimated, are more likely to be conveyed obliquely—often, as we have seen, by using heuristic devices—than by explicit statement. This nuanced rhetorical strategy, however, in no way betrays theological heterodoxy. The theology of Judges

---

Ideological Dispute and Religious Transformation," *SEL* 29–30 (2012–2013): 137–58; Susan Ackerman, *Under Every Green Tree: Popular Religion in Sixth-Century Judah*, HSM 46 (Atlanta: Scholars Press, 1992), 139–43; Logan, "Rehabilitating Jephthah"; Levenson, *Death and Resurrection*, 4–5.

[65] Levenson, *Death and Resurrection*, 14.

[66] Stavrakopoulou, *King Manasseh*, 195; Stavrakopoulou, "Jerusalem Tophet," 147–48.

[67] Compare Levenson, *Death and Resurrection*, 15.

[68] Richter, "Die Überlieferungen um Jephtah," 513; Ackerman, *Under Every Green Tree*, 117.

[69] Ackerman, *Under Every Green Tree*, 120–25; Frank Moore Cross, "A Phoenician Inscription from Idalion: Some Old and New Texts Relating to Child Sacrifice," in *Scripture and Other Artifacts: Essays in Honor of Philip J. King*, ed. Michael D. Coogan, J. Cheryl Exum, and Lawrence E. Stager (Louisville: Westminster John Knox, 1994), 93–107.

[70] Like Gideon and Samson, Jephthah is mentioned in the New Testament (Heb 11:32–34) in a discourse on what mortals can effect by faith in God (cf. Jas 5:17–18). These men appear on account of their faith, not necessarily their righteousness, as Chrysostom recognized long ago: "Some find fault with Paul, because he puts Barak, and Samson, and Jephthah in these places…. For do not tell me of the rest of their life, but only whether they did not believe and shine in Faith" (John Chrysostom, *Hom. Heb.* 27 [*NPNF* 1/14:488]).

is that of a strict Yahwist writing in the seventh century BCE, probably, as Alice Logan contends, during Manasseh's reign.[71] One of her arguments for ascribing this date to the text is precisely that child immolation as a religious rite was a feature of that king's rule (2 Kgs 21:6, 23:10).[72] It therefore possessed a topicality at that time that is given expression in the Jephthah account, as blood pollution also is. In one of the few references elsewhere in the Bible to the era of the judges, the exilic Ps 106 (vv. 34–39) associates this time with child sacrifice and the blood pollution of the land.[73] Of all the individuals mentioned in Judges, Jephthah alone is identified with this combination of deeds. The psalmist regarded the combination as the nadir of wickedness and a metonym for all that YHWH condemned in Israelite conduct.[74] One may conclude, then, that in the exilic period and, on the evidence of Deuteronomy (12:31), Jeremiah (7:30–32, 19:5, 32:35), and Ezekiel (16:21, 20:31, 23:39), in the period that preceded it, such Yahwists considered child sacrifice an abomination. The Judges author is no exception.

The treatment of Jephthah in Judges reveals an individual who, with each step, strays farther from YHWH's standards. The holocaust of his child leads to the event that concludes his story, namely, the Gileadite–Ephraimite war (12:1–6).[75] Overshadowed, as it is, by the pathos of the daughter sacrifice, this war has attracted less attention. In addition, the appearance of "shibboleth" in the report has tended to divert attention from the story itself. Yet it is as great a transgression against normative Yahwism as the paedicide. In this conflict, Jephthah oversees the slaughter of 42,000 Israelites. This, as Butler observes, constitutes a greater body count than all the foreign enemies killed by all the judges combined.[76] The blood pollution, which began on a limited scale in Gideon's assault on Succoth and Penuel and then escalated during Abimelech's three years, becomes endemic as a result of Jephthah's actions. God acted to purge the land of Abimelech's defilement by the inflicted deaths of the perpetrators. But in the aftermath of the orgy of idolatry in which the Israelites participate before the Jephthah section, YHWH declares, "You have left me and served other gods. Therefore, I will no longer save you" (10:13). YHWH does not intervene again to cleanse the land but withdraws increasingly from it and

---

[71] Logan, "Rehabilitating Jephthah," 668, 684–85.

[72] Abraham J. Heschel, *The Prophets* (1962; repr., New York: Harper Perennial Modern Classics, 2001), 529.

[73] On the date of the psalm, see Tzvi Novick, "Law and Loss: Response to Catastrophe in Numbers 15," *HTR* 101 (2008): 1–14, here 9–10.

[74] Compare Bennie H. Reynolds, "What Are Demons of Error: The Meaning of שידי טעותא and Israelite Child Sacrifices," *RevQ* 22 (2006): 593–613, here 607–11.

[75] Exum, *Tragedy and Biblical Narrative*, 53.

[76] Butler, *Judges*, 300. It also very significantly exceeds the total of Benjaminites killed by Israel in the final and bloodiest of the civil wars described in Judges (20:35, 46). Webb holds that the number of Benjaminite casualties was 50,100 (*Book of Judges*, 340 n. 93), but this overlooks the fact that the entire Benjaminite force at the commencement of hostilities was 26,700 (20:15–16).

his people. Psalm 78:55–60, another text that treats the settlement era, describes YHWH abandoning his people in response to their provocation and idolatry. William Schniedewind argues compellingly that the text derives from Hezekiah's reign.[77] If so, the notion that, in the latter part of the settlement era, the Israelites experienced divine abandonment was current in the theological discourse in Jerusalem at the time Judges was composed.

If Jephthah's offenses were limited to the pollution of the land through a prohibited act of child sacrifice and the extermination of a vast number of Israelites, they would be grave enough. But he compounds these deeds to promote factionalism. Again, the precursor of this aspect of his story is found in Abimelech's actions. To achieve his ambition, Abimelech incites a conflict between the maternal and paternal branches of his family. Jephthah takes this further, championing tribalism rather than the unity of Israel. His appeal is in any case limited to Gilead and Manasseh (the tribe of Abimelech), and, although he claims to have called on the Ephraimites to join him in the battle against the Ammonites, the text belies this (11:29, 12:2–3).[78] Webb acutely describes the way in which Jephthah turns the vexatious complaint that the Ephraimites level against him into an intertribal conflict, aggravating already febrile intercommunal relations.[79] In a morbid caricature of the united Israelites vanquishing their Moabite oppressors at the Jordan fords, the narrative relates that "all the men of Gilead," marshaled by Jephthah, "battled the Ephraimites and the men of Gilead struck Ephraim.... Gilead captured the Jordan fords.... The men of Gilead said, 'Are you an Ephraimite?' If he replied, 'No,' they said to him, 'Then say "shibboleth."' ... Then they seized him and slaughtered him [שחט] at the Jordan fords" (12:4–6).

The slaughter of the Ephraimites demonstrates that the integrity of Israel as one people composed of twelve tribes united in the worship of one God was no longer valued. It portended the violent fragmentation of the Israelites along tribal lines and ultimately the eradication of the concept of the Israelites as a living entity.[80] The consequences of this development would be played out in a variable geometry for the rest of Judges and through the books of Samuel and Kings, until the ten tribes, which included both combatants of Judg 12, are torn from the land in the Assyrian deportations—in recent memory of the writer. It is, perhaps, significant that among the first to go, in the deportations carried out by Tiglath-pileser III, were the Israelite inhabitants of Gilead.[81] Furthermore, the Transjordanian tribes

---

[77] William M. Schniedewind, *Society and the Promise to David: The Reception History of 2 Samuel 7:1–17* (Oxford: Oxford University Press, 1999), 66–69.

[78] Soggin, *Judges*, 207; Willis, "Nature of Jephthah's Authority," 42–43; Block, *Judges, Ruth*, 382.

[79] Webb, *Book of Judges*, 339; see also Hertzberg, *Die Bücher Josua, Richter, Ruth*, 218.

[80] Baker, *Hollow Men*, 242.

[81] E. W. Heaton, *The Hebrew Kingdoms*, NCB.OT 3 (Oxford: Oxford University Press, 1968), 101–2; K. Lawson Younger Jr., "The Repopulation of Samaria (2 Kings 17:24, 27–31)," in *The*

are not included in the list of those who, in Jeremiah's prophecy, would offer sacrifices in the Jerusalem temple (17:26).[82]

V. Conspicuous Lisps

The mention of the Assyrians and shibboleth brings me to the consideration of their place in the narrative. Scholars who seek in the shibboleth story an excoriation of Ephraim to support an assertion that Judges represents a polemic against the northern kingdom are right only insofar as the narrative looks forward.[83] But it looks forward further than such verdicts allow. It does not end with the kings of Israel but has in view the destruction of the twelve tribes as a community through the deportations of the late eighth century, as intimated by the remark about them in 18:30. This verse constitutes the sole reference to a datable near-contemporary event in Judges.

Important work has been done in analyzing the sound processes that may have caused the reported dialect difference in the pronunciation of word-initial /š/ in pre-high vocalic position in the word šibbōlet/שבלת. Whether the articulatory phenomenon manifested in the Ephraimites' irregular pronunciation is best explained as the result of a phonological process or simply as phonetic variation awaits resolution.[84] To my understanding, though, the writer's purpose in relaying this episode was not chiefly to record a curiosity of Hebrew historical dialectology, albeit one with savage consequences. Rather, he inserts it into his composition because of the resonance it would have for his (immediate) readership. Consistent with the theological and prophetic purpose with which he approached his task, the writer uses šibbōlet to cast light on the vast implications of Jephthah's sin. The writer has already prepared the ground with the play on pivotal words with initial /š/ that differentiate Jephthah and Samson from their successful

---

Future of Biblical Archaeology: Reassessing Methodologies and Assumptions; The Proceedings of a Symposium, August 12–14, 2001, at Trinity International University, ed. James K. Hoffmeier and Alan Millard (Grand Rapids: Eerdmans, 2004), 254–80, here 254–55.

[82] Bustenay Oded, "II Kings 17: Between History and Polemic," *Jewish History* 2 (1987): 37–50, here 41–42.

[83] Brettler, "Book of Judges: Literature," 408; of Judges more generally as an anti-Ephraimite polemic, see Brian P. Irwin, "Not Just Any King: Abimelech, the Northern Monarchy, and the Final Form of Judges," *JBL* 131 (2012): 443–54, https://doi.org/10.2307/23488248; Block, *Judges, Ruth*, 384, 386; Younger, *Judges and Ruth*, 274. Note also Alexander Rofé, "Ephraimite versus Deuteronomistic History," in *Storia e tradizioni di Israele: Scritti in onore di J. Alberto Soggin*, ed. Daniele Garrone and Felice Israel (Brescia: Paideia, 1991), 221–35.

[84] The weight of opinion is toward the latter. See Ronald S. Hendel, "Sibilants and šibbōlet (Judges 12:6)," *BASOR* 301 (1996): 69–75; Robert Woodhouse, "The Biblical Shibboleth Story in the Light of Late Egyptian Perceptions of Semitic Sibilants: Reconciling Divergent Views," *JAOS* 123 (2003): 271–89.

predecessors. To underscore the connection he inserts another, שחט, as discussed above, precisely in the sentence that follows שבלת. Then, in the following verse, he positions שפט in the (for this study) focal clause "and Jephthah judged Israel for six years" (12:7). The phoneme /š/, which the event at the Jordan fords has exposed as deadly in the world in which Jephthah holds sway, shooshes through the phrase שש שנים (šēš šānîm, "six years"). Moreover, to reinforce the connection between /š/, the six years, and Jephthah with death, the next statement in the narrative is, in literal translation, "and died Jephthah the Gileadite."

Of all the lexemes with initial /š/ in Biblical Hebrew, why was שבלת the password of choice?[85] The Judges author deployed it in the knowledge that his audience would bring to their reception of his tale associations with the term that they already possessed.[86] With allusions between biblical texts, there is often the conundrum of relative chronology. In the case in question, however—the story describing the relations between the original Israelites, the ancestors of the twelve tribes—the relationship between Judges and the source goes well beyond general allusion. Specific lexemes from the Genesis narrative are exploited artfully by the writer to provide a "sacred-historical" context for the Judges account, indicating that he was familiar with a text not dissimilar from the version we know.[87] It is this narrative that furnishes the first mention of שבלת in the Bible, in the episode recounting Pharaoh's dreams, specifically that of the seven lush and good *heads of grain* (שבלת)

---

[85] Compare Klein, *Triumph of Irony*, 97; Arthur E. Cundall and Leon Morris, *Judges, Ruth: Introduction and Commentary*, TOTC (London: Tyndale, 1968), 151.

[86] Among the many examples of discussions of artful parallels with other biblical texts found in Judges, see Burney, *Book of Judges*, 443–45; Moshe Garsiel, "Homiletic Name-Derivations as a Literary Device in the Gideon Narrative: Judges VI–VIII," VT 43 (1993): 302–17, here 314–16; Walter Beyerlin, "Geschichte und heilsgeschichtliche Traditionsbildung im Alten Testament: Ein Beitrag zur Traditionsgeschichte von Richter VI–VIII," VT 13 (1963): 1–25, here 9–10; Geoffrey P. Miller, "Verbal Feud in the Hebrew Bible: Judges 3:12–30 and Judges 19–21," JNES 55 (1996): 105–17, here 110–12; Webb, *Judges: An Integrated Reading*, 148–53; Mieke Bal, *Lethal Love: Feminist Literary Readings of Biblical Love Stories*, ISBL (Bloomington: Indiana University Press, 1987), 29–33; A. Graeme Auld, "Gideon: Hacking at the Heart of the Old Testament," VT 39 (1989): 257–67, here 257–58; Ken Stone, "Gender Criticism: The Un-manning of Abimelech," in Yee, *Judges and Method*, 183–201, here 197–88; Gregory T. K. Wong, "Gideon: A New Moses?," in *Reflection and Refraction: Studies in Biblical Historiography in Honour of A. Graeme Auld*, ed. Robert Rezetko, Timothy H. Lim, and W. Brian Aucker, VTSup 113 (Leiden: Brill, 2006), 529–46.

[87] Eckart Frahm posits that this narrative in Genesis was written in the wake of King Esarhaddon's accession to the Assyrian throne (680 BCE), that is, during the reign of Manasseh ("'And His Brothers Were Jealous of Him': Surprising Parallels between Joseph and King Esarhaddon," *BAR* 42.3 [2016]: 43–64). If he is correct, the Genesis narrative is roughly contemporary with Judges. See also Jan Joosten, "The Distinction between Classical and Late Biblical Hebrew as Reflected in Syntax," HS 46 (2005): 327–39, here 339; Joosten, "YHWH's Farewell to Northern Israel (Micah 6, 1–8)," ZAW 125 (2013): 1–15, here 7–8. Schniedewind avers that explicit textual citation of the type evinced by Judges with regard to the Joseph narrative begins only from the seventh century (*Society and the Promise*, 70). He, too, dates the Joseph account to that century (101–2).

followed by the seven wasted *heads of grain* blasted by the east wind, which swallowed up the former (Gen 41:5-7). Pharaoh repeats this to Joseph (41:22-24). In all, the word in its plural form שבלים appears ten times and thus corresponds to the number of brothers who come to seek grain from Joseph. The result of his interpreting the dream in which שבלת is the focus makes the difference between life and death, as in Judg 12.[88] Joseph is given an Egyptian wife, Asenath, and she bears him two sons, Manasseh and Ephraim, in Egypt. We are explicitly told that both are born in the years of plenty, the years of the good שבלים before the desiccating wind blows from the east (41:50). Joseph names the first Manasseh because God had enabled him to forget his vexation and "all his father's house" and the second Ephraim because God had caused him to be fruitful. Thus, the divinely inspired handling of שבלת provided Joseph's passport from prison to vizier and the engendering of Ephraim, as well as Israel's passage from famine and certain death to plenty. Judah declares the position plainly: "we will go [to Egypt] that we might live and not die, we, you [Jacob], and our children" (Gen 43:8). The dream interpretation also, ultimately, brought about the reunification of the Israelites, ruptured by their betrayal of Joseph. In Judges, the term "house of Joseph" applies exclusively to Ephraim (1:22, 35).[89] The correspondence between Judg 12 and the Joseph narrative is echoed in another lexical root that is pivotal in the scene at the Jordan fords: פלט. In Joseph's account of his divinely ordained role, he affirms that "God sent me before you to cause you to live by means of a great *escape*" (Gen 45:7). Thus, the section that begins with the appearance of the שבלים is concerned throughout with the vivification and unification of the Israelites.

Jephthah's slaughter of the members of the house of Joseph is the mirror image of Joseph's life-saving act toward Jephthah's forebears. He dealt death to the escapees, and this deed, as discussed above, signaled the destruction of the Israelites as an entity, thereby reversing Joseph's divine achievement. Moreover, the Genesis narrative features the word יפתח(ו) ([*wa*]*yiptaḥ, jephthah*) at critical points in the plot. Following the report of the birth of Ephraim (41:52), Joseph "*opened* all the storehouses" (41:56), a phrase that, as it were, juxtaposes the two names: יפתח(ו) יוסף. It was this act that led to his brothers' journey to Egypt (41:57). The lexeme occurs when the brothers open their sacks (42:27, 43:21), and its final attestation is in the denouement of the tale of Joseph and his brothers when sacks are again opened and Benjamin's contains Joseph's cup (44:12).

The evidence indicates, then, that the Judges writer harnessed the text that contains the birth of Ephraim, the reunification of the Israelites after their first

---

[88] For a discussion of wordplay in the accounts of dreams interpreted by Joseph, see André Caquot, "Les Songes et leur interprétation selon Canaan et Israel," in Serge Sauneron et al., *Les Songes et leur interprétation: Egypte ancienne, Babylone, Hittites, Canaan, Israël, Islam, peuples altaïques, Persans, Kurdes, Inde, Cambodge, Chine, Japon*, ed. Anne-Marie Esnoul et al., SOr 2 (Paris: Seuil, 1959), 99–124, here 112–15.

[89] Gray, *Joshua, Judges, Ruth,* 240; Zecharia Kallai, "The Settlement Traditions of Ephraim: A Historiographical Study," *ZDPV* 102 (1986): 68–74, here 70.

rejection of (the house of) Joseph,⁹⁰ and the act of YHWH-inspired deliverance performed by Joseph for Israel to project in sharp relief the scale of Jephthah's sin and of its deleterious consequences for the cohesion of God's people. Jephthah became the death-delivering east wind for Israel. The parallel treating the beginning of the tribes reinforces the conclusion reached above regarding the meaning of the double number of Abimelech's years attributed to Jephthah: it conveys that Jephthah was "evil times two" in the injury he caused Israel.

The account of the Ephraimites' pronunciation of /š/ as /s/ in the shibboleth episode had an additional resonance for the writer's contemporary audience, one that was especially topical. As Brettler notes, "Ephraim" functioned as synecdoche for the northern kingdom.⁹¹ At the time Judges was composed, the ten tribes constituting "Ephraim" had been uprooted and removed to the reaches of the Assyrian Empire.⁹² The degree of assimilation of these Israelites to their Assyrian environments appears to have been both great and rapid: "Israel is swallowed up; now they are found among the peoples, a vessel undesired. They have gone up to Assyria" (Hos 8:8–9a).⁹³ As the good שבלים were swallowed up (בלע) by the bad, so these tribes were swallowed up (בלע) by Assyria, the paradigmatic "unclean land" (Amos 7:17).⁹⁴ As a consequence of processes that have their roots in Judges, Ephraim, whose name celebrates Joseph's fruitfulness in the land of his affliction, was exiled in affliction and made barren: "Within sixty-five years, Ephraim will be destroyed from being a people" (Isa 7:8a).

What is the link between this and the Ephraimites' pronunciation of /š/ as /s/? An innovation that distinguishes the Assyrian dialect of Akkadian from other varieties is the sound change š > s.⁹⁵ Consequently, as Robert Woodhouse comments,

---

⁹⁰ Levenson, *Death and Resurrection*, 143–69. The description "bratty upstart," with which Brettler characterizes the Ephraimites in Judges ("Book of Judges: Literature," 408), is apt for the precocious Joseph. It fueled his rejection by his brothers (Gen 37:8).

⁹¹ Ibid.; see also Heath D. Dewrell, "Yareb, Shalman, and the Date of the Book of Hosea," *CBQ* 78 (2016): 413–29, here 428–29.

⁹² Bustenay Oded, *Mass Deportations and Deportees in the Neo-Assyrian Empire* (Wiesbaden: Reichert, 1979), 30. That the number of tribes deported equals the number of mentions of שבלים in the Genesis account perhaps invites reflection.

⁹³ "The relative low number of Israelite deportees traced back might be an indication of the process of assimilation to the culture of Assyria. It can be surmised that during this process parents increasingly gave their children non-YHWH-istic names, and even Assyrian names" (Bob Becking, *The Fall of Samaria: An Historical and Archaeological Study*, SHANE 2 [Leiden: Brill, 1992], 93). See also Shalom M. Paul, "Sargon's Administrative Diction in II Kings 17:27," *JBL* 88 (1969): 73–74, https://doi.org/10.2307/3262835; Oded, *Mass Deportations*, 31, 85; H. W. F. Saggs, *The Might That Was Assyria*, Great Civilization Series (London: Sidgwick & Jackson, 1984), 263–64.

⁹⁴ Julian Morgenstern, "Amos Studies I," *HUCA* 11 (1936): 19–140, here 54, 94.

⁹⁵ Stephanie Dalley, "ᵈNIN.LÍL = *mul(l)is(s)u*, the Treaty of Barga'yah, and Herodotus' Mylitta," *RA* 73 (1979): 177–78; Michael L. Barré, "The First Pair of Deities in the Sefîre I God-List," *JNES* 44 (1985): 205–10, here 205, 207 n. 11; Paul V. Mankowski, *Akkadian Loanwords in Biblical Hebrew*, HSS 47 (Winona Lake, IN: Eisenbrauns, 2000), 61, 156.

the Assyrians "heard all West Semitic /š/ as /s/."[96] Thus, "the Hebrew name Hosea, realized as ᵐú-si-a, ᵐú-se-eʾ and ᵐú-si-i, in Neo-Assyrian cuneiform, is lemmatized as Ūsēaʾ [in the *Prosopography*], even though it was certainly pronounced Hōšēaʿ in Hebrew.... The correlation Ūsēaʾ = Hōšēaʿ shows that the NA /s/ corresponds to the Hebr. /š/."[97] We may confidently assert, therefore, that the Assyrian pronunciation of *šubultu*, "ear of barley," the Akkadian cognate of *šibbōlet*,[98] had word-initial /s/. The Assyrians manifested the feature that distinguished the Ephraimites cornered by Jephthah. Put differently, in the narratology of Judges, the Ephraimites' pronunciation of *šibbōlet* as *sibbōlet* symbolizes the destiny of all the northern tribes known by the collective designation "Ephraim," as assimilated to Assyria, "swallowed up" in an alien culture, and removed forever from the promised land.[99] They were, thus, ultimately destroyed by "the king of Mesopotamia," the successor of their first oppressor. As Hosea proclaims, Ephraim "will not return to the land of Egypt; the Assyrian will be his king" (Hos 11:5).[100]

---

[96] Woodhouse, "Biblical Shibboleth Story," 276–77, esp. nn. 20 and 21.

[97] S. Parpola, "Guidelines of the Transcription System," *The Prosopography of the Neo-Assyrian Empire* [*PNA*], 1.1, ed. Karen Radner, Publications of the Foundation for Finnish Assyriological Research 4 (Helsinki: Neo-Assyrian Text Corpus Project, 1998), xxii–xxvii, here xxii; see also xxiv.

[98] *CAD* 17.3:186.

[99] There is robust evidence that the seventh-century scribal community in Jerusalem was familiar with Akkadian and recognized Assyrian dialect traits. In Isa 20:1, the name of the Assyrian king Sargon II is given as *sargôn*, reproducing the Assyrian dialect treatment of the initial phoneme, rather than reflecting *šarru-kēnu/šarru-kīn*, the Babylonian form used in Assyrian royal inscriptions (D. G. Lyon, *Keilschrifttexte Sargon's, Königs von Assyrien [722–705 v. CHR.]*, AB 5 [Leipzig: Hinrichs, 1883], ix–x; A. Fuchs, "Šarru-kēnu, Šarru-kīn, Šarru-ukīn," *PNA* 3.2, ed. Heather D. Baker, 1239–40; Alan Millard, "'Take a Large Writing Tablet and Write on It': Isaiah—a Writing Prophet?," in *Genesis, Isaiah, and Psalms: A Festschrift to Honour Professor John Emerton for His Eightieth Birthday*, ed. Katharine J. Dell, Graham Davies, and Yee Von Koh, VTSup 135 [Leiden: Brill, 2010], 105–17, here 114). Assyrian and Babylonian were fertile sources of lexical borrowings into Hebrew (Mankowski, *Akkadian Loanwords*); Mesopotamian literary models influenced biblical textuality (David M. Carr, *The Formation of the Hebrew Bible: A New Reconstruction* [New York: Oxford University Press, 2011], 304). Christopher B. Hays argues that a knowledge of Akkadian informed First Isaiah (*Death in the Iron Age II and in First Isaiah*, FAT 79 [Tübingen: Mohr Siebeck, 2011], 25); see also Noam Mizrahi, "The Textual History and Literary Background of Isa 14,4," *ZAW* 125 (2013): 433–47, here 444–47. In the eighth and seventh centuries BCE, the influence of the Assyrian legal system on commerce in Syro-Palestine was immense. After the destruction of the northern kingdom, Assyrian garrisons were located in proximity to Jerusalem (Mordechai Cogan and Hayim Tadmor, *II Kings: A New Translation*, AB 11 [Garden City, NY: Doubleday, 1988], 210–11; Hermann Spieckermann, *Juda unter Assur in der Sargonidenzeit*, FRLANT 129 [Göttingen: Vandenhoeck & Ruprecht, 1982], 308; Mordechai Cogan, "Into Exile," in *The Oxford History of the Biblical World*, ed. Michael D. Coogan [Oxford: Oxford University Press, 1998], 242–75, here 254, 257; Schniedewind, *Society and the Promise*, 56–57, 96–97).

[100] Compare Anthony R. Ceresko, "The Function of Chiasmus in Hebrew Poetry," *CBQ* 40

VI. Concluding Remarks

The list in Judg 10:6 of the gods of the surrounding nations to which Israel adhered in preference to YHWH is unprecedented in its detail. Moreover, it forms the literal center of the book of Judges according to the masoretic verse count. In the composition's rhetorical plan, similarly, it constitutes the fulcrum in the account of the relations between YHWH and his people.[101] The worship of these deities and the syncretistic application of aspects of their cults to normative Yahwism provoke the response from Israel's god that he will deliver them no more and that they should "appeal to the gods you have chosen" for deliverance. This rupture in the relationship sets the scene for Jephthah's ascendancy. The Gileadites, in extremis, take the initiative to engineer a human solution to a divine problem by approaching Jephthah, a social outcast with proven leadership and combat skills.[102] As detailed above, Jephthah's attitudes and deeds, far from redressing the balance, legitimized a syncretistic practice of the most baneful kind. His understanding of YHWH was profoundly flawed. He desecrated the land with Israelite blood unjustly and prodigiously shed, rendering it inhospitable to YHWH, thus exacerbating his people's alienation from YHWH and depriving the land of rest. He fanned the flames of internecine friction, which then engulfed any semblance of unity in Israel. He died, denied of descendants by his own hand and unlamented, his only memorial an annual festival to mourn the daughter he killed. The symptoms and consequences of the dynamic between YHWH and his people depicted in 10:6–16 are thus echoed dramatically in Jephthah's brief six years "judging Israel." It is a time when the principles enunciated in Jeremiah's declaration are vividly enacted: "I will first recompense those who have defiled my land double for their iniquity and their sin. They have filled my inheritance with the corpse of their abominations and detestable practices" (16:18).

(1978): 1–10, here 3; John Day, "Asherah in the Hebrew Bible and Northwest Semitic Literature," *JBL* 105 (1986): 385–408, here 404, https://doi.org/10.2307/3260509.

[101] Compare Mullen, "'Minor Judges,'" 196–97. Possibly the writer's play on the word-medial radical in the crucial lexical set שפט-שקץ through the book's central section subtly points to the key function that its literal center fulfills in elucidating its meaning. On the role of "extended" paronomasia in the Hebrew Bible, see Jack M. Sasson, "Wordplay in the Old Testament," *IDBSup*, 968–70; Scott B. Noegel, "'Sign, Sign, Everywhere a Sign': Script, Power, and Interpretation in the Ancient Near East," in *Divination and Interpretation of Signs in the Ancient World*, ed. Amar Annus, OIS 6 (Chicago: University of Chicago Press, 2010), 143–62, here 149. On the hermeneutical significance of the midpoint of biblical compositions, see Yehuda T. Radday, "Chiasmus in Hebrew Biblical Narrative," in *Chiasmus in Antiquity: Structures, Analysis, Exegesis*, ed. John W. Welch (Hildesheim: Gerstenberg, 1981), 50–117, here 51, 57; Douglas, *Leviticus as Literature*, 50; Douglas, *In the Wilderness*, 117.

[102] Exum, *Tragedy and Biblical Narrative*, 47–48.

New and Recent Titles

THE FIRST URBAN CHURCHES 3
Ephesus
James R. Harrison and L. L. Welborn, editors
Paperback $46.95, 978-0-88414-234-8   382 pages, 2018   Code: 064209
Hardcover $61.95, 978-0-88414-236-2 E-book $46.95, 978-0-88414-235-5
Writings from the Greco-Roman World Supplement Series 9

READING AND TEACHING ANCIENT FICTION
Jewish, Christian, and Greco-Roman Narratives
Sara R. Johnson, Rubén R. Dupertuis, and Christine Shea, editors
Paperback $40.95, 978-1-62837-196-3   338 pages, 2018   Code: 064212
Hardcover $55.95, 978-0-88414-261-4 E-book $40.95, 978-0-88414-260-7
Writings from the Greco-Roman World Supplement Series 10

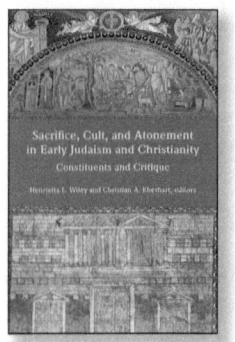

PEDAGOGY IN ANCIENT JUDAISM AND EARLY CHRISTIANITY
Karina Martin Hogan, Matthew Goff, and Emma Wasserman, editors
Paperback $49.95, 978-1-62837-165-9   424 pages, 2017   Code: 063548
Hardcover $64.95, 978-0-88414-208-9 E-book $49.95, 978-0-88414-207-2
Early Judaism and Its Literature 41

SACRIFICE, CULT, AND ATONEMENT IN EARLY JUDAISM AND CHRISTIANITY
Constituents and Critique
Henrietta L. Wiley and Christian A. Eberhart, editors
Paperback $56.95, 978-1-62837-155-0   434 pages, 2017   Code: 060393
Hardcover $76.95, 978-0-88414-191-4 E-book $56.95, 978-0-88414-190-7
Resources for Biblical Study 85

REDESCRIBING THE GOSPEL OF MARK
Barry S. Crawford and Merrill P. Miller, editors
Paperback $89.95, 978-1-62837-163-5   708 pages, 2017   Code: 064520
Hardcover $109.95, 978-0-88414-204-1 E-book $89.95, 978-0-88414-203-4
Early Christianity and Its Literature 22

SBL Press • P.O. Box 2243 • Williston, VT 05495-2243
Phone: 877-725-3334 (toll-free) or 802-864-6185 • Fax: 802-864-7626
Order online at www.sbl-site.org/publications

New and Recent Titles

Biblical Archaeology Society 2017 Publication Award Winner
A POLITICAL HISTORY OF THE ARAMEANS
From Their Origins to the End of Their Polities
K. Lawson Younger Jr.
Paperback $97.95, 978-1-58983-128-5   886 pages, 2016   Code: 061713
Hardcover $117.95, 978-1-62837-080-5   E-book $97.95, 978-1-62837-084-3
Archaeology and Biblical Studies 13

FIGHTING FOR THE KING AND THE GODS
A Survey of Warfare in the Ancient Near East
Charlie Trimm
Paperback $89.95, 978-1-62837-184-0   748 pages, 2017   Code 060394
Hardcover $109.95, 978-0-88414-238-6   E-book $89.95, 978-0-88414-237-9
Resources for Biblical Study 88

SARGON II, KING OF ASSYRIA
Josette Elayi
Paperback $41.95, 978-1-62837-177-2   310 pages, 2017   Code: 061722
Hardcover $56.95, 978-0-88414-224-9   E-book $41.95, 978-0-88414-223-2
Archaeology and Biblical Studies 22

HOUSEHOLD AND FAMILY RELIGION IN PERSIAN-PERIOD JUDAH
An Archaeological Approach
José E. Balcells Gallarreta
Paperback $33.95, 978-1-62837-178-9   208 pages, 2017   Code: 062822
Hardcover $48.95, 978-0-88414-226-3   E-book $33.95, 978-0-88414-225-6
Ancient Near East Monographs 18

LIFE IN KINGS
Reshaping the Royal Story in the Hebrew Bible
A. Graeme Auld
Paperback $39.95, 978-1-62837-171-0   330 pages, 2017   Code 062632
Hardcover $54.95, 978-0-88414-212-6   E-book $39.95, 978-0-88414-211-9
Ancient Israel and Its Literature 30

SENSING WORLD, SENSING WISDOM
The Cognitive Foundation of Biblical Metaphors
Nicole L. Tilford
Paperback $34.95, 978-1-62837-175-8   258 pages, 2017   Code 062634
Hardcover $49.95, 978-0-88414-220-1   E-book $34.95, 978-0-88414-219-5
Ancient Israel and Its Literature 31

SBL Press • P.O. Box 2243 • Williston, VT 05495-2243
Phone: 877-725-3334 (toll-free) or 802-864-6185 • Fax: 802-864-7626
Order online at www.sbl-site.org/publications

2 Kings 6:24–30: A Case of Unintentional Elimination Killing

KRISTINE GARROWAY
kgarroway@huc.edu
Hebrew Union College–Jewish Institute of Religion, Los Angeles, CA 90007

Second Kings 6:24–30 presents an astonishing narrative wherein two Israelite mothers agree to eat their children. The city of Samaria is under siege and food is scarce, but this hardly lessens the shock of the mothers' cannibalism. Scholars view this text as describing a world where everything has gone awry, where violence in society becomes a call for social change. Scholarship has failed, however, to connect the mothers' act to the events immediately following their actions: the king has a revelation, Elisha announces that the siege will end, and indeed the enemy retreats. This part of the narrative, 2 Kgs 7:1–7, provides a new way of reading the text. The women have saved the city by unintentionally offering a child sacrifice and, in doing so, have lifted the siege and restored order and harmony. The sacrifice can be read as a veiled polemic against child sacrifice and the religious depravity running rampant in the northern kingdom.

Second Kings 6:24–30 presents an astonishing narrative wherein two Israelite mothers agree to eat their children. Granted, the city of Samaria is under siege and food is scarce, but this hardly lessens the shock of the mothers' cannibalism. Modern critical commentaries identify this story as a part of a larger narrative describing the siege of Samaria in 2 Kgs 6:24–7:20. Within this framework, scholars have taken various approaches, including literary and sociohistorical, to try to explain why a siege narrative includes a story about cannibalism. Literary perspectives suggest that the cannibalistic mothers are a metaphor or plot device used to demonstrate the dire state of the Samarians. The structure of the larger text reveals that the narrative forms a chiasm in which the mothers' actions are paired with those of the lepers mentioned in 2 Kgs 7:3–16. The former story describes the state of the siege and famine, while the latter explains how the siege and famine ended.[1] A literary approach also supports viewing the narrative as a type-scene, in which the mother's plea is part of the type of the wise woman, epitomized by the wise woman

---

[1] Robert L. Cohn, *2 Kings*, Berit Olam (Collegeville, MN: Liturgical Press, 2000), 48.

of Tekoa.² A sociohistorical critique concentrates more on the historical context and the ruler under whose reign these horrific actions occurred. In such a reading, the siege becomes the focus of the exegesis and the resulting cannibalistic act, the fallout.³ Various scholars point out that cannibalism in times of siege-related famine was not unheard of in the ancient Near East.⁴ The treaties of Esarhaddon, as well as the Bible itself, attest to such practices during wartime.⁵ By placing the events of 2 Kgs 6 in their historical context and demonstrating that cannibalism is not unprecedented, a sociohistorical reading downplays the violence against the children and makes the biblical text appear less dreadful.

At the other end of the spectrum are readings that highlight the violence instead of suppressing it. Consider the readings offered by Gina Hens-Piazza and Stuart Lasine, who focus on the people harmed in the aftermath of a societal collapse.⁶ For both scholars, the mothers become vulnerable victims of war. Hens-Piazza points out that the nameless women are forced to eliminate their own future by killing their children. In killing and eating a child, the women become dislocated in society as they lose not only their humanity but their status and credibility as mothers.⁷ While the children face a literal death, the mothers face a social death.

I. Childist Interpretation

I offer a childist or child-centered reading, which, as the name suggests, focuses on children in the biblical text. The field of child-centered interpretation is in its nascent stages. Works by Julie Faith Parker, Laurel Koepf Taylor, Naomi Steinberg, and myself, among others, have begun to explore the lives of children in the biblical and ancient Near Eastern texts.⁸ Mirroring the elder hermeneutic of

---

² Walter Brueggemann, *1 and 2 Kings*, SHBC (Macon, GA: Smyth & Helwys, 2000), 356–57; Cohn, *2 Kings*, 49.

³ John Gray, *I and II Kings: A Commentary*, OTL (Philadelphia: Westminster, 1963), 460–67; Mordechai Cogan and Hayim Tadmor, *II Kings: A New Translation with Introduction and Commentary*, AB 11 (New York: Doubleday, 1988), 79–84; Volkmar Fritz, *1 and 2 Kings*, trans. Anselm Hagedorn, CC (Minneapolis: Fortress, 2003), 268–69.

⁴ Gray, *I and II Kings*, 466; Cogan and Tadmor, *II Kings*, 80; Fritz, *1 and 2 Kings*, 269.

⁵ "Treaties of Esarhaddon," lines 448–50, 547–50, in *The Ancient Near East: An Anthology of Texts and Pictures*, ed. James Pritchard (Princeton: Princeton University Press, 2011), 221, 223; Deut 28:52–57, Jer 19:9, Ezek 5:10, Lam 2:20, 4:10.

⁶ Gina Hens-Piazza, "Forms of Violence and the Violence of Forms: Two Cannibal Mothers before a King (2 Kings 6:24–33)," *JFSR* 14 (1998): 91–104; Stuart Lasine, "Jehoram and the Cannibal Mothers (2 Kings 6.24–33): Solomon's Judgment in an Inverted World," *JSOT* 50 (1991): 27–53. Walter Brueggemann also notes the vulnerability of the mothers (*1 and 2 Kings*, 353–56).

⁷ Hens-Piazza applies this stigma to both women; however, only the first mother lost her child. I would argue that, while the second mother still technically holds the title "mother," one may categorize her, in light of her cannibalistic actions, as an unfit mother.

⁸ Kristine Garroway, *Children in the Ancient Near Eastern Household*, EANEC 3 (Winona

feminist analysis, a childist approach brings to the fore the suppressed other, the child, reassigning agency and a voice to the silent child. As with feminist interpretations, there is no single methodology utilized by scholars researching children. For example, Parker crafted a six-step methodology based on literary theory for examining children in the Elisha cycle, whereas Steinberg's methodology applies a sociological lens to interpret children in the biblical text.[9] Recognizing the value of various theoretical approaches, childist interpretations most often bring a multidisciplinary approach to the text, combining sociohistorical criticism, gender theory, literary theory, and various anthropological theories.[10] Childist readings might also consider how the archaeological record and ethnographic studies can aid our understanding of the child in biblical Israel.[11] An approach that combines both the sciences and humanities has been called "processual-plus" by archaeologists and a "coffeehouse" model by Koepf Taylor.[12] While the data from a single

---

Lake, IN: Eisenbrauns, 2014); Laurel W. Koepf Taylor, *Give Me Children or I Shall Die: Children and Communal Survival in Biblical Literature*, Emerging Scholars (Minneapolis: Fortress, 2013); Julie Faith Parker, *Valuable and Vulnerable: Children in Hebrew Bible, Especially the Elisha Cycle*, BJS 355 (Providence, RI: Brown Judaic Studies, 2013); Naomi Steinberg, *The World of the Child in the Hebrew Bible*, HBM 51 (Sheffield: Sheffield Phoenix, 2013). New Testament scholars have also begun focusing specifically on children; see A. James Murphy, *Kids and Kingdom: The Precarious Presence of Children in the Synoptic Gospels* (Eugene, OR: Pickwick, 2013); and Cornelia B. Horn and John W. Martens, *"Let the Little Children Come to Me": Children and Childhood in Early Christianity* (Washington, DC: Catholic University of America Press, 2009).

[9] Parker's first three steps engage in three aspects of literary theory: setting, characters, and plot. The remaining three steps provide the core of her childist interpretation. Step 4 is a child-centered analysis of the text. This leads into step 5: insights about the children in the text. Step 6 connects the child under investigation to other children in the Bible as a way of demonstrating possible avenues for future research (Parker, *Valuable and Vulnerable*, 77–90; Steinberg, *World of the Child*, 45–97).

[10] Koepf Taylor, *Give Me Children*, 1–32; Jonathan Valk, "They Enjoy Syrup and Ghee at the Tables of Silver and Gold: Infant Loss in Ancient Mesopotamia" (paper presented at the Institute for the Study of the Ancient World at New York University spring conference, New York, NY, 17 April 2015); Shawn Flynn, *Children in Ancient Israel: The Hebrew Bible and Mesopotamia in Comparative Perspective* (Oxford: Oxford University Press, 2018); David A. Bosworth, *Infant Weeping in Akkadian, Hebrew, and Greek Literature*, Critical Studies in the Hebrew Bible 8 (Winona Lake, IN: Eisenbrauns, 2016).

[11] Kristine Garroway, "Gendered or Ungendered? The Perception of Children in Ancient Israel," *JNES* 71 (2012): 95–114; Garroway, *Children in the Ancient Near Eastern Household*, 16–47; Garroway, *Growing Up in Ancient Israel: Children in Biblical Texts and Material Culture*, ABS (Atlanta: SBL Press, forthcoming); Rona Avissar-Lewis, "Childhood and Children in the Material Culture of the Land of Israel from the Middle Bronze Age to the Iron Age" [in Hebrew] (PhD diss., Bar-Ilan University, 2010).

[12] Michelle Hegemon, "Setting Theoretical Egos Aside: Issues and Theory in North American Archaeology; Special Section: Mapping the Terrain of Americanist Archaeology," *American Antiquity* 68 (2003): 231–43; A. Jones, "Archaeometry and Materiality: Material-Based Analysis in Theory and Practice,'" *Archaeometry* 46 (2004): 327–38. Koepf Taylor points to the importance of the conversation between multiple disciplines, hence her decision to call this approach a

discipline offers much, combining data from various disciplines can produce even more insights concerning children and their place in biblical Israel.

My childist reading of 2 Kgs 6 engages the coffeehouse model in order to highlight the children in the text and reassign them agency; it draws on anthropological, archaeological, and literary theory to illuminate this troubling passage. My interpretation is spurred on by a statement from Hens-Piazza: "They [the two women] and their children represent an expiatory offering bearing the iniquities of the whole society."[13] While drawing attention to the women as victims of social decay, her words provide a starting point for a childist reading of the text, which views the dead child as the expiatory offering. The offering is not a metaphor for social and moral decay, nor is it a reference to the ills of the patriarchy. The death of the child is a literal, expiatory offering. Moreover, the child's death does not typify actions during the siege, as a sociohistorical reading might imply; rather, the child's death is the conduit by which the siege is lifted. The implications here are significant, for this childist reading suggests that the child sacrifice was effective.

My conclusion that the mothers' actions in 2 Kgs 6 served as an expiatory sacrifice may seem a bit far-fetched at the outset, but it is grounded in textual and archaeological materials that link child sacrifice to a siege. My childist reading, therefore, begins with biblical, Canaanite, and Ugaritic depictions of child sacrifice during a siege. After presenting these materials, I turn to an anthropological perspective to discuss why people sacrifice and the difference in the kinds of sacrifices offered. I then address why a child would be used as a sacrificial victim and survey debates about the legitimacy of child sacrifice in biblical Israel. I conclude by applying the anthropological and archaeological data to a literary analysis that examines the use of terminology surrounding child sacrifice, specifically the terminology used in 2 Kgs 6. Through this analysis, it becomes clear that 2 Kgs 6:26–30 is a unit bracketed by *Wiederaufnahme* (resumptive repetition) that uses coded language for child sacrifice. The insertion of this unit functions as a polemic against the northern kingdom concerning the north's place in the covenant and the place of child sacrifice in the cult of YHWH. Thus, a childist reading of these few verses leads to the conclusion that the death of a single child ended a siege and called the northern kingdom to task concerning its religious practices.

II. Child Sacrifice in the Ancient Near East

Evidence of child sacrifice during times of siege is found in both biblical and extrabiblical texts. Consider, for example, the narrative in 2 Kgs 3:24–27. Here the

---

"coffeehouse" method wherein voices from each approach are in dialogue with each other (Koepf Taylor, *Give Me Children*, 9).

[13] Hens-Piazza, "Forms of Violence," 102.

king of Israel is trying to quell an uprising by the Moabites. He destroys towns, ruins fields, stops up springs, and cuts down trees. The Israelites then lay siege to the one remaining Moabite town. Seeing few options left, Mesha, the king of the Moabites, appeals to the deity by sacrificing his son on the city wall. The deity responds by routing Israel back to their own land, thus lifting the siege on the Moabite city. That the Hebrew Bible would preserve a record describing Israel's defeat at the hand of a foreign god is surprising.[14] Even more surprising is that "no theological judgment or critique" is offered.[15] Directly following these events, the narrative drops the war context and moves to the domestic realm, where Elisha performs wonders. The matter-of-fact presentation of Mesha's offering leads Francesca Stavrakopoulou to call child sacrifice of this nature "an effective ritual."[16]

Second Kings 3 places the expiatory killing in the hands of foreigners. The Moabites, however, are not the only foreigners to have offered their children on a city wall. Reliefs from Karnak and a text from Ugarit suggest that this type of ritual was well known in Bronze Age Canaan. During the Late Bronze Age, the land of Canaan came under Egyptian hegemony. To commemorate their victories in their ever-expanding empire, the Egyptian kings Seti I, Ramesses II, Merenptah, and Ramesses III all inscribed reliefs on the walls of the Karnak temple complex. These reliefs show Canaanite cities under siege by the Egyptian army. Men stand atop the city walls with arms outstretched to the heavens, while women are kneeling in a prayer position below them. One man holds a brazier with burning incense, while another man dangles a child over the city wall. These scenes are interpreted as depicting a Canaanite ritual similar to that found in 2 Kgs 3:26–27. Since the brazier appears similar to those used in the service of Baal Hammon, this scene is understood as a plea to the deity.[17] Baal is invoked to lift the siege of the city. Along with the incense, the inhabitants attempt to capture Baal's attention by sacrificially throwing a child over the city wall.

The interpretation of the Karnak reliefs is influenced by a text from Ugarit that prescribes an eerily similar set of events to be carried out when a city is under siege.[18]

---

[14] In this foreign context, the reader is meant to assume that the Moabite king was sacrificing to Kemosh, the Moabite god. Yet, since the text does not specify the deity to whom the king of Moab sacrifices his son, one could insert YHWH as the possible respondent. This would keep the narrative consistent with YHWH as the only God. While this opens a theological can of worms, it is not without precedent that God acts against Israel or uses a foreign entity to do so, as with Pharaoh, Nebuchadnezzar, and Cyrus. In all cases, Israel suffers in order to bring glory to YHWH (Exod 3:19, 4:21, Isa 45:1–25, Jer 25:1–11).

[15] Francesca Stavrakopoulou, *King Manesseh and Child Sacrifice: Biblical Distortions of Historical Realities*, BZAW 338 (Berlin: de Gruyter, 2004), 176–77.

[16] Ibid.

[17] Anthony John Spalinger, "A Canaanite Ritual Found in Egyptian Relief," *JSSEA* 7 (1978): 47–60; Armin Lange, "They Burn Their Sons and Daughters—That Was No Command of Mine," in *Human Sacrifice in Jewish and Christian Tradition*, ed. Karin Finsterbusch, Armin Lange, and K. F. Diethard Römheld, SHR 112 (Leiden: Brill, 2007), 120–24.

[18] RS 24:266, VI D = *CTU* 1:119, V 26–35.

It calls for the inhabitants to cry out to Baʿlu and to offer the following items: a sanctified bull, a vow, a sanctified firstborn, a *ḥtp* offering, and a feast. The people will ascend to the temple of Baʿlu with these items, and in return Baʿlu will hear their prayer and defeat the enemy and/or lift the siege. Scholars agree that child sacrifice is a part of the ritual—which part, however, is still debated. Armin Lange follows Dennis Pardee's translation, understanding the "firstborn" to refer to a firstborn child.[19] Baruch Margalit, on the other hand, argues that the unknown *ḥtp* should be read as the well-known word *ḥtk*, "offspring."[20] Following Margalit, "firstborn" parallels "offspring," making it clear that a firstborn human, not an animal, is part of the ritual enacted to lift the siege.

Both the Canaanite and Ugaritic materials suggest that people of the ancient Near East carried out an elaborate ritual in times of extreme duress. Whether the writer of 2 Kings was aware of this particular Bronze Age ritual is impossible to know. The text in 2 Kgs 3:26–27, however, contains strong echoes of such a ritual: a city is under siege, and the king has no recourse but to offer up an ancient Hail Mary, as it were, and sacrifice his son on the city walls.

III. An Anthropological View

To understand the ritual in 2 Kgs 3 as well as a childist reading of 2 Kgs 6, one must grasp the purpose and function of ancient sacrifices and the thought process that goes into picking a sacrificial victim. These questions of why and who can best be addressed through the lens of religious anthropology.

The Rationale of Sacrifice

The biblical text attests to a rich array of sacrifices: burnt offering (עלה), grain offering (מנחה), sacred gift of greeting (זבח שלמים), sin offering (חטאת), and guilt or reparation sacrifice (אשם).[21] Religious anthropology defines sacrifice as a plea to the divine. A plea fulfills one of two purposes: it is a request either for communication with the divine or for separation from the divine.[22] If communication is desired, the individual performs a sacrifice through an offering. Sacrifice through

---

[19] Lange, "They Burn Their Sons and Daughters," 122; Dennis Pardee, *Ritual and Cult at Ugarit*, WAW 10 (Atlanta: Society of Biblical Literature, 2002), 53, 149–50.

[20] Baruch Margalit, "Why King Mesha of Moab Sacrificed His Oldest Son," *BAR* 12.6 (1986): 62–63, 76.

[21] For "sacred gift of greeting," I follow Baruch A. Levine, who arrives at this translation based on the Akkadian cognate *shulmānu* and the Ugaritic *shalamūma* (*Leviticus* ויקרא: *The Traditional Hebrew Text with the New JPS Translation*, JPS Torah Commentary [Philadelphia: Jewish Publication Society, 1989], 14).

[22] See Hubert Seiwert, "Opfer," *HRWG* 4:268–84; Beate Pongratz-Leisten, "Ritual Killing and

offerings occurs on a regular basis and inside a sacred space.²³ In this category we may place the עלה, מנחה, and זבח שלמים. Baruch Levine suggests that the עלה, and its cheaper alternative the מנחה, acted as a means of getting God's attention.²⁴ While the function of the זבח שלמים has been debated, Levine suggests that it, too, has a communicative purpose—to express "the fellowship experienced by the worshipers and priests in God's presence, as they greeted their divine guest."²⁵

The second purpose of sacrifice is the one most pertinent to the present discussion, a ritual killing, or eliminatory sacrifice, which has a distancing function and includes an eliminatory ritual to dispel evil.²⁶ Whereas the offering sacrifice takes place in a sacred space, an eliminatory sacrifice occurs outside the sacred arena.²⁷ In the ancient Near East, eliminatory sacrificial rituals are found in myths, ritual texts, and historiographical narratives.²⁸ The child sacrifice in 2 Kgs 3 and, as I will demonstrate, the one in 2 Kgs 6 both fulfill the requirements of an eliminatory sacrifice: they are done outside the sacred space in order to rid society of an evil. Ritual killings or eliminatory sacrifices can also request societal restructuring from the divine.²⁹ Again, both passages in Kings ask for societal reordering with the hope that the eliminatory killing will jolt the currently misaligned social order back into place.

Ellen Morris points out that ritual becomes more popular when there is a need to establish order.³⁰ A new social order is desired in both 2 Kgs 3 and 2 Kgs 6. In

---

Sacrifice in the Ancient Near East," in Finsterbusch, Lange, and Römheld, *Human Sacrifice*, 3–34, here 10–11.

²³ Beate Pongratz-Leisten, "Sacrifice in the Ancient Near East: Offering and Ritual Killing," in *Sacred Killing: The Archaeology of Sacrifice in the Ancient Near East*, ed. Anne M. Porter and Glenn M. Schwartz (Winona Lake, IN: Eisenbrauns, 2012), 289–302, here 295–96. Such offerings often work on a gift-giving system; they are given out of gratitude and serve an economic function.

²⁴ This suggestion is supported by Gen 8:20 and the extrabiblical flood narratives (e.g., Atrahasis and Enuma Elish), wherein the aroma of sacrifices catches the attention of the gods.

²⁵ Levine, *Leviticus*, 15.

²⁶ The last two types of Levitical sacrifices, the חטאת, which atones for unwitting sin, and the אשם, for sins against God and his sancta, both have this expiatory function. See Mark E. Biddle, "The 'Endangered Ancestress' and Blessing for the Nations," *JBL* 109 (1990): 599–611, https://doi.org/10.2307/3267365.

²⁷ Pongratz-Leisten, "Sacrifice in the Ancient Near East," 291.

²⁸ Consider Tiamat's death in the Enuma Elish epic (tablet IV) and the scapegoat ritual in the biblical text (Lev 16:10–22). Since the Levitical חטאת and אשם both occur in a sacred space, they do not present analogous examples.

²⁹ Other purposes for eliminatory killings include transformation, or reintegration. For examples of each, see Pongratz-Leisten, "Sacrifice in the Ancient Near East," 292–94.

³⁰ Ellen Morris examines the graves of First Dynasty Egypt, noting the orderly nature of the ritual remains contrasted with the more messy graves in other contemporaneous societies. She concludes that societal reordering demands orderly conduct ("Sacrifice for the State: First Dynasty Royal Funerals and the Rites at Macramallah's Rectangle," in *Performing Death: Social Analyses of Funerary Traditions in the Ancient Near East and Mediterranean*, ed. Nicola Laneri, OIS 3 [Chicago:

the relationship between ritual and the violence enacted to obtain order, the process of sacrifice represents an entire society's desire for violence.[31] Because a sacrifice is socially acceptable and controlled, the violence is channeled into an admissible form.[32] Yet, even if sacrifice is socially acceptable, such violence is still the result of the vicious circle created by "the privileging of the powerful and the empowering of the privileged."[33] When one considers the victims of sacrifice in both 2 Kgs 3 and 2 Kgs 6, this circle of privilege becomes more obvious.

The Victims of Sacrifice

Anthropological theory contends that sacrificial victims are not chosen at random. As a stand-in for the sacrificer, the victim must be similar to other members of the society yet marginal enough to avoid a revenge killing. The closer the victim is to the one sacrificing, the better.[34] For example, because of the time and effort associated with domesticating animals, domesticated animals are better victims than nondomesticated animals.[35] But a human victim trumps all. Indeed, even

---

Oriental Institute of the University of Chicago, 2007], 15–38). While the situation in 2 Kings does not demand the start of a new dynasty, it nevertheless demands the restart of a kingdom once the war has ended and turns to a ritual—elimination killing.

[31] Glenn Schwartz, "Archaeology and Sacrifice," in Porter and Schwartz, *Sacred Killing*, 1–32, here 5.

[32] In the biblical text, the tribe of Levi seems to represent a group of people with a thirst for blood and violence. While the Levites are eventually sanctioned to do animal sacrifice, their ancestors are men who seek blood, as evidenced in Gen 34:25–31. Levi and his brother Simeon avenge Dinah and blot out the memory of the sin against her by killing all the men of Shechem. Likewise, in Exod 32:26–29 the Levites volunteer to commit mass murder against their fellow idolatrous Israelites in the name of YHWH. Even after the tribe of Levi is given the priesthood and the sacrificial duties therein (Exod 28:1, 40:12–15; see also the various tasks in Leviticus and Num 18), Levites still commit violence as a way to solve issues. Phinehas resorts to extreme violence in the name of the Lord (Num 25:10–12). Striking down an Israelite having intimate relations with a Midianite woman, he skewers them through their bellies (Num 25:8). Violence is again linked to the Levite family in Judg 19. An unnamed Levite stops for the night with his concubine, who is raped and killed by the men of Gibeah. In response, the Levite cuts the woman up with the same kind of knife Abraham intended to use on Isaac, a מאכלת, "meat cleaver" (Judg 19:29, Gen 22:10) and sends her body parts to the twelve tribes of Israel. In each case the Levite men demonstrate a thirst for violence and vengeance. Their killings are all horrifying. Yet the macabre nature of these passage is almost glossed over. The grisly deaths, if not socially acceptable, are ideologically acceptable; in the narrator's opinion, the killings are sacrifices that restore order.

[33] Hens-Piazza, "Forms of Violence," 91.

[34] For a bibliography on appropriate sacrificial victims, see Schwartz, "Archaeology and Sacrifice," 5. See also John Beattie, "On Understanding Sacrifice," in *Sacrifice*, ed. M. F. C. Bourdillon and Meyer Fortes (New York: Academic Press, 1980), 41–44; René Girard, *Violence and the Sacred*, trans. Patrick Gregory; new ed. (London: Continuum, 2005); Henri Hubert and Marcel Mauss, *Sacrifice: Its Nature and Function*, trans. W. D. Halls (Chicago: University of Chicago Press, 1964), 52.

[35] This hierarchy is evidenced in the biblical text with preference placed on sacrificing a

for humans there is a hierarchy. Humans with minimal power and legal rights make the best victims,[36] and the ultimate victim is a biological child.[37] As an issue of the sacrificer's own body, a child has the closest association with the sacrificer while at the same time fulfilling the prerequisites of low social status and minimal legal rights.

Applying this anthropological frame to the biblical text, one finds that the sacrifices follow the same general schema. Yet a closer look at the sacrificial beings highlights another important aspect—the desirability of the victim. The sacrificer must be attuned to the divine desires and then determine what will best fulfill that desire. In the biblical text, the most commonly referenced sacrifice is an animal (Lev 5:6, 7) with emphasis on the unblemished animal (Exod 12:5; Lev 4:3, 23, 32; 5:15, 18). The owner spends not only money but time and valuable resources raising the animal and watching over it to keep it safe and unblemished, to keep it desirable. There also appears to be a personal and emotional attachment in play. Although the stolen lamb of the prophet Nathan's parable was not a sacrifice, the parable suggests that owners could be quite attached to their animals and might consider some animals like family members (2 Sam 12). How much more, therefore, would be the value of a child to a parent. The narratives describing Mesha's *firstborn* son (2 Kgs 3:27), Abraham's *beloved* son (Gen 22:2), and Jephthah's *only* daughter (Judg 11:34) emphasize the value of these children to their parents.

Once the victim, animal or human, is specifically designated or marked for a particular sacrifice, the victim is sanctified.[38] The transformation of the once profane into a sacred being/object allows the victim to be a conduit for

---

stall-fed calf. Such a calf is not a lean, free-range cow but one kept inside the family confines so that it fattens up. While fatty and tender, the stall-fed calf may also be used in sacrifices due to its close association with the family (1 Sam 28:24, Jer 46:21, Amos 6:4, Mal 4:2). See Philip King and Lawrence Stager, *Life in Biblical Israel*, LAI (Louisville: Westminster John Knox, 2001), 34.

[36] Schwartz, "Archaeology and Sacrifice," 8.

[37] The Inca viewed children as the most effective messengers to the divine. Archaeologists have found evidence of child sacrifice in high-altitude Incan tombs where the children were interred as ice mummies (Schwartz, "Archaeology and Sacrifice," 7; Maria Constanza Ceruti, "Frozen Mummies from Andean Mountaintop Shrines: Bioarchaeology and Ethnohistory of Inca Human Sacrifice," *BioMed Research International*, vol. 2015 [2015], http://dx.doi.org/10.1155/2015/439428).

The controversial Tophet at Carthage is geographically and temporally closer to Israel. Its vast quantity of cremated infant remains has led scholars to suggest that it was either a cemetery for infants or a place of infant sacrifice (Patricia Smith et al., "Aging Cremated Infants: The Problem of Sacrifice at the Tophet of Carthage," *Antiquity* 85 [2011]: 859–75; J. H. Schwartz et al., "Bones, Teeth, and Age of Perinates: Carthaginian Infant Sacrifices Revisited," *Antiquity* 86 [2012]: 738–45). Renewed analysis of over 320 charred remains shows that the majority of infants buried there were under two months old, favoring the hypothesis that it was a place of infant sacrifice (Patricia Smith et al., "Age Estimates Attest to Infant Sacrifice at the Carthage Tophet," *Antiquity* 87 [2013]: 1199–1207). In contrast to the Inca ice mummies, the specific reason for the sacrifices at Carthage remains unclear.

[38] Pongratz-Leisten, "Sacrifice in the Ancient Near East," 292.

communication between the sacred and the profane.³⁹ The victim can then carry out the intended purpose of the sacrifice—to offer thanks to the gods in an offering sacrifice or to cry out for help as part of an eliminatory ritual killing. The choice of a child for sacrificial purposes both privileges and empowers the powerful while at the same time disempowering the child.

2 Kings 3:24–27 and 2 Kings 6:24–7:20 as Eliminatory Sacrifices

Returning to the example of 2 Kgs 3:24–27, one can see that all the elements needed for an eliminatory killing are in place. The community is under siege, and the city is running out of options. The killing serves as a last-ditch cry for help and is done outside of the sacred arena on the city wall. The king offers the most valuable victim he can, his firstborn son. As 2 Kgs 3 states, the eliminatory killing works, the siege is lifted, and social order is reset. In 2 Kgs 6:24–7:20, a similar pattern develops. A city under siege experiences communal distress. As a result, two women kill a child. This is where a childist reading differs from previous readings of the text, for it focuses on the victim and views the women's actions as a sacrifice. While their actions may well be reflective of the siege conditions, as other scholars suggest, the killing also functions as an unintentional sacrifice precipitating the events leading to the end of the siege. Herein lies the disquieting fact, for it is one thing to say that the foreign gods of the Moabites, Canaanites, or Hittites paid attention to child sacrifice but quite another to assert that YHWH, God of the Israelites, acknowledged the (unintentional) sacrifice and lifted the siege.⁴⁰ To make this claim requires an investigation into whether the biblical text suggests that YHWH ever acknowledges child sacrifice.

IV. Child Sacrifice in the Bible

The relationship between child sacrifice and the Israelite cult is complicated. Legal passages condemn the practice outright,⁴¹ but other texts suggest that child sacrifice once held a legitimate, albeit tenuous, place in the cult.⁴² One can add to these the narrative passages of Jephthah's daughter (Judg 11) and possibly the

---

³⁹ Henri Hubert and Marcel Mauss, *Sacrifice: Its Nature and Function*, trans. W. D. Halls (Chicago: University of Chicago Press, 1964), 97.

⁴⁰ By unintentional, I mean that the mothers in the narrative did not act with the intention of following a Bronze Age ritual. Their actions become a means by which the writer is able to construct a polemic against child sacrifice. More about the polemic and the unintentional nature of the sacrifice follows below.

⁴¹ Lev 18:21, 20:3, Deut 12:20–31, 18:10, Isa 7:31, Jer 19:5, and 32:35.

⁴² Karin Finsterbusch, "The First-Born between Sacrifice and Redemption in the Hebrew Bible," in Finsterbusch, Lange, and Römheld, *Human Sacrifice*, 85–108. See also Exod 22:28 and Ezek 20:25.

Akedah (Gen 22), which, through their various redactional layers, hint that child sacrifice in the Israelite cult is, at best, ambiguous.[43]

Seeking to bring some clarity to the Bible's position on child sacrifice, scholars have offered explanations for the contradictions. James L. Kugel borrows Shakespeare's reasoning that the Bible "doth protest too much"; therefore, child sacrifice must be happening.[44] Mark S. Smith, Jon D. Levenson, and Susan Niditch, among others, present a more nuanced version of Kugel's intuition. These scholars hold that, at one point in time, child sacrifice was indeed a legitimate part of YHWH worship for a portion of the population.[45] At a later stage, child sacrifice became taboo. Saul Olyan furthers this position by explaining how the Deuteronomists intentionally distorted the terminology for and references to child sacrifice as a polemic against the practice by associating what some considered a legitimate part of the YHWH cult with the foreign cult of Baal.[46] Whether the practice is a distant memory or itself the victim of an elaborate cover-up operation, one thing seems evident: the biblical authors were highly concerned with Israelites engaging in child sacrifice.

Part of the ambiguity concerning child sacrifice stems from the language used to describe such sacrifices; texts are often vague and at times confusing. If the text were to use the terms designated for animal sacrifice, such as שחט ("slaughter") and זבח ("ritually slaughter"), we would be on firmer ground. Instead, the Bible records warnings such as being forced "to eat" (אכל) one's children or "to offer up" (עלה) a child.[47] The most common terms are the *hiphil* of עבר, "to cause to pass through/over" (Lev 18:2, Jer 32:35, Ezek 20:25–26), נתן, "to give/donate" (Lev 20:3), שרף + באש, "to burn through the fire" (Deut 12:30–31), and עבר + באש "to cause to pass over in fire" (Deut 18:10, Jer 7:31, 19:5). To complicate matters further, Stavrakopoulou points out that these passages may not necessarily describe child sacrifice. One could interpret the passages as rituals describing nonlethal rites, technical language describing a ritual, euphemisms for an uncomfortable practice,

---

[43] Michaela Bauks, "The Theological Implications of Child sacrifice in and beyond the Biblical Context in Relation to Genesis 22 and Judges 11," in Finsterbusch, Lange, and Römheld, *Human Sacrifice*, 65–86; Jon D. Levenson, *Death and Resurrection of the Beloved Son: The Transformation of Child Sacrifice in Judaism* (New Haven: Yale University Press, 1993), 111–24; Heath Dewrell, *Child Sacrifice in Ancient Israel*, EANEC 5 (Winona Lake, IN: Eisenbrauns, 2017), 108–15; Flynn, *Children in Ancient Israel*, 163–69.

[44] James L. Kugel, *How to Read the Bible: A Guide to Scripture Then and Now* (New York: Free Press, 2008), 131.

[45] Levenson, *Death and Resurrection*, 5; Susan Niditch, *War in the Hebrew Bible: A Study in the Ethics of Violence* (Oxford: Oxford University Press, 1995), 47; Mark S. Smith, *The Early History of God: Yahweh and the Other Deities in Ancient Israel*, Biblical Resource Series (Grand Rapids: Eerdmans, 2002), 172–78. See also Susan Ackerman, *Under Every Green Tree: Popular Religion in Sixth-Century Judah*, HSM 46 (Atlanta: Scholars Press, 1992), 137.

[46] Saul M. Olyan, *Asherah and the Cult of Yahweh in Ancient Israel*, SBLMS 34 (Atlanta: Scholars Press, 1988), 13–14, 38–61, 74.

[47] Deut 28:53–57, Jer 19:9, Lam 2:20, 4:10, 2 Kgs 3:27, Jer 19:5.

nonritual infanticide, or simply metaphors.[48] Yet the preponderance of texts referring to child sacrifice in some form seems to suggest that, even if metaphorical, such a practice was known.[49] As with other social institutions in biblical Israel, the biblical text refers to the event without describing the details of the event. For example, with marriage a man "takes" (לקח), "knows" (ידע), or "sleeps with" (שכב) a woman and the two are considered married. So, too, with child sacrifice. Depending on the context, a child is understood to be sacrificed when offered up, passed through the fire, given to a god, or donated as an offering. Second Kings 3:27 describes a sacrifice: King Mesha took (לקח) his firstborn son, who was to reign after him, and offered him up (ויעלהו) upon the wall (על־החמה). The context demands that we read it "offered him up [as a sacrifice] upon the wall." The same applies to Judg 11:31, where Jephthah vows to offer up as a burnt offering (עולה והעליתהו) the first one to cross his threshold and subsequently "did to her [his daughter] as he vowed" (ויעש לה את־נדרו).[50] While the text leaves out a detailed description of the sacrifice, in both examples, the reader must use the context and the language provided to comprehend what happens; we are to understand that Mesha's son and Jephthah's daughter were sacrificed by their parents.

V. Child Sacrifice in 2 Kings 6:25–30: A Literary Critique

As in Mesha's and Jephthah's stories, rhetoric and context are important for understanding 2 Kgs 6:24–30 as an eliminatory sacrifice. In 2 Kgs 6:28–29, the Kings writer uses language that echoes that used to describe child sacrifice as a regular religious rite.[51] The "cannibalistic mothers" have the following conversation: "Give/donate your son, and let us eat him today, and we will eat my son tomorrow. So we boiled my son and ate him." The absurdity of such a dialogue

---

[48] Stavrakopoulou, *King Manasseh*, 142–43.

[49] Dewrell acknowledges the different terms surrounding child sacrifice and argues that a variety of child sacrifices took place in ancient Israel (*Child Scarifice*, 4–36, 72–147).

[50] Despite the discomfort with the biblical text, Dewrell notes a near consensus among scholars regarding the term עלה: "This near consensus is surprising, since it is difficult to understand 'I will offer up a burnt offering' (והעליתהו עולה) as meaning anything other than sacrifice" (*Child Sacrifice*, 110).

[51] It has become increasingly difficult to know what is meant when the term *Deuteronomistic* is employed, as Martin Noth's initial identification of the Deuteronomistic scribal school has been called into question (Martin Noth, *The Deuteronomistic History*, 2nd ed., JSOTSup 15 [Sheffield: JSOT Press, 1991]; Marvin A. Sweeney, "The Critique of Solomon in the Josianic Edition of the Deuteronomistic History," *JBL* 114 [1995]: 607–22, here 607–8, https://doi.org/10.2307/3266477; John Van Seters, "The Deuteronomistic History: Can It Avoid Death by Redaction?," in *The Future of the Deuteronomistic History*, ed. Thomas Römer, BETL 147 [Leuven: Leuven University Press, 2000], 213–22). Instead, this article adopts the term "Kings writer," following Stavrakopoulou (*King Manasseh*, 21–22), to refer to the writer of Kings. This designation addresses the final form of the text of Kings and puts aside issues of dating.

causes the reader to perk up. The reader's expectations are not met; one does not expect the solution to "I am hungry" to be "let us eat a child." On a simple level, the conversation serves as a metaphor for the dire circumstances surrounding the siege. On a deeper level, however, one finds that specific words in 2 Kgs 6:26–30 link the reader to other passages concerning child sacrifice.

The author gives the reader a few clues to what is going on. The first hint is the setting. The conversation between the mother and the king occurs while the king is עבר על החמה (2 Kgs 6:26). In a *peshat* reading, we would say that the king is "pacing on the wall." But the choice of עבר here is significant. The most common word for movement in the Hebrew Bible is הלך ("walk, go"). As we have seen, the root עבר often describes acts of child sacrifice, "crossing over" to or for Molech/the king (מלך) or through or over the fire. Whereas passages related to child sacrifice use the *hiphil* of עבר, in 2 Kings עבר appears in the *qal*.[52] The king is crossing over (עבר) upon the wall. Note, too, the second part of this phrase, על החמה. The last time these words appear is three short chapters earlier when they describe the very place where the Moabite king sacrificed his son (2 Kgs 3:27). Using the phrase עבר על החמה to set the conversation between the king and the mother clues the reader into a sacrificial context.

The phrase תני את־בנך, "Give your son" (2 Kgs 6:28b), again recalls the rhetoric of child sacrifice. While the verb נתן has a wide semantic range, when used in a sacrificial context it means to give or donate an item to the deity by killing it.[53] Consider Lev 18:21, which exhorts the Israelites ומזרעך לא תתן להעביר למלך, "do not allow any of your offspring to be offered up to Molech/as a *mlk* sacrifice," and Lev 20:3, which states that God will cut himself off from those who מזרעו נתן למלך, "give any of his offspring to Molech/as a *mlk* sacrifice."[54] Other sacrificial contexts include the verb נתן as well; Exod 22:28–29 states that YHWH requests the sacrifice

---

[52] For the purposes of this argument, the stem is not important, but the root is. My argument here builds on the tenets of literary theory wherein the biblical author gives us clues to how the text should be read. In examining the redactional side of literary criticism, Gary Rendsburg describes how different theme words, or *Leitworte* ("catch words," to use his terminology), appear in the text for the purpose of linking or bridging certain texts together. Such words fall into one of four categories: (1) the same word, (2) different words or inflections from the same root, (3) like-sounding words from different roots, (4) words with similar meanings or connotations (*The Redaction of Genesis* [Winona Lake, IN: Eisenbrauns, 1986], 4–5).

[53] Deuteronomy 28 also plays with the concept of "giving children." It identifies YHWH as the giver or provider (נתן־לך) of children, but נתן is also used to describe the action whereby one "gives" or "sacrifices" a child to YHWH. Read ironically, Deut 28 seems to be saying that the one who gave you children will cause you to destroy them.

[54] The translation of the term מלך has been debated in recent years, and scholars have determined that it refers to a specific kind of offering that was a part of the YHWH cult, the *mlk* offering. For the reading of מלך as *mlk* sacrifice rather than as the god Molech, see Stavrakopoulou's discussion and extensive bibliography (*King Manasseh*, 283–99). See also Lange, "They Burn Their Sons and Daughters," 129; Bennie H. Reynolds, "Molek: Dead or Alive? The Meaning and Derivation of mlk and *mlk*," in Finsterbusch, Lange, and Römheld, *Human Sacrifice*, 133–50.

of the firstborn child, along with the firstfruits and animals. The language there, בכור בניך תתן־לי, "give me your firstborn sons," recalls the mother's demand in 2 Kgs 6:28: תני את־בנך, "give (me) your son." Exodus 22:30 goes on to explain what kind of flesh the people should eat (אכל). As in 2 Kgs 6:28–29, the verb אכל appears in close proximity to "offering" (נתן) a son.[55]

How the women go about eating the child is also important, for it has to do with how the sacrifice is carried out. Again, the author hides a clue within the mother's complaint. She tells the king, "We boiled [בשל] my son, and we ate [אכל] him."[56] Boil (בשל) is another coded link to child sacrifice. While none of the texts connected with child sacrifice say that parents boiled their children to death, many texts reference passing sons and daughters over/through the fire. To boil an object requires you to place it in boiling water, and to boil water requires placing a pot over a fire. The mother's statement in 2 Kgs 6:29, נבשל את־בני ונאכלהו, "we boiled my son and ate him," could also be read according to the actions that took place; the mothers took the son and placed/passed him over the fire. By using key words such as "boil," "eat," "crossing," "upon the wall," "give/donate," and "your son," the author taps into known sacrificial language and a known sacrificial context.

In addition to these linguistic links, the Kings writer employs another literary technique in order to highlight the uniqueness of the passage at hand. Second Kings 6:26–30 is placed into the siege narrative via a *Wiederaufnahme*. The resumptive clause הוא [מלך ישראל] עבר על־החמה, found in verses 26 and 30, signals to the reader that the text within has been inserted. Without the insertion, the text states that the king of Aram besieged Samaria, causing food to become scarce and expensive. The king of Israel's response was to rend his clothes and wear sackcloth. If the "cannibalistic mothers" text can be bracketed out, one might wonder why the Kings writer chose to include this vignette. Most commentators conclude that the insertion simply functions to clarify the extremity of the famine. The repeated use of words linked to child sacrifice, however, pushes the reader to search for another meaning.

VI. The Purpose of Eliminatory Killing: Biblical Polemic

Ostensibly, the plight of the Samarians in 2 Kgs 6:24–7:20 comes as a direct result of the people breaking the covenant with God (Deut 28:53–58). The people

---

[55] The words אכל and צרר in 2 Kgs 6 also stand out, as they immediately echo the curses from Deut 28:52–57. That passage describes the dire straits the Israelites will fall into in times of war when cities are besieged (צרר). Like the mothers in 2 Kgs 6, the mothers will be forced to eat (אכל) their children (בניך ובנתיך) in secret. Rather than sacrifice to YHWH, the mothers here will have to sacrifice their children to save their own lives. In Deut 28, cannibalism becomes a punishment for breaking the covenant. See also Jer 19:9.

[56] The curse in Lam 4:10 echoes this narrative.

have sinned, and now their city is under siege. One may therefore ask what part of the covenant the northern kingdom has broken. I suggest that the author hints at a sin so dark that he must veil it. In using code language and framing 2 Kgs 6:26–30 using a *Wiederaufnahme*, the entire narrative of 2 Kgs 6:25–7:20 functions as a hidden polemic against child sacrifice.

The biblical text is rife with hidden polemics.[57] Polemics indicate ideological struggles, presenting arguments and disagreements. One might call a polemic a war of words or a war of opinions. Analyzing biblical polemics, Yairah Amit states:

> The argument within a text defined as polemical, and pertaining to some war of ideas, is intended to strengthen or to reject an explicit or covert position taken by that text, in other biblical texts dealing with the same subject, or in frameworks external to the Bible.[58]

Polemics must also have a bearing on reality. In using a polemic, the author offers critiques of society and a "desire to correct and to shape" the ideology of the world he is commenting on. A variety of polemics are used within the Hebrew Bible. For example, a polemic might be explicit, stating the subject and the polemical stance forthrightly. A polemic might also be implicit, stating the subject and guiding the reader in such a way that the reader arrives at the implied stance seemingly on their own. A third way of employing a polemic is to hide it. In this case, the subject is either not explicitly mentioned or not addressed in a conventional manner. A polemic can be considered hidden if it fits the following criteria: (1) the subject is not explicitly mentioned; (2) other biblical texts address a polemic on the same subject; (3) a variety of code words are present that can guide the reader to uncover the polemic; and (4) other biblical texts reference the polemic. An author might hide a polemic as part of a rhetorical strategy meant to strengthen the persuasiveness of the argument. Fear of censorship might also drive the writer to hide a polemic in order to ensure that it will be preserved.

That child sacrifice would qualify as fuel for an explicit polemic should come as no surprise.[59] The plethora of biblical texts concerning child sacrifice are controversial if somewhat ambiguous. The text of 2 Kgs 6, however, employs a hidden polemic. It provides many signs to identify the polemic. Code words and context point the reader to other stories in the Bible that are clearly concerned with child sacrifice. If the narrator had confined his polemic to an explicit one, to the story of

---

[57] The assumption that a text should have a singular view is a contemporary Western way of thinking. Ancient authors and editors may not have operated under this assumption. Consider, for example, duplicate stories that contradict each other (creation, sister wife, double naming of Jacob). Consider also the writing of the Chronicler, which can be understood as evidence of a literary tradition that includes editorial freedom (Yairah Amit, *Hidden Polemics in Biblical Narrative*, trans. Jonathan Chipman, BibInt 25 [Leiden: Brill, 2000], 33).

[58] Ibid., 7. The material in this paragraph depends on Amit, *Hidden Polemics*, 4, 7, 56–58, 93–98.

[59] Ibid., 45.

the "cannibalistic mothers," the polemic would be fairly straightforward and not that outrageous. The Kings writer, a scribe from Judah, pens tales about the northern kingdom and accuses them of participating in child sacrifice.[60] But the Kings writer goes one step further, creating a hidden polemic.

As noted above, a hidden polemic becomes necessary when censorship is involved and a need exists for concealing the polemic.[61] On the surface, the Kings writer may have had little trepidation about including an explicit polemic against child sacrifice in the northern kingdom; the fact that the northern kingdom was engaged in alternative forms of religious expression was well known (see 2 Kgs 17:1–23). There would seem to be no need to hide this critique, yet this narrative goes one step further than a simple condemnation of child sacrifice. It implies the efficacy of such a sacrifice.

The plot elements within the larger narrative (2 Kgs 6:25–7:20) are the following: the king of Aram lays siege to Samaria; conditions in Samaria are dire; the king feels helpless; a son is eaten; the king feels extremely helpless and sends for Elisha; Elisha predicts the end of the siege; lepers report that the Arameans have fled; the narrator relates that they have fled due to divine intervention; the siege ends. The cause of the divine intervention is not immediately evident and not explicitly stated. Yet if one looks at the narrative in this step-by-step manner, recognizing the *Wiederaufnahme* in 6:26, 30, the cause-and-effect relationship linking the child sacrifice and the end of the siege starts to appear.

The anthropological model for elimination killing further bolsters the case for the efficacy of the mothers' actions in 2 Kgs 6. Such a killing takes place outside of a sacred precinct and subsequently seizes the attention of the deity, who then dispels evil from the community so that peace can be restored and the social order reset.[62] Proof that eliminatory killings were known to the Kings writer comes three chapters earlier with the child sacrifice performed by the Moabite king. Second Kings 3:26–27 does not disguise the fact that the Moabite king sacrifices his son on the city wall as a last-ditch effort to garner the attention of the deity, who then causes a plague, thus ending the siege. Similarly, the mothers in 2 Kgs 6 (unintentionally) sacrifice a son while the king walks on the city walls. This causes the king to summon Elisha, the conduit to YHWH, who then pays attention to the Samarians. YHWH responds by tricking the Arameans, thus ending the siege.

Connecting the mothers' actions to those of the Moabite king in 2 Kgs 3 through *Leitworte* and context illuminates the events in 2 Kgs 6 as an eliminatory

---

[60] On the southern nature of the so-called Deuteronomistic History, see Israel Finkelstein, *The Forgotten Kingdom: The Archaeology and History of Northern Israel*, ANEM 5 (Atlanta: Society of Biblical Literature, 2013), 1–6.

[61] Amit, *Hidden Polemics*, 97.

[62] Pongratz-Leisten, "Sacrifice in the Ancient Near East," 293; Schwartz, "Archaeology and Sacrifice," 1–32.

killing.⁶³ Nevertheless, there are some differences between 2 Kgs 3 and 2 Kgs 6. First, two different nations are involved—Moab and Israel—meaning (presumably) that two different deities are at work. More importantly, in the second narrative the child sacrifice garners the immediate attention of the king, not the deity. I would argue that this second difference is due to the first. The Kings writer is playing with the notion of foreignness in the polemic. The reason for the biblical prohibition against child sacrifice is that child sacrifice is foreign.⁶⁴ Placing the cannibal mothers so close in the narrative to the tale of Mesha, the Kings writer associates the two as eliminatory sacrifices. Yet, if the Kings writer were to state outright that the Samarians were engaging in an eliminatory child sacrifice, he would be opening a theological can of worms. Instead, by associating the Samarian eliminatory killing with that of the Moabites in the previous chapter, the Kings writer subtly lashes out against the northern kingdom, associating them not only with aberrant religious practices but also with foreigners. Foreigners engage in idolatrous actions, are accused of religious depravity, and, most importantly, are not a part of the covenant between YHWH and Israel.

If the Kings writer were to make such an accusation openly, he might face severe repercussions. He needs to walk a fine line in this polemic, making sure the reader understands both 2 Kgs 3 and 2 Kgs 6 as eliminatory killings without equating YHWH's response to the sacrifice with that of the Moabite god. In order to ensure that his critique is included in the narrative, he creates a hidden polemic. By switching the order of events in the two stories and having the mothers' sacrifice capture the *king*'s attention and not *YHWH*'s attention, the Kings writer is able to create the required distance between the actions and the expected result. Rather than have an immediate effect such as the Moabites witnessed, the mothers' actions are separated from their effect. The king falls into mourning, he blames Elisha and YHWH for the current state of Samaria, and Elisha predicts a turn of events. In the end, the narrative appears to be about trusting YHWH, not about the effectiveness of child sacrifice. By presenting a coded narrative wherein child sacrifice allegedly becomes a side effect of war, the Kings writer hides the polemic concerning the efficacy of child sacrifice, instead making the text ostensibly about the foreign nature of the northern kingdom.⁶⁵

---

⁶³ While the text in 2 Kgs 3 makes it clear that King Mesha killed his son as a sacrifice, one could debate the role of intentionality in the passage in 2 Kgs 6. It is clear that the mothers both mean to kill their sons (6:28–29b), but, according to the narrative, the mothers do not do so as a sacrifice. The Kings writer places the sacrificial layer over the text through the use of the coded words.

⁶⁴ For evidence that the prohibition is due to the foreign rather than the unethical nature of the practice, see Stavrakopoulou, *King Manasseh*, 148–49. See also Deut 12:19–31, 2 Kgs 17:25–28. Stavrakopoulou also points out that the Kings writer identifies people who engage in child sacrifice as either foreign or deviant Israelites: 2 Kgs 3:26–27; 16:3; 17:17, 31; 21:3–6.

⁶⁵ Amit argues that the Hebrew Bible contains hidden polemics against the northern

VII. Conclusions: Focusing on the Children

Whereas previous readings view the children as helpless, ineffectual victims, a childist reading of 2 Kgs 6:24–30 presents children as the solution. The son who is eaten becomes the solution on two levels. On an immediate level, the death of the child allows the mothers to fill their bellies. On a meta-level, the death of the child causes the end of the war. God recognizes the act of boiling the child for what it is, a sacrificial cry for help. God is not silent or hidden in the face of such an act; God immediately responds to the child's death by dispatching Elisha and bringing mayhem to the Aramean camp. On this reading, the importance of the child should not be underestimated. The child is not a passive object acted upon and forgotten. The child, silent though he is, becomes an agent of change. What the Samarian army could not do, a young boy's death did—it stopped the siege.

In an ironic twist, the very thing that should not have been happening—child sacrifice—is what saves Samaria. If one wants to argue about the efficacy of child sacrifice in Israel's narrative, one need look no further than this text; the Kings writer states that it works.[66] Just because it works, however, does not mean that people should do it. Child sacrifice should be relegated to the realm of foreign gods, and the Kings writer bases his hidden polemic on this fact. YHWH does not want his cult to be associated with this foreign practice. One could argue that the prohibition against child sacrifice is an effort to separate Israel from its neighbors, to make sure YHWH is not associated with meaningless pagan rituals.

A childist reading of the story also pushes us to ask why the Kings writer includes an effectual child sacrifice to make his point. The answer again centers on the children. Children are valuable not just economically and socially but intrinsically as well. Each member of the covenant is important to YHWH, no matter what his or her age. Thus, each member of the covenant, each Israelite child, has inherent value, and the sacrifice of a young boy cannot be ignored. Even so, the Kings writer reminds the reader that YHWH does not desire a child's death, for in the words of Jeremiah "it is no commandment" of his (Jer 7:31).

---

kingdom with respect to its religious depravity (*Hidden Polemics*, 99–129). The 2 Kgs 6 text falls in line with other examples of veiled polemics addressing the evils of the northern kingdom.

[66] Nowhere does the Hebrew Bible say that child sacrifice is ineffectual, but at some point it became undesirable to YHWH (Gen 22, Ezek 20:25–26, Lev 18:21, 20:3, Deut 12:30–31, 18:10, Mic 6:7, Isa 30:27–33, Jer 7:31, 19:5, 32:35).

Transformations in Translation: An Examination of the Septuagint Rendering of Hebrew Wordplay in the Fourth Book of the Psalter

ELIZABETH BACKFISH
lbackfish@jessup.edu
William Jessup University-Rocklin Campus, Rocklin, CA 95765

The translation technique of the Septuagint version of the Psalter has been characterized in various ways, but little attention has been given to the translators' handling of poetic features such as wordplay. This study builds on Theo A. W. van der Louw's work on LXX "transformations," that is, changes between the source and target languages made to better represent both the content and the form essential to the message of the source text. Recognizing the LXX translators' ability to represent the Hebrew wordplays in Pss 90–106, often by using transformations, contributes to a more nuanced understanding of the relationship between the LXX, its *Vorlage*, and the MT.

Wordplay, like most poetic devices, is not easily translated from a source to a target language, and this fact created a formidable responsibility for the Septuagint translators. At stake were both the semantic equivalent and the style of the text, which are both important for communicating the original message. Characterizing the translation technique used in the LXX is vital in order to illuminate the nature of the LXX and its value in textual criticism. The dominant issues of identifying the *Vorlage* of the LXX and determining whether the translation technique was literal or free or whether it should be analyzed qualitatively or quantitatively have given way in the past few decades to a more nuanced and holistic approach.[1] This approach seeks to widen the criteria used for characterizing translation technique from lexical, grammatical, and syntactical choices of the translators to include rhetorical elements and poetic features such as wordplay. According to Anneli Aejmelaeus,

[1] Scholars, however, have not altogether ignored the role of wordplay in translation; see, e.g., Emanuel Tov, "Loan-Words, Homophony, and Transliteration in the Septuagint," *Bib* 60 (1979): 216–36; Jan de Waard, "'Homophony' in the Septuagint," *Bib* 62 (1981): 551–61.

"What one needs in order to gain a more reliable and complete picture of this translator, as well as others of his kind, is new and other criteria for the characterization of 'translation technique.'"[2]

Hans Ausloos, Bénédicte Lemmelijn, and Valérie Kabergs argue for "content-related" criteria for characterization, examining such features as jargon, *hapax legomena*, and etiological wordplays in order to describe more fully the translation technique employed in the LXX.[3] This article contributes to this broader approach of translation technique characterization by analyzing specifically how the translator rendered or represented Hebrew wordplay in his own target language. More specifically, I will show that these renderings were often made possible through what Theo A. W. van der Louw describes as "transformations," slight alterations to the sense or surface structure of the source text.[4] Before offering some examples of these transformations, I will outline the study's methodology and provide a summary analysis of the data.

I. Methodology

Scholars define wordplay in various ways. For Stefan Kjerkegaard, it is "an interaction between a semiotic deficit and a semantic surplus,"[5] which is to say that the economy of language requires more meanings than signs. Knut Heim writes, "Wordplays are playful but significant uses of one and the same word or phrase with different meanings or of different words or phrases with the same 'meanings.'"[6]

---

[2] Anneli Aejmelaeus, "Characterizing Criteria for the Characterization of the Septuagint Translators: Experimenting on the Greek Psalter," in *The Old Greek Psalter: Studies in Honour of Albert Pietersma*, ed. Robert J. V. Hiebert, Claude E. Cox, and Peter J. Gentry, JSOTSup 332 (Sheffield: Sheffield Academic, 2001), 54–73, here 55–56.

[3] Hans Ausloos, Bénédicte Lemmelijn, and Valérie Kabergs, "The Study of Aetiological Wordplay as a Content-Related Criterion in the Characterization of LXX Translation Technique," in *Die Septuaginta: Entstehung, Sprache, Geschichte; 3. Internationale Fachtagung veranstaltet von Septuaginta Deutsch (LXX.D), Wuppertal, 22.–25. Juli 2010*, ed. Siegfried Kreuzer, Martin Meiser, and Marcus Sigismund, WUNT 286 (Tübingen: Mohr Siebeck, 2012), 273–94.

[4] Theo A. W. van der Louw, *Transformations in the Septuagint: Towards an Interaction of Septuagint Studies and Translation Studies*, CBET 47 (Leuven: Peeters, 2007).

[5] Stefan Kjerkegaard, "Seven Days without a Pun Makes One Weak: Two Functions of Wordplay in Literature and Literary Theory," *Journal of Literature, Language and Linguistics* 3 (2011): 1–9, here 1.

[6] Knut Heim, "Wordplay," in *Dictionary of the Old Testament: Wisdom, Poetry and Writings*, ed. Tremper Longman III and Peter Enns (Downers Grove, IL: InterVarsity Press, 2008), 925–29, here 925. Derek Attridge defines wordplay (or puns, specifically) in a similar way, as either one word with two meanings or as two homophones "in a particular context made to coalesce" ("Unpacking the Portmanteau, or Who's Afraid of Finnegans Wake?," in *On Puns: The Foundation of Letters*, ed. Jonathan Culler [Oxford: Blackwell, 1988], 140–55, here 144). Wilfred G. E. Watson posits, "Wordplay is based on lexical ambiguity which is simply a way of saying that words can be

These explanations refer specifically to semantic wordplay. Luis Alonso Schökel aptly includes both the semantic and phonetic dimensions of wordplay: "Plays on words exploit the polivalence [sic] of meaning of one word, or the similarity of sound of various words."[7] In this study I assume Schökel's broader definition.

Kabergs and Ausloos offer a thorough discussion of the definition of wordplay, helpfully distinguishing it from the word *paronomasia*. Although the two words have often been confused or used interchangeably,[8] Kabergs and Ausloos argue that wordplay is the broader category, while paronomasia is a type of wordplay wherein the poet uses "the proximity of two words with a different meaning but a similar sound pattern."[9] I maintain that same distinction, using wordplay as the umbrella

---

polyvalent" (*Classical Hebrew Poetry: A Guide to Its Techniques*, JSOTSup 26 [Sheffield: JSOT Press, 1984], 237). Watson's more general definition is fleshed out with examples and categories, but, as it stands, the definition is simultaneously too broad and too limited. It is too broad because polyvalency in itself is not wordplay; rather, the author's exploitation of a word's polyvalency for a particular purpose is wordplay. Moreover, lexical ambiguity exists only when the context does not demarcate a word's intended sense; wordplay exists only when such ambiguity is intentionally not immediately disambiguated or when secondary meanings are potentially suggested. Watson's definition is too limited because it excludes all wordplays that play on sound rather than meaning, which excludes many forms of paronomasia.

Geoffrey H. Hartman offers a memorable definition of wordplay in relation to homonymic (and homophonic) plays and polysemantic plays: "You can define a pun as two meanings competing for the same phonemic space or as one sound bringing forth semantic twins, but however you look at it, it's a crowded situation" ("The Voice of the Shuttle: Language from the Point of View of Literature," in *Beyond Formalism: Literary Essays, 1958-1970* [New Haven: Yale University Press, 1970], 337-55, here 347).

[7] Luis Alonso Schökel, *A Manual of Hebrew Poetics*, SubBi 11 (Rome: Pontifical Biblical Institute, 1988), 29.

[8] Immanuel Moses Casanowicz's 1892 dissertation, "Paronomasia in the Old Testament" (published in 1894 by J. S. Cushing in Boston), was the first monograph-length work on Hebrew wordplay. While this work was an important foundation for future studies, Casanowicz used paronomasia as the broader term and wordplay as specifically a play on meaning, that is, a pun, which he considered inferior to plays on sound (*Paronomasia in the Old Testament*, 12). Subsequent scholars, including J. J. Glück ("Paronomasia in Biblical Literature," *Semitics* 1 [1970]: 50-78), Alfred Guillaume ("Paronomasia in the Old Testament," *JSS* 9 [1964]: 282-90), and Baruch Halpern and Richard Elliott Friedman ("Composition and Paronomasia in the Book of Jonah," *HAR* 4 [1980]: 79-92), either followed Casanowicz's lead or interpreted the Greek components of "paronomasia"—παρά and ὀνομασία, meaning "by the side of" and "naming," respectively—to denote wordplay in general. According to Anthony J. Petrotta, "In classical usage, paronomasia usually refers to words in proximity that differ only slightly in form and have a different meaning" (*Lexis Ludens: Wordplay and the Book of Micah*, AmUStTR 105 [New York: Lang, 1991], 6); Ausloos and Kabergs, "Paronomasia or Wordplay? A Babel-Like Confusion Towards a Definition of Hebrew Wordplay," *Bib* 93 [2012]: 1-20, here 7).

[9] Kabergs and Ausloos, "Paronomasia or Wordplay?," 7. While Kabergs and Ausloos limit wordplay to only those figures that play on both meaning and sound, I include plays that are, or appear to be, playing only on sound (ibid., 14). The reason for this broader definition is twofold. First, it includes figures that many other scholars have dubbed wordplay; in other words, many

term for both paronomasia (play on sound) and polysemany (play on meaning). Paronomastic wordplays play on phonetic similarity and include alliteration,[10] metaphony, parasonancy, and root letter transposition, whereas polysemantic wordplays play on semantic ambiguity and include double entendre and punning repetition.

Although this type of analysis requires an element of subjectivity, there are certain guidelines and criteria that will prove helpful in identifying true wordplay in both the MT and the LXX.[11] For Hebrew wordplays, the identification of paronomasia requires that the second word being played upon should contain at least two of the consonants of the first, and, if those two consonants do not constitute half of the letters, supplementary evidence of wordplay is required.[12] The use of *hapax legomena* or unexpected words when more common or expected words would fit the context, as well as words that cause imbalance in a colon, could also support the identification of wordplay. Other contextual indicators of wordplay

---

scholars use this broader definition. Second, and more critical, it is often very difficult to discern whether a play on meaning is intentional. Many words used in paronomasia, for example, are clearly juxtaposed for their similarity in sound (and thus a wordplay by our definition), but the function or purpose of the play is not always clear. It could be merely aesthetics, it could be to maintain the readers' interest, or it could be a play on meaning. Sometimes, however, the play on meaning is not obvious and can only be speculated.

[10] In this study, for both Hebrew and Greek analysis, only alliteration that involves the repetition of more than one phoneme will qualify as wordplay.

[11] A completely objective system of identifying true wordplay is impossible, and, as with many hermeneutical endeavors, such an exercise necessarily requires an artful and imaginative close reading of the text. In explaining his own safeguards in interpreting deliberate ambiguity in the Psalms, Paul Raabe summarizes well this subjective nature: "I doubt, however, that we will ever be able to formulate such scientifically precise rules so as to remove all scholarly disagreement. There will always be some, well, ambiguity" ("Deliberate Ambiguity in the Psalter," *JBL* 110 [1991]: 213–27, here 227, https://doi.org/10.2307/3267083). Despite these helpful guidelines for identifying wordplays, it is important to remember that the line between true and contrived wordplay is not always clear. According to Catherine Bates, "the difference is one of degree but not of kind" ("The Point of Puns," *Modern Philology* 96 [1999]: 421–38, here 432). The recognition of wordplay is often dependent on one's interpretative style; some readers are willing to be riskier and occasionally create their own "wordplays," whereas other readers may be safer and occasionally overlook or deny true wordplays. While ideal readers need to be careful not to say more than Scripture, they also must not say less than Scripture. Bates points out that a particularly important advantage of the "risky" interpreter is that he or she "knows the nature of the market better" and "may in the end be better at playing the game" (435). J. J. M. Roberts likewise encourages openness in his study on double entendre in First Isaiah: "While one must remain aware of the danger of overreading … it is far more likely that our lack of familiarity with the wider connotations of classical Hebrew words and phrases will result in underreading, of missing intentional *double entendres*" ("Double Entendre in First Isaiah," *CBQ* 54 [1992]: 39–48, here 40). As with many interpretative analyses, it is probably best to begin a study with openness and to distinguish true wordplays from potential ones through careful study.

[12] Edward L. Greenstein, "Wordplay, Hebrew," *ABD* 6:968–71, here 969.

include irregular syntax, gender, or inflection.[13] If a word pair in a potential wordplay is related structurally (e.g., in an *inclusio*, chiastic pattern, or parallelism), this relationship could also support its identification as a wordplay. Hebrew morphology often produces end rhyme and other forms of phonemic similarity that are a product not always of wordplay but of grammatical necessity.[14] Finally, if the author could not have said the same thing another way, or if it would have been a strain to do so, the phenomenon is very likely accidental and not a wordplay.

The criteria for identifying wordplay in the LXX of the Psalter are slightly less rigid because of the relative limitations of rendering poetry but also because the sense of the source language is very different from that of the target language. Thus, the repetition of two or more phonemes in close proximity will support the identification of wordplay, but additional evidence will be required to determine the intentionality of the translator. If a translator typically used one Greek lexeme for a particular Hebrew term, straying from this consistency may indicate his acknowledgment of the wordplay and an attempt at his own. Another key factor is the element of choice: did the translator have another semantic or grammatical option that he could have chosen?[15]

One final point of methodology that is relevant to the data below is the potential of finding false positives in the LXX translation of MT wordplay. If the LXX were replete with wordplays and if the translator had used wordplay in the Greek where it does not appear in the Hebrew, then the correlations argued for in this study would be merely coincidental. Yet the translator seldom uses wordplay independent from where it is found in the MT, and the majority of the instances of wordplay in the LXX render wordplays in the MT.

II. Analysis of the Data

An overview of this study's findings should help to define the landscape of the texts under consideration. The Hebrew psalms of book 4 of the Psalter contain an impressive seventy-one wordplays, 87 percent of which are paronomastic wordplays and 13 percent of which are polysemantic. Table 1 illustrates the distribution of these wordplays in the MT and summarizes their representation in the LXX.

---

[13] Heim, "Wordplay," 927; Raabe, "Deliberate Ambiguity," 227; Stephen Ullmann, *Semantics: An Introduction to the Science of Meaning* (New York: Harper & Row, 1979), 168–69.

[14] Schökel believes that end rhyme produced through morphology is "poor" but can be effective if amassed (*Manual of Hebrew Poetics*, 23). See also one of Casanowicz's more lasting contributions on "intentional and accidental congruence of sound"(*Paronomasia in the Old Testament*, 27–28).

[15] Staffan Olofsson, *The LXX Version: A Guide to the Translation Technique of the Septuagint*, ConBOT 30 (Stockholm: Almqvist & Wiksell, 1990), 14.

TABLE 1. Distribution of LXX Translation Tendencies in Individual Psalms

| | Unrepresented Wordplay | | Represented Wordplay | | | % of |
| | LXX Renders the Sense | LXX Contains a Textual Variation | LXX Creates a Similar Wordplay | LXX Replicates the Same Wordplay | Total Word-plays in MT | Wordplays Repre-sented in LXX |
Psalm						
90	8	1	5		14	35.7
91	6		2		8	25.0
92			1	1	2	100.0
93	1	1			2	0
94	3		1		4	33.3
95	1	1		1	3	33.3
96	1		2		3	66.6
97	1		2	1	4	75.0
98						
99						
100						
101				1	1	100.0
102	9		1		10	10.0
103	3				3	0
104	2		1	1	4	50.0
105	3	1			4	0
106	4	1	4		9	44.4
Total	42	5	19	5	71	33.8

The LXX was able to represent twenty-four, or 33.8 percent, of the Hebrew wordplays in Pss 90–106. In five cases, the translator was able to replicate the wordplay by using the same terms and the same category of wordplay in his target language. In nineteen cases, he was able to create a similar wordplay, either translating the same words using a different category of wordplay or using the same category of wordplay but adjacent words in order to best represent the phenomenon in the Hebrew text.

Given the difficulty of translating wordplay into a target language, these are impressive numbers; however, if the LXX is replete with wordplays of its own, these data are far less convincing. To test against false positives, it is essential to analyze the total distribution of LXX wordplays in comparison to the distribution of wordplays in the MT, paying particular attention to the number of independent LXX wordplays and the percentage of LXX wordplays used to render MT wordplays. The following table evinces a clear correlation between wordplay in the MT and the LXX, showing that the majority of wordplays in the LXX render wordplays in the MT:

TABLE 2. LXX Wordplay Translation Compared with LXX Overall Wordplay Use

Psalm	Total MT WP	Total LXX WP	LXX Rendering of MT WP	LXX WP Excluding MT WP	% of LXX WP Used to Render MT WP
90	14	5	5	0	100.0
91	8	2	2	0	100.0
92	2	2	2	0	100.0
93	2	0	0	0	NA
94	4	2	1	1	50.0
95	3	2	1	1	50.0
96	3	2	2	0	100.0
97	4	3	3	0	100.0
98	0	0	0	0	NA
99	0	0	0	0	NA
100	0	0	0	0	NA
101	1	1	1	0	100.0
102	10	2	1	1	50.0
103	3	0	0	0	NA
104	4	3	2	1	66.6
105	4	4	0	4	0
106	9	4	4	0	100.0
Total Number of Wordplays	71	32	24	8	
Percentage			33.8	25.0	75.0
Total Number of Wordplays Excluding Ps 105	67	28	24	4	
Percentage Excluding Ps 105			35.8	14.3	85.7

Notice that 75 percent of wordplays in the LXX render wordplay in the MT, leaving only 25 percent of the total LXX wordplays independent of the MT wordplays. Independent wordplays are not surprising, given the translator's aptitude for the poetic device, and their scarcity (eight total in the entire corpus) supports the thesis that the LXX translator was indeed attempting to represent the trope in his source text. Of these eight independent wordplays, half (four) are found in Ps 105, where, moreover, the translator did not represent any of the Hebrew wordplays. This makes Ps 105 a bit of an anomaly for book 4, which is why the final two rows in the table calculate the data without respect to Ps 105. If Ps 105 is considered an outlier, statistically speaking, the data are even more convincing: 85.7 percent of the LXX wordplays render MT wordplays, and only 14.3 percent (four total) are unrelated to the Hebrew wordplay.

Van der Louw has written a significant study on the translation technique of the LXX, paying particular attention to transformations, which he defines as "shifts or changes (linguistic or other) with respect to an invariant core that occur in translation from source text to target text."[16] If the target text differs significantly from the assumed source text (MT in this case), interpreters usually conclude that (1) the target text differed from the MT, (2) the translator was incompetent or had ideological motives for changing the text, or (3) scribal error was involved. Van der Louw proposes a more nuanced approach in assessing these differences, arguing that transformations were made because a literal translation would not be feasible or adequate. He categorizes many transformations, the most relevant for this study being stylistic translation, compensation, addition, and explication.[17] He also notes that stylistic translation and compensation are common in poetry because the form is more important than the semantic equivalence.[18] Thus, when the LXX translator is attempting to represent wordplay in his target language, it should not be surprising that he uses various transformations to do so, which is exactly what we see in many of the cases where the LXX differs from the MT or where the LXX seems to use an unexpected or inconsistent lexeme.[19] Table 3 presents the distribution of transformations in book 4 of the Psalter, in both the paronomastic and polysemantic wordplays that the translator was able to represent.

---

[16] Van der Louw, *Transformations in the Septuagint*, 383.
[17] Ibid., 61–62. For detailed descriptions of each category, see his elaboration in 62–92.
[18] Ibid., 84.
[19] De Waard takes a similar approach to the LXX translation of Isaiah, showing how various phonological translations create semantic and grammatical variants ("'Homophony' in the Septuagint," 551–61).

TABLE 3. Distribution of LXX Transformations in Individual Psalms

Psalm	Wordplay is Represented in the LXX	Wordplays Involving Transformations	Percentage of Transformations
90	5	3	60.0
91	2	2	100.0
92	2	1	50.0
94	1	1	100.0
95	1	0	0
96	2	0	0
97	3	1	33.3
101	1	1	100.0
102	1	0	0
104	2	1	50.0
106	4	2	50.0
Total	24	12	50.0

In exactly half of the total renderings, the translator used some sort of transformation, some sort of alteration to the surface structure of the source text in order to render the wordplay effectively in his target language. These transformations and their motives are too often overlooked, which results in at least two problems: (1) the inclination to overlook true and nuanced motives of transformations (such as those used to render style); and (2) the failure to appreciate the skill involved in the translator's efforts to render such poetic features. The translator is thus criticized for being too literal, too free, ignorant of Hebrew vocabulary or grammar, or just in error, creating an overall negative view of his skills as a translator. Attention to the translator's regard for the style of the communication facilitates a more nuanced and holistic picture of the LXX translation technique.

III. SELECTED EXAMPLES OF TRANSFORMATIONS IN THE LXX TRANSLATION OF WORDPLAY IN PSALMS 90–106

The following examples of LXX translation of Hebrew wordplay are limited to cases wherein the LXX translator had to make some sort of transformation or an unexpected lexical choice that, far from being an indicator of his ineptitude or a variant parent text, actually highlights his skill in both interpreting and representing the original wordplay.

In Ps 91:6a and 7a, the Hebrew poet uses parasonancy between בָּאֹפֶל ("in the darkness"), יִפֹּל ("he/it will fall"), and אֶלֶף ("one thousand").

מִדֶּבֶר בָּאֹפֶל יַהֲלֹךְ	6a	[Nor] of the plague that walks in the darkness,
מִקֶּטֶב יָשׁוּד צָהֳרָיִם	6b	[Nor] of the destruction that destroys at midday.
יִפֹּל מִצִּדְּךָ אֶלֶף	7a	A thousand will fall from your side,
וּרְבָבָה מִימִינֶךָ	7b	And ten thousand from your right hand.
אֵלֶיךָ לֹא יִגָּשׁ	7c	To you they will not come near.

All three words share a פ and ל, and additionally two share either a defective *holem* or an א. The author also chose a rare word for darkness (אֹפֶל, which occurs only nine times in the Hebrew Bible) when he could have used a much more common word (חֹשֶׁךְ, which occurs ninety-eight times). The effect of this parasonancy (אֹפֶל and יִפֹּל) on the surface level and root letter transposition (אֹפֶל and אֶלֶף) on the deep level is both aesthetic and structural, linking the bicolon of verse 6 with the tricolon of verse 7.

The LXX translator uses the standard Greek equivalents for these words, none of which exhibit any similarity in sound. He had the opportunity, however, to represent the wordplay by rendering יִפֹּל מִצִּדְּךָ אֶלֶף ("a thousand may fall from your side") thus:

90:7a πεσεῖται ἐκ τοῦ κλίτους σου χιλιάς
One thousand will fall from your side.

Both words share a λ and a final ς, and the phonetic similarity between κ and χ suggests that the translator chose κλίτους ("side")[20] for its phonetic similarity to χιλιάς ("one thousand"). Moreover, the translator could have used πλευρά, which most often refers to the side of a human, whereas κλίτους is used almost exclusively of a region or side of an inanimate object, often referring to articles or areas in the temple.[21] This example illustrates how an apparently inconsistent lexical choice is better understood as a transformation for the sake of rendering wordplay.

The Hebrew wordplay in Ps 97:7 is a case of paronomastic end rhyme between הַמִּתְהַלְלִים ("the ones who boast") and בָּאֱלִילִים ("in [the] vain things")[22] in the second line of the tricolon:

---

[20] Johan Lust, Erik Eynikel, and Katrin Hauspie, *Greek-English Lexicon of the Septuagint*, rev. ed. (Stuttgart: Deutsche Bibelgesellschaft, 2003), 344, s.v. κλίτος.

[21] BAGD, s.v. "πλευρά"; GELS, s.v. "κλίτος."

[22] According to Erich Zenger, אֱלִילִים is "probably an artificially constructed diminutive of אֵל or אלהים, 'God,' and means, in an ironic sense, 'little god.'" Its only other use in the plural is in Ps 96:5 (Frank-Lothar Hossfeld and Erich Zenger, *Psalms 2: A Commentary on Psalms 51–100*,

יֵבֹשׁוּ כָּל־עֹבְדֵי פֶסֶל	7a	Let all who serve an idol be ashamed!
הַמִּתְהַלְלִים בָּאֱלִילִים	7b	Those who boast in vain things!
הִשְׁתַּחֲווּ־לוֹ כָּל־אֱלֹהִים	7c	Worship him, all you gods!

End rhyme is often a natural byproduct of conjugational necessity and, thus, incidental, but the end rhyme combined with the double ל, along with the immediate proximity of the words, marks this wordplay as a true wordplay. Moreover, this is the only verse in the Hebrew Bible where both of these terms are used.[23] The function of the usage is probably aesthetic, structural, and theological. It binds the second line together in such a way as to show that the boasters themselves are much like the vain things they worship, drawing together two ideas in an ironic way. The repeated use of ל in this strophe (nine occurrences) further highlights the wordplay between הַמִּתְהַלְלִים and בָּאֱלִילִים.

The LXX translator attempted his own paronomasia in the place of the Hebrew rhyme in 96:7b:

7a   αἰσχυνθήτωσαν πάντες οἱ προσκυνοῦντες τοῖς γλυπτοῖς

7b   οἱ ἐγκαυχώμενοι ἐν τοῖς εἰδώλοις αὐτῶν

7c   προσκυνήσατε αὐτῷ πάντες οἱ ἄγγελοι αὐτοῦ

7a   Let anyone who bows down to carved images be ashamed!

7b   Those who boast in their idols!

7c   Worship him, all his angels!

The threefold repetition of the κυν/χυν syllable is reinforced by the similar-sounding χωμ syllable in verse 7b.[24] The translator's choice of προσκυνοῦντες ("those who bow down/worship")[25] in verse 7a to render עֹבְדֵי ("those who serve") is unique in the LXX. Of its 288 occurrences, it is almost exclusively used to render חוה ("to bow down") as in verse 7c and occasionally the similar סגד ("to do homage/bow down") in Aramaic. The translator's desire to simulate the Hebrew wordplay would also explain the explicating transformation in the LXX; "bows down" specifies the means by which idolaters "serve" false gods.[26] This wordplay has the

---

trans. Linda M. Maloney, Hermeneia [Minneapolis: Fortress, 2005], 475). This may further support the intentionality of wordplay.

[23] Isaiah 2:18 employs a similar wordplay using וְהָאֱלִילִים כָּלִיל יַחֲלֹף: אֱלִיל ("And the idols will entirely pass away").

[24] That the translator used the entire tricola to represent a wordplay limited to the second colon of the source text should not be surprising given the difficulty of the translator's task. Nor is it unlikely that the translator would use the line preceding the MT's wordplay to begin his own wordplay, as though the translator would not or could not have read the strophe before translating it.

[25] GELS, s.v. "προσκυνέω"; LEH, s.v. "προσκυνέω."

[26] The many variants in the verse between the MT and the LXX (including grammatical and

effect of emphasizing and explicating the contrast between idolatrous worship (v. 7a) and Yahwistic worship (v. 7c).

In Ps 101:3b, the MT uses alliteration in three words:

לֹא־אָשִׁית לְנֶגֶד עֵינַי דְּבַר־בְּלִיָּעַל 3a I will not set before my eyes a worthless thing.

עֲשֹׂה־סֵטִים שָׂנֵאתִי 3b I hate the work of transgressors.

לֹא יִדְבַּק בִּי 3c It will not cling to me.

Every word in verse 3b is either part of or contributes to the wordplay. The words סֵטִים and שָׂנֵאתִי share three phonetic equivalents (ס/שׂ, ט/ת, and י◌), and the initial infinitive עֲשֹׂה reinforces the wordplay. While these three phonemes are common in the Hebrew alphabet, their prevalence in the colon and close proximity mark this as a true wordplay. Moreover, the noun סֵט is a *hapax legomenon*, even though several other words in the semantic field of evil works or evildoers could have been chosen (e.g., פֹּעֲלֵי אָוֶן, עֹשֵׂה הָרָעָה).

This wordplay links the words of this line and adds poetic beauty to the strophe. It also emphasizes the line and the psalmist's rejection of anything ungodly, which is further underscored by the *inclusio* of negatives (לֹא) in the preceding and following lines: "I will not set before my eyes a worthless thing" (v. 3a), and "It will not cling to me" (v. 3c). Use of the rare word סֵט also brings to mind the more common verb שׂוּט (שֵׂטִים), meaning "to despise," thereby creating a polysemantic play emphasizing the depth of the psalmist's hatred toward evildoers.[27]

The LXX creates alliteration between two of these equivalent words, as well as four of the words in the preceding line:

100:3a οὐ προεθέμην πρὸ ὀφθαλμῶν μου πρᾶγμα παράνομον

3b ποιοῦντας παραβάσεις ἐμίσησα

3a I have not set before my eyes an unlawful thing.

3b I have hated those who commit transgressions.

The fivefold repetition of the π and the fourfold repetition of the π and ρ together mark this as a wordplay. Moreover, προτίθημι ("to set before")[28] occurs only twelve times in the LXX, only eight of which are in the Hebrew Bible. Likewise, παράβασις

---

semantic) are well known and not pertinent to the relevant wordplays. For a good discussion of these, see Marvin E. Tate, *Psalms, 51–100*, WBC 20 (Nashville: Nelson, 1990), 517.

[27] The editors of *BHS* suggest that the LXX *Vorlage* of παραβάσεις is שֵׂטִים, which occurs only once in the Old Testament (Hos 5:2), and according to *HALOT*, s.v. "סֵט," the form שֵׂטִים in Hos 5:2 should actually be read סֵטִים.

[28] LEH, s.v. "προτίθημι."

("transgression")[29] is a *hapax legomenon* in the Hebrew Bible and occurs only twice in the apocryphal books (2 Macc 15:10; Wis 14:31). In addition, παράνομον ("unlawful")[30] and ποιοῦντας ("those who do/work") are not standard translation equivalents, and they could even be construed as variants were the translator not making a purposeful transformation in order to create a wordplay. The phrase πρᾶγμα παράνομον is used to render the MT's דְּבַר־בְּלִיָּעַל ("a worthless thing"), and the participial phrase ποιοῦντας παραβάσεις is used to render the MT's nominal use of the infinitive construct עֲשֹׂה־סֵטִים ("works of transgression/faithless men"), thus shifting focus from the deeds to the doers.[31] These lexical and syntactic choices enabled the translator to create as much alliteration as possible and should thus be explained as style, compensation, accidence, and word-class transformations rather than true variants.

In Ps 104:12, the Hebrew poet plays on עוֹף ("birds") and their dwelling place עֳפָאיִם ("foliage") by using paronomasia:

עֲלֵיהֶם עוֹף־הַשָּׁמַיִם יִשְׁכּוֹן   12a   The birds of the heavens dwell with them.
מִבֵּין עֳפָאיִם יִתְּנוּ־קוֹל   12b   From among the foliage they lift up a voice.

Both words share ע and פ, making this a case of alliteration. Both words are also second in their lines and syntactically parallel in that both lines begin with a prepositional phrase. As is common in wordplay, עֳפָאיִם, from עֳפִי, is a *hapax legomenon*, even though the poet could have used other words, such as שִׂיחַ ("bush" or "shrub"), as he does in verse 34.[32] This wordplay serves effectively to connect the subjects (birds of the heavens) with their setting (the foliage).

The LXX translator is able to replicate this same wordplay, translating the same Hebrew words with the same alliterative device:

---

[29] Ibid., s.v. "παράβασις."
[30] Ibid., s.v. "παράνομος."
[31] Willem VanGemeren also notes this variant (*Psalms*, EBC 5 [Grand Rapids: Zondervan, 2008], 746). It is unclear whether the *hapax legomenon* סֵטִים refers to the unfaithful acts or the perpetrators of those acts. For interpretive options, see John Goldingay, *Psalms*, 3 vols., BCOTWP (Grand Rapids: Baker Adademic, 2006–2008), 3:138; Leslie C. Allen, *Psalms 101–150*, WBC 21 (Waco, TX: Word, 1983), 2.
[32] The *hapax legomenon* עֳפָאיִם is usually translated as "foliage" based on the Aramaic cognate; however, Mitchell Dahood proposes the meaning "ravens" based on the parallelism with עוֹף־הַשָּׁמַיִם and similar Hebrew roots meaning "dark" or "black" (*Psalms: Introduction, Translation, and Notes*, 3 vols., AB 16, 17, 17A [Garden City, NY: Doubleday, 1966–1970], 3:38–39; cf. Frank-Lothar Hossfeld and Erich Zenger, *Psalms 3: A Commentary on Psalms 101–150*, trans. Linda M. Maloney, Hermeneia [Minneapolis: Fortress, 2011], 51).

103:12a	ἐπ' αὐτὰ τὰ πετεινὰ τοῦ οὐρανοῦ κατασκηνώσει
12b	ἐκ μέσου τῶν πετρῶν δώσουσιν φωνήν
12a	The birds of the heaven[s] will dwell among them.
12b	From the midst of the rocks they will lift up a voice.

Just as in the MT, the Greek word pair directly follows the prepositional phrase. Both words begin with the syllable πετ-, ending (or nearly ending) with ν. The translator's choice of πετρῶν ("rocks") suggests that he either did not recognize the Hebrew *hapax legomenon* עֳפָאיִם or was intentionally using a different word for the sake of creating a parallel wordplay. If the translator did not recognize the word and was merely using the context to make an educated guess, as Frank-Lothar Hossfeld suggests,[33] then one might expect a better guess, since trees and foliage are more obvious dwelling places for birds (cf. vv. 16–17).[34] It is more likely that this is in fact a wordplay, an example of a modification transformation, substituting a word of equivalent specificity for the original, in this case for the purpose of making a compensational transformation and wordplay.

In Ps 106:23, the poet uses alliteration (with הֻשׁ and שֻׁה) with four different lexemes:

וַיֹּאמֶר לְהַשְׁמִידָם	23a	And he said [that he would] destroy them,
לוּלֵי מֹשֶׁה בְחִירוֹ	23b	Had not Moses, his chosen one,
עָמַד בַּפֶּרֶץ לְפָנָיו	23c	Stood in the breach before him,
לְהָשִׁיב חֲמָתוֹ מֵהַשְׁחִית	23d	To turn his wrath from destroying [them]
וַיִּמְאֲסוּ בְּאֶרֶץ חֶמְדָּה	24a	And they despised the delight of the land.

The fourfold repetition of the ה/שׁ combination and the twofold repetition of the מ/ח repetition mark this as a wordplay. Additionally, the poet chose two words for "destroy," שמד and שחת, both of which employ the ה/שׁ combination in the *hiphil* and both of which bracket the verse and stand in contrast, the first as a reference to God's determination to destroy Israel and the second as the retraction of that destruction because of Moses's intercession. Thus, four key words in this verse are highlighted through alliterative paronomasia: לְהַשְׁמִידָם ("to destroy them"), מֹשֶׁה ("Moses"), לְהָשִׁיב ("to turn back"), and מֵהַשְׁחִית ("from destroying [them]"). Similarly, the words חֲמָתוֹ ("his wrath") and חֶמְדָּה ("delight") are related through sharp contrast. Emphasizing these key theological concepts, the poet is able to highlight the Lord's turning of his wrath only for Israel to reject what was actually pleasant.[35]

---

[33] Hossfeld and Zenger, *Psalms 3*, 59.

[34] Goldingay even sees a chiastic connection between the mention of birds and trees in verses 12–13 and then again in verses 16–17 (*Psalms*, 3:186).

[35] Watson cites the play between חֲמָתוֹ ("his wrath") in verse 23d and חֶמְדָּה ("pleasant") in

The LXX attempts a similar wordplay using different words:

23a καὶ εἶπεν τοῦ ἐξολεθρεῦσαι αὐτούς
23b εἰ μὴ Μωυσῆς ὁ ἐκλεκτὸς αὐτοῦ
23c ἔστη ἐν τῇ θραύσει ἐνώπιον αὐτοῦ
23d τοῦ ἀποστρέψαι τὴν ὀργὴν αὐτοῦ τοῦ μὴ ἐξολεθρεῦσαι

23a And he said that he would destroy them,
23b Had not Moses, his chosen one,
23c Stood in the destruction before him,
23d In order to turn his wrath to not destroy them.

The LXX uses the same word (ἐξολεθρεύω) to translate both לְהַשְׁמִידָם and מֵהַשְׁחִית. Although ἐξολεθρεύω is used often to translate both of these verbs, the translator had other options, such as καταφθείρω or ἀπόλλυμι, that he could have used to maintain the variation of the Hebrew and the preference for variety evinced in the LXX. The word choice of ἀποστρέψαι (with its similar phonemic blend, τρ) also underscores this phonetic repetition. Most significantly, the translator renders בַּפֶּרֶץ ("in the breach") with ἐν τῇ θραύσει ("in the destruction"). It is unlikely that the LXX was unfamiliar with the Hebrew *Vorlage*, as פֶּרֶץ occurs eighty-three times in the Hebrew Bible.³⁶ More likely, the translator is trying to replicate the MT's alliteration with his own repetition of θρ.³⁷ His choice of τῇ θραύσει is an example of explication as well. Willem VanGemeren explains the Hebrew expression:

> The metaphor "stood in the breach" derives from military language and signifies the bravery of a soldier who, standing in the breach of the wall, is willing to give his life to ward off the enemy (cf. Eze 22:30). So Moses stood bravely in the presence of Almighty God on behalf of Israel.... The Lord responded to Moses' intercession by not destroying the people.³⁸

Thus, the LXX word choice is not only an apt selection to communicate the wordplay but an explication for his readers.

---

verse 24a as chiastic paronomasia (*Traditional Techniques in Classical Hebrew Verse*, JSOTSup 170 [Sheffield: Sheffield Academic, 1994], 381).

³⁶ According to Hossfeld, "the LXX does not know what to do with the 'breach.' Throughout the verse it stays within the verbal field of 'rooting out'" (*Psalms 3*, 94). What Hossfeld attributes to the translator's ignorance may be better understood as his attempt at creating a wordplay similar to that in the MT and his theological understanding of what the "breach" signified, showing his recognition of and skill with wordplay, as well as his knowledge of Hebrew semantics.

³⁷ This repeated consonant blend is also followed by a diphthong in each case, which may be an additional, albeit weak, correspondence in sound.

³⁸ VanGemeren, *Psalms*, 786.

IV. Conclusion

According to Ausloos, "it is one of the most difficult problems for a translator to adequately render wordplay from a source language into a target language."[39] From this analysis, it should be clear that the Greek translator(s) of book 4 of the Psalter often went to great lengths to translate and replicate Hebrew wordplays, showing adroitness and appreciation for the trope. Their task required complex choices. They considered poetic style to be an integral part of the poet's message, giving interpreters a better understanding of LXX translational technique and also a reminder of the importance of poetic devices when interpreting the Hebrew text.

---

[39] Hans Ausloos, "Judges 3:12–30: An Analysis of the Greek Rendering of Hebrew Wordplay," in *Text-Critical and Hermeneutical Studies in the Septuagint*, ed. Johann Cook and Hermann-Josef Stipp, VTSup 157 (Leiden: Brill, 2012), 53–68, here 53.

A Call to Law: The Septuagint of Isaiah 8 and Gentile Law Observance

ALEX P. DOUGLAS
adouglas@post.harvard.edu
Miami, FL 33186

Though much recent research has focused on the Septuagint of Isa 8, the majority of these studies have analyzed the text in individual units, which creates numerous problems of interpretation. This article reexamines the broader text and context of Isa 8 LXX and argues that the translator transformed this pericope into an extended dialogue between the righteous Israelites and the gentiles. The translator did so to bring out his larger concern that gentiles should not only worship YHWH but should also observe the entirety of Mosaic law. The translator's interpretation of the need for gentile law observance gives us a second-century BCE view into a debate that continues through Judaism and Christianity beyond the end of the Second Temple period.

The Septuagint of Isa 8 has received considerable attention in recent scholarship. Due in large part to the significant divergence between the Greek and Hebrew texts, this passage has been analyzed for its role in illuminating the larger text of the Isaiah LXX, as well as for how the translator's treatment of the *Vorlage* sheds light on broader questions of translation technique, septuagintal origins, and our understanding of diaspora Judaism in the Second Temple period.[1] To give but a few

---

[1] See, e.g., Rodrigo Franklin de Sousa, *Eschatology and Messianism in LXX Isaiah 1–12*, LHBOTS 516 (London: T&T Clark, 2010), 31–40; Jean Koenig, *L'herméneutique analogique du Judaïsme antique d'après les témoins textuels d'Isaïe*, VTSup 33 (Leiden: Brill, 1982), 118–35; Johan Lust, "The Demonic Character of Jahweh and the Septuagint of Isaiah," *Bijdr* 40 (1979): 2–14; Ronald Troxel, *LXX-Isaiah as Translation and Interpretation: The Strategies of the Translator of the Septuagint of Isaiah*, JSJSup 124 (Leiden: Brill, 2008), 152–72, 234–45; Arie van der Kooij, "Accident or Method? On 'Analogical' Interpretation in the Old Greek of Isaiah and in 1QIsᵃ," *BO* 43 (1986): 366–76; van der Kooij, "Isaiah in the Septuagint," in *Writing and Reading the Scroll of Isaiah: Studies of an Interpretive Tradition*, ed. Craig C. Broyles and Craig A. Evans, 2 vols., VTSup 70 (Leiden: Brill, 1997), 2:513–29; van der Kooij, "The Septuagint of Isaiah and the Mode of Reading Prophecies in Early Judaism: Some Comments on LXX Isaiah 8–9," in *Die Septuaginta—Texte, Kontexte, Lebenswelten: Internationale Fachtagung veranstaltet von Septuaginta Deutsch (LXX.D), Wuppertal 20.–23. Juli 2006*, ed. Martin Karrer and Wolfgang Kraus, WUNT 219

of many examples, studies have variously explained Isa 8 LXX as an instance of fulfillment interpretation (*Erfüllungsinterpretation*), contextual exegesis, or atomistic translation, and commentators have attributed a wide range of theological agendas to the translator.[2] Most scholars agree in seeing this passage as an extended reworking by the translator to deal with the topic of Mosaic law, but beyond this basic agreement there is little that is firmly settled in the continuing academic debate.[3]

Yet despite the extensive treatment Isa 8 LXX has received, modern analyses have tended to focus narrowly on small sections of the passage, often at the expense of the larger context. When scholars do take a more holistic approach, such as studying the translator's view of law, these discussions often concentrate exclusively on the role of law within Judaism, completely ignoring the role this passage might play in non-Jewish legal contexts. As I will show, this narrow focus leads to numerous difficulties in interpretation. By taking a broader view we can see how the entirety of Isa 8 LXX functions as a coherent whole, as well as how this chapter sheds light on Jewish beliefs surrounding law observance—not by other Jews but by gentiles.

I. Interpretations in Modern Scholarship

The Hebrew text of Isa 8 opens with a description of impending judgment upon Damascus, Samaria, and Judah by means of the king of Assyria, and this judgment is explained through a series of wordplays on the names Maher-shalal-hash-baz and Immanu-el. Judah is upbraided for rejecting YHWH's help, and Isaiah is warned against walking "in the way of this people" (Isa 8:11). The ensuing oracle again describes the coming judgment upon Judah, and Isaiah commands, "Bind up the testimony, seal up the teaching [תורה] among my disciples" (v. 16), as he expresses his faithfulness to "YHWH, who hides his face from the house of Jacob" (v. 17) and speaks of the role he and his children play as signs in Israel.

(Tübingen: Mohr Siebeck, 2008), 597–611; van der Kooij, "Zur Theologie des Jesajabuches in der Septuaginta," in *Theologische Probleme der Septuaginta und der hellenistischen Hermeneutik*, ed. Henning Graf Reventlow, VWGTh 11 (Gütersloh: Kaiser, 1997), 9–25; and J. Ross Wagner, "Identifying 'Updated' Prophecies in Old Greek (OG) Isaiah: Isaiah 8:11–16 as a Test Case," *JBL* 126 (2007): 251–69, https://doi.org/10.2307/27638434.

[2] See the discussion below.

[3] Nothing in Isa 8 LXX is explicitly Mosaic, and νόμος has a much wider semantic range in the LXX than simply Mosaic law. See esp. Laurent Monsengwo Pasinya, *La notion de* NOMOS *dans le Pentateuque grec*, AnBib 52 (Rome: Biblical Institute Press, 1973); Jacob Neusner, *Torah: From Scroll to Symbol in Formative Judaism*, BJS 136 (Atlanta: Scholars Press, 1988); Alan F. Segal, "Torah and *Nomos* in Recent Scholarly Discussion," *SR* 13 (1984): 19–27; and Stephen Westerholm, "*Torah*, *Nomos*, and Law: A Question of 'Meaning,'" *SR* 15 (1986): 327–36. Nevertheless, for reasons explained below, I agree with the consensus that the law addressed in Isa 8 LXX is specifically Mosaic.

The LXX version of this section, to the extent that it can be reconstructed,[4] looks quite different. In Isa 8 LXX, rather than Isaiah being warned against walking in the way of this people, now it is an unspecified "they" who reject this people's way (v. 11). The addressee is told not to call something "hard" (v. 12), and the command to seal up the teaching is transformed into a statement that "those who seal up the law, so as not to learn, will be made manifest" (v. 16). Numerous verbs and pronouns have different referents, and the passage culminates in the statement that God "gave the law as a help" (v. 20).

Nearly every modern commentator agrees that the LXX passage shows a heightened concern for the place of Mosaic law.[5] The description of "those who seal up the law, so as not to learn," in 8:16 is understood to provide an interpretive key for the entire pericope, particularly the author's exhortation: "Do not say 'hard,' for whatever this people says is hard" (v. 12). In this view, the passage is an extended criticism of an unknown group that has called for an abandonment or relaxation of Mosaic law and has endeavored to prevent its study.

Aside from these basic facts, modern scholars disagree over just about everything else in the passage. Isac Leo Seeligmann saw the pericope as a case of fulfillment interpretation regarding "an anti-dogmatic movement" in Alexandria that "qualif[ied] the precepts of orthodox Judaism as hard and oppressive, and consider[ed] those who adhered to these precepts as having been caught in a snare."[6] Arie van der Kooij likewise sees this as fulfillment interpretation, but he locates the antinomian party in Jerusalem rather than Alexandria: "LXX Isa 8:11–16 ... makes perfect sense if understood as a prophecy that could (and should) be read as

---

[4] The term *Septuagint* is problematic in many respects, as has long been noted (see esp. Gert Steyn, "Which 'LXX' Are We Talking about in NT Scholarship? Two Examples from Hebrews," in Karrer and Kraus, *Die Septuaginta*, 697–707). To be more precise, the text discussed in this article is the reconstructed archetype that lies behind the various later septuagintal traditions of the Greek text of Isaiah (Alexandrian, Lucianic, Hexaplaric, etc.)—a text that is not necessarily identical with the original second-century translation (see Jennifer M. Dines, *The Septuagint*, ed. Michael A. Knibb, Understanding the Bible and Its World [London: T&T Clark, 2004], 59, on the so-called Göttingen gap). In this article I use the term *Septuagint* (LXX) to describe our best reconstruction of that archetype, and, though it remains problematic, the term is still useful in distinguishing this tradition from other translations or revisions. All quotations from the LXX in this article reflect my own translation and are based on the critical Göttingen edition, except for noted instances where I differ in how best to reconstruct the text. In Isa 8:21–22, versification differs in editions of the text; I follow the Göttingen versification.

[5] See below.

[6] Isac Leo Seeligmann writes, "Assuming that we are to explain this as being the words used by an anti-dogmatic movement, then such a movement would qualify the precepts of orthodox Judaism as hard and oppressive, and consider those who adhered to these precepts as having been caught in a snare, and in a cave; for men such as these, God has become a stone of offence, a stumbling-block. Man should not let himself be confused and led into a superstitious fear (of all these precepts and laws)" (*The Septuagint Version of Isaiah and Cognate Studies*, ed. Robert Hanhart and Hermann Spieckermann, FAT 40 [Tübingen: Mohr Siebeck, 2004], 273–74).

predicting the policy of Hellenistic leaders in Jerusalem, in the first half of the second century BCE, and its failure."[7] In van der Kooij's view, verse 11 ("with a strong hand they reject the course of the way of this people") is best understood as a description of the leaders in Jerusalem who advocated abandoning Mosaic law.[8]

Other scholars reject fulfillment interpretation altogether. As J. Ross Wagner points out, the supposed links between Isa 8:11–16 LXX and the contemporaneous situation in Alexandria or Jerusalem are vague, and these features of the text can be better explained as "a serious effort to interpret the text … within the wider context of Isaiah."[9] Ronald Troxel agrees that, "although [the translator's] translation reflects pervasive concern for the Torah, the argument that he read Isa 8:11–16 as condemnation of an antilegalist group in his day is based on little more than serendipitous associations in modern readers' minds."[10] For these authors, we need to be able to provide much more specific ties between the text and contemporaneous events before positing fulfillment interpretation, especially since, as Johan Lust points out, "nothing is known of an anti-Law movement [within Judaism itself] in this period."[11]

Still others see this pericope neither as fulfillment interpretation nor as an example of contextual exegesis but as the translator's best attempt to understand an opaque text. Rodrigo Franklin de Sousa writes,

> The significant deviations between the LXX and MT versions of Isa 8:11–16 do not originate in an insightful rewriting of the oracle, *but in the misreading of a difficult Hebrew text*. The translator's expectation that the prophecy was directed to his generation, his theological and ideological worldview, and actual encounters with opposition to the law, would have provided the necessary backdrop against which his reading would have made sense.[12]

---

[7] Van der Kooij, "Isaiah in the Septuagint," 529. Florian Wilk takes a similar view in "Between Scripture and History: Technique and Hermeneutics of Interpreting Biblical Prophets in the Septuagint of Isaiah and the Letters of Paul," in *The Old Greek of Isaiah: Issues and Perspectives; Papers Read at the Conference on the Septuagint of Isaiah, Held in Leiden 10–11 April 2008*, ed. Michaël van der Meer and Arie van der Kooij, CBET 55 (Leuven: Peeters, 2010), 189–209, here 193.

[8] Van der Kooij states, "So, in the view of the leaders, which is clearly rejected in our pericope, the only condition to live in security and safety is to honour God in his temple; the ethical demands of the law are considered as not being required" ("The Septuagint of Isaiah: Translation and Interpretation," in *The Book of Isaiah/Le livre d'Isaïe: Les oracles et leurs relectures; unité et complexité de l'ouvrage*, ed. Jacques Vermeylen, BETL 81 [Leuven: Leuven University Press, 1989], 127–33, here 133).

[9] Wagner, "Identifying 'Updated' Prophecies," 267. He writes, "When Isa 8:11–16 is read with attention to this broader context, the evidence for van der Kooij's claim that the translator has 'actualized' or 'updated' this prophecy in order to speak to a specific situation in his own day evaporates" (ibid.).

[10] Troxel, *LXX-Isaiah as Translation and Interpretation*, 246.

[11] Lust, "Demonic Character," 10.

[12] De Sousa, *Eschatology and Messianism*, 31–32 (emphasis added).

Jean Koenig takes the exact opposite view, claiming that the control of the translator's approach, along the lines that Koenig outlined elsewhere, "proves understanding, whereby the Greek diverged from the Hebrew not by confusion or error, but knowingly and deliberately."[13]

There is no reason a priori to exclude *Erfüllungsinterpretation* as a potential explanation for the text, but Wagner, Troxel, and Lust are correct in pointing out that we do not have enough specific ties between the text and contemporaneous events to make a compelling case for fulfillment interpretation. Instead, Isa 8 LXX is best understood as a learned reworking of the Hebrew text that draws from themes elsewhere in Isaiah to create a coherent message. And as we will see below, this message is central to the translator's understanding of foreign nations and their relation to the law.

II. Internal Structure

Part of the debate regarding Isa 8 LXX concerns how we understand the passage's flow and internal structure. If, for example, we understand verse 16 as belonging with the following verses rather than with the preceding, this can have a great impact on whether we interpret the preceding verses in light of law rejection.

Most scholars have seen Isa 8:5–10 LXX as a separate unit from 8:11–16, and their interpretations have tended to focus on only one of these units. This division is based on the natural conclusion formed by the *inclusio* of verses 8 and 10 ("God is with us ... for the Lord God is with us"), as well as on the fact that verse 11 has an introductory formula, "Thus says the Lord."[14] For the section beginning with verse 11, one of the most noticeable differences between the Hebrew and Greek text is that in Greek verse 16 has been more closely tied with the preceding verses through the introduction of τότε ("then").[15] Subsequent to van der Kooij's analysis of this section, most scholars have focused exclusively on 8:11–16 as a unit on its own.

Wagner was the first to argue that taking 8:11–16 alone is insufficient for understanding this text. He proposed that the section beginning in verse 11 actually extends through verse 22, as indicated by the addition of καὶ ἐρεῖ in verse 17, "marking vv. 17–18 not simply as a 'new section' unrelated to what precedes (as van der

---

[13] In Koenig's words, "Nous avons vu plus haut que ce contrôle prouve l'intellection, d'où il résulte que G a divergé par rapport à H, non par embarras ou erreur, mais en connaissance de cause et de propos délibéré" (*L'herméneutique analogique*, 120).

[14] See Troxel, *LXX-Isaiah as Translation and Interpretation*, 240.

[15] Van der Kooij explains that "vs 16 is linked up with vs 15 (and not with vs 17 as in MT), because, first of all, τότε ... refers to the situation described in vs 15, and secondly, the first words of vs 17 (καὶ ἐρεῖ, not in MT) mark the beginning of a new section" ("Septuagint of Isaiah," 129). See also Lust, "Demonic Character," 9; and Seeligmann, *Septuagint Version of Isaiah*, 273.

Kooij implies), but more importantly, as the prophet's response to the oracle."[16] In addition, the phrase καὶ ἐὰν ἐπ' αὐτῷ πεποιθὼς ᾖς in verse 14 seems to have been drawn from verse 17,[17] further indicating the close connection between verses 17–22 and the preceding verses, and the debate between "they" and "you" in verses 19–22 "draws on the key term contested by the parties in vv. 11–16: νόμος."[18] Thus, any analysis that excludes verses 17–22 will be skewed or, at best, incomplete.[19]

I find Wagner's analysis convincing, but I believe the boundaries of this unit need to be extended even further to include verses 5–10. As Wagner himself recognizes, the identification of "this people" in verses 11–12 draws directly from the negative portrayal of "this people" in verse 6—a connection that exists in Greek as well as in Hebrew. Moreover, beyond the dependence of one section upon another, 8:11–22 does not make sense when cut off from the previous verses. This can be seen in the endless debates about who "they" and "this people" are in this passage, but the problem can be seen most clearly in verses 11–12. In Isaiah LXX these verses read,

> [11]Thus says the Lord: with a strong hand they reject the course of the way of this people, saying: [12]Do not say "hard," for whatever this people says is hard. But do not fear their fear, nor be troubled.

When the passage is taken on its own, who could the addressee of verse 12 be? It cannot be "this people," since the addressee is warned against fearing "their" fear. Nor can it be those who reject the way of this people, since they are the speakers of this verse. We might assume that the reader is being addressed, but it would be highly unusual for a character within the book of Isaiah to address the reader directly. When we take verses 11–12 together with verses 5–10, however, this problem disappears, and the meaning of the pericope is cast in an entirely new light.

III. Taking the Passage Together

As I argue in detail below, Isa 8 LXX cannot be understood unless verses 5–22 are taken together as one complete unit. To show the internal structure of the passage, I have reproduced the text below, with each section followed by analysis and discussion. Differences between the Greek and Hebrew texts are shown in bold.[20]

---

[16] Wagner, "Identifying 'Updated' Prophecies," 259.
[17] Ibid., 260.
[18] Ibid., 259.
[19] As Wagner points out, this is simply an extension of van der Kooij's "contextual approach," which is one reason why he believes the identification of this passage as *Erfüllungsinterpretation* fails, even using van der Kooij's own method.
[20] As is well known, there is no one Hebrew text from the period of translation (ca. second century BCE) against which we could measure divergences, and reconstruction of a *Vorlage* is

Account of Israel's Rebellion

⁵The Lord spoke to me yet again:
⁶On account of this people's not wanting the water of Siloam that flows gently, but wanting to have Rasson and the son of Romeliou **as king**[21] **over you**, ⁷therefore, behold, the Lord is bringing upon you[22] the many and strong waters—the king of Assyria and his glory—and he will go up upon all your valleys, and he will walk on all your walls.
⁸**And he will take away from Judah a man**[23] **who can lift his head or who can accomplish something**,[24] and his encampment will be such as to fill the breadth of your land; God is with us.

This opening section sets the stage for the dialogue that occupies much of the rest of this chapter, and it begins with a description of Israel's rebellion and their desire for a foreign king. "This people" (τὸν λαὸν τοῦτον) is introduced as rebellious, as a group that "do[es] not want" what God wants (v. 6), and they are referred to continually in the verses that follow. At times they are mentioned explicitly, as in verses 11 and 12, where "this people" is held up as an example of wicked conduct, but elsewhere the wicked are simply referred to as "they." "They" say everything is "hard" (v. 12); they "seal up the law" (v. 16); "they seek the dead among the living" (v. 19; cf. Hebrew); and "they will look to the earth beneath, and behold: affliction" (v. 22). The identification of the wicked with an unnamed, third-person plural group is consistent throughout the chapter, starting in these verses.

The rebellion incited by "this people" against God serves as a springboard for the exhortation in the following verses.

---

speculative. Therefore, words shown in bold represent those areas where the LXX departs from all known Hebrew variants or from a significant portion of the Hebrew tradition. If there are any known variants that might lie behind these readings, they are given in the notes.

[21] It is difficult to determine how the translator may have based this on the Hebrew text. Perhaps he read ומשוש as משיח, but this is uncertain.

[22] The second-person address (ἐφ' ὑμᾶς) is different from the Hebrew tradition (עליהם), but there is some rabbinic evidence for second-person pronouns in Hebrew here.

[23] Or "any man."

[24] ἀφελεῖ ἀπὸ τῆς Ιουδαίας ἄνθρωπον ὃς δυνήσεται κεφαλὴν ἆραι ἢ δυνατὸν συντελέσασθαί τι. Again, this is difficult to trace back to the Hebrew text, which reads: וחלף ביהודה שטף ועבר עד־צואר יגיע והיה מטות כנפיו מלא רחב־ארצך עמנו אל. Presumably the idea of a river overflowing would not have been negative in an Egyptian culture dependent on the overflowing Nile, so the translator may have taken more liberty than usual in translating the sense of the passage rather than focusing on semantic equivalents. Although the translation of חלף with ἀφαιρέω does not occur elsewhere in the LXX, the equivalence fits within the semantic range of the Hebrew verb. The idea of a man who can lift his head and accomplish something evidently arose from שטף ועבר עד־צואר, but the translation is so stretched that *BHS* even proposes inserting ואיש לא יוכל לשאת ראשו ולעשות מעשה ("and a man will not be able to lift his head or do anything") into the Hebrew text.

Exhortation from the Righteous to the Gentiles: Learn from Israel's Rebellion, and Submit to God's Will

(The Righteous):
⁹"**Learn, peoples, and submit!**²⁵ Listen, to the ends of the earth! **O strong ones, submit! For if again you become strong, again you will** be brought to submission.²⁶
¹⁰And whatever counsel you may counsel, **the Lord** will scatter;²⁷ and whatever word you may speak, it will surely not remain **with you,**²⁸ for God²⁹ is with us."

In the Hebrew text, this section begins an account of judgment on the nations, but in the LXX, in contrast to being told to band together (רעו), the nations are commanded to "learn," or perhaps "take note" (γνῶτε), reading the Hebrew as if it were דעו.³⁰ The rebellion against God recounted in the previous section now serves as a negative example to the other nations, who are told instead to "learn," "submit," and "trust in him" (vv. 9, 14). In wanting a foreign king, Israel has implicitly rejected God's sovereignty, but the nations are commanded to submit to God, no matter how strong they may be. Israel had its own desires (διὰ τὸ μὴ βούλεσθαι, v. 6), and

---

²⁵ There is a general tendency to translate ἡττάομαι as "to be defeated," but the word has a much broader semantic range than simply defeat in battle. As Michaël van der Meer notes, if we base our definition on "the daily use of the verb ἡττάω in the documentary papyri from Greek and Roman Egypt," in a legal context the word can mean "to lose a lawsuit" or "to be the unsuccessful party" ("Papyrological Perspectives on the Septuagint of Isaiah," in van der Meer and van der Kooij, *Old Greek of Isaiah*, 107–33, here 114), and dictionaries list many other definitions, such as "to give way," "to yield," "to be proved inferior," and "to be overcome" (see, e.g., LSJ, LEH). In light of the fact that the context of this passage is ambiguous, I choose to translate ἡττᾶσθε as "be brought to submission" and "submit" in order to leave open the possibility for multiple interpretations. In Isaiah LXX, ἡττάομαι is the most frequent equivalent of חתת.

²⁶ The Hebrew here reads התאזרו וחתו התאזרו וחתו, and the translator evidently understood התאזרו as relating to strength, as seen in his rendering of מאזרי זיקות (Isa 50:11) with κατισχύετε φλόγα. A similar equivalent can be found in 2 Kgdms 22:40, which renders ותזרני חיל with καὶ ἐνισχύσεις με δυνάμει. As for the addition of ἐὰν γὰρ πάλιν ... πάλιν, Martin Karrer and Wolfgang Kraus posit that the repetition of התאזרו וחתו suggested to the translator "eine Wiederholung des Vorgangs in späterer Zukunft (nicht nur z.Z. von Achaz und Ezekias)" (*Septuaginta Deutsch: Erläuterungen und Kommentare zum griechischen Alten Testament*, 2 vols. [Stuttgart: Deutsche Bibelgesellschaft, 2011], 2:2524).

²⁷ The Hebrew here reads עצו עצה ותפר, and in the masoretic tradition the verb is taken as passive. The translator evidently construed ותפר as active and supplied the subject to clarify the sense.

²⁸ The Hebrew tradition contains only ולא יקום.

²⁹ The Göttingen Septuagint leaves κύριος in the main text, but it is missing from almost the entire Lucianic recension, O, oI, oII, Marchalianus, the Catena texts, and a number of other manuscripts. Every surviving Hebrew witness reads עמנו אל.

³⁰ This reading is in fact attested in 4QIsaᶠ and possibly 4QIsaᵉ, where the manuscript is damaged.

in a play on words the nations are told not to rely on their own counsel (ἣν ἂν βουλεύσησθε βουλήν, v. 10). Finally, the speaker is identified as a group on the Lord's side ("God is with us," v. 10), presumably the righteous Israelites. The command to learn and submit takes on new significance in this context, as the futility of gentile self-sufficiency is contrasted with God and righteous Israel as the true source of strength. Whatever word the gentiles might speak, they are told, "it will surely not remain *with you* [missing in Hebrew], for God is *with us.*"

This section sets up a pattern that will recur throughout Isa 8 LXX. On the one hand, we see the beginning of an address to the gentiles, or ἔθνη. The translator has changed numerous verbs and pronouns to make much of this chapter into a prolonged address "to you" (pl.), an address that will carry on into the verses that follow. In addition, not only are gentiles addressed in this section, but they are commanded to learn from the wicked. This happens again in verse 12 ("Do not say 'hard,' for whatever this people says is hard"), as well as in verses 19–20, where the wicked people's words "to you" are held up as an example of misunderstanding the law ("And if they say to you, 'Seek'.... Why do they seek the dead among the living? For he gave the law as a help"). The next section builds on this pattern to address the main topic of the pericope: law observance.

The Righteous Reject Israel's Rebellion against God and the Law, and They Exhort the Gentiles to Submit to Both

[11]Thus says the Lord: **with a strong hand**[31] **they** [the righteous] **reject**[32] the course of the way of this people [the wicked], saying:

(The Righteous):
[12]"Do not say '**hard**,' for whatever this people says is **hard**. But do not fear their fear, nor be troubled.
[13]Sanctify the Lord himself, and he will be your [sg.][33] fear.

---

[31] The Hebrew tradition is divided here. While most masoretic manuscripts attest כחזקת היד, some read בחזקת היד, which seems to lie behind the LXX reading.

[32] The *Vorlage* behind this reading is uncertain. Our best reconstruction of the Hebrew is ויסרני מלכת בדרך העם־הזה, but while ויסרני does seem to be the original reading, the Hebrew tradition preserves multiple readings here. 1QIsa[a] reads יסירנו, while Reuchlinianus similarly reads ויסירני. The translator evidently construed this verb as deriving from either סור or סרר, and it is possible that he understood the verb as plural by taking the *nun* as representing the Aramaic ending *-ûn* (see Koenig, *L'herméneutique analogique*, 328). As Koenig points out, there is a rich tradition of "misreading" this verb in Hebrew, Greek, and even daughter translations, and he concludes: "c'est que cette leçon n'était pas particulière à Qa. Elle représente donc une tradition exégétique qui a connu une certaine extension et une certaine autorité" (325). Van der Kooij illustrates this through 4QFlor, which "offers a 'sectarian' interpretation of Isa 8,11 which presupposes the reading of Q[a]" ("Accident or Method?," 375).

[33] The singular rendering here is odd, since the Hebrew witnesses are unanimous in reading מוראכם. In the Greek text, the addressee is envisioned as the ἔθνη, and the singular rendering of

¹⁴**And if you** [gentile] **trust in him,**³⁴ he will be to you as a sanctuary, and **you will not encounter him**³⁵ as a rock of stumbling, **nor** as a stone of falling. But the house of Jacob³⁶ **is in** a trap, and the inhabitants of Jerusalem **are in** a pit. ¹⁵Therefore many among them [the unrighteous Israelites] will **become weak,**³⁷

σου might be due to the ease with which groups can be addressed as a collective in Greek and Hebrew (cf. pentateuchal legislation). The singular rendering might have arisen due to the singular ἧς in 8:14 (discussed in n. 34 below), though of course we cannot rule out the possibility that the translator's (real or imagined) *Vorlage* read מוראך.

³⁴ This is derived from והוא מערצכם at the end of the previous verse. Richard Ottley thought the translator may have read מערצכם as deriving from some form of עזר and that "πέποιθα is one of those words which the LXX. seem to have used as a stop-gap when in doubt" (*The Book of Isaiah according to the Septuagint [Codex Alexandrinus]*, 2 vols. [London: Cambridge University Press, 1904], 2:149). Most scholars today follow Koenig in seeing this as a derivation from the Aramaic רחץ ("to trust"), arrived at through confusion of the gutturals ע/ח and metathesis (*L'herméneutique analogique*, 124; see also Karrer and Kraus, *Septuaginta Deutsch*, 2:2525). As Wagner points out, the phrase seems to have been influenced by 8:17, וקויתי־לו/καὶ πεποιθὼς ἔσομαι ἐπ' αὐτῷ ("Identifying 'Updated' Prophecies," 260), which likewise probably accounts for the switching between singular and plural in the LXX verses 13–14. The influence of verse 17 here will be discussed below. The Targum to this verse reads similarly (ואם לא תקבלון, "And if you do not receive him"), reflecting another instantiation of this interpretive tradition.

³⁵ The mechanism by which the translator arrived at this rendering is unclear. The Hebrew reads והיה למקדש ולאבן נגף ("he will be as a sanctuary and as a stone of striking"), and perhaps the translator read ולאבן ("and as a stone") as ולא לאבן ("and not as a stone") through letter duplication, mirroring another potential change in verse 16 (where בלמדי seems to have been read as בל למד). As to why this change was made, Koenig claims that the differences "s'expliquent par le souci révérenciel d'éviter tout risque d'interprétation litholâtrique," which he claims also accounts for why the Hebrew phrase "he will be" has been rendered in Greek as "you will encounter him" (*L'herméneutique analogique*, 125). Lust explains it as stemming from a general discomfort with how YHWH is portrayed in this passage: "Through the insertion of a negation … the Septuagint not only seems to have smoothed out the text but also to have eliminated the theologically problematic presentation of Jahweh as a cause of sin for his own people" (Lust, "Demonic Character," 9). The presentation of YHWH in the Hebrew text as simultaneously sanctuary and a stumbling block is odd, and it is worth noting that some Hebrew manuscripts try to resolve this tension. Manuscript 96 reads למוקש ("as a snare") instead of למקדש ("as a sanctuary"), while the Kennicott Bible reads והיה להם לאבן ("he will be for them as a stone"). *BHS* even proposes to emend למקדש to למקשיר ("as one who conspires"), presumably to bring this in line with קשר in verse 12, though this has no manuscript support. This is not to suggest that these readings were in the *Vorlage*, but they do attest to a degree of discomfort with this verse, even within the Hebrew tradition.

³⁶ The Hebrew tradition here reads לשני בתי ישראל, and, while the Göttingen text reads οἶκοι, there is ample evidence for οικοι (O''-Qᶜ ᵉᵗ ᵐᵍ L''⁻⁹³-311-46-233-456 C 403' Syp Tht.). I do not know of anyone who claims that this difference was theologically motivated. Troxel writes that the difference "should be compared to τὸν οἶκον τοῦ Ισραηλ || בית יעקב in 2:6, which shows the reverse interchange. Moreover, the appearance of מבית יעקב in v. 18 [sic for 17] may have influenced a scribe" (*LXX-Isaiah as Translation and Interpretation*, 244).

³⁷ The Greek reads ἀδυνατήσουσιν. The Hebrew reads וכשלו בם רבים, and the translator evidently understood the semantic range of כשל as encompassing weakness, as seen in his

and they will fall, and they will be crushed, and **those in safety**[38] **will draw near**[39] and be taken.

[16]**Then those who**[40] seal up the law, **so as not to learn,**[41] will be **made manifest.**"[42]

In this section, the Lord introduces an unspecified "they" who reject the course of the way of "this people" (v. 12).[43] The unspecified "they" go on to address a plural audience, warning this audience against the evil ways of "this people" (v. 12), speaking about the fallen state of the house of Jacob, and commanding them to "sanctify the Lord." This is the same pattern we saw in verses 9–10, where a righteous group commands a plural audience not to follow the example of "this people" (v. 6), and it seems most reasonable, therefore, to assume that both verses 9–10 and verses 12–16 are spoken by the same group, which I label "the righteous."[44] In this same

---

rendering of Isa 40:30 (ובחורים כשול יכשלו/καὶ ἐκλεκτοὶ ἀνίσχυες ἔσονται). This is in keeping with the root's translation in the broader LXX, in which the most frequent equivalent for כשל is ἀσθενέω.

[38] This apparently derives from reading צור (the first word in the following verse) as the subject of the preceding verbs and taking the idea of "rock" to mean "a place of safety" or "a place of refuge" (cf. the Hebrew, ונפלו ונשברו ונוקשו ונלכדו). See Ottley, *Book of Isaiah*, 2:149–50; and Karrer and Kraus, *Septuaginta Deutsch*, 2:2525. As Troxel points out, "The fact that ἄνθρωποι ἐν ἀσφαλείᾳ ὄντες follows Greek word order rather than Hebrew suggests that this is [the translator's] own formulation" (*LXX-Isaiah as Translation and Interpretation*, 245).

[39] The verb נוקשו was apparently taken as נגשו on the basis of these words' phonetic similarity. De Sousa sees the two changes in this verse primarily as "an explanatory note on the weakening and inability of the 'many' at the beginning of the verse. LXX Isaiah displays numerous examples of paraphrastic additions intended to clarify obscure passages" (*Eschatology and Messianism*, 38).

[40] The Hebrew reads צור תעודה חתום תורה בלמדי, and it is possible that the translator read חתום as a participle, חותם.

[41] The term בלמדי was evidently interpreted as בל למד, בל למוד (with the final י being read as ו and metathesizing with ד), בלי למד, or מלמד.

[42] This was possibly derived through reading תעודה as a *hiphil* or a *hophal* of ידע.

[43] In van der Kooij's interpretation, this unspecified "they" refers to the leaders in Jerusalem: "The expression 'with a strong hand' points to a position of power and might of those who 'disobey'. It is likely therefore that leaders of the people are meant" ("Septuagint of Isaiah," 130). In response, de Sousa rightly points out, "While this is certainly plausible, one must not forget that τῇ ἰσχυρᾷ χειρί simply represents כחזקת היד and one must, therefore, be careful about drawing specific conclusions" (*Eschatology and Messianism*, 34).

[44] Van der Kooij argues that "the course of the way of this people" is positive and that the speakers' rejection is seen negatively by the translator. After comparing the use of πορεύομαι in Isa 65:2, he writes, "Just as in this text in 8:11 the right way is meant, as is indicated by the verb ἀπειθέω (in MT, quite the opposite is the case; there 'the way of this people' conveys a negative meaning)" ("Septuagint of Isaiah," 130). Wagner offers a convincing rebuttal through the translator's use of the phrase "this people" in Isa 8:6 and 9:16 LXX: "The appellation 'this people' underscores the sharp distancing of God from his people on account of their sin.... The Greek translator has not only recognized but even enhanced the contrast between 'this people' and 'my people'" ("Identifying 'Updated' Prophecies," 261–62; see also Troxel, *LXX-Isaiah as Translation*

vein, if this is a continuation of the speech begun above, the most natural antecedent for the addressee of verses 12–16 is the ἔθνη addressed in verses 9–10.

As with the previous verses, the force of this section is quite different from the Hebrew text. In the Hebrew tradition, the primary concern is with alliances or conspiracies, but the LXX focuses instead on not calling something "hard," presumably reading קשר as if it were קשה.[45] In the Hebrew, God is portrayed as both a sanctuary and a stumbling block, but now the addressee is assured that he will *not* encounter God as a rock of stumbling or a stone of falling. Israel is portrayed as already in a pit, and the final verse speaks of sealing up the law.

In the broader context of a conversation between righteous Israelites and gentiles, how should we understand these verses? What might the gentiles be in danger of calling "hard," and what might they otherwise encounter as a stumbling block? Modern scholars have been nearly unanimous in seeing these verses as referring to Mosaic law, in large degree based on the section's conclusion regarding "those who seal up the law, so as not to learn" (v. 16).[46] The wicked do not want the addressees to learn the law, which they call "hard," but the gentiles have been told back in verses 9–10: "Learn, peoples, and submit … for the Lord God is with us."

---

and Interpretation, 242). The use of ἀπειθέω is similarly problematic as the basis for seeing "the course of the way of this people" as negative, since "it is the object against which one rebels that determines whether ἀπειθέω carries a positive or negative connotation. If 'this people' denotes the unfaithful in Israel, then to 'reject walking in the way of this people' must in this instance be a mark of fidelity to the Lord" (Wagner, "Identifying 'Updated' Prophecies," 263). The identification of this group as "the righteous" is further bolstered by Wagner: "The absence of any explicit quotation formula indicating a shift of speakers after v. 12 (contrast καὶ ἐρεῖ in 8:17) would seem to favor this view, as it suggests that it was not important to the translator to distinguish sharply between the words of the unnamed speakers in vv. 12–14 and the words of the Lord" (260).

[45] Alternative explanations have been put forward, however, such as that the translator understood קשר as קרס (Koenig, *L'herméneutique analogique*, 131) or that קשר was understood as a passive participle (van der Kooij, "Isaiah in the Septuagint," 524).

[46] Lust, for example, writes, "Verse 16 states that God condemns those who refuse to study the law. Verses 11–15 are to be understood in the light of this statement. They articulate the point of view of that section of the people who in this period refused to study the law and who qualified the precepts of orthodox Judaism as 'hard'" ("Demonic Character," 9). According to Koenig, this verse "contient une allusion à l'austérité de la vie sous le joug de la Loi : elle est 'dure, difficile!'" (*L'herméneutique analogique*, 131; see also Wagner, "Identifying 'Updated' Prophecies," 257; and Troxel, *LXX-Isaiah as Translation and Interpretation*, 241). Karrer and Kraus offer one of the main dissensions from this view, claiming that "mit 'hart' ist dabei wohl nicht das schwere Joch des Gesetzes benannt (so Seeligmann, 1948, 106; Koenig, 1982, 121; van der Kooij, 1989, 130), sondern die unnachgiebige Ausübung politischer Herrschaft" (*Septuaginta Deutsch*, 2:2525). In other words, they agree that "law" is still the referent of "hard," but they claim that a political rather than a religious view of law is meant. This latter interpretation seems less likely given that the wicked seal up the law "so as not to learn." What these authors call "politischer Herrschaft" is usually something imposed upon a people, not willingly learned by them.

A Gentile Responds

[17] **And one will say**,[47] "I will wait upon God, who has **turned** his face **away**[48] from the house of Jacob, and I will trust in him. [18] Here am I and the children whom God gave me, and **they** will be[49] signs and wonders in Israel[50] from the Lord Sabaoth, who dwells on Mount Zion."

After the righteous describe the fall of the unrighteous,[51] their weakened state, and their sealing up the law, a new speaker is introduced in verse 17 with the words καὶ ἐρεῖ. If we take verses 9–22 as an extended dialogue between the gentiles and righteous Israelites, as I propose here, καὶ ἐρεῖ in verse 17 would most naturally introduce a gentile response to the Israelites' words. The previous section opened with a command to the gentiles not to say certain words (Μήποτε εἴπητε, v. 12), and now we are given what the gentile will say (καὶ ἐρεῖ, v. 17). The gentile was earlier encouraged to trust in the Lord (ἐὰν ἐπ' αὐτῷ πεποιθὼς ᾖς, v. 14), and here he expresses his trust in language drawing from the speech of the righteous: πεποιθὼς ἔσομαι ἐπ' αὐτῷ (v. 17). As Wagner points out, these two sections have been deliberately brought into parallel in Isaiah LXX, a relationship that does not exist in the Hebrew text.[52] The gentile's description of his children as "signs and wonders in Israel" now takes on an entirely different meaning from that of the Hebrew text, in which both Isaiah and his children are the signs. In Isaiah LXX, the presence of gentile children

---

[47] It is difficult to see how this could have been derived from the Hebrew witnesses we have, all of which lack a corresponding text here. Most likely it was inserted in the LXX to help give the passage internal structure (cf. וכי יאמרו/καὶ ἐὰν εἴπωσι in v. 19), though in theory this change could have happened at the level of the *Vorlage* as well.

[48] Hebrew: ליהוה המסתיר פניו. Although the translator does render סתר with κρύπτω elsewhere, he also seems to have seen ἀποστρέφω as a viable translation option for this root (e.g., Isa 50:6, 54:8, 57:17, 59:2, and 64:6).

[49] Although this differs from the usual English translation of the Hebrew (אנכי והילדים אשר נתן־לי יהוה לאתות ולמופתים, "I and the children whom YHWH has given me are for signs"), this does represent a valid reading of the consonantal text.

[50] The Hexaplaric, Lucianic, and Catena traditions all attest ἐν τῷ οἴκῳ Ισραηλ here, though most see this as a later addition (see Mirjam van der Vorm-Croughs, *The Old Greek of Isaiah: An Analysis of Its Pluses and Minuses*, SCS 61 [Atlanta: SBL Press, 2014], 248–49).

[51] The phrase "many among them" in verse 15 most likely refers back to "the house of Jacob … and the inhabitants of Jerusalem" in the previous verse, as Troxel points out. Troxel takes verses 14b–16 as being spoken by the Lord, but his broader point is still valid: "In this construal, the announcement of the Kyrios in 14b–16 *concurs* with the statements by the speakers in vv. 11–14a by acknowledging that 'the way of this people' has led them into a snare and trap" (*LXX-Isaiah as Translation and Interpretation*, 241–42 [emphasis original]).

[52] Wagner, "Identifying 'Updated' Prophecies," 260. Another example of this is the description of God as one "who has turned his face away from the house of Jacob" (v. 17), parallel to the righteous ones' claim that "the house of Jacob is in a trap" (v. 14). Wagner writes, "This verbal connection is due to the translator's decision to render 'the two houses of Israel' in v. 14 (לִשְׁנֵי בָתֵּי יִשְׂרָאֵל) as 'the House of Jacob,' borrowing the terminology of v. 17" (260–61).

among Israel will be (note the future tense, and cf. the theme of *Völkerwallfahrt* seen elsewhere in Isaiah) for signs and wonders from God.

The Righteous Exhort the Gentiles Not to Listen to the Rebellious in Israel or Transgress the Torah

[19]"And if they [the unrighteous Israelites] say to you, 'Seek those who speak from the earth, and ventriloquists, those who speak emptily from their belly;[53] is not a people to its god?'[54]—why do they[55] seek the dead among the living?" [20]For he gave the law as a help,[56] so that[57] they may speak not as this word, concerning which there are no gifts to give.[58]

Following this response, verse 19 picks back up with an address to a plural audience, again exhorting them not to listen to what "they say" (ἐὰν εἴπωσι πρὸς ὑμᾶς). The parallel to verse 12 is strong, where a plural audience is warned not to listen to what "this people" says (ὃ ἐὰν εἴπῃ ὁ λαὸς οὗτος), and once again the overriding concern is for the status of the law (cf. v. 20, "he gave the law as a help"). On the basis of these parallels in content and form, it makes sense to see the addressee once again as the gentiles and the speakers as the righteous Israelites. This conclusion is reinforced by the unspecified "they" in verse 19. Note that in verse 16, the wicked are accused of sealing up the law, and here "they" try to persuade the addressee to seek out diviners and mediums—in direct contradiction to Mosaic law (cf. Lev 19:31, Deut 18:10–11, etc.). The righteous Israelites respond again by emphasizing the goodness of the law.

---

[53] The Hebrew here is difficult (דרשו אל־האבות ואל־הידענים המצפצפים והמהגים), and Ottley notes that Isaiah LXX "is more explanatory" in this section (*Book of Isaiah*, 2:150). There is no reason to see any major divergence here, however.

[54] This divides the Hebrew text differently than MT does, but it is still (mostly) faithful to the consonantal text. The MT has הלוא־עם אל־אלהיו ידרש בעד החיים אל־המתים, with the *athnaḥ* indicating the division after ידרש, whereas the Greek presupposes a division following אלהיו: הלוא־עם אל־אלהיו ידרש בעד החיים אל־המתים. The only difference is in Isaiah LXX's insertion of τί, which was probably done to make sense of the verse in this division.

[55] Reading ידרש as ידרשו. This was probably done to agree with the plural in the following verse (יאמרו/εἴπωσιν).

[56] The Hebrew takes verses 19 and 20 together: הלוא־עם אל־אלהיו ידרש בעד החיים אל־המתים לתורה ולתעודה, "Should not a people consult its God/gods, on behalf of the living to the dead, for instruction and confirmation?" The LXX apparently reads לתעודה as some form of עזר, through ז/ו and ד/ר interchange. Both γάρ and ἔδωκεν seem to have been added to clarify the sense. Alternatively, as Karrer and Kraus suggest, perhaps the translator read לתעודה as לתת עזרה ("to give help"). Cf. the targum: לאוריתא דאתיהיבת לנא לסהדו ("to the law which was given to us").

[57] This is the only instance in which Isaiah LXX translates אם as ἵνα, assuming this is what was in the *Vorlage*. Regardless, this fits well with the translator's tendency to add connecting words in order to smooth out the syntax in Greek.

[58] Reading שחר as שחד ("bribe").

The Righteous Predict a Time When the Gentiles Will Give Up Idolatry and the Wicked Israelites Will Be Punished

²¹And a difficult famine[59] will come upon **you**, and when **you** are hungry, **you** will be grieved, and **you** will speak evil of **the ruler** and **idol**.[60] And they [the unrighteous Israelites] will look **to the heaven** above,
²²and they will look to the earth **beneath**,[61] and behold: affliction, and distress, and darkness, narrow difficulty and darkness **so as not to see**.[62] **And he in distress will not be at a loss for a time**.[63]

In the final section, the righteous continue their address to the plural audience and speak of a time when "you will speak evil of the ruler and idol" (v. 21). The Hebrew אלהיו is ambiguous, for the word could refer to either YHWH or foreign gods, but the LXX passage has specified that this is an idol (παταχρα) that the addressees will one day curse. This change, in addition to change of suffix to second-person plural, casts the addressees as foreigners, in line with the gentile addressees of verses 9–10, 12–16, and 19–20. That these are not idolatrous Israelites is implied by the continued reference to the wicked "they" throughout this pericope: "whatever this people says is hard. But do not fear their fear.... The house of Jacob is in a trap, and the inhabitants of Jerusalem are in a pit. Therefore many among them will become weak.... And if they say to you..." (vv. 12–19). Immediately after the prediction that "you will speak evil of the ruler and idol," we learn that "they"—that is, the wicked who have been spoken of in third person throughout this section—will be

---

[59] Reading רָעָב instead of רָעֵב (MT).

[60] If the translator read במלכו, as the Hebrew tradition unanimously attests, not only did he change the suffix from third-person masculine singular to second-person masculine plural, but he also understood "king" loosely to refer to a ruler. The transliterated παταχρα is from the Aramaic פתכרא ("idol"), and it arose from understanding ובאלהיו—itself ambiguous in the Hebrew text—as referring to a pagan god. The targum takes this verse similarly (וילוט ויבזי שום פתכריה וטעותיה, "he will curse and scorn the name of his image and idol"). Many Greek manuscripts read πατρια here, though this seems to be a secondary correction stemming from confusion surrounding the transliterated παταχρα.

[61] Both "beneath" and "to the heaven" (in the previous verse) were most likely added to increase the parallelism within this clause. As Mirjam van der Vorm-Croughs ("LXX Isaiah and the Use of Rhetorical Figures," in van der Meer and van der Kooij, *Old Greek of Isaiah*, 173–88, here 184) and Joseph Ziegler (*Untersuchungen zur Septuaginta des Buches Isaias*, ATA 12.3 [Münster: Aschendorff, 1934], 58) note, this is typical of Isaiah LXX.

[62] It is unclear how the translator arrived at this, given the Hebrew tradition (מעוף צוקה ואפלה מנדח, "darkness, distress, and scattered darkness"). The idea of "going away" or "not being seen" is associated with the root נדח in Job 6:13 LXX (= ἄπειμι), or perhaps מנדח was read as having to do with light (= נר, "lamp," [Karrer and Kraus]) or as מראה (see Ottley, *Book of Isaiah*, 2:151).

[63] καὶ οὐκ ἀπορηθήσεται ὁ ἐν στενοχωρίᾳ ὢν ἕως καιροῦ. This translates 8:23, כי לא מועף לאשר מוצק לה כעת, understanding מועף as coming from עיף, "to be weary."

punished: "they will look to the heaven above, and they will look to the earth beneath, and behold: affliction, and distress" (vv. 21–22).

When taken together, Isa 8:5–22 LXX presents one coherent conversation between the righteous and the gentiles, and the translator has made numerous changes to make the passage fit this scheme. He has changed pronouns, introduced speakers, and brought internal sections into greater parallel in order to create a flowing discourse regarding the righteous, the example of the wicked, the gentiles, and the law. In each case, the referents never change: "you" are the gentiles explicitly addressed in verse 9; "they" are the wicked among the Israelites; and the speakers are the righteous whose view is endorsed by the translator.[64] In 8:9–22, the only time this pattern is broken is in verse 11, where the Lord speaks directly to affirm the righteous group's view.

III. Implications

When Isa 8 LXX is understood according to the approach presented here, the passage takes on an entirely new meaning relative to gentiles and the law, a meaning that has been overlooked by previous scholarship. Scholars have long noted the emphasis Isa 8 LXX places on Mosaic law, but these studies assume that the passage deals exclusively with Jewish law observance, not gentile observance. When the entire pericope is read together, however, the passage can be seen as an extended dialogue addressing an important question: when gentiles come to worship God, are they simply *included* in Israelite worship (i.e., worshiping God as gentiles), or should they fully convert and observe the law?[65] This question is particularly

---

[64] In my opinion, there are two major arguments in favor of seeing these changes as originating with the translator. First, Isa 8 LXX presents a relatively smooth and coherent Greek text. Second, it is striking that almost every difference between the Hebrew and Greek can be traced back to possible variants within—or manipulations of—the Hebrew text. For example, רעו was read as דעו (v. 9), קשר was read as קשה (v. 12), מערצכם was read as מרחצכם (v. 14), נוקשו was read as נגשו (v. 15), שחר was read as שחד (v. 20), and so on. These types of variations—all clustered within a few verses and taken together to produce one coherent text—are clear examples of the type of scribal hermeneutic laid out in Koenig's and Teeter's works, and modern scholars have been practically unanimous in ascribing these divergences to the translator (see David Andrew Teeter, *Scribal Laws: Exegetical Variation in the Textual Transmission of Biblical Law in the Late Second Temple Period*, FAT 92 [Tübingen: Mohr Siebeck, 2014], esp. 199–200). The intimate connection between so many Hebrew variants and the Greek text argues against ascribing these changes to later Greek scribes, and the fact that the Greek text is so smooth—and that it fits so well with the translator's theology as seen elsewhere in Isaiah LXX, as I argue here—further keeps us from ascribing the interpretive work of this section to the Hebrew *Vorlage*.

[65] For a fuller discussion of levels of gentile adherence to Mosaic law and the spectrum between inclusion and a fully converted, "Jewish" identity, see Scot McKnight, *A Light among the Gentiles: Jewish Missionary Activity in the Second Temple Period* (Minneapolis: Fortress, 1991), 101.

pressing in Isaiah, where it is foretold that, in the last days, law will go out to the nations and gentiles will worship alongside Israelites in the temple (Isa 2:2–3, 56:6–7). The Hebrew text of Isaiah never clarifies what this law entails or how exactly the foreign nations will "walk in [YHWH's] ways" (Isa 2:3), and Isaiah LXX directs the reader toward an answer centered on acceptance and observance of Mosaic law.

In the late Second Temple period, multiple groups within Judaism and nascent Christianity wrestled with this very question. If gentiles are to join Israel—whether through present conversion or in the eschatological future—how much of the law should they be expected to keep? The New Testament shows the heated dispute between Paul and his contemporaries on this question, and stories such as the conversion of King Izates show a similar debate among other Jewish groups.[66] My analysis of Isa 8 LXX does not settle this debate, and it is unclear how the author might have envisioned complete gentile law observance in practice.[67] But understanding the message of Isa 8 LXX does help us recognize at least one approach to this question in the second-century diaspora. According to Isaiah LXX, the answer is clear: gentiles should embrace and keep Mosaic law—even those aspects that might be considered "hard."

This reading is in line with the increased concern that pervades Isaiah LXX regarding law observance, and it sheds new light on a number of other passages. For example, Isa 24:16 MT reads, "the treacherous deal treacherously, and with treachery the treacherous deal treacherously," but in the LXX this verse is rendered as a curse on law rejection: "Woe to those who reject, those who reject the law."[68] Isaiah 8 LXX builds on this, showing that the translator was concerned not only that Israelites might reject the law but also that the nations might reject it on the grounds that it is "hard" or a "stumbling block." Isaiah 26:9 LXX similarly reflects an increased focus on law observance, as the Hebrew text (כאשר משפטיך לארץ צדק למדו ישבי תבל) is rendered, "your commands are light upon the earth. Learn righteousness, you who dwell on the earth!"[69] The imperative directed at the earth's

---

[66] See, e.g., Mark D. Nanos, "The Question of Conceptualization: Qualifying Paul's Position on Circumcision in Dialogue with Josephus's Advisors to King Izates," in *Paul within Judaism: Restoring the First-Century Context to the Apostle*, ed. Mark D. Nanos and Magnus Zetterholm (Minneapolis: Fortress, 2015), 105–52; Josephus, *Ant.* 20.2.4 §§41–45; Marc Hirshman, "Rabbinic Universalism in the Second and Third Centuries," *HTR* 93 (2000): 101–15; and Christine E. Hayes, *Gentile Impurities and Jewish Identities: Intermarriage and Conversion from the Bible to the Talmud* (Oxford: Oxford University Press, 2002).

[67] Does gentile acceptance of the law, for example, include full observance of Jewish dietary practice? Would gentile converts be indistinguishable from native-born Israelites, or would they retain their separate status? If they remained somehow distinguishable from native Israelites, would this distinction find halakic expression, and what would this expression entail? Such specifics are never broached in Isaiah LXX.

[68] For discussion, see Troxel, *LXX-Isaiah as Translation and Interpretation*, 235; and Seeligmann, *Septuagint Version of Isaiah*, 270.

[69] See Karrer and Kraus, *Septuaginta Deutsch*, 2:2569; and Koenig, *L'herméneutique analogique*, 140–41.

inhabitants to "learn righteousness" in the context of God's law looks strikingly similar to the imperative in Isa 8:9 LXX: "Learn, peoples!" Twice in Isaiah LXX God commands the nations: "Consecrate yourselves to me, islands" (41:1, 45:16), while the Hebrew looks quite different.[70] Individually, these commands could be interpreted in a number of different ways, but taken together with the overriding concern for law in Isa 8 LXX, they bespeak the translator's desire that the nations come to God and keep his law.

As scholars have long noted, Isaiah LXX is hardly the end point in this stream of tradition; the book of Isaiah is among the most frequently quoted books in Second Temple Judaism, and the approach of Isaiah LXX to the question of gentile law observance undoubtedly influenced subsequent interpretation. As one example, Paul's description in Rom 9:32–33 of the law as a stumbling block and the importance of faith draws directly from Isa 8:14 LXX, where the gentiles are told that through trust (ἐὰν ἐπ' αὐτῷ πεποιθὼς ᾖς; cf. the MT) they will not encounter the law as a stumbling block (οὐχ ὡς λίθου προσκόμματι συναντήσεσθε). Clearly, Paul does not entirely adopt the view of Isaiah LXX on this question, as he argues against gentiles' wholly adopting the practices of Mosaic law, but the influence of Isaiah LXX on his thinking opens up promising new avenues of research on what is still a divisive discussion.[71] By taking a broader approach to Isa 8 LXX, as argued here, we can better understand not only the LXX text of Isaiah itself but also the wider world of the Second Temple period, including those groups that argued for full gentile inclusion and observance of Mosaic law.

---

[70] Isaiah 41:1 reads החרישו אלי איים, and 45:16 reads הלכו בכלמה חרשי צירים. See van der Vorm-Croughs, *Old Greek of Isaiah*, 349.

[71] The influence of Isaiah on Paul has been treated extensively (see, e.g., Florian Wilk, *Die Bedeutung des Jesajabuches für Paulus*, FRLANT 179 [Göttingen: Vandenhoeck & Ruprecht, 1998]; and Steve Moyise and Maarten J. J. Menken, eds., *Isaiah in the New Testament*, NTSI [London: T&T Clark, 2005]), but little attention has been given to Isaiah LXX's unique contributions to the debate on law observance or to how these contributions may have influenced Pauline theology.

New and Recent Titles

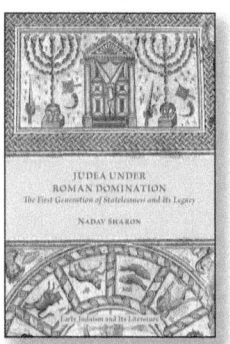

JUDEA UNDER ROMAN DOMINATION
The First Generation of Statelessness and Its Legacy
Nadav Sharon
Paperback $79.95, 978-1-62837-176-5   552 pages, 2017   Code 063547
Hardcover $99.95, 978-0-88414-222-5 E-book $79.95, 978-0-88414-221-8
Early Judaism and Its Literature 46

REFLECTIONS OF EMPIRE IN ISAIAH 1–39
Responses to Assyrian Ideology
Shawn Zelig Aster
Digital open access, 978-0-88414-272-0
https://www.sbl-site.org/publications/Books_ANEmonographs.aspx
Paperback $54.95, 978-1-62837-201-4   382 pages, 2017   Code: 062823
Hardcover $74.95, 978-0-88414-273-7 Ancient Near East Monographs 19

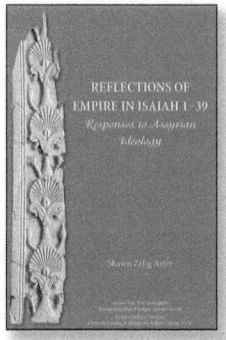

THE SBL COMMENTARY ON THE SEPTUAGINT
An Introduction
Dirk Büchner, editor
Paperback $37.95, 978-1-62837-187-1   280 pages, 2017   Code 060466
Hardcover $52.95, 978-0-88414-244-7 E-book $37.95, 978-0-88414-243-0
Septuagint and Cognate Studies 66

READING THE BIBLE IN ANCIENT TRADITIONS AND MODERN EDITIONS
Studies in Memory of Peter W. Flint
Andrew B. Perrin, Kyung S. Baek, and Daniel K. Falk, editors
Paperback $82.95, 978-1-62837-191-8   746 pages, 2017   Code: 063546
Hardcover $102.95, 978-0-88414-254-6 E-book $82.95, 978-0-88414-253-9
Early Judaism and Its Literature 47

WHEN TEXTS ARE CANONIZED
Timothy H. Lim, editor
Paperback $29.95, 978-1-946527-00-4   188 pages, 2017   Code: 140359
Hardcover $44.95, 978-1-930675-95-7 E-book $29.95, 978-1-930675-99-5
Brown Judaic Studies 359

SBL Press • P.O. Box 2243 • Williston, VT 05495-2243
Phone: 877-725-3334 (toll-free) or 802-864-6185 • Fax: 802-864-7626
Order online at www.sbl-site.org/publications

THE CULMINATING WORK OF A LEADING ARCHAEOLOGIST OF THE BIBLICAL WORLD

BEYOND THE TEXTS

An Archaeological Portrait of Ancient Israel and Judah
William G. Dever

William G. Dever offers a welcome perspective on ancient Israel and Judah that prioritizes the archaeological remains to render history as it was—not as the biblical writers argue it should have been. Drawing from the most recent archaeological data as interpreted from a nontheological point of view and supplementing that data with biblical material only when it converges with the archaeological record, Dever analyzes all the evidence at hand to provide a new history of ancient Israel and Judah that is accessible to all interested readers.

FROM SBL PRESS
More than 80 maps and illustrations
Hardcover ISBN 978-0-88414-218-8
E-book ISBN 978-0-88414-217-1
Hardcover or E-book $49.95

Order online at
https://tinyurl.com/SBLPressDeverBeyond

Phone: 877-725-3334 (toll-free) or 802-864-6185
Fax: 802-864-7626

SBL PRESS

The End of Exile: The Reception of Jeremiah's Prediction of a Seventy-Year Exile

STEVEN M. BRYAN
steve.bryan@sim.org
Trinity International University, Deerfield, IL 60015

An increasingly common assessment of the Second Temple period posits a widespread belief, even among Jews living in Judea, that Israel remained in a state of ongoing exile long after the sixth-century return from exile following the decree of Cyrus. This essay evaluates that claim in relation to the reception of Jeremiah's prophecy that the exile would last for seventy years. The texts that reflect on the prophecy of seventy years do not adopt exegetical strategies that greatly extend the length of the exile, as if the return under Cyrus were not the "real return from exile." This is true even in Daniel, where the literal fulfillment of Jeremiah's prophecy of a seventy-year exile and Daniel's penitent preparation for that fulfillment serve as a starting point and a model for reflecting on another hoped-for experience of God's mercy at the end of seventy weeks of years. Though the texts that refer to Jeremiah's prediction of a seventy-year exile do not handle the seventy years in a completely uniform way, the fulfillment of Jeremiah's prophecy is placed firmly in the past, reflecting the belief that the exile had ended. Not all the texts examined regard the period following the seventy-year exile as a time of unremitting punishment. Texts that do assess the period following the exile in negative terms do not view that period as an extension of exile. Rather, the literal fulfillment of Jeremiah's prophecy that the exile would come to an end inspires hope that the God who was faithful to keep his promise would also keep his promise of an ultimate restoration that would far outstrip the initial jubilee (Dan 9:25), "the brief moment of favor" (Ezra 9:8) that had brought the exile to an end.

In his recent book *Paul and the Faithfulness of God*, N. T. Wright has renewed his oft-repeated contention that the Second Temple period was widely understood as a period of ongoing exile. In his view, this idea is one that "ought by now to be non-controversial but which continues to be stubbornly resisted in certain quarters."[1] Despite Wright's latest effort to root out the resistance, important strands of

[1] N. T. Wright, *Paul and the Faithfulness of God*, 2 vols., Christian Origins and the Question of God 4 (Minneapolis: Fortress, 2013), 139.

evidence cannot be tidily accommodated within the overarching narrative he lays out.[2] In this essay, I consider one strand of evidence by examining Second Temple reflection on the return from exile in relation to Jeremiah's prediction that Israel would serve the king of Babylon for seventy years (Jer 25:11–12).

Central to Wright's ongoing scholarly project is the idea that the New Testament is best understood in relation to the basic Second Temple Jewish worldview. This worldview was shaped by the belief that the historic return from exile did not bring the exile to an end; it was not "the real return from exile" because it did not bring with it the promised restoration.[3] If one accepts Wright's understanding of "exile" as nonrestoration, I am in complete agreement. Wright, however, goes beyond this understanding to assert that consciousness of ongoing exile was so much a part of Second Temple Jewish self-awareness that its influence can be assumed even when it is not mentioned.[4]

It is my contention that Jews in the postexilic period were concerned not so much with the continuation of exile but with its end: the exile had ended, but full restoration had not followed. Thus, far more formative for Second Temple Judaism was the dissonance created by the fact that the pattern of sin–exile–restoration had not unfolded as expected. This is exactly the opposite of the assertion of Robert P. Carroll, whom Wright quotes to launch his case: "Much of the literature of the Second Temple period recognizes a category of exile after the destruction of Jerusalem in 587/86, but it does not recognize any return in subsequent centuries. This literature … represents Israel as being in exile for centuries; virtually permanent exile."[5]

But is it true that the literature of the Second Temple period "does not recognize any return" from exile? The way that postexilic biblical and Second Temple Jewish literature handled the prophet Jeremiah's prediction that the exile to Babylon would last for seventy years is evidence of the belief that the exile had ended with the return from Babylon. Although the prediction of a seventy-year exile is not interpreted uniformly, there is considerable consistency in viewing the exile as limited in duration and completed at the time of the return from Babylon under Cyrus. This is true even of texts that cast the Second Temple period in generally negative terms. Often these texts sustain a hope for further action by God, but this hope does not typically reflect a sense that the exile had not come to an end.

---

[2] Wright responds at length to critics of his view (ibid., 139–62), focusing especially on an excursus in my *Jesus and Israel's Traditions of Judgement and Restoration*, SNTSMS 117 (Cambridge: Cambridge University Press, 2002), 12–20.

[3] Wright, *Paul and the Faithfulness*, 117.

[4] For examples, see the treatment of the parable of the prodigal son in N. T. Wright, *Jesus and the Victory of God*, Christian Origins and the Question of God 2 (Minneapolis: Fortress, 1996), 126, and his interpretation of Gal 3:10–14 in Wright, *Paul and the Faithfulness*, 867.

[5] Robert P. Carroll, "Israel, History of (Post-Monarchic Period)," *ABD* 3:567–76, here 575, cited by Wright, *Paul and the Faithfulness*, 139.

I. "Exile": Geographical Displacement or a Political and Theological State?

In attempting to discern whether there was in Second Temple Judaism a sense of ongoing exile, it is important to be clear about what is meant by the term. The normal sense of *exile*, both in the Hebrew Scriptures and in modern parlance, has to do with removal, usually by force, from one's homeland.[6] Yet many, including Wright, use the term to describe Israel's experience of captivity to foreign powers regardless of whether that enslavement is experienced outside of Israel's homeland.[7] Wright regards continuing exile "as a political and theological state rather than a geographical one."[8] The equation of exile with subservience to foreign powers and the perception of divine disapproval was evident in an early article by Michael A. Knibb, and its continuing influence is illustrated in a more recent article by James C. VanderKam.[9] VanderKam surveys the meanings of the term *exile* in the Hebrew Scriptures. After examining ways in which the term is used to describe literal or historical experiences of removal from the land, he identifies an additional sense "in which the language of dispersion and captivity may be used ... as an ongoing, still unfinished experience for Judeans living after the so-called restoration."[10] In the Hebrew Scriptures, however, the "language of dispersion"—whether "exile" or any similar expression—is never used of Israelites living in their own land either before or after the exile. Further, although the language of captivity is used to describe Israel's national experience at various times in its history, that

---

[6] See, e.g., Amos 7:11, 17: "Israel must surely go into exile, away from its land."

[7] Wright rejects the idea that he is using the term *exile* as a metaphor, because he understands this political and theological state as an extension of the geographical exile. Somewhat confusingly, however, he endorses Carroll's designation of the term as a "*symbol* for the alienation of the group (or sect) from power in Jerusalem" (*Paul and the Faithfulness*, 140; emphasis added) and chides those who resist speaking about "metaphorical uses of 'exile'" (142 n. 272). By contrast, Martien A. Halvorson-Taylor embraces the idea that "exile" came to be used as a metaphor for experiences of divine displeasure other than geographical displacement—a usage whose origin she traces to the association of exile with other forms of divine punishment in the curse texts of Deut 28 and Lev 26. Although she succeeds in showing that other forms of divine punishment were associated with the historic exile, she assumes rather than shows that the language of geographical displacement came to be used as a metaphor for divine displeasure *that took other forms*, for example, subservience to foreign powers (*Enduring Exile: The Metaphorization of Exile in the Hebrew Bible*, VTSup 141 [Leiden: Brill, 2011], 6).

[8] Wright, *Paul and the Faithfulness*, 139.

[9] Michael A. Knibb, "The Exile in the Literature of the Intertestamental Period," *HeyJ* 17 (1976): 253–72; James C. VanderKam, "Exile in Jewish Apocalyptic Literature," in *Exile: Old Testament, Jewish, and Christian Conceptions*, ed. James M. Scott, JSJSup 56 (Leiden: Brill, 1997), 89–109, here 89.

[10] VanderKam, "Exile in Jewish Apocalyptic Literature," 89.

captivity is associated with the term *exile* only when it involves physical removal from the land.

The text cited by VanderKam as evidence for a political and theological as opposed to geographic sense of exile is Ezra 9:7, a text that is also important to Wright: "From the days of our ancestors to this day we have been deep in guilt, and for our iniquities we, our kings, and our priests have been handed over to the kings of the lands, to the sword, to captivity, to plundering, and to utter shame, as is now the case." The passage does not refer to ongoing "exile," however, but to the ongoing experience of foreign domination, which had been a continuous part of Israel's experience from the nation's earliest history and not just beginning with the exile to Babylon. When Ezra speaks of "exile," as he does in 6:21, it is in reference to an experience from which the people of Israel have recently returned. This illustrates a key problem: if all of Israel's experiences of foreign domination that are depicted in the Hebrew Scriptures are labeled "exile," then we must speak of the nation's many experiences of preexilic "exile."

Although the Hebrew Scriptures do not use the term *exile* as a metonym for subservience to foreign powers, some Second Temple Jews seem to have regarded Israel's experience as one of divine punishment that had not ended with the end of exile. This belief, however, was far from uniform, and, even where the belief was held, the exile could be isolated as the first part of Israel's punishment. Many Second Temple texts had a strong sense that the exile had come to an end in fulfillment of Jeremiah's prophecy, which suggests the need for a more complex way of describing Second Temple Jewish self-understanding.

II. The Completion of the Exile in Biblical Literature

A significant body of evidence suggests that the sixth-century BCE return from exile was regarded as an important fulfillment of one part of the divine promise that Israel would be restored following exile. Some of this evidence is biblical. We will look first at biblical texts in which the seventy-year prophecy is appropriated in a straightforward way, before turning to Daniel, where the prophecy is widely regarded as having been reinterpreted.

Jeremiah

Already within Jeremiah there is evidence for the durability of the prophecy of seventy years of desolation of the land and service to the king of Babylon (25:11–12). Jeremiah 25 places the original prophecy in the fourth year of Jehoiakim and the first year of Nebuchadnezzar, that is, just prior to the exile in 605. If false prophets in Judea had dismissed Jeremiah's warning of punishment prior to the exile, false prophets in Babylon following the exile scorned the idea that it would last anything like seventy years. As a result, Jeremiah reaffirms the original prediction of seventy years of service in the form of a letter preserved in chapter 29: only when the seventy years were complete would the exile come to an end.

In its narrative setting, the rearticulation of the prediction strengthens the polemic against those who resist the decreed punishment for Judah. Those who have stayed behind in Judah will not be exempt from punishment. Although they have not been sent into exile for seventy years (29:16), they will nevertheless suffer a full measure of covenantal curses: "I am going to let loose on them sword, famine, and pestilence, and I will make them like rotten figs that are so bad they cannot be eaten" (29:17 NRSV). Jeremiah's letter thus distinguishes between punishment outside the land, which is exile, and punishment inside the land, which is not. Even when God casts those "who did not go with [the others] into exile" out of the land (29:16–18), they are not counted as "exiles." Rather, the "exiles" are those on whom God "will set his eyes ... for good" (24:6). Those who initially remained in Judah will be expelled from the land, but their expulsion is permanent; like rotten figs, they will be cast away until they are "utterly destroyed" (24:10).[11] Jeremiah is aware of "exiles" to lands other than Babylon and frames the promise of restoration as a promise to gather the exiles "from all the nations and all the places" where the Lord had driven them (29:14). The dispersion of those who had originally stayed behind, however, adds not to the number of exiles but to the number of those destroyed from the land.

2 Chronicles/Ezra

Despite ambiguities in dating the onset of the seventy years, the biblical literature outside of Jeremiah consistently regards the oracle as a premier example of fulfilled prophecy. In 2 Chr 36:20–23 (2 Chr 36:22–23 // Ezra 1:1–2) we read:

> [Nebuchadnezzar] took into exile in Babylon those who had escaped from the sword, and they became servants to him and to his sons until the establishment of the kingdom of Persia, to fulfill the word of the LORD by the mouth of Jeremiah, until the land had made up for its sabbaths. All the days that it lay desolate it kept sabbath, to fulfill seventy years. In the first year of King Cyrus of Persia, in fulfillment of the word of the LORD spoken by Jeremiah, the LORD stirred up the spirit of King Cyrus of Persia so that he sent a herald throughout all his kingdom and also declared in a written edict: "Thus says King Cyrus of Persia: The LORD, the God of heaven, has given me all the kingdoms of the earth, and he has charged

---

[11] Michael Fishbane argues that the hopeful tone of Jer 29 expresses "a more conciliatory (post-exilic) concern" and reflects the reinterpretation of the seventy-years prophecy "as a prophecy of hope for the diasporic community" (*Biblical Interpretation in Ancient Israel* [Oxford: Clarendon, 1985], 480). The rearticulation of the seventy-years prophecy, however, functions as a warning against those who resist the decreed punishment. It is difficult to see how the prediction would have functioned as a prophecy of hope for a diaspora community in a *postexilic* setting.

me to build him a house at Jerusalem, which is in Judah. Whoever is among you of all his people, may the LORD his God be with him! Let him go up." (NRSV)

Here the Chronicler portrays the return from Babylon and "all the kingdoms of the earth" as the literal fulfillment of the promise that Israel's exile would last seventy years and places the fulfillment firmly in the past. Under the influence of Lev 26:34–35, the Chronicler understands the seventy years as compensation to the land for the sabbatical years that Israel had neglected. Anticipating the discussion of Dan 9, these sabbatical years are repaid consecutively, not just once in seven years. The Chronicler interprets Jeremiah "quite literally: seventy years meant seventy years."[12]

Zechariah

In Zech 1, the completion of Jeremiah's seventy years prompts the question of verse 12: "O LORD of hosts, how long will you withhold mercy from Jerusalem and the cities of Judah?" (NRSV). The question is asked after those sent throughout the earth find the whole world at peace (1:11). This peace corresponds to the short time anticipated by Haggai that would pass before the Lord would once more shake the heavens and the earth, bringing the wealth of the nations to Jerusalem to establish a temple of surpassing glory (Hag 2:6–9). Both Zechariah and Haggai see the fulfillment of these hopes in the offing, even as they recall the nation's former ways as a warning that the fulfillment might yet be compromised. In reply to the question "how long?" (Zech 1:11), the Lord speaks "gracious and comforting words" (1:13) and declares that he has "returned to Jerusalem with compassion" (1:16). If subsequent events would frustrate the hopes associated with the return of the exiles, these texts nevertheless evince a strong conviction that the exile had ended.

Some have suggested that, unlike the Chronicler, Zechariah regarded the seventy years as complete with the reconstruction of the temple in 516/515. Thus, Michael Fishbane dates the oracle of 1:12 to 520/519 and thinks it "conceivable that the anticipated fulfilment of a seventy-year oracle believed to have been effective from the second Judaean exile (in 587/6) may have actually fuelled national energies towards the restoration of the Temple."[13] Yet the angel's question—"How long will you withhold mercy from Jerusalem and the cities of Judah with which you have been angry these seventy years?"—is better understood as a response to the perception of divine delay. It makes little sense as a cry for mercy expected but not received if the allotted time of punishment has not yet come to completion. The question of 1:12, then, is an expression of bewilderment that the expected concomitants of the return from exile have not yet been experienced despite the fact

---

[12] Ibid., 481.
[13] Ibid. Cf. Devorah Dimant, "The Seventy Weeks Chronology (Dan 9,24–27) in the Light of New Qumranic Texts," in *The Book of Daniel in the Light of New Findings*, ed. A. S. van der Woude, BETL 106 (Leuven: Leuven University Press, 1993), 64.

that the seventy-year exile had ended some time before. On either understanding of the text, Jeremiah's oracle is taken at face value.

The reference to Jeremiah's oracle in Zech 7 places the fulfillment of the seventy-year prophecy firmly in the past. The people query the priests whether they should continue the fasts they had practiced during the exile, now that the seventy years have ended and the exiles have returned to the land (7:5). The Lord responds by asking whether the fasts were truly for him or more of the same religious formalism denounced by the prophets prior to the exile. The ensuing review of the exile serves as an implied warning that the balance of God's work to bring about Israel's restoration could yet be delayed, but the return from exile in fulfillment of Jeremiah's prophecy augurs better things.

Daniel

A common approach to Dan 9 suggests that the prophecy of seventy weeks of years is an attempt to cope with the failure of Israel's restoration to materialize following the seventy years of exile. Thus, Daniel is told "that the seventy years meant seventy weeks of years."[14] In his influential study of this perceived transformation, Fishbane argues that the seventy years of Jeremiah had already been read by the Chronicler through the lens of Lev 25, which resulted in an understanding of the seventy years as recompense to the land for its sabbaths (2 Chr 36:19–21; cf. Lev 26:34–35). Fishbane contends that 2 Chronicles thus provided the exegetical basis for Daniel's transformation of Jeremiah's seventy years into seventy sabbatical cycles: Daniel reckons Jeremiah's seventy years by counting only the seventh year in each sabbatical cycle.[15]

There are several reasons to question this assessment. First, 2 Chronicles, the supposed basis for the transformation detected by Fishbane, says just the opposite: the seventy years *were* the lost sabbatical years. From the point of view of the Chronicler, the sabbatical years had already been repaid. Second, to regard the seventy weeks as a reinterpretation of the seventy years makes little sense of the narrative setting in relation to Daniel's prayer of repentance. In 9:2, Daniel understands from his reading of Jeremiah's scroll that the exile was to last seventy years. This prompts Daniel's prayer of repentance. The prayer is set in the first year of Darius, that is, at the passing of imperial power from the Babylonians to the Medo-Persians. In the narrative, the collapse of Babylonian hegemony is the sign that points to the impending fulfillment of Jeremiah's prediction that Jerusalem would be desolate for seventy years. Some have read the prayer as though it functions as Daniel's response to his inability to understand Jeremiah's prediction. Thus, for example, Fishbane states that Daniel searched the books and found Jeremiah's

---

[14] VanderKam, "Exile in Jewish Apocalyptic," 90.
[15] Fishbane, *Biblical Interpretation*, 482–83.

prophecy, "whose comprehension eluded him."¹⁶ In fact, 9:2 says that Daniel prayed after he had "understood" Jeremiah's prophecy. Hence, the following prayer is not a prayer for illumination, as some have suggested, but a prayer of corporate repentance.¹⁷ Daniel's conviction that the time for the fulfillment of Jeremiah's prediction has arrived prompts the penitential prayer.

The prayer is constructed according to the stipulations of Lev 26 and 1 Kgs 8, which had mandated corporate prayers of repentance as the condition for God to "cause their conquerors to show them mercy" (1 Kgs 8:50; cf. Lev 26:40–45). In this context, the prayer reconciles the tension between the belief that God's mercy toward Israel was conditional upon Israel's repentance and the implication of Jeremiah's prophecy that restoration would occur according to a fixed timetable. Daniel's prayer is the penitential means by which Jeremiah's prophecy is brought to fulfillment. By contrast, on Fishbane's reading, the prayer effects only the revelation of an alternative timetable that pushes restoration into the distant future.¹⁸ But the setting of the prayer at a time just prior to the end of the seventy years, the explicit indication that Daniel understood the seventy-years prophecy, and the construction of the prayer on the basis of texts promising that God would respond in mercy to corporate repentance suggest that the prayer functions as the means by which the devastation of the seventy years is brought to an end. The prayer serves as a model for the prayer of those who suffer the afflictions of the seventieth week. It could do so because it was effective first as a means of ending the exile at the end of Jeremiah's seventy years.

Third, the view that Daniel transforms the seventy years diverges sharply from the book's positive use of Jeremiah's prediction. The text specifies the end of the seventy years as the end of Jerusalem's desolation (9:2) and then designates a period of seventy weeks to bring Israel's punishment to completion (9:24). But the seventy years do not become seventy weeks. This is evident from the role the initial seventy-year period plays in the seventy-week scheme. In the breakdown of the seventy weeks into three periods, the first period lasts only seven weeks; the second period, sixty-two weeks; and the third period, a single week. In the effort to sort out the referents of the events associated with the final week, the significance of this first period of seven weeks is often overlooked. Knibb, for instance, dismisses the initial

---

¹⁶ Ibid., 487–88. Cf. Reinhard G. Kratz, "The Visions of Daniel," in *The Book of Daniel: Composition and Reception*, ed. John J. Collins and Peter W. Flint, 2 vols., VTSup 83 (Leiden: Brill, 2001), 1:91–113, here 105; Rodney Alan Werline, *Penitential Prayer in Second Temple Judaism: The Development of a Religious Institution*, EJL 13 (Atlanta: Scholars Press, 1998), 72.

¹⁷ On this, see esp. John S. Bergsma, "The Persian Period as Penitential Era: The 'Exegetical Logic' of Daniel 9:1-27," in *Exile and Restoration Revisited: Essays on the Babylonian and Persian Periods in Memory of Peter R. Ackroyd*, ed. Gary N. Knoppers and Lester L. Grabbe, LSTS 73 (London: T&T Clark, 2009), 51–58.

¹⁸ Fishbane, *Biblical Interpretation*, 488–89.

seven-week period, which he claims weighs lightly in the seventy-week scheme.[19] Wright disregards it altogether. But, given the focus on the seventieth week, the remarkable thing is not that the seventh week weighs lightly in the seventy-week scheme but that it was marked at all. But what does the initial seven-week period signify?

While the seven weeks (forty-nine years) do not correlate precisely with the seventy years of Jeremiah, they do specify a shorter period of time at the beginning of the seventy weeks. It is important to note that the seventy-week scheme designates both a period of sevenfold punishment, arising from Jeremiah's seventy years, and a tenfold deliverance, arising from the length of a single forty-nine-year jubilee. Thus, the initial break at seven weeks within the seventy-week scheme is the length of a single jubilee. The segmentation of the seventy weeks, then, highlights the correlation between an initial jubilee of forty-nine years and the full jubilee of 490 years.

Further, the significance of the first forty-nine years in the 490-year scheme goes beyond the fact that it is the first of ten jubilees. The author seems also to see the completion of the first jubilee as corresponding to the end of the first of seven seventy-year periods.[20] This is indicated by the fact that the seventy years begins with the *desolation* of Jerusalem according to the word of the Lord (9:2) but that the first jubilee begins with the word of the Lord concerning the *rebuilding* of Jerusalem (9:25).[21] By staggering the start times of the two ways of reckoning time, the first seven-week period marks an initial convergence of two methods of calculating time—either as a sequence of jubilees measured in forty-nine-year increments or as periods of punishment marked in seventy-year blocks—just as the end of the seventy weeks marks the ultimate convergence of the completed punishment (7 × 70 years) and the full deliverance (10 × 49 years).[22] The relationship between the seventh week and the seventieth week confirms that the author of Dan 9 did not

---

[19] See Knibb, "Exile in the Literature," 255.

[20] For another example in which a brief period of seventy years is marked at the beginning of a 490-year scheme, see the discussion of 4Q390 below.

[21] The referent of the "word" concerning the rebuilding of Jerusalem in Dan 9:25 is disputed but is best understood as a designation of Jeremiah's prophecy regarding the restoration of Jerusalem in Jer 30–31, which follows the prophecy in chapter 29 of the city's desolation. So, e.g., Ernest Lucas, *Daniel*, ApOTC (Nottingham: Apollos, 2002), 243. Lucas dates the oracles of desolation to 605 BCE (Jer 25:12) and 597 BCE (Jer 29:10), preceding the oracles of restoration, which date to 587 (Jer 30:18–22, 31:38–40). Bergsma defends the view that the "word" refers to the edict of Cyrus that permitted the return of the exiles ("Persian Period as Penitential Era," 58–60). Yet the fact that the chapter begins with Daniel's meditation on the "word" of the Lord to Jeremiah suggests that the "word" of 9:25 also refers to a word of the Lord to Jeremiah. Moreover, if the "word" refers to the edict of Cyrus, it is difficult to explain why the end of the first seven weeks is marked in the seventy-week scheme.

[22] The exegetical warrant for a sevenfold punishment probably stemmed from Lev 26:18, as others have noted. See John J. Collins, *Daniel: A Commentary on the Book of Daniel*, Hermeneia

seek so much to transform the seventy years as a way of lengthening the time of the exile as to exploit the end of exile as a model for how God's mercy might again be experienced in a later generation, that is, through the penitential prayers of the righteous.[23] The serendipity of the first convergence as an anticipation of the second convergence at the end of the 490-year period doubtless reduced whatever tension, if any, the author may have felt in staggering the start times of the initial jubilee and Jeremiah's seventy years. In such schemes, prescient chronography trumps precise chronology. The point, in other words, is "not about a strict chronology but about constructing a meaning for the exile and a way of understanding the prophecy of Jeremiah as having been fulfilled."[24] This meaning is found in the twinned convergence: just as the first jubilee brought about the prophesied end to the exile in response to Daniel's prayer of repentance, so also the ultimate jubilee that will end Israel's punishment must be sought through repentance.[25]

By marking different starting points for the first jubilee and the seventy-year exile, the return from exile is highlighted as an initial act of deliverance that underwrites the promise of an ultimate deliverance. In a stroke of chronographic insight, Daniel understands (9:22) that the seventy-year exile presages a longer punishment brought to sevenfold fullness and corresponds to a forty-nine-year jubilee brought to tenfold completion.[26] It is unlikely, then, that the seventy weeks is a reconception of the length of the exile. Rather, the exile ends in the seventh week, and this initial experience of deliverance anticipates the full liberation that must await the seventieth week. Daniel's prayer of corporate repentance serves as a means by which the seventy-year exile comes to an end and thus as a model for the way in which a later generation might also experience the mercy of God.

III. Jeremiah's Seventy Years in the Septuagint

Perhaps the earliest response to Jeremiah's seventy years outside the Hebrew Scriptures is that of the Septuagint. The relationship between the LXX and the MT

(Minneapolis: Fortress, 1993), 352. There is no need to resort to Fishbane's hypothesis that only sabbatical years counted toward the completion of the seventy years.

[23] Largely because of the initial seven-week period, Carol A. Newsom (*Daniel: A Commentary*, OTL [Louisville: Westminster John Knox, 2014], 305), referring to Knibb, cautions against "importing" into the text the idea that Daniel regards the exile as having not come to an end.

[24] Ibid., 300.

[25] Bergsma suggests that the relationship between the seventy years and the seventy weeks arises from the impenitence of the people: because they have not repented, the fulfillment of Jeremiah's prophecy is delayed by a factor of seven ("Persian Period as Penitential Era," 55–58). This, however, overlooks the fact that Daniel's prayer is a prayer of *corporate* repentance. As such, the prayer functions as the means by which the initial jubilee is realized.

[26] On the issue of chronography, see Lester L. Grabbe, "Chronography in Hellenesitic Jewish Historiography," in *Society of Biblical Literature 1979 Seminar Papers*, ed. Paul J. Achtemeier, 2 vols., SBLSP (Missoula, MT: Scholars Press, 1979), 2:43–68.

of Jeremiah is notoriously complex, but it is possible to detect in the LXX a process of reflection on the seventy years. Though there are significant differences between the LXX and the MT in Jer 25:11–12, these do not affect the specified length of time. It is perhaps significant that, in contrast to the MT, in which Israel and the surrounding nations will serve the Babylonian king for seventy years, the LXX says more simply that Israel "will serve in the nations for seventy years." In the LXX no mention is made of service specifically to the Babylonian king or of service rendered by nations other than Israel; rather, Israel serves "in the nations" for seventy years. This contrasts with the MT, which does not specifically mention Israel's exile either to Babylon or in the nations. The silence of the LXX in regard to Babylon and its king is characteristic, though the devastation of Israel is clearly wrought by a single nation. Somewhat surprising, then, is the indication that Israel's servitude is *in the nations*. Though the relationship between the textual traditions at this point has been variously understood, textual development is evident in one or both of the traditions. Yet the reference to the seventy years remained untouched.

Of greater importance for our purposes is the reference to the seventy years in Jer 29:10 (36:10 LXX). It is widely recognized that the translation of Jer 29–52 stems from the hand of someone other than the person responsible for chapters 1–28.[27] It is not surprising, therefore, to find that the reference to the seventy years is handled somewhat differently in Jer 36:10 LXX than in 25:11–12. The Hebrew text of Jer 29:10 reads: "Only when Babylon's seventy years are completed will I visit you" (מלאת לבבל שבעים שנה אפקד אתכם). The Greek text, however, reflects a subtle difference: "When seventy years *are about to be* fulfilled for Babylon, I will visit you" (ὅταν μέλλῃ πληροῦσθαι Βαβυλῶνι ἑβδομήκοντα ἔτη ἐπισκέψομαι ὑμᾶς). The amelioration in the translation of the LXX is not without difficulties, particularly for Jeremiah, where the *Vorlage* of the LXX differs substantially from the textual tradition represented by the MT. Recent studies have suggested that ameliorative translation is a significant feature in the LXX of Jeremiah.[28] Furthermore, both the immediate context and the line in question indicate very close correspondence between the LXX and its *Vorlage*, on the one hand, and the MT, on the other. The LXX, like the Hebrew, uses an infinitive for the opening temporal clause, and the following, idiomatic clause (והקמתי עליכם את־דברי הטוב להשיב אתכם אל־המקום הזה, "And I will establish my good word over you to return you to this place") is mirrored quite literally in the LXX (καὶ ἐπιστήσω τοὺς λόγους μου ἐφ᾽ ὑμᾶς τοῦ τὸν λαὸν ὑμῶν ἀποστρέψαι εἰς τὸν τόπον τοῦτον, "And I will establish my words over you to return your people to this place").[29] Thus, the presence of μέλλῃ before πληροῦσθαι is unexpected. The fact that the seventy years does not correspond

---

[27] See Sven Soderlund, *The Greek Text of Jeremiah: A Revised Hypothesis*, JSOTSup 47 (Sheffield: JSOT Press, 1985), 153–92.

[28] See Andrew G. Shead, *The Open Book and the Sealed Book: Jeremiah 32 in Its Hebrew and Greek Recensions*, JSOTSup 347 (Sheffield: Sheffield Academic, 2002), 256.

[29] The single significant variation in this clause is the presence of the adjective הטוב following דברי.

precisely to any fixed dates for Babylonian hegemony over Israel has long troubled commentators. It may also have troubled the translator, who introduced μέλλῃ to reduce the chronological difficulty. The translator's rendering encourages the reader to understand the seventy years as a round figure. If so, the translator, working in the second or third century BCE, clearly regarded Jeremiah's prediction as fulfilled.

IV. Jeremiah's Seventy Years at Qumran

Explicit references to Jeremiah's seventy years are rare in the Qumran writings. In 4Q243 (4Qpseudo-Daniel[a–c] ar) frag. 16, there is a possible reference to a group "oppressed for seventy years" immediately followed by mention of divine deliverance. The word *seventy* is fully present only in reconstruction but remains a probable reading. If the reference is to a seventy-year exile followed by God's deliverance, the passage may be especially significant, since it is part of a collection of fragments based on the book of Daniel. John J. Collins and Peter W. Flint aver that the "'seventy years' does not necessarily refer to the Babylonian exile."[30] Yet a reference to the seventy-year Babylonian exile is probable: the fragment depends on Daniel, and, apart from the reference to Jeremiah's prediction of a seventy-year exile in Dan 9:2, there are no other references in Daniel to a period of seventy years. It is possible, then, that we have in 4Q243 frag. 16 an indication that the reference to the seventy years in Dan 9 was regarded by the author of 4Qpseudo-Daniel as literally fulfilled.

Devorah Dimant identifies the fragments of 4Q390 as part of a larger work that she calls the Apocryphon of Jeremiah C.[31] In the first fragment, we read:

> [and]be[fore me and a]gain I shall [deliver them]into the hand of the sons of Aar[on]seventy years
>
> And the sons of Aaron will rule over them, and they will not walk [in]my [wa]ys, which I command you so that you may warn them. And they too will do what is evil in my eyes, like all that which the Israelites had done in the former days of their kingdom, except for those who will come first from the land of their captivity to build the Temple. And I shall speak to them and I shall send them commandments, and they will understand everything which they and their fathers had abandoned. And from (the time) when that generation comes to end, in the seventh jubilee of the devastation of the land, they will forget statute and festival and Sabbath and covenant. And they will violate everything and they will do what

---

[30] John J. Collins and Peter W. Flint, "Pseudo-Daniel," in *Qumran Cave 4.XVII: Parabiblical Texts, Part 3*, DJD XXII (Oxford: Clarendon, 1996), 134.

[31] Devorah Dimant, "Apocryphon of Jeremiah," in *Qumran Cave 4.XXI: Parabiblical Texts, Part 4: Pseudo-Prophetic Texts*, DJD XXX (Oxford: Clarendon, 2001), 91–260.

is evil in my eyes. Therefore I shall hide my face from them and deliver them into the hands of their enemies… (4Q390 frag. 1, lines 2–9)[32]

Dimant's reconstruction of this work locates the time of the ostensible revelation to Jeremiah in the aftermath of the destruction of 586 BCE. Despite the fact that Dimant places the transition from past to future in the aftermath of the destruction of 586, however, she asserts that 4Q390 1 refers to the early Second Temple period.[33] Thus, she understands the period of seventy years mentioned in line 2 as a reference to events in the third century BCE.[34] This makes little sense. The seventy-year period in line 2 is followed by a reference to return from exile in lines 5–7. Furthermore, the people on whom the seventy years of judgment falls are those warned by Jeremiah (lines 3–4). Those who return are regarded as exceptions among the people who revert to the evil done in the former days of the kingdom. All of this suggests that the seventy years in this text are the seventy years predicted by Jeremiah.

Of particular interest is the fact that the returnees to whom God sends his commandments and who "understand everything which they and their fathers abandoned" are described as a generation that comes to an end "in the seventh jubilee of the devastation of the land" (lines 7–8). Dimant rightly points out that this is part of a ten-jubilee or 490-year scheme mentioned in 4Q387 2 II, 3–4. This is significant. If the devastation begins with the Babylonian invasion of Judea, the seventh jubilee and the return of the people to evil does not occur until the third century BCE. The generation of the return from exile is regarded as having lasted as much as three hundred years.[35] If this is accurate, the seventy years are regarded as the length of exile, in keeping with the prophecy of Jeremiah. The devastation of the land, however, lasts for a much longer time despite the end of the exile and the righteousness of the generation of the return.

The second reference to seventy years occurs in 4Q390 frag. 2, col. I. Here the seventy years is the length of time during which a group "will begin to quarrel among themselves … from the day of the violation of the [oath and the] covenant which they will have violated." Dimant cites evidence indicating "at least three or four columns separated 4Q390 1 from 2."[36] In a document that sets forth an overview of history, this would seem to suggest that frag. 2 describes a period significantly later than that of frag. 1. Though the historical referents are vague, Dimant may be correct that the mention of several features that are prominent in

---

[32] Ibid., 238 (Dimant's translation).

[33] Ibid., 97.

[34] Ibid., 116.

[35] For a discussion of a number of texts in which the term *generation* (דור) embraces a salvation-historical grouping across an extended period of time, see Bryan, *Jesus and Israel's Traditions*, 81–85.

[36] Dimant, "Apocryphon of Jeremiah," 249.

second-century sectarian polemics may point to a later date.[37] This may suggest that Jeremiah's prediction has been taken up typologically to describe a period in the second century BCE.

V. The Seventy-Year Exile in the Old Testament Deuterocanonical and Pseudepigraphical Works

1 Esdras

The reference to the fulfillment of Jeremiah's prophecy in 1 Esd 1:57–58 occurs in a section that corresponds to 2 Chr 35–36, but 1 Esdras does not quote Chronicles precisely. Though 1 Esdras generally truncates the Chronicler, in this passage there is expansion. Two alterations stand out. First, 1 Esdras attributes to Jeremiah the Chronicler's comment that the time of desolation was compensation for neglected Sabbath years. Second, in keeping with the reformulation of the Chronicler's sabbatical rationale for the exile, the language has been brought into closer conformity with Lev 26:34–35. These alterations are significant in a composition usually dated to the two centuries prior to the turn of the Common Era. Alongside the other modifications of 2 Chr 35–36, they indicate that the author was not merely passing on received tradition. Far from muting or refuting Jeremiah's prophecy, 1 Esd 1:57–58 highlights its acuity.

Letter of Jeremiah

In the Letter of Jeremiah, the putative author writes to Jews about to be sent into exile to urge them to avoid the idolatry of Babylon. The warning gains intensity with the assertion that return from Babylon will not be speedy: God will not bring them back from Babylon "for a long time, up to seven generations" (6:3). It is clear both that the author was familiar with Jeremiah's prediction and that the seven generations stand in the place of the seventy years. Reinhard G. Kratz has demonstrated the very close literary dependence of the Letter of Jeremiah on canonical Jeremiah;[38] however, the relationship between the seven generations and the seventy years is uncertain.

Many deny a direct link. This is true especially of those who use the reference to seven generations as a way of dating the book. An average generation of forty years would suggest that the book stems from the late fourth century BCE.[39] If it is

---

[37] Ibid., 244.

[38] Reinhard Gregor Kratz, "Die Rezeption von Jeremia 10 und 29 im pseudepigraphen Brief des Jeremia," *JSJ* 26 (1995): 2–31.

[39] E.g., Carey A. Moore, *Daniel, Esther, and Jeremiah: The Additions; A New Translation with Introduction and Commentary*, AB 44 (Garden City, NY: Doubleday, 1977), 335. Moore reckons the seven generations from 597.

true that forty years would have been regarded as the standard length of a generation and that seven generations have displaced Jeremiah's seventy years, the conclusion must be that the seven generations (i.e., 280 years) were not derived from the seventy years. Indeed, such a transformation lacks exegetical warrant in the text and, in any case, would be not so much a reinterpretation as a straightforward denial of the seventy-year prediction.

Few, if any, think that the Letter of Jeremiah is directly dependent on Daniel, that is, that the seven generations derive from Daniel's seventy weeks. This would require an understanding of a generation as seventy years in length—an idea for which there is little support. More importantly, the specification of seven generations contradicts the book of Jeremiah, which explicitly states that not seven but three generations will render service to Babylon in exile (27:7, 29:6).

Over a century ago, C. J. Ball suggested that the reference to the three generations in Jeremiah might be the key to the problem posed by the specification of seven generations in the Letter of Jeremiah. Ball registered the possibility "that a Hebrew ג (= 3) has been confused with ז (= 7) in the original text of our Epistle."[40] Ball regarded as more probable the assumption of forty-year generations but offered no explanation of how a period of three generations might have been derived from Jeremiah's seventy years. Perhaps, as in Jeremiah itself, the author assumed that three generations would be affected by a seventy-year exile. If Ball's emendation is correct, it may reflect a preference for vagueness in designating the length of the exile: the exile was complete, but because its duration was not precisely seventy years, the author may have preferred Jeremiah's more stylized reference to a punishment of three generations.

Sibylline Oracle 3

The third Sibylline Oracle is widely thought to have been composed in the second century BCE. In 3:265–294, Israel's experience of exile and return is recalled, partly in reference to Jeremiah's prediction of seventy years. Because of Israel's disobedience and idolatry, the land and temple will lie desolate for "seven decades." Thereafter, "a good end and very great glory await," when God will raise up a king—probably Cyrus—and the temple will be rebuilt with the help of the kings of Persia.[41] This restoration does not have overt eschatological significance; the eschatological climax comes much later in the book, after the restored and beautified temple is subject to attack. In Sib. Or. 3, the seventy years are understood as an accurate chronology of the exile and its end. It is not the length of the exile but rather the nature and complexity of the eschatological climax that have been reconceived. The exile may have ongoing significance in its typological anticipation of the

---

[40] C. J. Ball, "Epistle of Jeremy," *APOT* 1:596–611, here 599.

[41] For the identification of the king in 3:286 as Cyrus, see John J. Collins, "Sibylline Oracles," *OTP* 1:317–472, here 368.

tribulation that will occur prior to eschatological dénouement, but the exile is not ongoing.[42]

Testament of Moses

The early first-century CE Testament of Moses comprises a survey of Israel's history, which reaches the exile in chapter 3. Moses foretells the fulfillment of his biblical predictions that the people's recalcitrance will lead inexorably to exile. Moses also prophesies that the people will be "slaves for about seventy-seven years." The reference is puzzling, not least because the author is quite probably aware of Jeremiah's prediction of a seventy-year exile. In the ensuing verses, the author indicates that the end of exile will come as a response to the penitent prayer of "one who is over them." If, as seems likely, this is a reference to Daniel, then the author would have known Jeremiah's prediction from Dan 9:2, if not also from Jeremiah.

There are several possible explanations for the designation of the exile as "about seventy-seven years." Though the work derives from a Semitic original, the text is poorly preserved in a single Latin manuscript that has been translated from the Greek. These factors greatly increase the possibility of errors in transmission or translation. Alternatively, if the "seventy-seven" is original, it may be symbolic: if the seventy years symbolizes the full punishment of Israel, then perhaps in its fulfillment seventy-seven represents complete punishment come to completion.[43] A more plausible solution is to see the "seventy-seven" as an attempt to adjust Jeremiah's round figure to the author's understanding of the actual chronology. If the author dates the start of the exile from the deportation of 597 BCE, then a seventy-seven-year period would place the end of the exile in 520 BCE—a commonly accepted date for the start of the rebuilding.[44]

That the author regards the exile as having reached a definite end emerges also from what follows. Moses prophesies that God will show compassion in response to Daniel's prayer (T. Mos. 4:5). In contrast to many modern interpreters of Daniel, the author of the Testament of Moses understands the answer to Daniel's prayer not as the angel's riddle but as the return from exile. The return from exile following the edict of Cyrus is significant, though not comprehensive: only "some parts

---

[42] See esp. John J. Collins, *The Apocalyptic Imagination: An Introduction to Jewish Apocalyptic Literature*, 2nd ed. (Grand Rapids: Eerdmans, 1998), 122.

[43] Cf. Johannes Tromp, *The Assumption of Moses: A Critical Edition with Commentary*, SVTP 10 (Leiden: Brill, 1993), 173–74; Norbert Johannes Hofmann, *Die Assumptio Mosis: Studien zur Rezeption massgültiger Überlieferung*, JSJSup 67 (Leiden: Brill, 2000), 59 n. 24.

[44] The Animal Apocalypse (1 En. 83–90) provides an interesting parallel in that, like the Assumption of Moses, it seems to regard the seventy years of Jeremiah as round or figurative and therefore susceptible to adjustment to mirror the author's understanding of the actual dates. If a seventy-seven-year exile dates the start of the exile from 597 BCE, the twelve week-hours (i.e., eighty-four years) in the Animal Apocalypse correspond to a start date of 605/604 BCE.

of the tribes" return to rebuild the city (4:7). But the partial nature of the return is not understood as an indication of ongoing exile or of unremitting wrath. As in Daniel, the text refers to the exile as the first punishment even as it anticipates "a second punishment ... even exceeding the former one" (9:2). The text indicates that this "second punishment" will be comparable to the scourges of the exile, but neither the second punishment nor the time before it is described in terms of exile.

4 Baruch (Paraleipomena Jeremiou)

This work was probably composed in the late first century or early second century CE. Fourth Baruch probably originated after the destruction of the Second Temple, but we consider it here because of the likelihood that it reflects ideas held before the Jewish War. At the heart of the account, Jeremiah pleads to God that the Ethiopian Abimelech, who had shown the prophet kindness by rescuing him from a pit, be spared amid the devastations about to befall Jerusalem. God responds to the prayer by sending Abimelech to the "vineyard of Agrippa," whereupon he falls into a deep sleep from which he does not awake for sixty-six years. When he does awake, he is led to Baruch, who sends a message by means of an eagle to Jeremiah in Babylon, who then leads the people out of Babylon and back to Jerusalem.

If, as commonly held, the work derives from an earlier Jewish work, the specification of the length of the exile as sixty-six years almost certainly stems from the earlier work. The best solution is perhaps the simplest one: in the narrative, Abimelech's sleep lasts for sixty-six years, but the subsequent return does not take place immediately; Jeremiah continues to teach the people to avoid the idolatry of Babylon (7:37) until "the day came in which the Lord led the people out of Babylon."[45] The truncation of the length of the exile from seventy years to sixty-six years thus accounts for the narrative gap between the waking of Abimelech and the completion of the full seventy years.

Less clear is whether the number had come to have paradigmatic significance. The destruction of Jerusalem by Nebuchadnezzar described in the book is widely regarded as a prototype for the destruction of 70 CE. The sixty-six years is then sometimes used to date the book to the time of Hadrian, just after the Bar Kokhba revolt. George W. E. Nickelsburg speculates that in its original Jewish form the work may have anticipated a second return of scattered Jews some seventy years after the second destruction.[46] If so, this would seem to require a post-70 CE date for the Jewish form of the book—a view to which even Nickelsburg is not inclined. More recently, a case has been made that the return to Jerusalem is a symbol for entry

---

[45] Christian Wolff, *Jeremia im Frühjudentum und Urchristentum*, TUGAL 118 (Berlin: Akademie, 1976), 115–16.

[46] George W. E. Nickelsburg, *Jewish Literature between the Bible and the Mishnah: A Historical and Literary Introduction* (Philadelphia: Fortress, 1981), 315.

into the heavenly city.⁴⁷ If so, there is nothing that makes the fall of Jerusalem in 70 CE a reference point for fixing the date of the work to the time of Hadrian, sixty-six years later.⁴⁸ Hence, the probability that Jeremiah's seventy years had paradigmatic significance fades considerably.

Fourth Baruch regards the historical exile as fixed in length. Whether it also takes the seventy years as paradigmatic for a literal regathering of the dispersion following the destruction of the temple in 70 CE is less certain.

VI. Jeremiah's Seventy-Year Exile in Josephus

For Josephus, the fulfillment of Jeremiah's prediction demonstrates the prophet's remarkable prescience. In an account that goes well beyond Jer 25, Jeremiah predicts not only that Israel would be led captive to Babylon but also that, on completion of the seventy years, the Persians and Medes would send the people back to the land (*Ant.* 10.7.3 §113). This *ex eventu* innovation highlights Josephus's utter confidence in the predictive powers of the prophets. *Antiquities* 11.1.1 §1 again highlights the precision of Jeremiah by equating the seventieth year of exile with the first year of Cyrus's reign. Such is Josephus's trust in the literal accuracy of the biblical prophets that he regards their predictions as basic data for dating events. The accuracy of the prophets is further underscored by the extrabiblical detail that the decision of Cyrus to allow the exiles to return was prompted by the king's amazement to find his own name mentioned in the book of Isaiah.

That Josephus regards the end of the seventy years not only as the end of exile but also as the end of punishment is suggested by his account of the report to Ezra that some of the returnees had taken foreign wives. In an extrabiblical addition, the men urge Ezra "to come to the aid of the laws lest God conceive anger at all of them alike and again bring misfortune upon them" (*Ant.* 11.5.3 §141). The concern is not merely that the individuals who had taken foreign wives might be punished but that their actions might stir another iteration of divine anger against the nation.

Josephus can occasionally speak of national calamities following the exile as instances of divine anger. But national disasters are not uniformly attributed to divine displeasure. In one striking passage he reports an extended period of drought and disease that struck during the thirteenth year of Herod's reign but expresses uncertainty whether such hardships were from God "being angry or because misfortune occurs in such cycles" (*Ant.* 15.9.1 §299; cf. 15.5.3 §144). Even in regard to the Jewish War, Josephus's after-the-fact rationalization for going over

---

⁴⁷ The case is conveniently summarized by Jean Riaud, "The Figure of Jeremiah in the *Paralipomena Jeremiae Prophetae*: His Originality, His 'Christianization' by the Christian Author of the Conclusion (9:10–32)," *JSP* 22 (2000): 31–44.

⁴⁸ Marinus de Jonge, "Remarks in the Margin of the Paper, 'The Figure of Jeremiah in the Paralipomena Jeremiae' by Jean Riaud," *JSP* 22 (2000): 45–49, here 47.

to the Romans has nothing to do with the perception that God was angry with the nation. Rather, it is his dream-induced realization that "fortune [had] wholly passed to the Romans" (*J.W.* 3.8.3 §§351–354). As he explains in recounting the speech by which he attempted to persuade his countrymen to lay down arms, "God who went the round of the nations, bringing to each in turn the rod of empire, now rested over Italy" (5.9.3 §367). If God was now angry for sins committed during the war, this further confirmed that the rebellion was destined for disaster.

Continuing his speech, Josephus makes one further reference to Jeremiah's seventy years:

> You know, moreover, of the bondage in Babylon, where our people passed seventy years in exile and never reared their heads for liberty, until Cyrus granted it in gratitude to God; yes, it was through him that they were sent forth and reestablished the temple-worship of their Ally. In short, there is no instance of our forefathers having triumphed by arms or failed of success without them when they committed their cause to God: if they sat still they conquered, as it pleased their Judge, if they fought they were invariably defeated. (*J.W.* 5.9.4 §§389–390 [Thackeray, LCL])

Josephus's self-stylization as a latter-day Jeremiah is well known, and it is possible that he regards the seventy years as a pattern to be repeated in his own day. Yet Josephus clearly designates the seventy years as the length of exile, which ends with God's deliverance through Cyrus. The folly of the rebellion is the failure to learn from history: Israel's subservience to foreign powers ends not with rebellion but when God induces foreign leaders to grant Israel liberty. That God, unaided by violent rebellion, had acted to end the exile in keeping with Jeremiah's prophecy was, for Josephus, a fact that trumped all arguments for war.

VII. Conclusion

An increasingly common way of assessing the Second Temple period posits a widespread belief that Israel remained in a state of exile long after the sixth-century return of the exiles under Cyrus. A comprehensive evaluation of this view would require a thorough examination of all references to the exile in Second Temple literature. My more modest aim has been to evaluate the reception of Jeremiah's prophecy that the exile would last for seventy years. The texts that reflect on the seventy-years prophecy do not adopt exegetical strategies that greatly extend the length of the exile, as if the return under Cyrus were not the "real return from exile." This is true even in Daniel, where the literal fulfillment of Jeremiah's prophecy of a seventy-year exile and Daniel's penitent preparation for that fulfillment serve as a starting point and a model for reflecting on another hoped-for experience of God's mercy at the end of seventy weeks of years. If the texts do not extend the length of the exile, it is also true that they do not handle the seventy years in a completely uniform way. For some, such as Josephus, the seventy years is precise, capable even of serving as a basic datum in the construction of an accurate chronology of events. Other texts, such as the LXX and, perhaps, the Letter of Jeremiah, seem to regard the prediction as basically accurate while making allowances for a lack of precision. There is only slight evidence that the seventy years was exploited in symbolic or typological fashion. Instead, the fulfillment of Jeremiah's prophecy is placed firmly in the past, reflecting the belief that the exile had ended. Not all the texts examined regard the period following the seventy-year exile as a time of unremitting punishment. Even texts that do assess the period following the exile in negative terms, however, do not view that period as an extension of exile. Rather, the literal fulfillment of Jeremiah's prophecy inspires hope that the God who was faithful to keep that promise would also keep his promise of an ultimate restoration that would far outstrip the initial jubilee (Dan 9:25) or "brief moment of favor" (Ezra 9:8) that had brought the exile to an end.

This conclusion does not call into question Wright's contention that a "continuous historical narrative" proved formative for the worldview of many in the Second Temple period. It does suggest, however, that the shape of that historical narrative was not mechanically read out of a "Deuteronomic view of history," divorced from actual historical events. Wright speaks of the early Christian revision of the historical narrative inherited from Second Temple Judaism: what the early Christians understood had happened as a matter of history led them to split the hope of resurrection in two.[49] The evidence surveyed here suggests that many Second Temple Jews had already done the same. Under the influence of the historical return from exile and the perceived delay in much of what they expected in the promised restoration, they revised the historical narrative, splitting the hope of restoration in two. What God had already done to end the exile after seventy years was not reinterpreted but was made the basis for hope of restoration yet to come.

---

[49] E.g., N. T. Wright, *The Resurrection of the Son of God*, Christian Origins and the Question of God 3 (Minneapolis: Fortress, 2003), 317.

The Elijah Forerunner Concept as an Authentic Jewish Expectation

ANTHONY FERGUSON
aferguson682@students.sbts.edu
Southern Baptist Theological Seminary, Louisville, KY 40280

Although many past scholars affirmed that the idea of Elijah as the forerunner of the messiah is an authentic Jewish expectation, recent scholars have questioned this notion. Morris M. Faierstein, in particular, evaluates the primary evidence and concludes that there is little support for this assertion. Moreover, he suggests that Christians may have originated this concept. In this article, I reevaluate the relevant evidence and point out methodological errors committed by those on both sides of the issue. I conclude that, although no direct pre-Christian textual evidence exists, there is abundant circumstantial evidence that indicates that the concept originated among Jews.

Past scholars generally agreed that ancient Jewish texts expressed the expectation that Elijah's coming would precede the coming of the messiah. Morris M. Faierstein and Joseph A. Fitzmyer, however, reexamined earlier scholars' argumentation and use of the primary evidence and concluded, to the contrary, that the expectation of Elijah is not widely attested in Second Temple Jewish literature.[1] Faierstein suggests that the expectation developed in Christian circles.[2]

The methodologies used by scholars on both sides of this issue, however, are problematic. Proponents of both views depend on inferences and assumptions about the evidence that negatively impact their evaluation of the sources. I argue that, although early direct evidence supporting Jewish origins is lacking, Jewish origins are still more likely because of *early and late circumstantial evidence*.[3]

---

[1] Morris M. Faierstein, "Why Do the Scribes Say That Elijah Must Come First?," *JBL* 100 (1981): 75–86, https://doi.org/10.2307/3265536; and Joseph A. Fitzmyer, "The Aramaic 'Elect of God' Text from Qumran Cave IV," *CBQ* 27 (1965): 348–72.

[2] Faierstein, "Why Do the Scribes Say?," 86.

[3] In this article, I define circumstantial evidence as evidence that *indirectly* supports the main thesis that Jews before the rise of Christianity expected Elijah to precede the messiah. The evidence is indirect because the conclusion does not necessarily follow but depends on further evidence or inferences.

I. Review of Literature

Scholars who hold to the traditional view—that Jews expected Elijah to be the forerunner of the messiah—appeal for support to the Hebrew Bible, the Apocrypha, Qumran writings, the New Testament, rabbinic sources, and Justin Martyr. Many find this concept adumbrated in Mal 3:23–24 (MT; LXX 3:22–23; Eng. 4:5–6), developed in Sir 48:10–12, and explicitly stated in Matt 17:10 and rabbinic literature such as b. ʿErub. 43a–b.[4] These scholars find additional support in Justin Martyr, *Dial.* 8.49–51.[5]

John A. T. Robinson argues against the idea of Elijah as a forerunner.[6] He contends that John did not see himself as Elijah but rather believed that Jesus was Elijah (Mark 1:7). Like Elijah (1 Kgs 18:30–39), Jesus was a man of fire (Matt 3:11; Luke 3:16).[7] According to Robinson, Acts 3:12–26 contains a primitive Christology that associates Christ with Elijah (3:26). In addition, Robinson accounts for the portrayal in the Synoptic Gospels of John as Elijah by asserting that these narratives originally referred to Jesus, not John. For example, he views Luke 1:69, which alludes to a "horn of salvation" raised up from the house of David, as a reference to Jesus, not John.[8]

Faierstein, likewise examining the primary evidence, especially Justin Martyr's *Dialogue with Trypho*,[9] sums up his critique of the traditional view by concluding that (1) Justin Martyr's *Dialogue* cannot be used to substantiate the traditional view because its trustworthiness is yet to be established; (2) late rabbinic passages that hope for the coming of Elijah and the messiah but do not specify the relationship between the coming of Elijah and the messiah do not prove the traditional view; and (3) the New Testament does not prove the traditional view because, as he states, it "is a case of circularity."

Dale C. Allison argues that, although the primary evidence may not suggest that this concept was widely held, the evidence still indicates that the concept originated among Jews, not Christians.[10] His argument is fivefold. First, he states that Faierstein does not adequately handle Mark 9:12–13, since he does not explain why

---

[4] George Foot Moore, *Judaism in the First Centuries of the Christian Era, the Age of the Tannaim*, 2nd ed., 2 vols. (Cambridge: Harvard University Press, 1927), 2:358; Dale C. Allison Jr., "Elijah Must Come First," *JBL* 103 (1984): 256–58, here 256, https://doi.org/10.2307/3260274.

[5] Moore, *Judaism in the First Centuries*, 2:360.

[6] John A. T. Robinson, "Elijah, John, and Jesus," in *Twelve New Testament Studies*, SBT 34 (Naperville, IL: Allenson, 1962), .

[7] Ibid., 29–31, 46–47, 48–52.

[8] See also Fitzmyer, "Aramaic 'Elect of God' Text," 355.

[9] Faierstein, "Why Do the Scribes Say,?" 75–86.

[10] See Allison, "Elijah Must Come First," 256–58.

Christians would attribute their own eschatological doctrine to the scribes. Second, Allison claims that Faierstein's conclusion about b. ʿErub. 43a–b is correct; namely, this passage does not demonstrate that this concept was widespread. This passage does demonstrate, however, that at least some rabbis believed this doctrine. Third, Allison remarks that the association of the messiah with the day of the Lord makes the traditional view a logical inference from Mal 3:23–24. Fourth, Allison asserts that rabbinic literature may have suppressed this doctrine because Christians adopted it. Fifth, Allison warns that fragmentary evidence should caution scholars against making statements about the extent to which the concept was known.

Fitzmyer responded to each of Allison's comments and concluded that Allison's argument does not undermine Faierstein's thesis.[11] First, Fitzmyer argues that Mark 9:12–13 does not discuss the concept of Elijah as the forerunner but refers to the idea that Elijah precedes the rising of the dead or the rising of the Son of Man. Moreover, this concept does not imply the Elijah forerunner concept because, according to Fitzmyer, Son of Man is not a messianic title. Second, according to Fitzmyer, b. ʿErub. 43a–b may indeed refer to the Elijah forerunner concept, but one cannot ascribe this rabbinic view to first-century Palestinian Judaism. Third, Fitzmyer contends that the Elijah forerunner concept is not a logical deduction of Mal 3:23–24 since no Second Temple writings relate the coming of a messiah on a day of the Lord. Fourth, Fitzmyer responds that, although Allison may be correct to suggest that rabbinic silence may be a reaction to Christian claims about Jesus and John, this silence does not undermine Faierstein's argument. Finally, Fitzmyer affirms Allison's warning that modern readers should be cautious when assessing eschatological expectations at the time of Jesus, but the need for caution per se does not undermine Faierstein's claim. On these grounds, Fitzmyer reasons that Allison's critique has not undermined Faierstein's central thesis.

II. Overview of the Evidence

Different scholars draw diametrically opposed conclusions from the same evidence. The debate underscores the absence of any direct Second Temple Jewish evidence for the view that Elijah is a forerunner of the messiah. Yet, when one accounts for the existence of both early and late circumstantial evidence, the data tip the scale in favor of the concept originating among Jews, not Christians.

---

[11] Joseph A. Fitzmyer, "More about Elijah Coming First," *JBL* 104 (1985): 295–96, https://doi.org/10.2307/3260970.

EVIDENCE FOR THE CONCEPT OF ELIJAH AS FORERUNNER

Primary Evidence	Traditional Evaluation	Nontraditional Evaluation	My Evaluation
1 Macc 4:46; 14:41/Sib. Or.	Yes, evidence of the concept/No Comment	No Comment	Uncertain
Uncertain Evidence from Qumran	Yes, evidence of the concept	No Comment	Uncertain
Mal 3:23–24	Yes, evidence of the concept	Dismissed: different concept is discussed	Early circumstantial evidence: concept is a logical inference
4Q558	Yes, evidence of the concept	Uncertain: fragmentary nature of evidence	Early circumstantial evidence: concept is a logical inference
Matt 17:10	Yes, evidence of the concept	Dismissed: evidence depends on circularity and wrong exegesis	Early circumstantial evidence: concept is a logical inference
Dial. 8.49–51	Yes, evidence of the concept	Dismissed: evidence may not be trustworthy	Late circumstantial evidence: the concept is discussed in a late text
b. ʿErub. 43a–b	Yes, evidence of the concept	Uncertain: evidence is late	Late circumstantial evidence: the concept is discussed in a late text

Uncertain Evidence

1 Maccabees

Joseph Klausner interprets 1 Macc 4:46 and 14:41 as evidence for the Elijah forerunner concept.[12] The former passage records the people's decision to put away the defiled stones of the old altar in a convenient place on the temple hill *until a prophet should come to tell what they should do with them* (4:45–46). The latter passage refers to the appointment of Simon son of Mattathias as prince of Israel: "Simon should be their leader and high priest forever, *until a true prophet should arise*" (14:41). Two points lead Klausner to understand these passages as evidence

---

[12] Joseph Klausner, *The Messianic Idea in Israel: From Its Beginning to the Completion of the Mishnah*, trans. W. F. Stinespring (New York: Macmillan, 1955).

for the Elijah forerunner concept. First, the phrase "until a true prophet should arise" is conceptually similar to the rabbinic phrase "it must be left until Elijah comes."[13] Second, he contends that the role of the unnamed prophet in 14:41, which is to bring an end to the Hasmonean reign and begin the Davidic dynasty anew, will be fulfilled by Elijah.[14]

The identification of the prophet in these texts, however, is uncertain. There are a number of possibilities: (1) 1 Maccabees might refer to a prophet other than Elijah—the text simply calls him a prophet; (2) the texts might in fact refer to Elijah, who, on the basis of Mal 3:23-24, was awaited; (3) the author might refer to a prophet like Moses, who, on the basis of Deut 18, was expected to return; (4) 1 Maccabees could refer to an authoritative prophet like Haggai, Zechariah, or Malachi. The unnamed prophet might be any of these figures. The fact that the phrase in the Maccabean text is similar to the rabbinic phrase cited above about Elijah is not conclusive, since rabbinic literature postdates 1 Maccabees by centuries. Moreover, it is possible that the rabbinic phrase could be a development of the phrase found in 1 Maccabees, the development being the identification of the prophet as Elijah.[15]

Klausner's identification of the unnamed prophet of 1 Maccabees as Elijah based on the prophet's function is inconclusive. Elijah was associated in Jewish literature with anointing past kings and with the future messiah.[16] Klausner argues that 1 Macc 14:41 indicates that the Hasmonean reign will end with the appearance of this prophet, yet one could argue that an authoritative prophet other than Elijah or a prophet like Moses could also bring an end to the Hasmonean reign.

The Sibylline Oracles

The Sibylline Oracles contain an original Jewish core but betray Christian influence.[17] Although the Elijah forerunner concept is attested implicitly in book 2, possible Christian influence weakens the assertion that this book testifies to this concept. In 2:187, Elijah's eschatological duties precede the messiah's.[18] The oracle refers to eschatological events, including the appearance of Elijah from heaven with

---

[13] Ibid., 260. See m. B. Meṣ. 1:8; 3:4; and b. Menaḥ. 3a, as cited by Klausner.

[14] Klausner, *Messianic Idea in Israel*, 260.

[15] See Jonathan A. Goldstein, *I Maccabees: A New Translation, with Introduction and Commentary*, AB 41 (Garden City, NY: Doubleday, 1976), 285. Goldstein identifies the prophet of 1 Macc 14:41 not as Elijah but simply as a true prophet (508).

[16] Elijah is commissioned to anoint Hazel to be king of Syria, Jehu to be king over Israel, and Elisha to be his successor (1 Kgs 19:15-16). Willis A. Shotwell argues that Judaism's priestly presentation of Elijah and Judaism's belief that he "will store the flask of oil which has existed from the days of the wilderness" makes Elijah's task of anointing the messiah a logical deduction (*The Biblical Exegesis of Justin Martyr* [London: SPCK, 1965], 72).

[17] See John J. Collins, "The Sibylline Oracles," *OTP* 1:317-472, here 330.

[18] J. L. Lightfoot, *The Sibylline Oracles: With Introduction, Translation, and Commentary on the First and Second Books* (Oxford: Oxford University Press, 2007), 480-81.

three signs that lead to catastrophic destruction and the separation of the impure from the pure (187–213). Following Elijah's work, God's angels lead all souls to the immortal God (214–220), the dead are resurrected (221–237), the Lord of hosts sits on a heavenly throne (238–240), and then Christ appears to judge the righteous and the wicked (241–251). Thus Elijah's eschatological duties are depicted as preceding the messiah's. Nonetheless, evidence of Christian influence foils using this section of the Oracles to establish pre-Christian authentic messianic expectations.[19]

Evidence from the Dead Sea Scrolls That Does Not Refer to Elijah Explicitly

Although evidence from Qumran does not necessarily prove that Jews expected Elijah to precede the appearance of the messiah, there are some possible hints at this concept. 1QS IX, 9b–11 alludes to the expectation of a future prophet and messiahs of Aaron and Israel; however, the text does not identify this prophetic figure specifically. References to an Interpreter of the Law (e.g., 4Q174 1–2, 21 I, 11) and a Messiah of Aaron (e.g., CD XII, 23) might evoke Elijah, since these figures resemble him. Correspondence between Elijah and these figures depends on Elijah's priestly status, which is rooted in the Hebrew Bible (1 Kgs 19:15–16) and is evidenced also in pseudepigraphical works, for example, LAB 48:1 and Liv. Pro. 21.[20] In addition, the Qumran Interpreter of the Law parallels the rabbinic portrayal of Elijah as one who resolves legal ambiguities.[21] Louis Ginzberg noted these similarities when he identified the Aaronide messiah as Elijah based on rabbinic and apocalyptic sources.[22] John C. Poirier also attempts to identify the Interpreter of the Law as Elijah and notes further correspondence between CD VII, 18–19 and 1 Kgs 19:15.[23] The evidence cited by Ginzberg and Poirier, however, does not provide a firm foundation for identifying either of these figures as Elijah. Ginzberg's appeal to rabbinic literature based on similar phraseology is insufficient since rabbinic literature postdates the rise of Christianity by centuries. Perhaps these phrases are related, but it is possible that the identification of the one who alleviates legal ambiguities as Elijah is a development of the phrase found in these Qumran texts. Moreover, contrary to Poirier's argument, the correspondence between CD VII, 18–19 and 1 Kgs 19:15 is slight: it depends on the figure "coming from Damascus."

---

[19] Collins, "Sibylline Oracles," 330. Collins observes six likely examples of Christian influence. Among these are 2:238–251, which includes the presence of angels accompanying Christ's appearance (Matt 25:31 is the only text that discusses this concept) and the statement that Christ's judgment results in the condemnation of all Hebrews born after Jeremiah.

[20] For a helpful survey of Elijah's priestly status in Judaism, see John C. Poirier, "The Endtime Return of Elijah and Moses at Qumran," *DSD* 10 (2003): 227–36.

[21] Elijah is often identified in rabbinic literature as a coming figure who will interpret the law on behalf of the people of Israel (see, e.g., b. Pesaḥ. 34a, b. Ber. 35b).

[22] Louis Ginzberg, *An Unknown Jewish Sect*, Moreshet Series 1 (New York: Jewish Theological Seminary of America, 1970), 209–56 (German original, 1911).

[23] Poirier, "Endtime Return of Elijah," 236.

Thus, the above evidence does not provide an adequate basis for identifying the Interpreter of the Law or the Messiah ben Aaron as Elijah.

Early Circumstantial Evidence

The Elijah Forerunner Concept: Two Eschatological Expectations

The Elijah forerunner concept can be divided into two beliefs: (1) the belief that Elijah will precede the day of the Lord and (2) the belief that the messiah will appear on the day of the Lord. Although Mal 3:23–24 [Eng. 4:5–6] does not establish both of these tenets, it does establish the first. The passage reads as follows:

²³הנה אנכי שלח לכם את אליה הנביא לפני בוא יום יהוה הגדול והנורא
²⁴והשיב לב־אבות על־בנים ולב בנים על־אבותם פן־אבוא והכיתי את־הארץ חרם

⁵Behold, I am going to send you Elijah the prophet before the coming of the great and terrible day of the Lord. ⁶He will restore the hearts of the fathers to *their* children and the hearts of the children to their fathers, so that I will not come and smite the land with a curse. [NASB]

According to this passage, God's people are to expect the end-time arrival of Elijah. When this text is viewed together with other passages (treated below) that refer to the expectation of the messiah's arrival on a future day of the Lord, the Elijah forerunner concept becomes a logical deduction.[24] Numerous sources demonstrate that the second tenet of the Elijah forerunner concept was an authentic Jewish expectation prior to the rise of Christianity. 4QpIsaᵃ (4Q161) 7–10, III, 22 interprets Isa 11 as referring to an eschatological "[shoot] of David" who arises in the *la*[*st days*], [רית הימים באחֿ]העומד דיוד [צמח].[25] 4QM (4Q285) 7, 2–4 develops the imagery of Isa 10:34–11:1 by discussing the appearance of the branch in the context of an eschatological war. This figure comes, judges, and puts Belial to death.[26] In addition, the Psalms of Solomon associate a messianic figure with a future day of the Lord.[27] Chapter 17 presents a υἱὸς Δαυιδ ("son of David") as a χριστὸς κυρίου ("messiah of the Lord") (v. 32). This son of David will gather a holy people (v. 26a)

---

[24] See Allison, "Elijah Must Come First," 257.

[25] John J. Collins, *The Scepter and the Star: Messianism in Light of the Dead Sea Scrolls*, 2nd ed. (Grand Rapids: Eerdmans, 2010), 63. For the date of 4Q161, see Maurya P. Horgan, "Isaiah Pesher 4 (4Q161 = 4QpIsaᵃ)," in *Pesharim, Other Commentaries, and Related Documents*, vol. 6B of *The Dead Sea Scrolls: Hebrew, Aramaic and Greek Texts with English Translations*, ed. James H. Charlesworth et al., PTSDSSP 6B (Tübingen: Mohr Siebeck, 2002), 83–97. On the basis of John Strugnell's description of the script of the document according to the categories of Frank Moore Cross, Horgan dates 4Q161 to the Herodian period (83).

[26] See Stephen J. Pfann and Philip S. Alexander, *Qumran Cave 4.XXVI: Cryptic Texts*, DJD XXXVI (Oxford: Clarendon, 2000), 232. They date 4Q285 to the end of the first century BCE. See Collins's discussion of this text in *Scepter and the Star*, 64–67.

[27] Robert Wright dates the Psalms of Solomon to the first century BCE (*The Psalms of*

and judge the tribes of the people set apart to the Lord (v. 26b). The nations will serve him (v. 30), and his kingdom will be characterized by the expulsion of unrighteousness: everyone will be holy, and the king will be the messiah of the Lord (v. 32).[28]

In light of the texts discussed above, Faierstein's analysis of Mal 3:23–24 is not entirely correct. Indeed, Mal 3:23–24 does not explicitly prove the Elijah forerunner concept, but this passage should not be ruled out as evidence for this concept.[29] Malachi 3:23–24 is evidence of an important expectation that, when taken together with other expectations, makes the Elijah forerunner concept a *reasonable inference* long before the rise of Christianity.

Elijah, an Elect One, and the Day of the Lord

An Aramaic text from Qumran that dates from the early to mid-first century BCE is important because it associates Elijah, eschatology, and a potential messianic figure called a בחיר (Elect One).[30] Due to the text's poor state of preservation, 4Q558 cannot be cited as direct evidence for the Elijah forerunner concept, since the exact relationship between Elijah and the Elect One is unclear. Nonetheless, it does function as early circumstantial evidence that makes the Elijah forerunner concept a reasonable inference. Lines 1–8 read as follows:[31]

Solomon: A Critical Edition of the Greek Text, Jewish and Christian Texts in Contexts and Related Studies 1 [New York: T&T Clark, 2007], 7).

[28] Other texts that associate a messianic figure with a future day of the Lord include the targum of Isa 11. The targum explicitly identifies the branch figure as משיחא (Tg. Isa. 11:1) and states that the restoration envisioned in Isa 11:6–9 takes place during the days of the messiah. It is difficult, however, to date the targum. For a discussion about the date of Targum Jonathan, see Martin McNamara, *Targum and Testament Revisited: Aramaic Paraphrases of the Hebrew Bible; A Light on the New Testament*, 2nd ed. (Grand Rapids: Eerdmans, 2010), 310–14. See also Bruce D. Chilton, *The Glory of Israel: The Theology and Provenience of the Isaiah Targum*, JSOTSup 23 (Sheffield: JSOT Press, 1983), 86–89. Here he argues that the targum's messianic interpretation of the "branch" is concurrent with and independent of Christianity.

[29] Faierstein, "Why Do the Scribes Say,?" 77–78.

[30] The identity of this figure is debated. Jean Starcky identifies this figure as messianic. He understands "the eighth" to refer to 1 Sam 16:10–13, where David is called the eighth son of Jesse and an anointed king ("Les quatre étapes du messianisme à Qumran," *RB* 70 [1963]: 481–505, here 498–99). I thank my friend Ben Tilson for helping me read several of the French sources cited here. Daniel Stökl Ben Ezra suggests that this figure may be messianic but proposes identifying this figure as an eschatological priest ("Messianic Figures in the Aramaic Texts from Qumran," in *Aramaica Qumranica: Proceedings of the Conference on the Aramaic Texts from Qumran in Aix-en-Provence [30 June–2 July 2008]*, ed. Katell Berthelot and Daniel Stökl Ben Ezra, STDJ 94 [Leiden: Brill, 2010], 515–44, here 522). Cf. Fitzmyer, who suggests that the Elect One may be a reference to Noah, who is described as an eighth in 2 Pet 2:5 ("Aramaic 'Elect of God' Text," 371 n. 28).

[31] Text and translation from *The Dead Sea Scrolls Study Edition*, ed. Florentino García Martínez and Eibert J. C Tigchelaar, 2 vols. (Leiden: Brill, 1997–1998), 2:1114–15.

1[...] באישין [...] 2 [...] הן די מ[...] 3 תמיניא לבחיר והא אנ[ה...]   4 לכן
אשלח לאליה קד[ם...] 5 תו[ק]ף {ס} ברקא וזי[קיא...] 6 [...][...][...]ז ואמ[...]
7 [...]עוד ...[...] 8 [...] ללא[...]

1 [...] evil [...] 2 [...] their [...] who ... [...] 3 the eighth as an elected one. And see, I [...]4 to you I will send Elijah, befo[re ...] 5 po[w]er, lightning and met[eors...] 6 [...] and... [...] 7 [...] again ... [...] 8 [...] ... [...]

This text is important to the Elijah forerunner concept because it associates Elijah with an Elect One. Evidence from 4Q534 (4QNoah[a] ar)[32] and the Enochic Book of Parables (1 En. 37–71) confirms that the title Elect One was a messianic title prior to the rise of Christianity. The passage in 4Q534 that describes a messianic figure called the בחיר אלהא (Elect of God), reads as follows:[33]

9 [וכו]ל חשבוניהון עלוהי יסופו ומסרת כול חייא שגיא תהוא 10 [...] ח[שבונוהי
כדי בחיר אלהא הוא מולדה ורוח נשמוהי 11 [...] ח[שבונוהי להוון לעלמין *vacat*

9 [And al]l their plans against him will come to nothing, although the opposition of all living things will be great 10 [...] his [p]lans. Because he is the elect of God, his birth and the spirit of his breath 11 [...] his [p]lans shall be for ever. *Blank 12*

Many scholars identify the Elect of God as Noah, though some think that it could refer to a messianic figure.[34] Fitzmyer favors a Noachian interpretation of this

---

[32] The paleography of 4Q534 is described by García Martínez as a round semiformal Herodian script dating from 30 BCE to 20 CE. See Florentino García Martínez, *Qumran and Apocalyptic: Studies on the Aramaic Texts from Qumran*, STDJ 9 (Leiden: Brill, 1992), 2. García Martínez understands this text as a copy of an original that was composed prior to Jubilees (3 n. 9).

[33] Text and translation from García Martínez and Tigchelaar, *Dead Sea Scrolls Study Edition*, 2:1070–71.

[34] On the one hand, Jean Starcky originally interpreted this figure as messianic ("Un texte messianique araméen de la grotte 4 de Qumrân," in *Mémorial du cinquantenaire, 1914–1964, École des langues orientales anciennes de l'Institut catholique de Paris*, Travaux de l'Institut catholique de Paris 10 [Paris: Bloud & Gay, 1964], 51–66). Fitzmyer, however, held that this figure is Noah ("Aramaic 'Elect of God' Text," 371–72), and Starcky later adopted this view ("Le Maître de justice et Jesus," *MdB* 4 [1978]: 53–57, here 53–55). Others who follow Fitzmyer include García Martínez (*Qumran and Apocalyptic*, 17–24) and Albert L. A. Hogeterp (*Expectations of the End: A Comparative Traditio-historical Study of Eschatological, Apocalyptic and Messianic Ideas in the Dead Sea Scrolls and the New Testament*, STDJ 83 [Leiden: Brill, 2009], 415). Still others argue that this figure may be identified as messianic. A sampling of these scholars includes Michael O. Wise, Martin G. Abegg Jr., and Edward M. Cook (*The Dead Sea Scrolls: A New Translation*, rev. ed. [San Francisco: HarperSanFrancisco, 2005], 539–40). They argue that this figure could possibly be identified as a messiah, if not *the* messiah, since the figure corresponds closely to a prophecy about a mighty priest in 4Q541. This assertion is nuanced slightly from the 1996 publication of this work, in which they state that the figure is clearly messianic (*The Dead Sea Scrolls: A New Translation* [San Francisco: HarperSan Francisco, 1996], 427–28). See also Craig A. Evans, who suggests that the

figure.³⁵ Among his reasons for this view are the following: (1) the term Elect One is not a messianic title in Second Temple literature; (2) the messianic use of the term in the Enochic Book of Parables is inconclusive because the Book of Parables may postdate the rise of Christianity; (3) there is a certain fascination with the birth of Noah in Second Temple literature; and (4) there is nothing in 4Q534 that cannot be applied to Noah.³⁶ Fitzmyer, therefore, understands the Elect of God of 4Q534 as a reference to Noah, not a messiah.

Although Fitzmyer argues for the identification of this figure as Noah, a messianic interpretation of the Elect of God in 4Q534 is still plausible. Several points support the interpretation of this figure as either a royal or a priestly messiah. First, the figure is described as one whose wisdom extends to the end of the earth. This characteristic might suggest a royal messiah, since the description evokes the image of Solomon (1 Kgs 10) and the promise of a shoot of Jesse who will be characterized by wisdom and will have a global reach (Isa 11).³⁷ The text, however, could also be interpreted as a reference to a priestly messiah. Edward M. Cook argues that this text evokes the future mighty priest whose teaching is like the will of God described in 4Q541 9 i, 3.³⁸ Second, that this figure knows the mysteries of all living things also echoes Solomon (1 Kgs 5:13).³⁹ In addition, the description resembles that of the expected mighty priest, since the future priestly figure likewise reveals hidden mysteries (4Q541 7, 1).⁴⁰ Thus, each of these characteristics can plausibly refer to either a royal or a priestly messianic figure. Furthermore, the setting of 4Q534 suggests interpreting this figure as messianic: it is an eschatological scene in which column 1 alludes to a conflict between the Elect of God and his opponents. The result of this conflict is that the plans of the Elect of God remain forever while those of his opponents fail.

Elect One may be messianic (*Jesus and His Contemporaries: Comparative Studies*, AGJU 25 [Leiden: Brill, 1995], 111–13). Stökl Ben Ezra observes that the identification of the Elect of God of 4Q534 as a messiah and as Noah may not be mutually exclusive, but he concludes that, since the text is not indisputably eschatological, the figure is likely not a messianic figure ("Messianic Figures," 526–27). For an alternative proposal, see André Caquot ("'4QMESS AR' 1 i 8–11," *RevQ* 15, no. 57/58 [1991]: 144–55). He argues that this figure is not a messianic figure, since he is neither royal nor a priest; rather, he suggests that this figure is Enoch redivivus (esp. 154–55).

³⁵ Fitzmyer, "Aramaic 'Elect of God' Text," 348–72.

³⁶ The color of Noah's hair, however, is identified as white in 1 En. 106:2, contrary to the red hair of this figure in 4Q534 1 I, 1–2. García Martínez does not see this fact as detrimental to the Noachian view. In his opinion, the reading of 4Q534 is original, and that of 1 Enoch is derived from a later tradition that associated the color white with the just (*Qumran and Apocalyptic*, 23).

³⁷ For other possible allusions to Isa 11 in 4Q534, see Craig A Evans, "Are the 'Son' Texts at Qumran Messianic: Reflections on 4Q369 and Related Scrolls," in *Qumran-Messianism: Studies on the Messianic Expectations in the Dead Sea Scrolls*, ed. James H. Charlesworth, Hermann Lichtenberger, and Gerbern S. Oegema (Tübingen: Mohr Siebeck, 1998), 135–53, here 144–45.

³⁸ Wise, Abegg, and Cook, *Dead Sea Scrolls* (2005), 539–40.

³⁹ Fitzmyer, "Aramaic 'Elect of God' Text," 365.

⁴⁰ Wise, Abegg, and Cook, *Dead Sea Scrolls* (2005), 539–40.

Contra Fitzmyer's second point, the messianic use of the term Elect One in the Enochic Book of Parables does provide a plausible reason for interpreting the title Elect of God messianically.[41] Fitzmyer was hesitant about citing the Book of Parables as evidence for a messianic interpretation of 4Q534 because its date is debated. He quoted J. T. Milik's opinion that the Book of Parables may derive from the first to second century CE. In a later work Milik suggests that a Christian authored the Book of Parables around 270 CE.[42] Most scholars, however, accept a date around the turn of the era, the date Fitzmyer later accepted.[43] Relevant evidence for the date of the Parables includes the following points. First, this section of the Enochic work is not attested among the Qumran writings. George W. E. Nickelsburg argues that the Parables' absence from Qumran, however, does not require the late date originally presumed by Fitzmyer, since the Book of Parables is dependent on the Book of Watchers (1 En. 6–36), which was composed prior to Qumran's settlement. The Book of Parables may have originated later but not necessarily after the rise of Christianity.[44]

Second, patristic evidence suggests a date earlier than that proposed by Milik. Several possible references to the Book of Parables are found in patristic writings.[45] In addition, Nickelsburg argues that a *possible* dearth of citations to the Book of

---

[41] A number of passages in these chapters use the term Elect One as a messianic designation (39:6; 40:5; 43:4, 5; 49:2, 4; 51:3, 5; 52:6, 9; 53:6; 55:4; 61:5, 8, 10; 62:1).

[42] J. T Milik, with the collaboration of Matthew Black, *The Books of Enoch: Aramaic Fragments of Qumrân Cave 4* (Oxford: Clarendon, 1976), 96.

[43] James H. Charlesworth, "Can We Discern the Composition Date of the Parables of Enoch?," in *Enoch and the Messiah Son of Man: Revisiting the Book of Parables*, ed. Gabriele Boccaccini (Grand Rapids: Eerdmans, 2007), 450–68. See also George W. E. Nickelsburg and James C. VanderKam *1 Enoch 2: A Commentary on the Book of 1 Enoch: Chapters 37–82*, Hermeneia (Minneapolis: Fortress, 2012), 60; and Paolo Sacchi, "The 2005 Camaldoli Seminar on the Parable of Enoch: Summary and Prospects for the Future Research," in Boccaccini, *Enoch and the Messiah Son of Man*, 499–512. Fitzmyer's endorsement of *Enoch and the Messiah Son of Man* reads, "They [the essays] show convincingly that the Parables were indeed an integral part of *1 Enoch* already in pre-Christian Palestinian Judaism and that the mention of a mysterious figure in them called 'Messiah' and 'Son of Man' forms a critical element in the history of ideas."

[44] Nickelsburg and VanderKam, *1 Enoch 2*, 60.

[45] Nickelsburg notes several allusions to the Book of Parables in the church fathers (e.g., Apoc. Pet. 4, 13 and Origen, *Cels.* 5.52–55). See Nickelsburg and VanderKam, *1 Enoch 2*, 76–78. Likewise, Daniel C. Olson argues that Irenaeus, *Haer.* 1.15.6 may allude to 1 En. 54:4–6 ("An Overlooked Patristic Allusion to the Parables of Enoch?," in Boccaccini, *Enoch and the Messiah Son of Man*, 492–96). A further possible reference to 1 En. 37:1 may be in Origen's *Commentary on John*; see Birger A. Pearson, "Enoch in Egypt," in *For a Later Generation: The Transformation of Tradition in Israel, Early Judaism, and Early Christianity*, ed. Randal A. Argall, Beverly A. Bow, and Rodney A. Werline (Harrisburg, PA: Trinity Press International, 2000), 216–31. Finally, Tertullian appears to allude to the Parables in *Cult. fem.* 1.3. See Paolo Sacchi, "Qumran and the Dating of the Parables of Enoch," in *The Bible and the Dead Sea Scrolls: The Second Princeton Symposium on Judaism and Christian Origins*, ed. James H. Charlesworth, 3 vols. (Waco, TX: Baylor University Press, 2006), 2:377–95, here 393.

Parables in Christian circles between the first and fourth centuries CE does not argue for late composition. This argument from silence assumes that the Book of Parables would have been cited if it had existed.[46]

Third, historical references and a potential sociological context suggest a date around the turn of the era. The historical references, according to Nicklesburg, restrict the date of composition to between 40 BCE and 40 CE. The first possible reference is the prediction of the Parthians' and Medes' invasion in 1 En. 56:5–8. This invasion resulted in the Parthians' and Medes' own destruction, not Jerusalem's. The inclusion of this reference would be unlikely if Jerusalem had been already destroyed.[47] Furthermore, a possible reference to Herod the Great's death (1 En. 67:8–13) restricts the date of composition to around 37 BCE–4 BCE.[48] James H. Charlesworth argues that the insistence in the Parables that landowners will be cursed depicts the sociological environment of the text's composition: the loss of farms of many Palestinian Jews during the time of Herod the Great (38:4; 48:8; 62:3–6, 9; 63:1).[49] Herod's seizure of land and heavy taxation led to such a crisis that a Jerusalemite named Eleazar owned one thousand villages.[50] These points suggest a date around the turn of the era.

Fourth, 1 En 71:14 identifies the Son of Man as Enoch, which confirms that the Parables originated among Jews, not Christians. It would be impossible for a Christian to identify Enoch as the Son of Man.[51]

Thus, the Elect of God of 4Q534 can plausibly be identified as a messianic figure. This identification and the certain messianic figure of the Parables provide evidence for interpreting the Elect One of 4Q558 as messianic. 4Q558 then likely associates Elijah and a messianic figure.

Moreover, this text—4Q558—not only associates Elijah with an Elect One but does so in the context of a future day of the Lord. The reference to the sending of Elijah in addition to possible correspondence with the imagery of the day of the Lord as described in Mal 3 suggest to Émile Puech that 4Q558 alludes to Mal 3:23.[52] Unfortunately, much of the correspondence that Puech cites between Mal 3 and

---

[46] In fact, Nickelsburg contends that there was little reason to quote the Parables because the messianic term "Son of Man" "was almost completely unattested in Greek and Roman literature of this time" (Nickelsburg and VanderKam, *1 Enoch 2*, 60).

[47] Ibid.

[48] Ibid., 61. Nickelsburg asserts that Herod the Great went to certain hot springs in order to be cured of a terminal illness. See 1 En. 67:8–10.

[49] Charlesworth, "Can We Discern the Composition Date?," 462.

[50] Ibid., 462–63.

[51] James R. Davila, *The Provenance of the Pseudepigrapha: Jewish, Christian, or Other?*, JSJSup 105 (Leiden: Brill, 2005), 134. I thank Brian Davidson for suggesting this point and this resource and several others to me.

[52] Émile Puech, *La croyance des Esséniens en la vie future: Immortalité, résurrection, vie éternelle? Histoire d'une croyance dans le judaïsme ancien*, 2 vols., EBib 21–22 (Paris: Lecoffre, Gabalda, 1993), 2:677–78.

4Q558 depends on readings that are at best suggestive. Albert L. A. Hogeterp suggests that the correspondence between 4Q558 and Mal 3:23–24 is that both allude generally to the day of the Lord and not that 4Q558 refers directly to Mal 3:23.[53] Whether 4Q558 refers to Mal 3:23 is uncertain, as is the relationship between Elijah's coming and the Elect One.

4Q558's poor state of preservation precludes citing it as direct evidence for the Elijah forerunner concept. Nonetheless, this text, like Mal 3:23–24, cannot be read in isolation from other Jewish sources. When 4Q558 is read together with passages such as Mal 3:23–24, the Elijah forerunner concept becomes a logical deduction.

The New Testament

Matthew 17:9–13 reads as follows:

⁹Καὶ καταβαινόντων αὐτῶν ἐκ τοῦ ὄρους ἐνετείλατο αὐτοῖς ὁ Ἰησοῦς λέγων·Μηδενὶ εἴπητε τὸ ὅραμα ἕως οὗ ὁ υἱὸς τοῦ ἀνθρώπου ἐκ νεκρῶν ἐγερθῇ. ¹⁰Καὶ ἐπηρώτησαν αὐτὸν οἱ μαθηταὶ λέγοντες·Τί οὖν οἱ γραμματεῖς λέγουσιν ὅτι Ἠλίαν δεῖ ἐλθεῖν πρῶτον; ¹¹ὁ δὲ ἀποκριθεὶς εἶπεν·Ἠλίας μὲν ἔρχεται καὶ ἀποκαταστήσει πάντα· ¹²λέγω δὲ ὑμῖν ὅτι Ἠλίας ἤδη ἦλθεν, καὶ οὐκ ἐπέγνωσαν αὐτὸν ἀλλὰ ἐποίησαν ἐν αὐτῷ ὅσα ἠθέλησαν·οὕτως καὶ ὁ υἱὸς τοῦ ἀνθρώπου μέλλει πάσχειν ὑπ᾿ αὐτῶν. ¹³τότε συνῆκαν οἱ μαθηταὶ ὅτι περὶ Ἰωάννου τοῦ βαπτιστοῦ εἶπεν αὐτοῖς.

⁹As they were coming down from the mountain, Jesus commanded them, saying, "Tell the vision to no one until the Son of Man has risen from the dead." ¹⁰And His disciples asked Him, "Why then do the scribes say that Elijah must come first?" ¹¹And He answered and said, "Elijah is coming and will restore all things; ¹²but I say to you that Elijah already came, and they did not recognize him, but did to him whatever they wished. So also the Son of Man is going to suffer at their hands." ¹³Then the disciples understood that He had spoken to them about John the Baptist. [NASB]

The traditional view understood the scribal opinion of Mark 9:11 // Matt 17:10 in light of the Elijah forerunner concept.[54] Therefore, when Peter, James, and John ask why the scribes say that Elijah must come first, the traditional view interprets "first" as referring to the *Messiah's coming*, but this conclusion is not immediately apparent. Only two things are clear from this phrase:[55] (1) the scribes believed that Elijah

---

[53] Hogeterp, *Expectations of the End*, 124.

[54] William Hendriksen, *Matthew*, vol. 9 of *New Testament Commentary* (Grand Rapids: Baker, 1973), 670; Leon Morris, *The Gospel according to Matthew*, PilNTC (Grand Rapids: Eerdmans:, 1992), 442–43; D. A. Carson, "Matthew," in *Matthew, Mark, Luke*, vol. 8 of *The Expositor's Bible Commentary*, ed. Frank Gaebelein (Grand Rapids: Zondervan, 1984), 388–89; Jeffrey A. Gibbs, *Matthew 11:2–20:34*, Concordia Commentary (St. Louis: Concordia, 2010), 864–66. Each of these commentators identifies this passage as referring to the Elijah forerunner concept.

[55] See John Nolland, *The Gospel of Matthew: A Commentary on the Greek Text*, NIGTC

must return; and (2) he will come first before something or someone else. The text does not state who or what must precede, but the referent is implied.

Some clarity about the implied referent is gained when one understands the nature of the disciples' confusion. The disciples are confused about what the resurrection may mean. This leads to the question concerning Elijah's coming (Matt 17:10 // Mark 9:11). Harmonizing these two facts—the resurrection of Jesus and the coming of Elijah—proves difficult. The disciples' prior expectation (the scribal opinion that Elijah comes to restore all things) does not fit with the present reality that the Messiah must suffer and rise again from the dead.[56] The disciples did not expect this, as illustrated by Peter's bold rebuke of Jesus in 16:22: "This shall never happen to you."[57] How can a restored kingdom coexist with a crucified and risen Messiah?[58] In the disciples' minds, Elijah's coming *first* to make restoration excludes the possibility that the Messiah will suffer, be killed, and then have to be raised from the dead.[59] Thus, the Elijah forerunner concept is implied.

Moreover, the scribal opinion that Elijah comes to restore all things entails the Elijah forerunner concept, since the final restoration of God's people depends in many Jewish contexts on the work of a messiah. For example, in 4QM (4Q285) 7, 3–4, the "branch" comes and judges the enemies of God's people while bringing joy to God's people. A similar motif is found in 1 En. 50:1–51:5, where the "Elect One" of 49:4 is presented as a judge whose decisions lead to the resurrection and restored life (see also 1 En. 69:29). Psalms of Solomon 17:21–32 discusses how the son of David will judge people and nations while gathering for himself a holy people. The Son of David inaugurates a time free from unrighteousness and makes a people holy. Thus, the scribal opinion implies the Elijah forerunner concept, since Elijah's task of restoration is linked to the coming of the messiah.

Late Circumstantial Evidence

Justin Martyr

The *Dialogue with Trypho* also provides evidence for the existence of the Elijah forerunner concept; *Dial.* 49.1–12 says:

Καὶ ὁ Τρύφων Ἐμοὶ μὲν δοκοῦσιν, εἶπεν, οἱ λέγοντες ἄνθρωπον γεγονέναι αὐτόν, καὶ κατ' ἐκλογὴν κεχρῖσθαι, καὶ Χριστὸν γεγονέναι, πιθανώτερον ὑμῶν λέγειν τῶν

(Grand Rapids: Eerdmans, 2005), 707–8. Nolland does not identify this passage as referring to the Elijah forerunner concept.

[56] Carson, "Matthew," 389.

[57] See Markus Öhler, "The Expectation of Elijah and the Presence of the Kingdom of God," *JBL* 118 (1999): 461–76, here 465, https://doi.org/10.2307/3268184. Öhler rightly emphasizes that the disciples' confusion results from Jesus's emphasis on the resurrection.

[58] Carson, "Matthew," 389.

[59] Morris, *Gospel according to Matthew*, 442.

ταῦτα ἅπερ φῆς λεγόντων. καὶ γὰρ πάντες ἡμεῖς τὸν Χριστὸν ἄνθρωπον ἐξ ἀνθρώπων προσδοκῶμεν γενήσεσθαι, καὶ τὸν Ἠλίαν χρῖσαι αὐτὸν ἐλθόντα. Ἐὰν δὲ οὗτος φαίνηται ὢν ὁ Χριστός, ἄνθρωπον μὲν ἐξ ἀνθρώπων γενόμενον ἐκ παντὸς ἐπίστασθαι δεῖ· ἐκ δὲ τοῦ μηδὲ Ἠλίαν ἐληλυθέναι, οὐδὲ τοῦτον ἀποφαίνομαι εἶναι.

And Trypho said, "Those who affirm him to have been a man, and to have been anointed by election, and then to have become Christ, appear to me to speak more plausibly than you who hold those opinions which you express. For we all expect that Christ will be a man [born] of men, and that Elijah when he comes will anoint him. But if this man appear to be Christ, he must certainly be known as man [born] of men; but from the circumstance that Elijah has not yet come, I infer that this man is not He [the Christ]. (*Dial.* 49.1–12 [*ANF* 1:219])

Chapters 49 and 8 in the *Dialogue* both allude to the Elijah forerunner concept.[60] There is, however, some doubt whether Justin accurately reflects genuine Jewish expectations. Many scholars have questioned the authenticity of the views attributed to Trypho, since Trypho concedes on points related to a suffering messiah, a messiah who is the Son of Man, and the two advents of the messiah—concepts that may or may not accurately reflect Jewish expectations.[61] Scholars further doubt Justin's trustworthiness because the form of the dialogue seems artificial and too long; Trypho is a stereotype who gives too many concessions, speaks too few words, and does not demonstrate enough knowledge of Scripture and Jewish teaching.[62]

Yet there are strong arguments in favor of Justin's trustworthiness. The audience of the *Dialogue* and its goal suggest that Justin accurately represents Jewish beliefs. Several factors support the notion of a Jewish audience and an evangelistic goal.[63] First, the stated goal of the dialogue is to profit Trypho, a Jew (*Dial.* 1). Second, Trypho and Justin both express an interest in converting the other. Third, Justin is willing to use only Scripture that Trypho recognizes as genuine (71). Fourth, Justin insists that Jews and Christians worship the same God. Fifth, the dialogue is more conciliatory than "the ancient literature of *Adversus Judaeos* from Barnabas to Chrysostom's homilies against the Jews." Sixth, Justin's belief that an eschatological remnant of the Jews will be saved points to a Jewish audience (32.2, 55.3, 64.2–3). Therefore, proper representation of Trypho's views is vital in light of

---

[60] *Dialogue* 8 states that the Christ has no power until Elijah comes to anoint him.

[61] See A. J. B. Higgins, "Jewish Messianic Belief in Justin Martyr's 'Dialogue with Trypho,'" *NovT* 9 (1967): 298–305.

[62] See Timothy J. Horner, *Listening to Trypho: Justin Martyr's Dialogue Reconsidered*, CBET 28 (Leuven: Peeters, 2001), 197. Horner argues that Trypho's concessions arise from his objective—he is less concerned about particular messianic definitions and instead wants to know if Jesus matches his own definitions or those of Justin (155). Horner also argues that Trypho's questions undermine Justin's argument (122). Horner further points out that Trypho uses sarcasm and wit (129). In addition, Trypho rejects several of Justin's arguments (196–98). Thus, there is plausible evidence that suggests an original, authentic dialogue.

[63] For these points, see Craig D. Allert, *Revelation, Truth, Canon, and Interpretation: Studies in Justin Martyr's Dialogue with Trypho*, VCSup 64 (Leiden: Brill, 2002), 44, 52, 57–59.

the most likely goal of the work (evangelism) and the most likely audience (Jews). Evidence suggests that Justin is at least attempting to reflect Jewish beliefs accurately.

Furthermore, Trypho's use of Son of Man as a messianic title in *Dial.* 32.1 has precedent in the Book of Parables of 1 Enoch (48:2; 46:3, 4; 48:2–7; 62:5–7, 9; 63:11; 69:26, 27, 29; 71:1, 14).[64] In addition, Trypho's statement about the superiority of the fate of a blameless philosopher over a Christian (*Dial.* 8.3) parallels a statement of Rabbi Joshua ben Hananiah in Midr. Ps. 9:15, which says that only the wicked among the nations will go into hell.[65] Thus, if Justin has accurately reflected Trypho on these occasions, he also could have represented accurately Jewish expectations about Elijah.

Two further facts suggest that the views attributed to Trypho about Elijah were genuine Jewish beliefs. First, Trypho initiates the discussion about Elijah as proof against Jesus as the Christ and is not persuaded by Justin's interpretation of Elijah. Second, there is precedent for Trypho's alleged Elijah views in wider Judaism. The concept of a hidden messiah, although not necessarily anointed by Elijah, is found in John 7:27, in 1 En. 62:7, and in a commentary on the Psalms, Midrash Tehillim. This concept is also hinted at in the Babylonian Talmud.[66] Willis A. Shotwell argues that Judaism's priestly presentation of Elijah and Judaism's belief that he "will store the flask of oil which has existed from the days of the wilderness" makes Elijah's task of anointing the messiah a logical deduction.[67]

Rabbinic Literature

The rabbinic literature articulates the Elijah forerunner concept explicitly in b. ʿErub. 43a–b:

תא שמע הריני נזיר ביום שבן דוד בא מותר לשתות יין בשבתות ובימים טובים

ואסור לשתות יין כל ימות החול אי אמרת בשלמא יש תחומין היינו דבשבתות ובימים טובים מותר אלא אי אמרת אין תחומין בשבתות ובימים טובים אמאי מותר שאני התם דאמר קרא הנה אנכי שולח לכם את אליה הנביא וגו' והא לא אתא אליהו מאתמול אי הכי בחול כל יומא ויומא נמי לישתרי דהא לא אתא

---

[64] Willis A. Shotwell, *The Biblical Exegesis of Justin Martyr* (London: SPCK, 1965), 73.

[65] See ibid., 73; see 71–90 for Shotwell's discussion of Justin's knowledge of postbiblical Judaism.

[66] In b. Yoma 19b, Elijah reveals the messiah, who is hidden from the world. In addition, Elijah functions as the herald of the messiah in b. Sanh. 98a, revealing him to the world. See Kristen H. Lindbeck, *Elijah and the Rabbis: Story and Theology* (New York: Columbia University Press, 2010), 125.

[67] See Sigmund Mowinckel, *He That Cometh: The Messiah Concept in the Old Testament and Later Judaism* (New York: Abingdon, 1954), 305; also Shotwell, *Biblical Exegesis*, 72. Shotwell states that Elijah is presented as storing the flask of oil in Tanḥ. Exod 16:33a.

אליהו מאתמול אלא אמרינן לבית דין הגדול אתא הכא נמי לימא לבית דין הגדול
אתא כבר מובטח להן לישראל שאין אליהו בא לא בערבי שבתות ולא בערבי
ימים טובים מפני הטורח קא סלקא דעתך מדאליהו לא אתא משיח נמי לא אתי
במעלי שבתא לישתרי אליהו לא אתי משיח אתי דכיון דאתי משיחא הכל עבדים
הן לישראל

> Come and hear: [If a man said,] 'Let me be a nazirite on the day on which the son of David comes,' he may drink wine on Sabbaths and festival days, [43b] but is forbidden to drink wine on any of the weekends. Now, if it is granted that the law of Sabbath limits is applicable, it is quite intelligible why the man is permitted [to drink wine] on Sabbaths and festival days; but if it be contended that the law of Sabbath limits is inapplicable why [it may be asked] is it permitted [for the man to drink wine] on Sabbaths and festival days?—There the case is different since Scripture said, *behold I will send you Elijah the prophet* etc. and Elijah, surely, did not come on the previous day. If so, even in the case of weekdays, [the drinking of wine] should be permitted on any day since Elijah did not come on the previous day? But the fact is that we assume that he appeared before the high court, then why should we not here also assume that he appeared before the high court?—Israel has long ago been assured that Elijah would not come either on Sabbath eves or on festival eves owing to the people's pre-occupation.
>
> Assuming that as Elijah would not come the Messiah also would not, why should not [the drinking of wine] be permitted on a Sabbath eve?—Elijah would not, but the Messiah might come because the moment the Messiah comes all will be anxious to serve Israel.[68] (b. ʿErub. 43a–b)[69]

This argument is difficult to interpret. It addresses the issue of the days on which a person can drink wine if that person declared that he will be a nazirite on the day when the Son of David comes. Two scenarios are envisioned. The first situation is regulated by the limits of the Sabbath law. If the limits are applicable, the text states that this person *can* drink on Sabbath and festival days. Under the second scenario, the question is asked again but slightly differently. What if the Sabbath limits are not applicable? The conclusion is that the person can still drink on Sabbaths and festivals days because of Mal 3:23. The Elijah forerunner concept is implied here. *Because Elijah will not come on Sabbath eve or festival eve, the messiah will not come on the Sabbath or festival day, the next day.* The same reasoning is applied to whether this person can drink wine on weekdays. He can as long as Elijah did not appear

---

[68] The second paragraph is ambiguous. The text appears to say that the messiah will not come on Sabbath eve but then says that he might. This is not a contradiction. The text assumes that the messiah will not come on Sabbath eve because Elijah will not come. This assumption is made so that this question might be asked: Can the person who took this vow drink on the Sabbath eve? The answer is no, since the messiah might appear on Sabbath eve. In this scenario, Elijah comes the day before the Sabbath eve.

[69] Hebrew text and English translation from Isidore Epstein, *Hebrew-English Edition of the Babylonian Talmud*, vol. 4 (London: Soncino, 1965), 85–86.

before the high court the previous day. The reason is that it is assumed that Elijah will appear before the high court. This baraita assumes that Elijah's coming affects the messiah's, so that, if Elijah does not come, neither will the messiah. In short, the Elijah forerunner concept effectively provides the ground for the proposed question.

An Early Date for the Tradition behind b. ʿErub. 43a–b

The dating of opinions found in rabbinic literature is challenging. In this case, some evidence exists for dating the Elijah forerunner concept early, possibly in the pre-Christian era. First, the Talmud discusses this concept as proof of a conclusion. In short, the concept is assumed throughout the discussion; if the concept did not exist, the conclusion would not follow. Since this concept is not self-evident, it must have been known prior to this discussion, but not necessarily prior to the rise of Christianity, or else it would hold little persuasive power. Second, the text asserts that Israel has long ago been assured that Elijah would not come either on Sabbath eves or on festival eves owing to the people's preoccupation.[70] Third, and most persuasively, it is unlikely that the rabbis would adopt a Christian development and appropriate it into their own eschatological framework.[71] If Faierstein's suggestion is correct—that Christians originated this concept—then Faierstein must convincingly account for the appearance of this concept in later rabbinic work. However, he does not. Gospel influence would be an unlikely explanation, especially in light of the pre-Christian evidence for this concept's existence discussed above. Although the first two reasons only indicate that the concept existed prior to the Talmud's codification, the third point suggests that this concept predates the rise of Christianity. The best explanation for the appearance of this concept in rabbinic literature is that the Elijah forerunner concept existed prior to and independent of Christianity.

III. Conclusion

The above survey has demonstrated that no text codified prior to the rise of Christianity directly states that Elijah will precede the messiah. There is persuasive circumstantial evidence, however, that this expectation was likely pre-Christian. Malachi 3:23–24, 4Q558, and Matt 17:9–13 all present early circumstantial

---

[70] This saying is found also in b. Pesaḥ. 13a. A similar phrase is attributed to the house of Hillel in y. Pesaḥ. 3:6, 30b. The view expressed here is that Elijah will not come on a Sabbath or on a holiday. The phrases are similar, but the relationship between them is not immediately apparent.

[71] Allison, "Elijah Must Come First," 256.

evidence that, once coupled with other pre-Christian expectations, imply the Elijah forerunner concept. In addition, there are later texts that attest to the Elijah forerunner concept: Justin, *Dial.* 8; 49.1–12; and b. ʿErub. 43a–b. Each individual piece of evidence may have some persuasive power, but, taken together, these texts point to the origination of the Elijah forerunner concept among Jews, not Christians, contrary to Faierstein's suggestion.[72]

[72] Faierstein, "Why Do the Scribes Say,?" 75–86.

New Titles from Liturgical Press

The Bible: From Late Antiquity to the Renaissance
Writing and Images from the Vatican Library
Edited by Ambrogio M. Piazzoni with Francesca Manzari
The scholars who contributed to this volume were given unprecedented access to the Vatican Library archive and, while focusing on the written and illustrative themes of the Bible, have created the most comprehensive chronology to date.
978-0-8146-4461-4 Hardcover with dust jacket, 366 pp., 9 ½ x 13, $79.95

Ephesians
Elisabeth Schüssler Fiorenza
In this commentary, Elisabeth Schüssler Fiorenza examines the political understandings of *ekklesia* and household in Ephesians as well as the roles that such understandings have played in the formation of early Christian communities and that still shape such communities today.
978-0-8146-8174-9 Hardcover with dust jacket, 232 pp., 6 x 9, $39.95

Evolving Humanity and Biblical Wisdom
Reading Scripture through the Lens of Teilhard de Chardin
Marie Noonan Sabin
"A book that fills a gap in Teilhard Studies. Contrary to some of his critics, Sabin affirms that Teilhard's insights were deeply biblical and Christian. I highly recommend this book."
Ilia Delio, OSF, Villanova University
978-0-8146-8452-8 Paperback 160 pp., 5 ½ x 8 ½, $19.95

LITURGICAL PRESS litpress.org • 800-858-5450

A Tense Discussion: Rethinking the Grammaticalization of Time in Greek Indicative Verbs

TIMOTHY BROOKINS
tbrookins@hbu.edu
Houston Baptist University, Houston, TX 77074

While linguists have long recognized that time is not encoded in Greek verb forms outside the indicative mood, many now argue that in the Hellenistic period (ca. 330 BCE–400 CE) time was not encoded in the Greek verbal system at all. According to this new perspective, Greek verbs grammaticalized not time but rather the semantic values of "aspect" and "space." In this article, I accept the emphasis of recent studies that Greek verbs grammaticalize aspect (and in some sense also space). On the basis of the cognitive-linguistic theories of "viewpoint," "mental space," and "conceptual blending," however, I argue that time also remained a grammaticalized, or semantic, feature of indicative verb forms. Focusing on the letters of Paul, I demonstrate that particular tense forms correspond invariably with particular times, relative to projected mental space: the imperfect, aorist, perfect, and pluperfect with anterior time; the present with contemporaneous time; and the future with posterior time. In short, Greek indicative verbs grammaticalize aspect as well as time and (in the cases of the perfect and pluperfect) distinctive configurations of mental spaces.

In 1992, classicist K. L. McKay opened an article with the declaration that "the inflexions of the ancient Greek verb signal aspect (as well as voice and mood) but not time."[1] McKay's declaration represented not only the conclusion of decades of his own research into Greek verbs but also the conclusion reached three years earlier by biblical scholar Stanley E. Porter in what became a seminal book for research in this area, *Verbal Aspect in the Greek New Testament* (1989).[2] While

---

[1] K. L. McKay, "Time and Aspect in New Testament Greek," *NovT* 34 (1992): 209–28, esp. 209.

[2] K. L. McKay, "The Use of the Ancient Greek Perfect Down to the Second Century A.D.," *BICS* 12 (1965): 1–21; McKay, *A New Syntax of the Verb in New Testament Greek: An Aspectual Approach*, Studies in Biblical Greek 5 (New York: Lang, 1994); Stanley E. Porter, *Verbal Aspect in the Greek of the New Testament with Reference to Tense and Mood*, Studies in Biblical Greek 1 (New York: Lang, 1989).

linguists have long recognized that Greek verb forms do not encode time outside the indicative mood,[3] the claim propounded by McKay and Porter was that in the Hellenistic period (ca. 330 BCE–400 CE) the Greek verbal system did not encode time at all. The chief problem with the "time" position, as this new perspective sees it, is that the time indicated by the context often disagrees with what is expected, under the traditional view,[4] given the tense forms provided. That is, present-tense forms do not always indicate present time (as with the "historical present") nor aorist-tense forms past time (as with the "epistolary aorist"); Hellenistic Greek exhibits numerous examples of this kind.[5] These anomalies or "exceptions," advocates of the new perspective argue, help prove that time is not grammaticalized by a verb's morphological features.

Despite sustaining widespread criticism over the last quarter century, including a number of recent critiques,[6] the "no-time" positon has continued to win over advocates, including Rodney Decker, Constantine Campbell, and a number of others.[7]

---

[3] This realization is credited to Georg Curtius, *Die Bildung der Tempora und Modi im Griechischen und Lateinischen sprachvergleichend*, Sprachvergleichende Beiträge zur griechischen und lateinischen Grammatik 1 (Berlin: Besser, 1846).

[4] For the traditional view, see as far back as Dionysius Thrax (second century BCE), *Gramm.* 15.

[5] McKay, "Time and Aspect," 209; Constantine R. Campbell, *Basics of Verbal Aspect in Biblical Greek* (Grand Rapids: Zondervan, 2008), 24; cf. Porter, *Verbal Aspect*, 75–108.

[6] Daryl D. Schmidt, "Verbal Aspect in Greek," in *Biblical Greek Language and Linguistics: Open Questions in Current Research*, ed. Stanley E. Porter and D. A. Carson, JSNTSup 80 (Sheffield: JSOT Press, 1993), 63–73; and, in the same volume, Moisés Silva, "A Response to Fanning and Porter on Verbal Aspect," 74–82; see also Daniel B. Wallace, *Greek Grammar beyond the Basics* (Grand Rapids: Zondervan, 1996), 504–12; Buist M. Fanning, "Greek Presents, Imperfects, and Aorists in the Synoptic Gospels," in *Discourse Studies and Biblical Interpretation: A Festschrift in Honor of Stephen H. Levinsohn*, ed. Steven E. Runge (Bellingham, WA: Logos Bible Software, 2011), 157–90; Steven E. Runge, "Contrastive Substitution and the Greek Verb: Reassessing Porter's Argument," *NovT* 56 (2014): 154–73. Even McKay was critical that Porter overstated his case ("Time and Aspect"). Porter has returned the favor in kind, with responses to both McKay ("Time and Aspect in New Testament Greek: A Response to K. L. McKay," in *Linguistic Analysis of the Greek New Testament: Studies in Tools, Methods, and Practice* [Grand Rapids: Baker Academic, 2015], 159–74) and Fanning ("Three Arguments Regarding Aspect and Temporality: A Response to Buist Fanning, with an Excursus on Aspectually Vague Verbs," in *Linguistic Analysis*, 175–94).

[7] Rodney Decker, *Temporal Deixis of the Greek Verb in the Gospel of Mark with Reference to Verbal Aspect*, Studies in Biblical Greek 10 (New York: Lang, 2000); Constantine R. Campbell, *Verbal Aspect, the Indicative Mood, and Narrative: Soundings in the Greek of the New Testament*, Studies in Biblical Greek 13 (New York: Lang, 2007); Campbell, *Basics of Verbal Aspect*; David L. Mathewson, *Verbal Aspect in the Book of Revelation: The Function of Greek Verb Tenses in John's Apocalypse*, Linguistic Biblical Studies 4 (Leiden: Brill, 2010); Wally V. Cirafesi, *Verbal Aspect in Synoptic Parallels: On the Method and Meaning of Divergent Tense-Form Usage in the Synoptic Passion Narratives*, Linguistic Biblical Studies 7 (Leiden: Brill, 2013); Douglas S. Huffman, *Verbal*

I make a case here for a different position: the cognitive-linguistic theories of perspective, mental space, and conceptual blending are able to account for the selection of verb forms more convincingly than both the no-time position and the conventional tense position, in the one case because these theories expose the so-called exceptions as being nothing of the kind and, in the other case, because they provide a theoretical framework that offers the qualifications the conventional explanation has lacked. In the first part of the article, I summarize in greater detail the new-perspective, or McKay-Porter-Campbell, account of indicative verbs and explain the linguistic frameworks within which each of us is working; here I identify my emphasis on cognitive linguistics as a pivotal difference between our perspectives. I then argue that spatiality does not, as Campbell and others have proposed, serve as an adequate substitute for temporality as an encoded value in Greek verb morphology. This theoretical discussion sets the stage for my argument that we need to understand Greek indicative verbs in relation to the "construal" phenomena of perspective, mental space, and conceptual blending as formulated in recent cognitive-linguistic studies and that in so doing we find that indicative verb morphology does, in fact, grammaticalize time.

I. The No-Time Position

Hellenistic Greek attests to six morphologically distinct indicative tense forms: the present, imperfect, future, aorist, perfect, and pluperfect. What semantic values are encoded in these tense forms, if not time? Advocates of the new perspective generally identify two such values. Indicative tense forms encode (1) aspect, or the speaker's subjective viewpoint of an action. Since Greek, however, attests to only two or three different aspects and six different tenses,[8] to account adequately for the differences among the latter a second value must also inhere. Advocates of the new perspective generally locate this value in (2) spatiality. Campbell, who takes this view, proposes that the present tense grammaticalizes "proximity" and the imperfect tense "remoteness" and, similarly, the perfect tense "heightened proximity" and the pluperfect "heightened remoteness."[9] Porter admits a "limited role" for spatiality as a grammaticalized feature, particularly as a means of distinguishing between the

---

Aspect Theory and the Prohibitions in the Greek New Testament, Studies in Biblical Greek 16 (New York: Lang, 2014).

In 2008, Campbell summarized the state of the debate in the following words: "The nontense position is still in the minority across those who teach and learn ancient Greek. Nevertheless, it is worth noting that among the major contributors in the modern debate, the nontense position is slightly dominant" (*Basics of Verbal Aspect*, 32).

[8] The different theories of aspect are discussed below.
[9] Campbell, *Verbal Aspect*, 14–16; Campbell, *Basics of Verbal Aspect*, 34–45.

present (-remoteness) and imperfect (+remoteness) and between the perfect (-remoteness) and pluperfect (+remoteness).[10] Allegedly, spatiality provides a better explanation for morphological differences than temporality because it circumvents the problem of the "exceptions" as well as explains the use of augmented tense forms in the use of counterfactual conditions.[11]

In grounding their rejection of time as a grammaticalized verbal feature, new-perspective advocates have often appealed to the distinction between semantics and pragmatics. Analogous to the distinctions between *langue* and *parole*, code and text, this opposition distinguishes between (a) what forms mean inherently and (b) what speakers do with forms in particular utterances. According to the new perspective, aspect is a semantic value, emerging from verb morphology, and time a pragmatic one, emerging from the context.[12] Campbell allows that the future tense alone is a true tense and time a semantic feature of future-tense forms, since these forms invariably denote times posterior to the speech-event.[13]

While I accept here the basic contribution that the new perspective has made to our understanding of verbal aspect,[14] I deny the claim that time is not grammaticalized in indicative verb morphology. Greek verbs grammaticalize both aspect and time. Specifically, among the six morphologically distinct tenses attested in the indicative mood, four grammaticalize *anteriority* (the imperfect, aorist, perfect, and pluperfect), one *contemporaneity* (the present), and one *posteriority* (the future). The differences among the four tenses that grammaticalize anteriority lie, as we shall see, in the structure of the action indicated, identified only in part in what we now call aspect. What one must offer in order to make the case for time, however, is some response to the problem of exceptions and, more specifically, to the charge that such phenomena belie the grammaticalization of tense.

II. Linguistic Frameworks

The linguistic approach I take here shares a great deal with the approaches of Porter, Campbell, and others who have addressed our topic. I move beyond these scholars, however, in my emphasis on the *cognitive* dimensions of language and in taking a more explicitly *constructivist* stance toward language.

---

[10] Porter, *Verbal Aspect*, 95; and still in *Linguistic Analysis*, 202.

[11] On the use of the tenses in conditions, see, e.g., Campbell, *Basics of Verbal Aspect*, 90, 136.

[12] For the "semantic" versus "pragmatic" distinction, see Porter, *Verbal Aspect*, 15; Campbell, *Basics of Verbal Aspect*, 22.

[13] Campbell, *Basics of Verbal Aspect*, 39, 132.

[14] Recent treatments of aspect have concluded that all the questions still have not been settled. See Trevor Evans, "Future Directions for Aspect Studies in Ancient Greek," in *Biblical Greek Language and Lexicography: Essays in Honor of Frederick W. Danker*, ed. Bernard A. Taylor et al. (Grand Rapids: Eerdmans, 2004), 199–206.

In the first instance, I assume, like Porter and Campbell, a social-semiotic and functionalist perspective on language. Such a perspective regards spoken language as constituting a system of signs, or a code, that transcends instantiations of language drawn from that system, and yet it regards such systems as being at the same time culturally shaped and therefore fluid. In that respect, while the code, *langue*, or semantics of a language may represent a more idealized version of the "rules" as reflected in particular utterances, that is, as reflected in particular texts, *parole*, or pragmatic instantiations of the language, the code is not absolute but is by its nature flexible. This does not mean that one cannot talk about grammaticalization in language at all, only that (and this point has not been sufficiently taken to heart in this debate) the line between semantics and pragmatics, or between grammaticalized features and ungrammaticalized ones, is not always a sharp one.

On the other hand, I assume that both Continental philosophy and cognitive linguistics have now effectively undermined an objectivist view of language. Language never corresponds strictly with reality but only represents it. Moreover, listeners do not simply decode in one-to-one fashion the thoughts expressed but rather construct them, often moving beyond the express elements used to channel the message. Cognitive linguistics in particular, since the 1970s, has emphasized the cognitive dimensions inherent in the construction of meaning. While cognitive-linguistic research long battled a dominant "antimentalist" approach to language,[15] now decades of empirically based research and data observation have validated this approach as a legitimately scientific and indeed illuminating approach to human language.[16] As an empirically based science, cognitive linguistics, on the one hand, views language as thoroughly embodied, or as grounded in common human experience in the body. On the other hand, cognitive linguistics accepts as a fundamental principle that meaning is not primarily a matter of relationships between language and the world but is instead primarily *cognitive*. Thus, cognitive linguistics seeks to understand the principles of meaning and grammatical organization through such notions as perspective, subjectivity, or point of view, notions that pertain not to the *object* of conceptualization but to its *subject*. It is this subjective element of language, which has now been explored in a wide variety of facets known collectively in the field as construal, through which I wish to address the issue of Greek verbs and the dimension of tense or time. I make use especially of the theories of perspective, mental space, and conceptual blending.

---

[15] Porter's work fits this characterization (*Verbal Aspect*, 93, 104).

[16] For emphasis that their theories are empirically supported, see, on "mental spaces" and "conceptual blending," Gilles Fauconnier and Mark Turner, *The Way We Think: Conceptual Blending and the Mind's Hidden Complexities* (New York: Basic Books, 2003), 55–56; and, on "conceptual metaphor theory," George Lakoff and Mark Johnson, *Metaphors We Live By* (Chicago: University of Chicago Press, 1980; with a new afterword, 2003), 246–64.

III. Space versus Time

As mentioned above, Campbell and others have suggested that the difference in meaning between the six indicative tense forms is a matter of aspect and *space*. Since, for instance, both the present and the imperfect tense forms grammaticalize imperfective aspect, Campbell has suggested that the dimension of space constitutes the remaining difference: while the present-tense form grammaticalizes proximity, the imperfect grammaticalizes remoteness. Similar differences are said to hold for the other tenses.[17]

This hypothesis has a number of weaknesses. The first is that it is extremely difficult to separate space and time cognitively.[18] As cognitive linguistics has now persuasively shown, people conceptualize time through orientational categories that emerge naturally through experience in their physical bodies. Perhaps we cannot do otherwise. Thus, as George Lakoff and Mark Johnson have shown, people tend to conceptualize time in terms of either of two TIME ORIENTATION metaphors, both of which utilize spatial categories.[19] These are (a) the TIME-SUBSTANCE metaphor, in which the observer is stationary and time is a substance moving toward the observer, and (b) the MOVING OBSERVER metaphor, in which time is stationary and the observer moves along time's path. The following expressions, for example, emerge out of the TIME-SUBSTANCE metaphor:

(1) "The time will come when …"

(2) "The time has long since gone when …"

The following examples, on the other hand, follow the structure of the MOVING OBSERVER metaphor:

(3) "As we moved further into the 1980s …"

(4) "As we approach the end of the year …"

Yet, in both variations, time (one category) is *conceptualized* in terms of space (another category). As embodied beings, humans necessarily employ bodily categories as at least an entry point into conceptualization. Thus, one finds that these spatial categories emerge naturally in virtually any attempt to conceptualize time.

---

[17] See Campbell, *Verbal Aspect*, 14–16; Campbell, *Basics of Verbal Aspect*, 34–45; Porter, *Verbal Aspect*, 95; Porter, *Linguistic Analysis*, 202.

[18] Campbell acknowledges that there is some connection between the two but seems innocent of discussions of space and time from cognitive linguistics (*Basics of Verbal Aspect*, 129–32).

[19] Lakoff and Johnson, *Metaphors We Live By*, 41–45; and Lakoff and Johnson, *Philosophy in the Flesh: The Embodied Mind and Its Challenge to Western Thought* (New York: Basic Books, 1999), 137–50.

Research has shown that the TIME IS SPACE metaphor is common in the world's languages, including a number of signed languages, and may in fact be universal among human cultures.[20] (This is not to deny that linguistic expression or metaphors in particularized forms are culturally shaped, but it is to affirm that there may be biological and environmental universals that help explain why the underlying conceptual framework for expressions of time across cultures remains so consistently similar.[21]) A more exhaustive search through ancient Greek sources would need to be conducted in order to confirm that the TIME IS SPACE metaphor was "universal" among first-century Greek speakers, but the metaphor was certainly known and used in Greco-Roman antiquity. Plato refers to the tenses, in the same context, as both "times" (χρόνοι) and "motions" (κινήσεις; *Tim.* 38A). Seneca, writing in Latin in the first century, employs both versions of the TIME ORIENTATION metaphor, referring, on the one hand, to "looking back" (*respicere*), "directing the mind backward" (*revocare*), "turning oneself back" (*retorquere*) toward the past, "roaming into all parts of life" (*Brev.* 10.2–5), and saying, on the other hand, that time "is always in motion, it flows [*fluit*] and hurries along" (*Brev.* 10.6). In short, on this view time *is* not space, but it is perhaps inevitably conceptualized *through* it.

A second, and perhaps more significant, reason to doubt the spatial explanation for the tense distinctions is that it fails to escape the original problem that the new perspective set out to resolve, namely, the deictic *relativity* of tense-morphological signification. McKay, Porter, Campbell, and others have denied the grammaticalization of time in Greek verbs precisely because tense forms do not consistently refer to specific times relative to the *embodied present*, that is, because present-tense forms, for example, do not always refer to the time of speaking. Yet the spatial explanation leaves us with precisely the same problem, for a "historical present" is "proximate" (to use Campbell's language) not relative to the *embodied present* but relative to the *projected* (past) event; the "futuristic present" is proximate not relative to the embodied present but relative to the projected (future) event. If what is sought, then, is an explanation for the differences between the tense forms that is absolute, that is, not relative to construal or projected mental space, then the spatial explanation fares no better than the temporal one and indeed fails

---

[20] Lakoff and Johnson observe that "a preliminary survey suggests that these [space-time] metaphors are common in the world's languages" (*Philosophy in the Flesh*, 150). Sherman Wilcox has added that a number of signed languages also use the TIME IS SPACE metaphor ("The Iconic Mapping of Space and Time in Signed Languages," in *Unfolding Perceptual Continua*, ed. Liliana Albertazzi, Advances in Consciousness Research (Amsterdam: John Benjamins, 2002], 255–81). Martin Haspelmath has argued that the TIME IS SPACE metaphor is universal (*From Space to Time: Temporal Adverbials in the World's Languages*, LINCOM Studies in Theoretical Linguistics 3 [Munich: LINCOM Europa, 1997]).

[21] On the relationship between cognitive linguistics and anthropological linguistics, see Gary B. Palmer, "Cognitive Linguistics and Anthropological Linguistics," in *The Oxford Handbook of Cognitive Linguistics*, ed. Dirk Geeraerts and Hubert Cuyckens (Oxford: Oxford University Press, 2007), 1045–73.

its own test. What advance has the new perspective made? We find a more adequate explanation for the selection of tense forms along the lines of cognitive mechanics and construal phenomena, to which we now turn.

IV. CONSTRUAL

Grammarians since antiquity have recognized that some linguistic units can be understood only in relation to temporal or spatial context. Such units are said to be deictic (from Greek δεικτικός), because they ground the subjective perspective in a specific point of origin. Traditionally deixis has been classified according to three types: personal (*I, you*), spatial (*here-there, this-that, come-go*), and temporal (*now-then*).[22] The standard characterization once depicted deictic scenarios as grounded in face-to-face interaction, with the (first-person) speaker as origo.[23] Cognitive-linguistic research, however, has revealed that deixis is not always anchored in the speaker's embodied perspective but is instead dependent on "construal," or subjective perspective. This point is crucial, for if projected or subjective representation of reality rules over an embodied perspective, grounded in the *hic et nunc* of speech, then either much that we generally consider grammaticalized, including not only tense but also *person*, is in fact *not* truly grammaticalized or the way in which one defines grammaticalization needs to be adjusted to take account of the pervasively subjective nature of meaning.

In what follows, I have collected examples from both English and Greek (in the latter case concentrating on the Pauline Epistles) in which deixis, or conceptual origo, is anchored not in the embodied situation but elsewhere. These examples illustrate not that deictic markers such as person, place, and time are not grammaticalized but that such grammatical markers, rather than correspond with reality, often merely project it.

Personal and Local Deixis

In grammar, *finiteness* refers to the limitation of a verb in terms of person: first ("I/we"), second ("you/you all"), third ("he/she/it/they"). In Hellenistic Greek, finiteness is inherent in all verbs that grammaticalize person, including all indicative verb forms.

Personal deixis, however, is not always anchored in the embodied present or in the perspective of the speaker. Since meaning is primarily cognitive and not, at bottom, a matter of relationships between language and the real world, person has

---

[22] To which has now been added social deixis.
[23] John Lyons, *Semantics*, 2 vols. (Cambridge: Cambridge University Press, 1977), esp. 1:180, 281.

to be assessed relative to what we call "perspective" and specifically to the "subject of conceptualization." In this regard, it is important to recognize that, while the subject of conceptualization, or the person whose perspective grounds the speech event, may be the speaker (and usually is), the subject of conceptualization is in many cases not the speaker himself or herself but rather the *listener*.

Arie Verhagen has captured this dynamic by distinguishing between conceptualizer 1 and conceptualizer 2. The former is the communicator, the latter the addressee. In many cases speech is grounded in the point of view not of the first person, or conceptualizer 1, but of the second person, or conceptualizer 2.[24] Thus, we may distinguish two subjects, or conceptualizers, each conceptualizing things from a different point of view, and two objects of conceptualization, each correlating with the point of view of a unique conceptualizer.

Shifts between proximate (*this, here*) and distal (*that, there*) deixis, for example, may indicate a shift in conceptual perspective. Verhagen provides the following example:

(5) When a physician investigating a sore spot on a patient utters *Is this where it hurts?* and the patient responds with *Yes, that is where it hurts*, the difference between *this* and *that*, and especially the patient's use of *that*, cannot be adequately characterized in terms of (non)proximity, since the spot referred to is on the patient's body. Rather, what the patient does is to indicate that the spot referred to is *not* as much in his/her focus of attention as it is in somebody else's, in this case, the physician's.[25]

The proximate and distal categories *this* and *that*, in other words, indicate that the speech event, for each speaker, is "alter-centered," grounded in the perspective of the second person, or conceptualizer 2.

This phenomenon is common enough in everyday speech:

(6) John is to meet his friends at the restaurant. Running late, he phones to ask if they have arrived. Jane, already at the restaurant, answers, "We're *there* now."

In this example, although the restaurant is in fact *here* for Jane, since she has already arrived, she has chosen to answer from the perspective of John, who is running late and from whose perspective the restaurant is, as Jane says, *there*.

The deictic center shifts in a similar way in the following example:

---

[24] Arie Verhagen, "Construal and Perspectivization," in Geeraerts and Cuyckens, *Oxford Handbook of Cognitive Linguistics*, 48–81.

[25] Verhagen ("Construal and Perspectivization," 66) borrows the example from Theo A. J. M. Janssen, "Deictic Principles of Pronominals, Demonstratives and Tenses," in *Grounding: The Epistemic Footing of Deixis and Reference*, ed. Frank Brisard, Cognitive Linguistics Research 21 (Berlin: de Gruyter, 2002), 151–93..

(7) I looked through the window and saw that the children were very nervous. In few minutes [*sic*], Santa Claus would come in.[26]

Here, conceptualization is at first grounded in the perspective of the first-person narrator (referred to with the personal pronoun "I"), who sits *outside* the house looking in. Perspectivization, however, shifts promptly to the perspective of the children, who reside *within* the house. Now, "Santa Claus *would come in.*" The first-person perspective has been "decentered" and reoriented from the children's perspective, or from a third-person perspective.

Pronoun referents are often misconstrued when shifts in conceptual perspective are neglected, as is familiar from everyday conversation. We find a comical example of this confusion in an episode from the satirical animated sitcom *The Simpsons*:

(8) Bart (eight years old), whiling away his time in a ski lodge, approaches a robotic statue of Smokey Bear. Bart presses a button located on the bear's belt buckle, and the bear asks, "Only *who* can prevent forest fires?" Looking to the console next to the bear, Bart locates the button labeled "You" and presses it. The bear responds: "You pressed 'You,' referring to me. That is incorrect. The correct answer is you." Bart kicks the bear.

Quite clearly, Bart has retained the bear's original perspective, thus conceptualizing the utterance from the perspective of conceptualizer 2, so that "you" in fact refers to Bart himself, who is pressing the button. The bear, however, shifts from its original stance to Bart's own perspective, evidently expecting him to answer from the perspective of conceptualizer 1. This is not a very cooperative way of conversing, of course, but one has a certain familiarity with this kind of interchange, which is precisely why the scene works as comedy.

We see something of the same sort where a speaker, or the first person, conceptualizes herself or himself as the *object* of conceptualization rather than as the subject, as in the following examples:[27]

(9) "Mommy is getting very irritated right now."

(10) "Was *Paul* crucified for you?!" (1 Cor 1:12)

---

[26] Verhagen, "Construal and Perspectivization," 73.

[27] Perspectivization may also explain what appear to be ungrammatical usages of personal and reflexive pronouns. For example, when the wife says to her husband, "I'm leaving you for *me*," one need not insist that she has incorrectly substituted the personal pronoun ("me") for the reflexive ("myself"). Rather, in this case we have an instantiation of the "split-self" metaphor, in which part of the self (I^1) serves as the subject of conceptualization ("*I'm* leaving you"), and another part (I^2) as the object of conceptualization ("for *me*"). As such, the first-person referent, "me" (or I^2), is not after all the subject of conceptualization but the object and, thus, from this perspective "third person."

Sometimes speakers even blend the perspectives of conceptualizer 1 and conceptualizer 2. We find numerous examples of this in the letters of Paul:

(11) whose glory was in their shame ... (Phil 3:19)

(12) you who are justified [δικαιοῦσθε] in the law have fallen away from grace (Gal 5:4)

(13) And those who are asleep in Christ are perished (1 Cor 15:18)

(14) false brothers, who slipped in to spy out our freedom ... (Gal 2:4)

It is doubtful that Paul's opponents in (11) thought that their "*glory* was in their *shame*"; rather what *they* considered "glory" the *speaker* considered "shame." In (12), Paul's statement blends the perspective of the listener/conceptualizer 2 (they are "justified by the law") with that of the speaker/conceptualizer 1 ("you have fallen from grace [and are *not* justified!]"). Paul's statement in (13) also blends the perspective of conceptualizer 1 (those who sleep are in fact "in" Christ, as Christ is in fact alive/raised) and conceptualizer 2 (they are perished and so not "in" Christ). And so on.

Plainly, the phenomenon of quotation involves a shift in the deictic center. While many written languages mark this change by punctuation (e.g., quotation marks in English) or by complementizers (e.g., ὅτι in Greek), these conventions do not nullify the simple fact that in quotation the first person is someone other than the current (embodied) speaker.

Many of the world's languages use particles or certain morphological features to indicate that the discourse is actually alter-centered, despite a lack of explicit attribution. Classical Greek, for instance, could use the optative mood in causal clauses to denote that a reason was only alleged or reported[28] and not stated on the authority of the speaker. In such cases, the alleged or reported reason conveys the past thought of a person *other* than the speaker, even though the thought is not introduced formally by a verb of saying or thinking. For example:

(15) ἔμεινεν ἐν τῇ πόλει ὡς οὐχ οἷος τ' εἴη γυναῖκα λιπεῖν.
He remained in the city *because* (*as he said*) he was unable to leave his wife.

(16) τοὺς στρατιώτας οὐκ ἐτίμων οἱ πολῖται ὅτι οὐκ ἐθέλοιεν μαχέσασθαι.
The citizens were not honoring the soldiers *because* (*as the citizens said*) they refused to fight.[29]

---

[28] Herbert Weir Smyth, *Greek Grammar*, rev. Gordon M. Messing (Cambridge: Harvard University Press, 1984), §2242.

[29] Examples (15) and (16) are drawn from Hardy Hansen and Gerald M. Quinn, *Greek: An Intensive Course*, 2nd rev. ed. (New York: Fordham University Press, 1992), 754, 770.

The "reason" in these examples is given from the perspective of what we might call conceptualizer 3, although neither the words nor the thoughts are attributed to the conceptual subject by explicit personal grammatical signifiers.

Recognizing these construal phenomena, applied here to personal and local deixis, is crucial to our point about the grammaticalization of time in Greek indicative verb morphology, for it demonstrates that the embodied first person is not always the origo for deictic relationships. It is crucial also because Porter has identified finiteness, or the limitation of an action according to *person*, alongside aspectuality as in fact a *semantic* category, as part of the unvarying "code" of the Greek language.[30]

Against Porter's point, we have seen that it is possible for the first person (speaker) to view matters from the conceptual perspective of the second person, as in (5) Is THIS WHERE IT HURTS and (6) WE'RE THERE NOW, or from the perspective of the third person, as in (7) SANTA CLAUS, (15) IN THE CITY, and (16) HONORING THE SOLDIERS. It is also possible for the speaker to blend the perspective of the first person with that of the third, as in (11) GLORY IN SHAME and (14) TO SPY OUT OUR FREEDOM. Moreover, the first person, by viewing himself as the *object* of conceptualization, can also view himself as the *second person*, as in (8) SMOKEY BEAR, or as the *third person*, as in (10) WAS PAUL CRUCIFIED?

This of course is not to say that in Greek ἐγώ does not always translate to "I" nor that the first-person personal ending -ν does not always translate to the same but rather that the *embodied* first person, that is, the speaker or conceptualizer 1, is not always the deictic center for conceptualization of propositions in which the first person may be the grammatical subject. Conceptual grounding, or origo, must be construed cognitively, with the help of certain grammatical prompts, to be sure, but not by means of grammatical person alone. We do not for that reason deny the grammaticalization of person. Moreover, this shifting away from the embodied present as the deictic center is precisely the reason for apparent exceptions to the rule of expected time, as we shall now see.

Temporal Deixis

Like personal and local deixis, temporal deixis is a matter of construal, of the *subjective* stance in which a discourse is grounded. Fundamentally, this idea is just an extension of a process that occurs and is easily understood in more imaginative exercises—as, for example, in reading history or fiction in which the narrator recounts past events in the present tense: one is *taken* there and imagines seeing the events as they unfold.[31] Cognitive linguistics has shown persuasively that the

---

[30] Porter, *Verbal Aspect*, 94; cf. 15, 97.

[31] Rutger J. Allan has examined classical Greek literature written from this point of view, that is, the so-called immediate diegetic point of view ("Towards a Typology of the Narrative Modes in Ancient Greek: Text Types and Narrative Structure in Euripidean Messenger Speeches,"

projection of mental spaces in the construction of meaning is not, however, a feature of cognition restricted to creative media like literature, art, music, and humor but that it is pervasive in everyday language and thought.

L. Michelle Cutrer and others have utilized "mental space" theory to explain tense and its local time-ordering function in relation to viewpoint and conceptual focus.[32] Thus, Cutrer distinguishes between Viewpoint space (S), Focus space (R), and Event space (E). To this one may add Base space (B), which serves as a possible starting point at a given moment for constructions of the other spaces.[33]

Let us look at the following example from Gilles Fauconnier:

(17) Max is 23. He has lived abroad. In 1990, he lived in Rome. In 1991, he would move to Venice. He would then have lived a year in Rome.

In this text, the 1990 space ("Max in Rome") becomes the Viewpoint from which perspective 1991 becomes the next Focus (and Event) space, with the content "Max move to Venice." "In 1991, he *would* move ..." puts 1991 in the future with respect to 1990. In the last sentence, "He would then have lived a year in Rome," 1990 remains the Viewpoint and 1991 the Focus, although the Event space ("live a year in Rome") resides in the past relative to the Focus 1991.[34]

The MAX IN ROME example illustrates, among other things, how English can prompt for a *future* event relative to the *past* ("he *would* move to Venice"). Most typically, Hellenistic Greek constructed frame shifts in this direction by using the IMPERFECT OF μέλλειν + INFINITIVE (e.g., "he was going to ..."), not, as with the other frame shifts we have seen, by using the simplex indicative relative to a decentered viewpoint space. It is *this*—the option of an auxiliary construction in grammaticalizing future-relative-to-past events—that explains why future-tense forms in the New Testament are invariably future-referring with reference to the time of speech and apparently never relative to the past. It is *not*, as Campbell suggests, that by the first century time has emerged as a grammaticalized value *only* for the future tense, since (as he says) it alone keeps consistent in its time reference.[35]

The following example provides another instance where time shifts relative to mental space:

(18) "Last night you were leaving tomorrow and now you are leaving the day after tomorrow! What I am supposed to believe?"[36]

---

in *Discourse Cohesion in Ancient Greek*, ed. Stéphanie J. Bakker and Gerry C. Wakker, Amsterdam Studies in Classical Philology 16 [Leiden: Brill, 2009], 171–204).

[32] L. Michelle Cutrer, "Time and Tense in Narratives and in Everyday Language" (PhD diss., University of California at San Diego, 1994).

[33] Gilles Fauconnier, "Mental Spaces," in Geeraerts and Cuyckens, *Oxford Handbook of Cognitive Linguistics*, 351–76.

[34] Ibid., 365–66.

[35] Campbell, *Basics of Verbal Aspect*, 39, 132.

[36] Example from Ronny Boogaart and Theo Janssen, "Tense and Aspect," in Geeraerts and Cuyckens, *Oxford Handbook of Cognitive Linguistics*, 803–28, esp. 809; citing Janssen.

In this example, the Base space is the time of speech. But the Viewpoint space shifts, first, from the perspective of "last night," at which time the addressee was planning to leave "tomorrow" (which is *today* relative to the Base space), to "now," at which time the addressee planned to leave "the day after tomorrow" (which is *the day after tomorrow* relative to the Base space). What results is a blended scenario, in which "last night" existed as a past event (hence the past tense "were leaving") and yet the same event is said to occur "tomorrow."

The English "future perfect" involves a familiar instance of deictic projection of time, as seen in the following example:

(19) By the close of 2017, the U.S. *will have spent* $1 billion fighting Zika.

The future perfect by its nature necessitates the projection of a future mental space, relative to which the event is construed as *past*. A few examples of the future perfect occur in the New Testament, although they occur only in periphrastic constructions (Matt 16:19, 18:18, Luke 12:52, Heb 2:13).

Frame-shifting of this nature explains all kinds of apparent tense "anomalies."[37]

(20) The boat *leaves* next week ("next week" provides the Viewpoint space).

(21) *I'm walking* down the street one day when suddenly this guy *walks* up to me … (the past provides the Viewpoint space).

(22) I can't go to the concert tonight. You'll have to tell me how it *was* (the future provides the Viewpoint space).

In each of these examples, the time is true to the tense form relative to the Viewpoint space prompted for by the "space-builders" in the discourse. Space-builders, or grammatical expressions that prompt for a new mental space or shift in Focus, come in many types: phrases ("next week"), adverbials ("tonight"), conjunctions + clause ("when this guy walks up to me"), as well as subject–verb complexes ("Max hopes").[38] Yet, as we have seen in the examples above, once the grounding mental space is recognized, the verbs signify consistent and predictable temporal functions relative to them.

As seen earlier in (18) LEAVING TOMORROW, the times projected in different mental spaces are sometimes blended. Vimala Herman provides an example from A. S. Byatt's novel *Possession*, in which Ash writes in a letter to Christabel,[39]

(23) "What will you be thinking of me now?"

---

[37] Examples (20), (21), and (22) are drawn from Fauconnier, "Mental Spaces," 370.

[38] On frame-shifting, see Seana Coulson, *Semantic Leaps: Frame-Shifting and Conceptual Blending in Meaning Construction* (Cambridge: Cambridge University Press, 2001).

[39] Vimala Herman, "Deictic Projection and Conceptual Blending in Epistolarity," *Poetics Today* 20 (1999): 523–41, esp. 535–36.

In this example, the Viewpoint space is set at the time of writing but the Focus and Event spaces at the time of Christabel's reading. Thus, we have blended time, where the future "thinking" is relative to Ash's Viewpoint space and the present "now" is relative to the projected event of reading.

Paul's quotation of Isa 22:13 LXX in 1 Cor 15:32 works similarly but now using a verb in the present tense:

(24) Let us eat and drink, for tomorrow we die [ἀποθνῄσκομεν].

The present, looking ahead to "tomorrow," serves as the Base space, but "tomorrow" sets up the future as the Viewpoint space, from which perspective the event becomes present: "we *die*."

The verb tense in the following examples as well has to be understood relative to a shift in mental space or viewpoint:

(25) And it shall be that, just as we bore [ἐφορέσαμεν] the image of the earthy human, we shall bear [φορέσομεν] also the image of the heavenly human. (1 Cor 15:49)

(26) But if you marry, you did not sin [ἥμαρτες], and if a virgin marries, she did not sin [ἥμαρτεν]. (1 Cor 7:28)

(27) and those whom he justified, these he also glorified [ἐδόξασεν]. (Rom 8:30 NRSV)

(28) It is by your holding fast to the word of life that I can boast on the day of Christ that I did not run [ἔδραμον] in vain or labor [ἐκοπίασα] in vain. (Phil 2:16 NRSV)

(29) But when I saw that they are not walking consistently [ὀρθοποδοῦσιν] with the truth of the gospel .... (Gal 2:14)

(30) The Scripture, having seen beforehand that God is justifying [δικαιοῖ] the gentiles by faith .... (Gal 3:8)

The first example (25) places the conceptualizer in the future, from which perspective he looks *back* (thus an instance of the proleptic aorist); yet the viewpoint promptly shifts back to the present, from which perspective the subject looks *ahead* to the future ("we shall bear ..."). The aorist in (26) also looks back, in this case from the future time of the condition's fulfillment. In (27), ἐδόξασεν could perhaps be debated: because of Paul's two-age, "already–not yet" perspective on God's work in Christ, it may be difficult to adjudicate between a proleptic aorist, in which the future serves as the Viewpoint space and the subject looks back, and a simple aorist, in which the Viewpoint is anchored in the present. But, especially because Paul exhibits marked eschatological restraint in the undisputed letters, we should almost undoubtedly prefer the former construal: from the viewpoint of the future, "... he *glorified*." (One could well ask whether in Col 2:12 and 3:1, "you *were raised* together with him," which uses the aorist indicative, cannot be understood likewise; so also in Eph 2:6, "he *raised* us up with him and *seated* us with him in the heavenly places.") The aorist in (28) likewise looks back from the viewpoint of the future. In (29), we find the viewpoint shifted into the past, relative to which the event becomes present; this of course may indicate that the event continues *into* the (actual) present, but the point is that the presentness of the action is anchored first in the past. In (30) the present tense is proleptic, being anchored in the past, from which point the Scripture had presaged the then-future event (for the Scripture "saw beforehand").

Quite often the future becomes the viewpoint for what then becomes a "present" event:

(31) We know that Christ, having been raised from the dead, never dies again [ἀποθνῄσκει]; death no longer has dominion over him. (Rom 6:9)

(32) Do you not know that the saints will judge the world? And if the world is to be judged [κρίνεται] by you, are you not competent to try trivial cases? (1 Cor 6:2)

(33) As the last enemy, death is destroyed [καταργεῖται]. (1 Cor 15:26)

(34) But someone will ask, "How are the dead raised [ἐγείρονται]? With what kind of body do they come [ἔρχονται]?" (1 Cor 15:35 NRSV)

(35) This is the third time I am coming [ἔρχομαι] to you. (2 Cor 13:1 NRSV)

It is important to emphasize that with such examples we do not have a present-tense verb with future meaning but rather an action that is *present* from the viewpoint of the future (see also 1 Cor 16:5).

Occasionally we find present-tense verbs that appear to be future referring because of the imagined future effects but that in fact place the emphasis on the present itself:

(36) Those who marry will have trouble in the flesh, and I *am sparing* [φείδομαι] you. (1 Cor 7:28)

Paul is *already* "sparing" them, for his advice, once spoken, he projects as being as good as taken.

References to the content of *texts* introduce a unique situation because the evaluative situation can then be viewed either from the time of writing or from the perspective of the text as an enduring artifact. Thus we have the "perfective present":

(37) he [God] says [λέγει] to Moses (Rom 9:15 NRSV)

(38) What does it [the Scripture] say [λέγει] (Rom 10:8 NRSV)

(39) it [the Scripture] does not say [λέγει] (Gal 3:16 NRSV)

Similarly, Herman has used the concepts of conceptual blending and deictic projection to explain the phenomenon of epistolarity, in which writers attempt to bridge temporal (and physical) separation from their addressees through the projection of common mental spaces.[40] We have already seen this in the Christabel example (23) above. The Greek "epistolary aorist" is another classic example. As seen in Gal 6:11, Paul uses the aorist tense with reference to his present act of writing because he is projecting a mental space anchored in the (later) viewpoint of his addressees:

(40) See with what large letters I wrote [ἔγραψα] to you in my own hand!

The cognitive-linguistic framework we have been using—which I have noted has both a firm empirical and a firm phenomenological basis—by all appearances provides a consistently satisfying answer to the supposed anomalies encountered in these examples. By contrast, the lack of regard for mental space in Porter's analysis has resulted in a confusing inconsistency in his interpretation of tense usages and often arbitrary decisions as to the time reference. For Porter, it seems that perhaps every tense in the indicative mood can have "timeless" reference: among the examples treated here, he so interprets the present tense in (32), the aorists in (26) and (27), and the perfect seen below in (45). McKay, who happens to share Porter's judgment that time is not encoded in Greek verbs, has nonetheless taken exception to Porter's rendering of time in a great number of instances. He lists several examples where Porter attributes timeless reference also to the imperfect tense, as in Rom 1:27 and 2 Cor 2:3.[41] But in fact we have in these two texts a habitual imperfect and a progressive imperfect, respectively, that is, truly past-referring imperfects:

(41) Men committed shameless acts with men and received in their own persons the penalty that *was necessary* [ἔδει] for their error. (Rom 1:27)

(42) And I wrote as I did, so that when I came, I might not suffer pain from those from whom it *was necessary* [ἔδει] for me to rejoice. (2 Cor 2:3)

A number of other texts where McKay criticizes Porter are worthy of mention.[42] The aorist ἔσχον in Phlm 7 is not present-referring (so Porter) but represents a true past, regarded from the viewpoint of the present:

(43) I had [ἔσχον] much joy and encouragement from your love (when you showed it) ... (Phlm 7)

In Rom 2:12 ἥμαρτον is not "timeless" (so Porter) but truly past referring,[43] for the future-tense form ἀπολοῦνται ("will perish") establishes the *final judgment* as the Viewpoint space, from which point the "sinning" in fact becomes a past event:

(44) All who sinned [ἥμαρτον] apart from the law will (at the judgment) also perish apart from the law ... (Rom 2:12)

---

[40] Herman, "Deictic Projection."
[41] McKay, "Time and Aspect," 218.
[42] Ibid., 212, 220, 224.
[43] Porter, *Verbal Aspect*, 197, 228, 236.

In sum, this discussion illustrates that the events described often take place in mental spaces anchored somewhere other than in the embodied present. The originary viewpoint for an action may be (a) a future mental space, from which point the action is viewed as either (i) present, as in (20), (24), (31), (32), (33), (34), and (35), or (ii) past, as in (19), (22), (25), (26), (27), (28), and (40); or (b) the viewpoint may originate in the past and, from that perspective, view some event as present, as in (21), or as future but still prior to the (speaker's) present, as in (17), or as future and contemporaneous with the (speaker's) present, as in (30).

None of these examples, therefore, constitutes a true anomaly or, at bottom, involves violations of expected meaning given conventional correlations of verb morphology and temporal reference—we have only to identify correctly the grounding mental space.[44] In the indicative mood, past-tense forms consistently encode *anterior* actions (and states), the present tense *contemporaneous* actions (and states), and the future tense *posterior* actions (and states). Admittedly, not every language breaks down into this kind of tripartite system. Some languages, for instance, reflect a bipartite, future versus nonfuture, past versus nonpast, or present versus nonpresent system,[45] and this has sometimes been alleged to describe ancient Greek.[46] D. N. Shankara Bhat identifies such bipartite systems as one way of circumventing the problem of some present-referring utterances (some events, even if spoken about immediately, are already left in the past) but not as the only

---

[44] The examples could be multiplied further. In some cases we have what might be called "time-lapse" compressions, where the verb tense places the action at one time, but contextual factors indicate that the action endures beyond that point. We find this frequently in the Pauline Epistles: "who also will strengthen you (such that you will be) blameless on the day of our Lord Jesus Christ" (1 Cor 1:8); "I suffer birth pangs over you (and will continue to) until Christ is formed in you (Gal 4:19); "from which day we heard, (we prayed and) we do not cease praying" (Col 1:9); "the Holy Spirit of God, with which you were marked (and which mark you will thus continue to bear) on the day of redemption" (Eph 4:30); and "through whom we received [ἐλάβομεν] the reconciliation (and have it still) now" (Rom 5:11). The frequency of this phenomenon in the Pauline corpus, as seen in 1 Cor 1:8, Gal 4:19, Col 1:9, and Eph 4:30, provides substantial justification for the above rendering of Rom 5:11: reception of the "reconciliation" took place in the *past* (hence the aorist), but the event is extended into the present through *ellipsis* in the thought, i.e., "... (and have it still) now." We need not resort then to Porter's understanding of the aorist ἐλάβομεν as *itself* present referring (Porter, *Verbal Aspect*, 228).

[45] D. N. Shankara Bhat identifies Kannada, Manipiri, and English (since the English future tense is formed using an auxiliary) (*The Prominence of Tense, Aspect, and Mood*, Studies in Language Companion Series 49 [Amsterdam: John Benjamins, 1999], 16–20). See also John Lyons, *Introduction to Theoretical Linguistics* (Cambridge: Cambridge University Press, 1968), 304–6, although he does not dispute the traditional, tripartite understanding of the Greek and Latin verb systems (306).

[46] E.g., Gerhard Mussies, *The Morphology of Koine Greek, as Used in the Apocalypse of St. John: A Study in Bilingualism*, NovTSup 27 (Leiden: Brill, 1971), 250–55.

solution languages have found for such problems;[47] hence the bipartite system is by no means universal. Grammarians, including ancient native speakers, have traditionally understood both Greek and its Indo-European sibling Latin in tripartite terms. Moreover, the present analysis has suggested that the tripartite framework fits the sampled data for Hellenistic Greek quite consistently.

My main qualification to this tripartite interpretation has been that (as we should expect given a constructivist understanding of language) these time correlations must be construed relative to the mental spaces in which the actions are projected as occurring. As we have seen, the same cognitive dimension applies to the conceptualization of *personal* deixis: the first person, or the embodied situation of the speaker, does not in every instance represent the origo or grounding space from which the objective situation is described. Thus, even though ἐγώ, for instance, encodes (grammaticalizes) a first-person (grammatical) subject, that "I" does not in every situation represent the (conceptualizing) subject.

If the fact that the embodied present does not always provide the ground for conceptualization leaves us no reason to deny the grammaticalization of person, I cannot see why this gives us any reason to deny the grammaticalization of time either.

V. Toward a Theory of Indicative Verbs

Any theory of the Greek tenses has to be able to explain the differences among them. My main argument in this article is that

1. Greek indicative verbs did grammaticalize time in the Hellenistic period. Yet, if there were only three times, as I am proposing, why were there six tense forms? The differences among the indicative tense forms cannot be accounted for by time alone. While these points cannot be treated in full here, I suggest that *two* further dimensions apply. (Future work can perhaps elaborate this more fully.)

2. With Porter and others, I share the conviction that aspect (the speaker's subjective conception of the state of an action) is one important distinguishing factor. Although there seems to be little agreement among scholars as to how many aspectual categories existed in the Greek verbal system (I tentatively accept the threefold distinction),[48] specialists have generally agreed on which aspectual category each of the six indicative tenses falls under: (a) the present and imperfect

---

[47] Bhat, *Prominence of Tense*, 17.

[48] Most suggest there are either two (internal/imperfective, external/perfective) or three (adding completed/stative). The discrepancy owes in part to disagreement over whether stativity is an aspect or an *Aktionsart*. Thus, Randall Buth says there are "two and one-half" aspects in Greek ("Verbs, Perception and Aspect: Greek Lexicography and Grammar," in Taylor et al., *Biblical Greek Language and Lexicography*, 177–98, esp. 192).

tenses both convey internal/imperfective aspect, instantiating actions viewed from within or actions in progress (e.g., λέγω, "I am speaking"); (b) the aorist tense conveys external/perfective aspect, instantiating actions viewed as a whole without regard to their internal structure (e.g., εἶπον, "I spoke"); and (c) the perfect and pluperfect tenses grammaticalize the aspectual value of stativity, indicating the state resulting from an action (e.g., εἴρηκα, "I have said"). The future tense is contested, being subsumed sometimes under the internal/imperfective category but more often under the external/perfective.[49]

3. I would add that, in addition to the element of aspect, two of the tense forms also grammaticalize distinctive configurations of mental space(s). Both the perfect and the pluperfect tenses encode such configurations. (a) The perfect tense prompts for *two* mental spaces, one in the past and one in the present, which, when integrated, signify a past action with an enduring result. As depicted in figs. 1 and 2, the focus of the action may be on either the mental space profiling the initiating act (Rom 5:5, 2 Cor 7:3) or on that profiling the intensive result (Rom 3:10, 2 Cor 1:24):

(45) God's love has been poured out [ἐκκέχυται] into our hearts … (Rom 5:5)

(46) I said beforehand [προείρηκα] … (2 Cor 7:3)

(47) as it is written [γέγραπται] … (Rom 3:10)

(48) For you stand firm in the faith [ἑστήκατε]. (2 Cor 1:24)

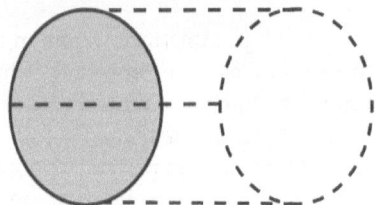

FIGURE 1. The "Extensive Perfect," as in (45) and (46)

---

[49] Wallace labels its aspect "external" (*Greek Grammar*, 501), and Campbell with the analogous label "perfective" (*Basics of Verbal Aspect*, 96). But Chrys C. Caragounis says it can be either "durative" or "instantaneous" (*The Development of Greek and the New Testament: Morphology, Syntax, Phonology, and Textual Transmission* [Grand Rapids: Baker Academic, 2006], 157–59), much as C. F. D. Moule had called it "mostly punctiliar" (*An Idiom Book of New Testament Greek* [Cambridge: Cambridge University Press, 1959], 6–10). On the ambiguity of the future, see also Coulter George, "Verbal Aspect and the Greek Future: ἕξω and σχήσω," *Mnemosyne* 69 (2016): 597–627.

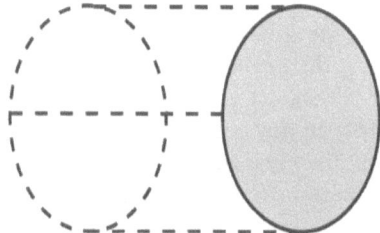

Figure 2. The "Intensive Perfect," as in (47) and (48)

(b) The pluperfect likewise prompts for two mental spaces, linked by the action's enduring or stative result, but now *both* spaces are set in the past (or the cognitive past).

In sum, indicative verb morphology encodes both (1) time and (2) aspect, while in the perfect and pluperfect tenses also (3) encoding mental-space duality. It is (2) and (3) that provide the needed distinctions among tenses that share the same time.

VI. Conclusions

Despite the persistence of those who have argued that Greek indicative verbs in the Hellenistic period lacked grammaticalized reference to time, the conclusion of the present assessment is that this new perspective, while justified in drawing attention to the problem of exceptions to expected time reference, is in fact mistaken in excluding time, on this basis, as an inherent grammatical value. During the Hellenistic period, and certainly in Paul's day, indicative verb morphology encoded both aspect *and* time (while in the case of the perfect and pluperfect, also encoding mental-space duality). The evidence points emphatically in this direction.

1. We have no way of knowing whether all Greek speakers of the classical and Hellenistic periods thought that Greek verbs grammaticalized time, but the people in those days who undertook reflective analyses of their own language—highly educated, native Greek speakers—attest that this is indeed how they understood their verbal system. Discussions have survived from grammarians and philosophers that reflect or fully elaborate a theory of verbs in terms of time and, in some cases, also of something like aspect.[50]

---

[50] Fourth century BCE: Plato, *Tim.* 38A; 47A–B; Aristotle, *Poet.* 20.1457a10–18; *De an.* 430b; cf. *Int.* 3.16b6; second century BCE: Dionysius Thrax, *Gramm.* 15; second century CE: Diogenes

2. Aspect alone is insufficient to distinguish Greek tense forms, particularly between forms that share the same aspect, as the present and the imperfect do, for example. As we have seen, the spatial-not-temporal explanation for the remaining differences lacks empirical support from cognitive linguistics, fails to recognize the virtual impossibility of separating space and time cognitively, and perhaps, most importantly, suffers from the *same problem of relativity* to projected mental space that it has alleged is problematic for the temporal view.

3. As statistics reveal, the time correlated with indicative tense forms is, in a vast majority of instances, as expected given the assumption that the tenses grammaticalize time: present-tense forms are present relative to speaking time about 70 percent of the time; aorist-tense forms are past relative to speaking time some 85 percent of the time;[51] and future-tense forms refer to the future, it has been said, 100 percent of the time. The percentages alone are worthy of consideration.

4. What we have sought to add here is a framework for understanding the time element of verbs that accommodates also the (smaller percentage of) supposed anomalies. It is a fundamental principle of modern linguistics that language does not correspond with reality so much as it attempts to project or construct it from particular subjective perspectives. Thus, tense, just as much as other deictic markers such as location and person—and indeed, just as much as syntax generally—must be assessed relative to projected mental spaces. This no more cancels tense as a semantic or grammaticalized feature of Greek indicative verbs than the decentering of personal deixis renders person an ungrammaticalized feature of indicative verbs.

Having focused here on verb tense primarily in the Pauline Epistles, I hope that these theoretical proposals about verb tense will also be taken up by Pauline theologians interested in Paul's general conceptions of time and especially in his conceptions of the *when* of certain salvation-historical or eschatological occurrences (e.g., as realized or as future; e.g., Rom 8:30).

Laertius, *Vit.* 7.141. Latin writers understood the tenses in terms of time as well, e.g., Seneca, *Brev.* 10.2.

[51] So Constantine R. Campbell, *Advances in the Study of Greek: New Insights for Reading the New Testament* (Grand Rapids: Zondervan, 2015), 114.

A Greek Papyrus Fragment with a Citation of Matthew 1:20

BRICE C. JONES
bricejones@me.com
University of Louisiana Monroe, Monroe, LA 71291

This article offers a critical edition of a Greek papyrus fragment recently identified as containing a partial citation of Matt 1:20. It is currently only the second known Greek papyrus to preserve this particular New Testament passage. If my argument is correct that this papyrus was most likely used as an amulet, it would become the only extant amulet to preserve Matt 1:20.

I. The Fragment

P.Mich. inv. 4944b is a light-brown Greek papyrus scrap that came to the University of Michigan in 1927 as part of a lot (inventory nos. 4926–4952) purchased in Egypt by Harold I. Bell and William L. Westermann from Maurice Nahman in the 1926/1927 season.[1] Bell's acquisition report ("Report on the Papyri in the Season 1926–1927") dated 9 May 1927 references the lot to which the fragment belongs:

> The third lot consists of the papyri bought by Prof. Westermann and myself from Nahman. These were acquired in one lot but consist of very various papyri purchased by Nahman at different times and of different vendors. Some had arrived recently; others were selected by me from boxes of fragments which had apparently been in stock for a long time.[2]

Thus, while we cannot say anything about the provenance of this papyrus, we can at least establish that it came from Nahman (or from another dealer in Nahman's

---

[1] The fragment was part of the acquisitions of the papyrus cartel or syndicate headed by the British Museum in the 1920s and 1930s, on which see James G. Keenan, "The History of the Discipline," in *The Oxford Handbook of Papyrology*, ed. Roger S. Bagnall (Oxford: Oxford University Press, 2009), 59–78.

[2] This report is accessible online at http://www.lib.umich.edu/papyrus-collection/report-papyri-season-1926-1927.

network), was purchased by Westermann and Bell, went to the British Museum, and was then dispatched to Michigan by Bell.[3]

The papyrus preserves a partial citation of Matt 1:20 in Greek. In this verse, an angel of the Lord appears to Joseph in a dream instructing him not to fear to take Mary as his wife. There is currently only one other papyrus in the official list of New Testament manuscripts that preserves this passage, namely, P.Oxy. 2 ($\mathfrak{p}^1$).[4] There are only nine majuscule manuscripts before the ninth century that preserve Matt 1:20, so if our dating is correct, our papyrus stands among the earliest textual evidence for this particular verse.[5] Besides a few orthographic variations, the text conforms to the NA^{28} edition of the Greek New Testament.

The papyrus measures 10.8 × 2.7 cm, is broken on all sides, and contains two incomplete but legible lines of text written with the fibers (→); the back is blank. Partial letter strokes visible along the upper and lower edges demonstrate that text preceded and followed the two partial lines that are preserved on the papyrus. A faint, vertical crease is present near the center of the fragment, suggesting that the papyrus may have been (deliberately?) folded at some point. Inorganic tremata are present over two initial vowels in line 2 (ϊωσηφ, ϋιος). Κυρίου in line 2 is written as a *nomen sacrum* with the typical supralinear stroke, while Δαυείδ (*l.* Δαυίδ) in line 3 exhibits *scriptio plena*. A middle dot occurs before the direct address of the angel in line 3. The script is a sloping pointed majuscule. The hand bears a close resemblance to the ones found in the following manuscripts: P.Oxy. 1374 (late sixth century CE),[6] P.Mich. 685 (seventh/eighth century CE),[7] PSI 1372 (first half of eighth century CE),[8] and P.Amst. 21 (first half of eighth century CE).[9] Thus, though tentative, a late sixth- to early eighth-century date seems plausible.

The biggest question concerns this papyrus's raison d'être. The fact that there is no text on the backside (↓) suggests that this is not a continuous text of the Gospel of Matthew. In New Testament textual criticism, a continuous manuscript is a manuscript "containing (originally) at least one New Testament writing in continuous fashion from beginning to end."[10] So what purpose did this scrap serve?

---

[3] Maurice Nahman (1868–1948) was a prominent Egyptian antiquities dealer based in Cairo through whom many of the Michigan papyri were purchased. See the brief biography in the premature obituary of Nahman by Jean Capart in *CdÉ* 22 (1947): 300–301.

[4] Leuven Database of Ancient Books (LDAB) no. 2940, http://www.trismegistos.org/text/61787.

[5] The nine majuscule manuscripts are: 01, 03, 04, 05, 07, 019, 024, 035, 042. Data retrieved 10 March 2016 from the online version of the *Kurzgefaßte Liste,* http://ntvmr.uni-muenster.de/liste.

[6] Guglielmo Cavallo and Herwig Maehler, *Greek Bookhands of the Early Byzantine Period A.D. 300–800*, BICSSup 47 (London: University of London, Institute of Classical Studies, 1987), pl. 42b.

[7] Image at http://quod.lib.umich.edu/a/apis/x-2879/6577r.tif.

[8] Cavallo and Maehler, *Greek Bookhands*, pl. 54b.

[9] Ibid., pl. 54c.

[10] Eldon Jay Epp, "The Papyrus Manuscripts of the New Testament," in *The Text of the New*

We are faced with a variety of possibilities. Is it a mere biblical extract, such as we find in de Hamel Gk. MS 389 (John 5:43; LDAB 113922), O.Sarga 5 (John 2:1; LDAB 2826), and P.Amh. 3b (Heb 1:1; LDAB 3475)? Or is it an excerpt from a biblical commentary, liturgical fragment, homily, or amulet? In fact, several characteristics point to the category of amulet.

Christians frequently inscribed New Testament passages on amulets in late antiquity.[11] Generally, these passages were chosen for their apotropaic value. In other words, they were used as a means to resolve individual crises, which often included protection from demons, fevers, scorpions, headaches, disease, the evil eye, and the like. The text inscribed on the medium (papyrus, pottery, leather, gem, etc.) was considered to be imbued with divine power that, when recited, could render some desirable effect on a human situation or circumstance. Often the circumstance prompting the ritual is not specified; only the words of power are inscribed, such as a single verse or abbreviated narrative from Scripture.[12]

For example, P.Oxy. 1077 (LDAB 2959), a fifth- to sixth-century Greek papyrus amulet, opens with the phrase "Curative Gospel according to Matthew," which is then followed by a citation of Matt 4:23-24—a narrative summary that depicts Jesus as a healer of every illness and infirmity.[13] This iatromagical ritual device appeals to Jesus's healing in an effort to activate supernatural power for protective effect for the one who wore the amulet.[14]

The gospel passage cited in our papyrus is, in fact, ritually charged: it exhibits an utterance of an "angel of the Lord" (i.e., "Do not fear..."). There are many Christian amulets from late antiquity that invoke the aid of angels (who are often named), and our fragment would fit with the ritual literature of the time.[15] Moreover, in

---

Testament in Contemporary Research: Essays on the Status Quaestionis, ed. Bart D. Ehrman and Michael W. Holmes, SD 46 (Grand Rapids: Eerdmans, 1995), 5.

[11] See Brice C. Jones, *New Testament Texts on Greek Amulets from Late Antiquity*, LNTS 554 (London: Bloomsbury T&T Clark, 2016).

[12] David Frankfurter has referred to these abbreviated narratives as *historiolae* in "Narrating Power: The Theory and Practice of the Magical *Historiola* in Ritual Spells," in *Ancient Magic and Ritual Power*, ed. Marvin W. Meyer and Paul A. Mirecki, RGRW 129 (Leiden: Brill, 1995), 457–76. This seminal article explains from a theoretical perspective how powerful words, episodes, or narratives draw sacred power into the realm of a ritual device's owner.

[13] For the most recent critical edition of P.Oxy. 1077, see Jones, *New Testament Texts*, 60–65.

[14] For a general discussion of Christian amulets, see Theodore S. de Bruyn and Jitse H. F. Dijkstra, "Greek Amulets and Formularies from Egypt Containing Christian Elements: A Checklist of Papyri, Parchments, Ostraka, and Tablets," *BASP* 48 (2011): 163–216; Ernst von Dobschütz, "Charms and Amulets (Christian)," *ERE* 3:413–30; Roy Kotansky, "Incantations and Prayers for Salvation on Inscribed Greek Amulets," in *Magika Hiera: Ancient Greek Magic and Religion*, ed. Christopher A. Faraone and Dirk Obbink (Oxford: Oxford University Press, 1991), 107–37; Joseph E. Sanzo, *Scriptural Incipits on Amulets from Late Antique Egypt: Text, Typology, and Theory*, STAC 84 (Tübingen: Mohr Siebeck, 2014).

[15] E.g., P.Princ. 107, P.Iand. 6, P.Vindob. G 29831, P.Oxy. 1151, P.Oxy. 5073, the latest editions of which are found in Jones, *New Testament Texts*.

antiquity dreams were vehicles of divine revelation and supernatural assistance, and we encounter them frequently in biblical literature, "pagan" literature, the Greek Magical Papyri, and beyond.[16] The fact that a divine being *speaks* to Joseph within a dream is, therefore, ritually significant.

There is one Christian amulet that serves as a good parallel. P.Oxy. 5073 is a small third-century Greek papyrus amulet that cites Mark 1:1–2, the second verse of which reads: "As it is written in the prophet Isaiah, 'See, I am sending my angel [ἄγγελον] ahead of you, who will prepare your way.'" While not a quotation from Isaiah, the phrase "I am sending my angel" is found in a couple passages in the Hebrew Bible, both of which are placed in the mouth of God (see Exod 23:20, Mal 3:1 LXX). The original editors were surely correct to say that this passage "serves as a guarantee of angelic protection, an assurance from beneficent angels."[17] While our papyrus does not specify the situation the amulet's words are meant to resolve or address, the angel in the Matthean account (and in our papyrus) tells Joseph not to be afraid (μὴ φοβηθῇς). It is possible, therefore, that this scriptural passage, like Mark 1:1–2 in P.Oxy. 5073, was reappropriated in the context of a protective ritual.

In summary, while other functions of this papyrus slip cannot be ruled out, the designation of amulet is supported by its ritually charged content (angelic encounter, dream) and format (written only on one side, folded). The extant text is of no real significance to textual criticism, but the papyrus is nonetheless a nice addition to our evidence of late antique Christian artifacts.

II. Text

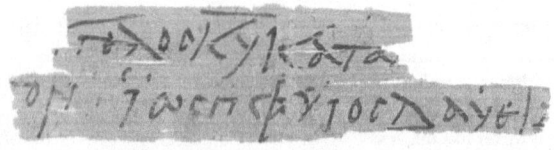

P.Mich. inv. 4944b, 10.8 ×2.7 cm, sixth–seventh century CE. Image digitally reproduced with the permission of the Papyrus Collection, Graduate Library, University of Michigan.

---

[16] On dreams in ritual contexts in antiquity, see Samson Eitrem, "Dreams and Divination in Magical Ritual," in Faraone and Obbink, *Magika Hiera*, 175–87.

[17] Geoffrey S. Smith and Andrew E. Bernhard, "5073," in *The Oxyrhynchus Papyri: Volume LXXVI (Nos. 5072–5100)*, ed. D. Colomo and Juan Chapa, EES.GRM 97 (London: Egypt Exploration Society, 2011), 19–23, here 20.

1
ἄ]γγελος κ(υρίο)υ κατ' ἄγ[α]ρ [ἐ]φ[άνη
αὐτῷ λέ]γον ·'Ιωσὴφ υἱὸς Δαυείδ
4   μὴ] φ[οβηθῆς

2. ὄναρ
3. λέγων | ἰωσηφ pap. | ὐιος pap. | Δαυίδ

An angel of the Lord appeared [to him] in a dream saying, "Joseph, son of David, do [not] fear."

III. Commentary

1 There is a vertical stroke visible toward the end of this line, perhaps the descending vertical of τ in ἐνθυμηθέντος.

2 ἄ]γγελος: ἰδού precedes ἄγγελος κυρίου in the New Testament passage. Based on the reconstruction above, there is room for this word. It is interesting to note that, in P.Oxy. 5073, mentioned above, the phrase ἀποστελῶ τὸν ἄγγελόν μου is also preceded by ἰδού.

ἄγ[α]ρ: Read ὄναρ. The left hasta of ν is visible following the initial α, signifying that the last α of κατά was elided. The descender of ρ is also visible and is positioned precisely where we would expect it to appear. The ο > α interchange, while not all that common, is noted by Francis T. Gignac, *Phonology*, vol. 1 of *A Grammar of the Greek Papyri of the Roman and Byzantine Periods*, TDSA 55 (Milan: Cisalpino-La Goliardica, 1976), 287–88, who cites ἀπόσης (for ὀπόσης) in P.Mil. Vogl. 98 and ἀνόματα (for ὀνόματα) in P.Cair.Isid. 29v; see also P.Oxy. 1478 (ἀνόματος), P.Oxy. 1566 (ἀνομασία), and P.Col. 181 (ἀνόματει).

[ἐ]φ[άνη: The long descending stroke of φ is visible; it descends into ι of Δαυείδ on the next line.

3 λέ]γον: As Gignac shows, the ω > ο vowel interchange "occurs frequently in all phonetic conditions throughout the Roman and Byzantine periods" (*Phonology*, 275).

Δαυείδ: Read Δαυίδ. As in 𝔓¹, the name is written in full here, but it appears as a *nomen sacrum* in Codex Sinaiticus, that is, Δα(υί)δ. In another Christian amulet citing Matt 1:1 (BKT 6.7.1),[18] Δαυίδ is found as Δα(υί)δ.

---

[18] Carl Schmidt and Wilhelm Schubart, eds. *Altchristliche Texte*, Berliner Klassikertexte 6 (Berlin: Weidmann, 1910).

4 φ[οβηθῆς: It is not impossible that the text ended here, especially if the papyrus functioned as an amulet. The practice of ending a citation before its logical conclusion was not unusual in amulet production; see Jones, *New Testament Texts*, 182 and the papyri cited there. It seems that material deemed irrelevant for the ritual carried out was sometimes omitted, which may be the case here (i.e., the reference to Joseph taking Mary as his wife).

JBL 137, no. 1 (2018): 175–191
doi: http://dx.doi.org/10.15699/jbl.1371.2018.283331

The Question of Punctuation in John 1:3–4: Arguments from Ancient Colometry

DAN NÄSSELQVIST
dan.nasselqvist@ctr.lu.se
Lund University, 221 00 Lund, Sweden

The question of how to punctuate John 1:3–4 has confounded both ancient and modern readers. Various textual and linguistic arguments have been used to support one of at least four suggestions about how to punctuate the passage. The present state of research, which supports both Reading A (ὃ γέγονεν belongs to the sentence in 1:4) and Reading B (ὃ γέγονεν belongs to the sentence in 1:3), is based primarily on textual evidence, whereas linguistic arguments have proven inconclusive and are used to confirm diametrically opposed readings. In this article, I apply recent developments in the study of ancient colometry and thus provide a firmer foundation for linguistic arguments based on the rhythm and length of lines. I conclude that balanced cola, approximate rhythm, and a successful beginning of the *gradatio* in 1:4–5 can be achieved only if the passage is punctuated according to Reading A. The case for understanding ὃ γέγονεν as part of 1:4 (Reading A) is more conclusively confirmed by both linguistic and textual evidence than by relying primarily on manuscript evidence. The fact that Reading A also provides the *lectio difficilior* and can explain the origin of Reading B makes it probable that it constitutes the original reading of John 1:3–4.

The question of punctuation in John 1:3–4 arose already in antiquity and continues to confound scholars today. The text-critical issue not only affects the structure of the passage but potentially leads to diametrically opposed interpretations.[1] The uncertainties about how to understand John 1:3–4 are increased by the

[1] Two attempts at more extensive interpretations of how the theology of the passage can be construed from a specific understanding of the punctuation are Ed. L. Miller, *Salvation-History in the Prologue of John: The Significance of John 1:3/4*, NovTSup 60 (Leiden: Brill, 1989); and John Nolland, "The Thought in John 1:3c–4," *TynBul* 62 (2011): 295–311. For the most recent analysis of the function of the Prologue as a unit, see Douglas Estes, "Rhetorical *Peristaseis* (Circumstances) in the Prologue of John," in *The Gospel of John as Genre Mosaic*, ed. Kasper Bro Larsen, Studia Aarhusiana Neotestamentica 3 (Göttingen: Vandenhoeck & Ruprecht, 2015), 191–208.

175

relative scarcity of punctuation in ancient manuscripts and may well have been the cause of early variation in interpretations and manuscript evidence.[2]

I. The *Status Quaestionis*

There are two common interpretations of the punctuation in John 1:3–4, both of which have found wide support,[3] as well as two additional suggestions with fewer adherents. The evidence used in support of the different proposals falls into two broad categories. Textual evidence involves arguments from manuscript witnesses, early translations, and church fathers.[4] Linguistic evidence involves arguments on the basis of grammatical, stylistic, and literary features. Whereas the textual evidence seems to favor one of the two interpretations, the linguistic evidence is less decisive.[5] Linguistic arguments are found primarily in older literature. More recent scholars argue mainly from the textual evidence or from the cogency of the interpretations rendered from different readings.

To avoid any confusion of terminology, I call the different proposals Readings A–D. The two common interpretations are usually designated Reading I and Reading II, but scholars have applied the same terminology to different proposals.[6] I follow and expand Peter van Minnen's terminology.[7] If my interpretation is correct, the designations Reading A, B, C, and D not only describe the various proposals but also arrange them in chronological sequence as well as in order of the strength of their accompanying linguistic and textual evidence.

The decision about which reading to choose has previously relied primarily on textual evidence. Ed. L. Miller even states that the linguistic arguments "tend to

---

[2] See, e.g., the argument in Kurt Aland, "Eine Untersuchung zu Joh. 1 3. 4: Über die Bedeutung eines Punktes," *ZNW* 59 (1968): 174–209.

[3] For helpful lists of scholars arguing for the two most common interpretations, see David J. MacLeod, "The Creation of the Universe by the Word: John 1:3–5," *BSac* 160 (2003): 187–201, esp. 194 n. 29; Nolland, "Thought in John 1:3c–4," 295–96 n. 1.

[4] See Miller, *Salvation-History*, 18.

[5] Ibid., 27, 43–44.

[6] For example, Peter M. Phillips uses the designation Reading I (as well as "Reading a.") to refer to what I call Reading A (Phillips, *The Prologue of the Fourth Gospel: A Sequential Reading*, LNTS 294 [London: T&T Clark, 2006], 162–63), but Miller uses the same term to refer to what I call Reading B (Ed. L. Miller, "P^{66} and P^{75} on John 1:3/4," *TZ* 41 [1985]: 440–43; Miller, *Salvation-History*, 13). John McHugh employs similar designations, Reading 1 and Reading 2, in the same sense as Phillips (McHugh, *A Critical and Exegetical Commentary on John 1–4*, ICC [London: T&T Clark, 2009], 14–15).

[7] Peter van Minnen, "The Punctuation of John 1:3–4," *FNT* 7 (1994): 33–42. He uses this terminology to refer to the same proposals as I do, although he mentions only Readings A, B, and C (his own suggestion).

cancel themselves out."⁸ In what follows I will review the four proposals of how to punctuate John 1:3–4 and advance a linguistic argument that involves length of lines and approximate rhythm. When this colometric argument is based on ancient compositional practices rather than employed intuitively, it provides much-needed linguistic evidence to support the already strong textual evidence about how to punctuate John 1:3–4.

Reading A: Punctuation after οὐδὲ ἕν

πάντα δι' αὐτοῦ ἐγένετο, καὶ χωρὶς αὐτοῦ ἐγένετο οὐδὲ ἕν. ὃ γέγονεν ἐν αὐτῷ ζωὴ ἦν, καὶ ἡ ζωὴ ἦν τὸ φῶς τῶν ἀνθρώπων·

All things came into being through him, and without him not one thing came into being. What has come into being in him was life, and the life was the light of all people. (NRSV)

In Reading A, the full stop comes after οὐδὲ ἕν, and ὃ γέγονεν thus introduces the sentence in 1:4. This reading is not present in the majority of English translations⁹ but is supported by strong textual evidence as well as by many modern scholars and commentators.¹⁰

The textual support for Reading A is substantial, both in terms of manuscript witnesses and quotations by church fathers. Already in the nineteenth century, B. F. Westcott concluded that "it would be difficult to find a more complete consent of ancient authorities in favour of any reading, than that which supports the second punctuation: *Without Him was not anything made. That which hath been made in Him was life.*"¹¹ All church fathers from the second century who discuss or quote John 1:3–4 relate the passage in line with Reading A. This is also true of many fathers from the third to the fifth centuries.¹² Since Westcott's assessment of the evidence, additional manuscript witnesses have strengthened the textual support. 𝔓⁷⁵, arguably the earliest punctuated witness to the Fourth Gospel,¹³ has an elevated

---

⁸ Miller, *Salvation-History*, 27.

⁹ Nevertheless, it lies behind the translations used in CEV, NAB, NJB, NRSV, and MSG [*The Message*].

¹⁰ For lists of supporters of this view, see MacLeod, "Creation of the Universe," 194 n. 29; Nolland, "Thought in John 1:3c–4," 295 n. 1; Phillips, *Prologue of the Fourth Gospel*, 162 n. 92.

¹¹ B. F. Westcott, *The Gospel according to St. John: The Authorized Version with Introduction and Notes* (London: Murray, 1896), 4. The original version was published in 1881 (iii).

¹² For a comprehensive list, see Miller, *Salvation-History*, 29.

¹³ For a recent and significant challenge to the traditional dating of 𝔓⁷⁵ (175–225 CE), see Brent Nongbri, "Reconsidering the Place of Papyrus Bodmer XIV–XV (𝔓75) in the Textual Criticism of the New Testament," *JBL* 135 (2016): 405–37, https://doi.org/10.15699/jbl.1352.2016.2803.

dot after οὐδὲ ἕν,[14] thus supporting Reading A.[15] Miller also concludes that p[66], although it has no punctuation in 1:3–4, "inclines slightly" toward Reading A.[16]

A further textual argument in favor of Reading A is that it constitutes the *lectio difficilior*.[17] This reading can also explain the origins of Reading B, which is predominantly found in manuscripts and church fathers of a later date. The difficulties in understanding 1:3–4 according to Reading A, which arise if one interprets ὃ γέγονεν as a reference to something created, probably led later church fathers to change the punctuation to Reading B. This also eliminated the possibility of interpreting 1:3–4 as a reference to the origin of the Ogdoad (a gnostic reading) or to prove that the Son had undergone change and thus was not equal to the Father (an Arian reading).[18] Reading A can thus account for the generation of Reading B due to its difficulty and popularity among opponents. It is harder to explain why an original Reading B was changed into the more difficult and theologically precarious Reading A (the *lectio difficilior*).

The linguistic arguments that have been suggested in favor of Reading A are not as convincing as the textual evidence. They regularly consist of arguments against reading B, which indirectly strengthens the case for Reading A.[19] There is, however, some linguistic justification in favor of Reading A. For example, Reading A produces an antithetic parallelism in 1:3, which resembles what we find in other Jewish literature, such as the Dead Sea Scrolls.[20] This similarity between the Greek and Hebrew texts cannot decide the interpretation of John 1:3–4, however, since there is no compelling evidence to suggest that the author actualized the potential for parallelism in John 1:3.[21]

---

[14] It is not a στιγμὴ τελεία (high dot), however, but a ὑποστιγμή (middle dot), which indicates a minor pause. See Bruce M. Metzger, *Manuscripts of the Greek Bible: An Introduction to Greek Paleography*, corrected ed. (Oxford: Oxford University Press, 1991), 32.

[15] Miller, "P[66] and P[75]," 441–42; Miller, *Salvation-History*, 36–39. Cf., however, Metzger's conclusion that (the original hand of) p[75] contains no punctuation in this passage (*A Textual Commentary on the Greek New Testament: A Companion Volume to the United Bible Societies' Greek New Testament (3d ed.)*, corrected ed. [Stuttgart: Deutsche Bibelgesellschaft, 1971], 167–68).

[16] Miller, "P[66] and P[75]," 440–41; Miller, *Salvation-History*, 35–36.

[17] Aland, "Eine Untersuchung zu Joh. 1 3. 4," 184–85; Miller, *Salvation-History*, 39. Cf. the conclusion drawn by Metzger (*Textual Commentary*, 168 n. 2): "Despite valiant attempts of commentators to bring sense out of taking ὃ γέγονεν with what follows, the passage remains intolerably clumsy and opaque."

[18] For an analysis of the origin of Reading B in Reading A, see Miller, *Salvation-History*, 45–51.

[19] These arguments are described in the context of Reading B, below.

[20] M.-E. Boismard, *Le prologue de saint Jean*, LD 11 (Paris: Cerf, 1953), 22; Ignace de La Potterie, "De interpunctione et interpretatione versuum Joh. 1,3.4," *VD* 33 (1955): 193–208, esp. 204–6. The parallelism is clearly visible in Greek:
πάντα δι᾽ αὐτοῦ ἐγένετο,
καὶ χωρὶς αὐτοῦ ἐγένετο οὐδὲ ἕν.

[21] Should we be able to confirm Reading A in another way, the likely parallelism of 1:3 will,

A comparable argument points out similarities within the Fourth Gospel that support Reading A.²² It is a common Johannine feature to end sentences or clauses with some form of οὐδείς, which works well with punctuation after οὐδὲ ἕν (or οὐδέν) in 1:3.²³ This argument, however, like the argument from similarities with the Dead Sea Scrolls, is conjectural to some degree. The author chose to end several sentences and clauses in this manner, but forms of οὐδείς are also found in other positions. We cannot be certain that οὐδὲ ἕν in 1:3 should necessarily be followed by punctuation, as in Reading A.²⁴

Another argument in favor of Reading A follows the assertion that "staircase" parallelisms, which may more exactly be referred to as examples of *gradatio*,²⁵ can be found throughout 1:1–5.²⁶ According to this argument, each line in 1:1–5 is connected through the repetition at the beginning of a line of an important word from the end of the previous line. Only if ὃ γέγονεν is taken with 1:4 can one hope to find such repetition throughout 1:3–4. While the rhetorical figure of *gradatio* is clearly used in 1:1 (in the repetition of λόγος ["word"] and θεός ["God"]) and 1:4–5 (in the repetition of ζωή ["life"], φῶς ["light"], and σκοτία ["darkness"]), it is difficult to argue convincingly for it in 1:2 and almost impossible in 1:3. Indeed, no words are repeated at the end and beginning of consecutive lines of 1:2–3.²⁷ Since

---

however, serve as further evidence of the rhetorically advanced composition of the Prologue in general and of 1:1–5 in particular.

²² Miller, *Salvation-History*, 25; Phillips, *Prologue of the Fourth Gospel*, 164.

²³ This is true regardless of whether one considers οὐδὲ ἕν or οὐδέν the original reading of 1:3. For a recent discussion of the issue, see Hartwig Thyen, *Das Johannesevangelium*, HNT 6 (Tübingen: Mohr Siebeck, 2005), 69. In the context of whether it is feasible to punctuate before ὃ γέγονεν, it does not matter whether οὐδὲ ἕν or οὐδέν is oldest, since both forms (as well as οὐδείς) are found numerous times at the end of sentences and clauses in the Fourth Gospel (5:30; 6:63; 8:15, 28; 9:33; 10:41; 11:49; 12:19; 14:30; 15:5; 16:23; 18:9, 20, 31; 21:3). I consider below the (slight) impact of either οὐδὲ ἕν or οὐδέν on each reading of the passage.

²⁴ It has also been argued that it is grammatically inconceivable—or even impossible—to end a sentence with οὐδὲ ἕν. See Theodor Zahn, *Das Evangelium des Johannes*, HNT 4 (Leipzig: Deichert, 1908), 52–53.

²⁵ On the different terms used for this rhetorical figure in John 1:1–5, see Dan Nässelqvist, *Public Reading in Early Christianity: Lectors, Manuscripts, and Sound in the Oral Delivery of John 1–4*, NovTSup 163 (Leiden: Brill, 2015), 185. For a definition of *gradatio*, see Heinrich Lausberg, *Handbuch der literarischen Rhetorik: Eine Grundlegung der Literaturwissenschaft*, 3rd ed. (Stuttgart: Steiner, 1990), §623.

²⁶ Raymond E. Brown, *The Gospel according to John: Introduction, Translation, and Notes*, 2 vols., AB 29, 29A (Garden City, NY: Doubleday, 1966-1970), 1:6; Martinus C. de Boer, "The Original Prologue to the Gospel of John," *NTS* 61 (2015): 448–67, esp. 449–51, 465; Alfred Loisy, *Le quatrième évangile* (Paris: Picard, 1903), 152.

²⁷ To argue for *gradatio* in these verses, one must claim that different words in other positions (such as θεόν in 1:2 and αὐτοῦ in 1:3) have identical referents and thus create a parallelism of thought rather than of words. Even if that were the case, which no one seems to argue any longer (although Phillips [*Prologue of the Fourth Gospel*, 163–64] comes close), such a correspondence

there is no *gradatio* in 1:3, one cannot successfully argue for Reading A on the ground that it preserves this rhetorical figure into 1:4.

The single persistent linguistic argument in favor of Reading A that I have found in earlier literature is an intuitive one; only if ὃ γέγονεν is taken with 1:4 do we maintain an approximate rhythm throughout 1:1–5 and avoid a single line becoming too long.[28] Although I sympathize with this argument, it has the drawback that proponents of Reading B have argued in the same way: the rhythm can be preserved only if we take ὃ γέγονεν with 1:3.[29] This type of reasoning cannot be conclusive as long it is based on subjective impressions of rhythm or balanced length of lines, especially if both sides can claim it for their interpretation. I will return to it below and examine whether it can be anchored in ancient compositional techniques in a manner that does not allow for it to be used in diametrically opposed readings of 1:3–4.

Reading B: Punctuation after ὃ γέγονεν

πάντα δι' αὐτοῦ ἐγένετο, καὶ χωρὶς αὐτοῦ ἐγένετο οὐδὲ ἕν ὃ γέγονεν. ἐν αὐτῷ ζωὴ ἦν, καὶ ἡ ζωὴ ἦν τὸ φῶς τῶν ἀνθρώπων·

> Through him all things were made; without him nothing was made that has been made. In him was life, and that life was the light of all mankind. (NIV)

In Reading B, the full stop comes after ὃ γέγονεν, which thus concludes the sentence in 1:3. This reading is regularly found in modern translations,[30] but it has slightly less support among scholars than Reading A.[31] Despite this, it seems to be the preferred reading among commentators on the Fourth Gospel.[32]

The textual support for Reading B is weaker than for Reading A. Some church fathers cite it, but they are fewer and later (mainly from the fourth century onward)

---

would not constitute an example of *gradatio*, which consists of verbal iterations at specific positions of successive lines.

[28] See, e.g., Aland, "Eine Untersuchung zu Joh. 1 3. 4," 206; Boismard, *Le prologue de saint Jean*, 28; de La Potterie, "De interpunctione et interpretatione," 204; Metzger, *Textual Commentary*, 167.

[29] See, e.g., Paul Gächter, "Strophen im Johannesevangelium," *ZKT* 60 (1936): 99–120, esp. 101–2.

[30] For English translations, see, e.g., ASV, ESV, ISV (International Standard Version), KJV, NASB, NCV (New Century Version), NET, NIV, NJB, NKJV, REB, RSV, and TLB (The Living Bible). For translations to other languages, see de Boer, "Original Prologue," 450 n. 12.

[31] For lists of supporters of Reading B, see MacLeod, "Creation of the Universe," 194 n. 29; Nolland, "Thought in John 1:3c–4," 295–96 n. 2.

[32] See Andreas J. Köstenberger, *John*, BECNT (Grand Rapids: Baker Academic, 2004), 29 n. 31, for a list of commentators supporting Reading B. Cf. van Minnen, who states, "This is the reading of the commentaries" ("Punctuation of John 1:3–4," 36).

than those who attest to Reading A. The same is true of the manuscript witnesses. Equal support for Reading B can be found only among the early translations.[33] It predominates in translations from the seventeenth century onward, primarily as a result of its being the chosen reading for the Textus Receptus.[34]

The linguistic arguments in favor of Reading B resemble those used to support Reading A, and they are correspondingly inconclusive in nature. They are often based on similarities with formulations used elsewhere in John or in other ancient literature. For example, some have argued that, since many sentences in the Fourth Gospel begin with a prepositional phrase with ἐν (e.g., 13:35, 15:8, 16:26)—which is also the case in 1:4—this supports Reading B.[35] Similarly, the phrase ἐν αὐτῷ ζωὴ ἦν has parallels elsewhere in the Fourth Gospel (5:26, 29; 6:53), which may suggest beginning a sentence without adding ὃ γέγονεν before it.[36] Others have argued that the use of ὃ γέγονεν to end 1:3 resembles formulations found in ancient Egyptian creation texts.[37] The fact that corresponding similarities have been used to support Reading A weakens this type of argument considerably.[38] If the recurrence of ἐν at the beginning of sentences points to Reading B and the frequency of οὐδείς at the end of clauses supports reading A, how can we hope to determine the punctuation of 1:3–4 on the basis of such similarities?

Others argue for Reading B more on the grounds of the difficulties in making sense of the phrase ὃ γέγονεν ἐν αὐτῷ ζωὴ ἦν (Reading A).[39] Besides the problem of understanding the theology implicit in Reading A,[40] the most common argument against it is that the perfect ὃ γέγονεν should have a verb in the present tense (ἐστιν) rather than in the imperfect (ἦν).[41] Van Minnen, for example, states that this combination of tenses is "awkward if not impossible."[42] This view follows from the

---

[33] For a list of church fathers, manuscripts, and translations that attest to Reading B, see Miller, *Salvation-History*, 28.

[34] De Boer, "Original Prologue," 450 n. 11.

[35] C. K. Barrett, *The Gospel according to St. John: An Introduction with Commentary and Notes on the Greek Text*, 2nd ed. (Philadelphia: Westminster, 1978), 156–57; Rudolf Schnackenburg, *Das Johannesevangelium*, 4 vols., HThKNT 4 (Freiburg: Herder, 1965–1975), 1:216–17.

[36] See Barrett, *Gospel according to St. John*, 157.

[37] Peder Borgen, "Logos Was the True Light: Contributions to the Interpretation of the Prologue of John," *NovT* 14 (1972): 115–30, esp. 126; Klaus Haacker, "Eine formgeschichtliche Beobachtung zu Joh. 1:3 fin.," *BZ* 12 (1968): 119–21, esp. 120.

[38] Cf. the comparable arguments above for Reading A from similarities with formulations found in other parts of the Fourth Gospel or in the Dead Sea Scrolls.

[39] A recent example of this tendency is Hartwig Thyen, "ὃ γέγονεν: Satzende von 1,3 oder Satzeröffnung von 1,4?," *Studien zum Corpus Iohanneum*, WUNT 214 (Tübingen: Mohr Siebeck, 2007), 411–17.

[40] Köstenberger states that Reading A "is hardly intelligible" (*John*, 29).

[41] See, e.g., Peter Cohee, "John 1.3–4," *NTS* 41 (1995): 470–77, esp. 474; J. Ramsey Michaels, *The Gospel of John*, NICNT (Grand Rapids: Eerdmans, 2010), 52; Thyen, "ὃ γέγονεν," 411–12.

[42] Van Minnen, "Punctuation of John 1:3–4," 36.

premise that, if ὃ γέγονεν opens the sentence in 1:4, it also functions as its subject, which is not necessarily the case.[43] Even if ὃ γέγονεν is considered to be the subject of 1:4 (and this is the most common interpretation of Reading A), it does not necessary follow that the predicate must be present tense. McHugh argues that ὃ γέγονεν is used in the sense of aorist, as a "resultative" (rather than a "present") perfect.[44] It therefore functions well with the imperfect verb (ἦν).[45] Several manuscripts nevertheless have ἐστιν in 1:4. This fact supports the notion that the original reading was ὃ γέγονεν ἐν αὐτῷ ζωὴ ἦν, since it explains why the variant (ἐστιν) would have been deemed necessary by some scribes or copyists.[46]

Reading C: Punctuation after ἐν αὐτῷ

πάντα δι' αὐτοῦ ἐγένετο, καὶ χωρὶς αὐτοῦ ἐγένετο οὐδὲ ἕν ὃ γέγονεν ἐν αὐτῷ. ζωὴ ἦν, καὶ ἡ ζωὴ ἦν τὸ φῶς τῶν ἀνθρώπων·

Everything came into being through him and without him not a thing came into being that exists in him. He was life. This life was the light of all people.[47]

In Reading C, the full stop comes only after ἐν αὐτῷ, which means that all of ὃ γέγονεν ἐν αὐτῷ belongs to the sentence in 1:3. I have not found this reading in any major English translation, and it is promoted by a single scholar, Peter van Minnen.[48] It has been mentioned and analyzed, however, by some earlier scholars.[49]

The textual support for Reading C is almost nonexistent. No manuscript or early translation gives witness to it, but it may be supported by one fourth-century church father. In his *Contra Eunomium*, Gregory of Nyssa twice quotes the passage up to and including ἐν αὐτῷ,[50] which may indicate that he thought that it should be punctuated after ἐν αὐτῷ.[51]

The linguistic arguments for Reading C are even more fragile than the textual support. Van Minnen does not so much argue in favor of it as simply state that Reading A and Reading B are impossible, which "leaves us with reading C."[52] He

---

[43] Cf. Cohee, "John 1.3–4," 473.

[44] McHugh, *Critical and Exegetical Commentary*, 15.

[45] He also argues for the possibility that the phrase may refer to Christ's work of salvation ("what came to pass in him was life") rather than to the creation ("what came into existence in him was life"), which further alleviates the difficulties (ibid.).

[46] Metzger, *Textual Commentary*, 168; cf. Miller, *Salvation-History*, 25–26.

[47] This translation is based on van Minnen, "Punctuation of John 1:3–4," 39. Note, however, that he does not translate the final clause of 1:3–4 (καὶ ἡ ζωὴ ἦν τὸ φῶς τῶν ἀνθρώπων).

[48] Van Minnen, "Punctuation of John 1:3–4."

[49] Aland, "Eine Untersuchung zu Joh. 1 3. 4," 179; Zahn, *Das Evangelium des Johannes*, 697.

[50] Gregory of Nyssa, *Contra Eunomium* 1.302–303 = 1.344 Migne (Jaeger 116.1–3, 10–11).

[51] Van Minnen, "Punctuation of John 1:3–4," 40–41.

[52] Ibid., 38.

also adds that the fact that so few have considered it makes it feasible that it was the original, intended reading:

> If we rank the three readings it is clear that reading B is the reading of convenience. Reading A is the *lectio difficilior* and has been treated as such in recent studies. In view of the fact that reading C has not been given serious consideration, at least for the past 1600 years, it is the *lectio difficilima*. It therefore has a good chance of actually being what John meant.[53]

Such a conclusion is neither convincing nor appended with any arguments. Recent commentaries consequently do not mention Reading C. Kurt Aland, however, calls it "offenbar absurd" and "nicht nur trivial, ja eigentlich unmöglich."[54]

Reading D: Punctuation after οὐδὲ ἕν and ὃ γέγονεν Is a Gloss

πάντα δι' αὐτοῦ ἐγένετο, καὶ χωρὶς αὐτοῦ ἐγένετο οὐδὲ ἕν. ἐν αὐτῷ ζωὴ ἦν, καὶ ἡ ζωὴ ἦν τὸ φῶς [τῶν ἀνθρώπων].[55]

All things came into being through him, and without him not one thing came into being. In him was life, and the life was the light [of all people].[56]

In Reading D, the full stop comes after οὐδὲ ἕν, just as in Reading A, but it also eliminates ὃ γέγονεν, which is considered to be a gloss. I have not found this reading in any major English translation. It is promoted by a single scholar, Peter Cohee, and does not seem to be mentioned in earlier works.[57] In contrast to Reading C, however, it has been discussed in some recent commentaries.[58]

The textual support for Reading D is even weaker than for Reading C. No early translation or church father gives witness to it, but the fact that some later manuscripts (primarily eighth to tenth centuries)[59] have dots both before and after ὃ γέγονεν can be interpreted as support for viewing the phrase as a gloss.[60] It is far

---

[53] Ibid., 37.

[54] Aland, "Eine Untersuchung zu Joh. 1 3. 4," 179 n. 7, 208.

[55] I have eliminated ὃ γέγονεν, since Cohee ("John 1.3-4," 476) considers it a gloss; in addition, he placed square brackets around τῶν ἀνθρώπων, since he believes that it may also be a gloss (in this he follows J. C. O'Neill, "The Prologue to St John's Gospel," *JTS* 20 [1969]: 41-52, esp. 42).

[56] This translation is based on the NRSV (which follows Reading A) but has been revised in accordance with Reading D (by eliminating ὃ γέγονεν and bracketing τῶν ἀνθρώπων). Cohee does not present a translation.

[57] Cohee, "John 1.3-4."

[58] Craig S. Keener, *The Gospel of John: A Commentary*, 2 vols. (Peabody, MA: Hendrickson, 2003), 1:382 n. 186; Köstenberger, *John*, 29 n. 30.

[59] These are (in chronological order): L, O, 211, Δ, F, G, H, Y, Π, Θ, K, V, M, ω, and S (based on the list in Aland, "Eine Untersuchung zu Joh. 1 3. 4," 188-89).

[60] Cohee draws this conclusion ("John 1.3-4," 476-77). He especially notes Codex Bezae,

from certain, however, that these dots indicate that the scribe deemed ὃ γέγονεν to be a gloss. In the ninth-century manuscript Δ (Codex Sangallensis 48), there are numerous dots in this passage, before and after most words.[61] No one has argued that ἐν αὐτῷ or ζωὴ ἦν are glosses on the basis of Δ. The only conclusive textual support for this reading comes from the tenth-century manuscript 0141, which does not include ὃ γέγονεν at all. It has an elevated dot after οὐδὲ ἕν, which is followed by ἐν αὐτῷ ζωὴ ἦν.

The linguistic argument for Reading D proceeds from the difficulties in making sense of the phrase ὃ γέγονεν ἐν αὐτῷ ζωὴ ἦν (Reading A). Cohee agrees with Aland and later scholars that this represents the *lectio difficilior* but draws the conclusion that the difficulties suggest that ὃ γέγονεν may be an intrusive gloss.[62] He proposes that "certain stylistic and syntactic features" of 1:1–5 and 1:10–11 make this plausible and then reiterates several arguments used against Reading A and Reading B[63] in order to assure that ὃ γέγονεν is best understood as a gloss.[64] The main thrust of Cohee's argument revolves around his identification of *gradatio* (although he uses the term λέξις εἰρομένη, "loose style" or "speech strung together") throughout 1:1–5 and 1:10–11.[65] He claims that the example of *gradatio* in 1:4–5 becomes much clearer and produces stylistic unity if ὃ γέγονεν is eliminated as a gloss.[66] The difficulties in identifying *gradatio* in 1:2–3 (see above), as well as the fact that the strong repetitions in 1:10–11 do not constitute *gradatio* at all,[67] argue against Cohee's conclusion.

II. Ancient Colometry

The presentation and critical review of the *status quaestionis* make it clear that, although only two of the four proposals have found wide support, the research on

---

although it may not have double punctuation at this point (see the discussion in Miller, *Salvation-History*, 33–35).

[61] Aland ("Eine Untersuchung zu Joh. 1 3. 4," 188) indicates four low dots (in the following positions: οὐδὲ ἕν ὃ. γέγονεν. ἐν αὐτῷ. ζωὴ ἦν.), yet a closer study of the manuscript shows that the phrase has five elevated dots as well as a low dot (οὐδὲ ἕν ὃ· γέγονεν· ἐν· αὐτῷ· ζωὴ· ἦν.). See St. Gallen, Stiftsbibliothek, Cod. Sang. 48, f. 318, http://www.e-codices.unifr.ch/en/list/one/csg/0048.

[62] Cohee, "John 1.3–4," 470.

[63] Most of these have been mentioned above, such as the notion that *gradatio* characterizes all of 1:1–5 and the fact that several sentences in the Fourth Gospel begin with ἐν.

[64] Cohee, "John 1.3–4," 470–74; quotation from 470.

[65] See above, under Reading A, for a discussion of *gradatio* and its presence in (parts of) 1:1–5.

[66] Cohee, "John 1.3–4," 476.

[67] The words in 1:10–11 are not repeated at the end and beginning of consecutive lines but rather in similar positions and without the "staircase" effect of changing words. The repetitions in this passage should rather be described as a combination of the rhetorical figures polyptoton, mesodiplosis, and paronomasia (Nässelqvist, *Public Reading*, 193).

the punctuation of John 1:3–4 has reached an impasse. The problem is compounded by the fact that only the textual arguments are grounded in facts from ancient (and medieval) sources, such as manuscript witnesses and statements by church fathers. The linguistic arguments, on the other hand, are often insightful and well argued but fundamentally based on subjective impressions of rhythm, rhetorical figures, similarities within and between texts, and how prescriptive grammar can invalidate formulations used in multiple ancient manuscripts.

In order to move beyond the present impasse, it is necessary to provide linguistic arguments that are as well rooted in ancient sources as the textual evidence. Linguistic arguments of the same type—regarding, for example, approximate rhythm or similarities within the Fourth Gospel—are presently used to validate conflicting readings of 1:3–4. It will be possible to find wider support for a specific reading only if it is confirmed by both textual and linguistic evidence that is firmly substantiated in ancient sources.

Recent developments in the study of ancient compositional techniques provide the opportunity for such a well-grounded linguistic argument on the punctuation of 1:3–4. Scholars engaged in "sound mapping," or "sound analysis," study sound structures in ancient Greek literary writings and have presented a method for analyzing a composition's sound.[68] In the context of studying ancient grammarians, rhetoricians, and literary critics on the fundamental structural components of literary writings, these scholars have established a firm basis for determining the boundaries of a composition's cola, or "lines."[69] This development advances the understanding of colometry beyond the conclusions of earlier research, which was primarily conducted in the early twentieth century.[70]

Lee, Scott, and Nässelqvist indicate that the colon functioned as the fundamental compositional unit for ancient prose literary writings in both Greek and

---

[68] The most significant contributions are by Margaret Ellen Lee and Bernard Brandon Scott (*Sound Mapping the New Testament* [Salem, OR: Polebridge, 2009]), who introduced the term *sound mapping*, and Nässelqvist (*Public Reading*), who uses the term *sound analysis* (see esp. *Public Reading*, 119–80). Earlier contributions include Margaret E. Dean, "The Grammar of Sound in Greek Texts: Toward a Method for Mapping the Echoes of Speech in Writing," *ABR* 44 (1996): 53–70; Dean, "Textured Criticism," *JSNT* 70 (1998): 79–91; Bernard Brandon Scott and Margaret E. Dean, "A Sound Map of the Sermon of the Mount," in *Treasures New and Old: Recent Contributions to Matthean Studies*, ed. David R. Bauer and Mark Allan Powell, SymS 1 (Atlanta: Scholars Press, 1996), 311–78; Jeffrey E. Brickle, *Aural Design and Coherence in the Prologue of First John*, LNTS 465 (London: T&T Clark, 2012).

[69] Lee and Scott, *Sound Mapping*, 136–51, 169–71; Nässelqvist, *Public Reading*, 124–33.

[70] Important contributions include Roland Schütz, "Die Bedeutung der Kolometrie für das Neuen Testament," *ZNW* 21 (1922): 161–84; Albert Debrunner, "Grundsätzliches über Kolometrie im Neuen Testament," *TBl* 5 (1926): 231–33; James A. Kleist, "Colometry and the New Testament," *ClB* 3 (1927): 18–19; 4 (1928): 26–27; Eduard Fraenkel, "Kolon und Satz: Beobachtung zur Gliederung des antiken Satzes," *NAWG* (1932): 197–213; (1933): 319–54. For a brief history of the few more recent publications that approach colometry, see Lee and Scott, *Sound Mapping*, 138–40.

Latin.[71] It is described both as a sense unit and as a breath unit. As a sense unit, the colon regularly consists of an entire clause with at least one verbal form and its related elements. It is thus adapted to its content and includes a complete thought or a complete part of a thought.[72] As a breath unit, the colon comprises no more than what one can pronounce in the duration of a single breath. It therefore has a limited extent. The ideal colon of prose is equivalent to a hexameter line and thus consists of twelve to seventeen syllables. In actual practice, however, its length can be considerably shorter or longer, although it is still far from limitless. I have examined cola that are presented as examples in ancient treatments of the colon and found that the acceptable length is seven to thirty syllables.[73]

Each colon should be characterized by "syntactical completion (at least a complete phrase), unitary thought, and a length that is a mean between 'too short' and 'too long.'"[74] These three general guidelines, which were based on Aristotle and remained in effect at least from the fourth century BCE up until the second century CE (and probably much longer),[75] can now be specified in greater detail. A colon should (1) consist of an entire clause, (2) include a complete thought or a complete part of one, and (3) be of acceptable length, which means that it comprises seven to thirty syllables. Cola that are longer than thirty syllables are not easily pronounceable in a single breath, whereas cola that are shorter than seven syllables are too brief to constitute a single line. Such a short expression is called a *comma* (plural *commata*), literally "that which is cut off," an indication of its fragmentary nature. Since a *comma* cannot constitute a line, several *commata* must be joined to form a colon.[76] This fact has important consequences for earlier interpretations on how to delineate John 1:3–4.

With this information about the colon, it is possible to examine linguistic arguments about the punctuation in John 1:3–4 that are based on the length of cola or the approximate rhythm in the passage. Below I display Readings A–D colometrically and discuss the merits of each reading according to these recent developments in colometry and sound analysis. The verse numbers are presented to the left of the text and the number of syllables found in each colon to the right. Reading A leads to the following colometric arrangement:

---

[71] Lee and Scott, *Sound Mapping*, 136; Nässelqvist, *Public Reading*, 124. The most common terms used to refer to a colon in the ancient sources are κῶλον and *membrum*.

[72] Lee and Scott, *Sound Mapping*, 169–70; Nässelqvist, *Public Reading*, 127–29, 132. Cf. Lausberg, *Handbuch der literarischen Rhetorik*, §930.

[73] Nässelqvist, *Public Reading*, 127, 129–31.

[74] Aristotle, *On Rhetoric: A Theory of Civic Discourse*, trans. George A. Kennedy, 2nd ed. (New York: Oxford University Press, 2007), 214. Quoted in Nässelqvist, *Public Reading*, 132.

[75] Nässelqvist, *Public Reading*, 131.

[76] Ibid., 124, 129. Ancient sources use the following terms to refer to *commata*: κόμμα, *caesum, comprehensio, incisum, particula,* and *articulus*.

1:3a	πάντα δι' αὐτοῦ ἐγένετο,	8
1:3b	καὶ χωρὶς αὐτοῦ ἐγένετο οὐδὲ ἕν.	12/11[77]
1:3c/4a	ὃ γέγονεν ἐν αὐτῷ ζωὴ ἦν,	10
1:4b	καὶ ἡ ζωὴ ἦν τὸ φῶς τῶν ἀνθρώπων·	11

In Reading A, with a full stop after οὐδὲ ἕν, the passage can be divided into four cola of similar length (8 + 12 + 10 + 11 syllables). If one reads οὐδέν, rather than οὐδὲ ἕν, the cola are even more balanced (8 + 11 + 10 + 11). Each colon meets the requirements of syntactical completion, unitary thought, and acceptable length.

The balanced cola of Reading A initiate the *gradatio*, or staircase parallelism,[78] of 1:4–5 without diminishing its effect. The paired words (ζωή, φῶς, and σκοτία) produce an approximate rhythm, as argued by earlier scholars.[79] The impression of balanced lines and approximate rhythm in Reading A can thus be confirmed by reference to ancient colometry and its identification of repeated words and sounds in parallel positions in cola of similar and acceptable length.[80] The *gradatio* in 1:4–5, which opens with ὃ γέγονεν, is best displayed colometrically (the paired words are underlined):

1:3c/4a	ὃ γέγονεν ἐν αὐτῷ <u>ζωὴ</u> ἦν,	10
1:4b	καὶ <u>ἡ ζωὴ</u> ἦν <u>τὸ φῶς</u> τῶν ἀνθρώπων·	11
1:5a	καὶ <u>τὸ φῶς</u> ἐν <u>τῇ σκοτίᾳ</u> φαίνει,	10
1:5b	καὶ <u>ἡ σκοτία</u> αὐτὸ οὐ κατέλαβεν.	12

The *gradatio* of 1:4–5 works well together with Reading A. It opens with a complete colon, which is followed by three lines of almost identical length. The repetition of paired words produces an approximate rhythm, and the similar colon length (ten to twelve syllables) bolsters it. Unlike the *gradatio* in 1:1–2, the paired words shift in each colon.[81] The impact is thus not as strong as in the opening lines of the Prologue, but the rhetorical figure in 1:4–5 nevertheless attracts attention through a combination of balanced cola, paired words, and assonance (due to a high concentration of similar long vowels in the first two cola).[82] Reading A, with its punctuation prior to ὃ γέγονεν, provides a fitting starting point for the *gradatio* in 1:4–5.

Reading B leads to a colometric arrangement that differs significantly from Reading A:

---

[77] The lower number of syllables is applicable if one reads οὐδέν instead of οὐδὲ ἕν.

[78] See the discussion of Reading A above in section I.

[79] Aland, "Eine Untersuchung zu Joh. 1 3. 4," 206; Boismard, *Le prologue de saint Jean*, 28; de La Potterie, "De interpunctione et interpretatione," 204; Loisy, *Le quatrième évangile*, 92; Metzger, *Textual Commentary*, 167; Miller, *Salvation-History*, 21.

[80] See the analysis in Nässelqvist, *Public Reading*, 187–90.

[81] The *gradatio* in 1:1–2 alternates between λόγος and θεός (although οὗτος is used at the beginning of 1:2).

[82] See Nässelqvist, *Public Reading*, 190.

1:3a	πάντα δι' αὐτοῦ ἐγένετο,	8
1:3b	καὶ χωρὶς αὐτοῦ ἐγένετο οὐδὲ ἕν ὃ γέγονεν.	16/15[83]
1:4a	ἐν αὐτῷ ζωὴ ἦν,	6
1:4b	καὶ ἡ ζωὴ ἦν τὸ φῶς τῶν ἀνθρώπων·	11

In Reading B the full stop is placed after ὃ γέγονεν, which produces a long second colon (1:3b; sixteen syllables) and a brief third line (1:4a; six syllables). The third line is so short that it cannot independently constitute a colon but rather acts as a *comma*. As such, it should be joined to one of the adjacent cola, in this case the final colon of the passage (1:4b), since the *comma* is preceded by a full stop.[84] The result is unbalanced cola (8 + 16 + 17 syllables) that hardly produce any rhythm.[85] Worse still, the *gradatio* of 1:4–5 will either start on a broken line of only six syllables or become partly ruined if the *comma* (1:4a) is joined with the following colon (1:4b), as shown below:

1:4	ἐν αὐτῷ ζωὴ ἦν, καὶ ἡ ζωὴ ἦν <u>τὸ φῶς</u> τῶν ἀνθρώπων·	17
1:5a	καὶ <u>τὸ φῶς</u> ἐν <u>τῇ σκοτίᾳ</u> φαίνει,	10
1:5b	καὶ <u>ἡ σκοτία</u> αὐτὸ οὐ κατέλαβεν.	12

In this case, the *gradatio* cannot begin with the repetition of ζωή, since the key words must be repeated in different cola (near the end of one and near the beginning of the next) to produce the rhetorical figure. Thus, the *gradatio* starts only with φῶς, the first of the paired words to appear in two adjacent cola.[86] In addition, the unbalanced lines (17 + 10 + 12 syllables) break the approximate rhythm and weaken the rhetorical figure.[87] Taken together, the weakened *gradatio*, disruption of rhythm, and unbalanced lines significantly lower the probability that Reading B constitutes the original reading of 1:3–4.

Reading C results in an even more unbalanced colometric arrangement:

1:3a	πάντα δι' αὐτοῦ ἐγένετο,	8
1:3b/4a	καὶ χωρὶς αὐτοῦ ἐγένετο οὐδὲ ἕν ὃ γέγονεν ἐν αὐτῷ.	19/18[88]
1:4b	ζωὴ ἦν,	3
1:4c	καὶ ἡ ζωὴ ἦν τὸ φῶς τῶν ἀνθρώπων·	11

---

[83] The lower number of syllables pertains to the reading οὐδέν rather than οὐδὲ ἕν.

[84] The whole point of Reading B indeed aims at separating ὃ γέγονεν from ἐν αὐτῷ ζωὴ ἦν, which also leads to the conclusion that ἐν αὐτῷ ζωὴ ἦν (the *comma*) should be joined with what follows it.

[85] Contra Gächter, "Strophen im Johannesevangelium," 101–2.

[86] For a comprehensive analysis of the use of *gradatio* in 1:1–5, which takes colometry into account, see Nässelqvist, *Public Reading*, 185–90.

[87] The assonance of 1:4, with its significant repetition of long vowels (see above), is not weakened, however, but rather is concentrated into a single colon. It may well attract more attention than the weakened *gradatio* that follows it.

[88] The lower number of syllables pertains to the reading οὐδέν rather than οὐδὲ ἕν.

Reading C, which positions the full stop after ἐν αὐτῷ, causes severely unbalanced lines. They differ between three and nineteen syllables in length (8 + 19/18 + 3 + 11). Van Minnen grants that the phrase ζωὴ ἦν comprises a "rather terse" line but argues that "in discourse short speech units are perfectly admissible—unlike long ones."[89] As the recent developments in colometry and ancient compositional technique have shown, however, that is not the case. Speech units of three syllables are extremely short even for *commata*,[90] and what van Minnen considers a "probably … too long" speech unit (one comprising eighteen syllables) is perfectly acceptable.[91]

Reading C thus builds on faulty notions of acceptable colon lengths in ancient literary writings. The brief phrase in 1:4b (ζωὴ ἦν) cannot constitute an independent line and thus needs to be combined with 1:4c. The result is similar to Reading B (yet comparatively worse) in terms of unbalanced lines, disruption of rhythm, and weakening of the *gradatio* in 1:4–5. Again, the repetition of ζωή occurs within a single colon and cannot be included in the rhetorical figure. There is no support for the notion that Reading C is the original reading of 1:3–4.

Reading D produces yet another colometric arrangement, due to the elimination of ὃ γέγονεν and the labeling of τῶν ἀνθρώπων as a potential gloss:

1:3a	πάντα δι' αὐτοῦ ἐγένετο,	8
1:3b	καὶ χωρὶς αὐτοῦ ἐγένετο οὐδὲ ἕν.	12/11[92]
1:4a	ἐν αὐτῷ ζωὴ ἦν,	6
1:4b	καὶ ἡ ζωὴ ἦν τὸ φῶς [τῶν ἀνθρώπων]·	7/11[93]

In Reading D, the full stop comes after οὐδὲ ἕν (or οὐδέν) and ὃ γέγονεν is eliminated as an intrusive gloss. The colometric result is similar to Reading B, since it consists of unbalanced cola and a *comma* in 1:4a. The length of lines (8 + 12/11 + 6 + 7/11 syllables) does not vary as much as in Reading B and Reading C (due the elimination of ὃ γέγονεν) but leads to the same disruption of *gradatio* and rhythm. The *gradatio* either begins with an incomplete line (the *comma* in 1:4a) or comprises the repetition of only two key words, φῶς and σκοτία (if the *comma* is joined with 1:4b to form a complete colon).[94]

From the perspective of ancient compositional practices and colometry, Reading D thus works slightly better than Readings B and C. Nevertheless, the

---

[89] Van Minnen, "Punctuation of John 1:3–4," 39.

[90] Nässelqvist, *Public Reading*, 129.

[91] Van Minnen, "Punctuation of John 1:3–4," 35. The speech unit in question is ὁ λόγος οὗτος ἦν ἐν ἀρχῇ πρὸς τὸν θεόν (from John 1:1–2).

[92] The lower number of syllables pertains to the reading οὐδέν rather than οὐδὲ ἕν.

[93] The length of this colon depends on whether τῶν ἀνθρώπων is considered to be a gloss. See n. 55.

[94] For this conclusion, see the colometric arrangement of 1:4–5 (under Reading B) and the discussion there.

hypothetical nature of Cohee's identification of certain phrases as glosses, the non-existent textual evidence in early manuscripts, and the fact that the reading has found no support among modern scholars strongly argue against the idea that Reading D constitutes the original reading of 1:3–4.

The examination of Readings A–D from the perspective of ancient colometry thus indicates that only Reading A fully corresponds to ancient compositional practices and results in balanced cola that meet the threefold requirements of syntactical completion, unitary thought, and acceptable length. Reading A also produces an intact *gradatio* in 1:4–5, which is strengthened by similar colon length (ten to twelve syllables throughout the rhetorical figure).

Readings B–D are impaired by the fact that in each reading one of the lines is incomplete and does not establish a complete colon. Readings B and D include a line made up of six syllables (ἐν αὐτῷ ζωὴ ἦν), and Reading C contains a line with only three syllables (ζωὴ ἦν). These brief lines lack the necessary length to constitute complete and independent cola. As a result, the *gradatio* in 1:4–5 either opens awkwardly with an incomplete line or is weakened by the repetition of ζωή within a single colon (if the brief phrase is combined with the rest of 1:4 to form a single line), instead of at the end of one colon and at the beginning of the next, as the staircase parallelism of *gradatio* demands. The unbalanced lines of Readings B–D also reduce the approximate rhythm produced by the paired words and rhetorical figures of 1:3–5.

III. Conclusion

The question of how to punctuate John 1:3–4 has confounded both ancient and modern readers. A number of textual and linguistic arguments have been raised in defense of the four different hypotheses on the original punctuation. Two of these hypotheses have found wide support among modern scholars. Despite strong textual evidence for Reading A, there is no consensus so far, partly because of the inconclusive nature of the linguistic arguments. Whereas the textual evidence distinctly points to Readings A and B (and indicates that Reading A is the oldest of these), similar linguistic arguments are used to support contrasting readings. For example, proponents of diametrically opposed readings argue that the rhythm of the passage cannot be preserved unless one follows their suggestion on punctuation.

The research on the punctuation of John 1:3–4 has thus reached an impasse. In order to move beyond it, the linguistic arguments must be as firmly substantiated in ancient sources as the textual arguments. Such methodological rigor will make it impossible to use the same type of argument to confirm opposing readings.

Recent developments in the study of ancient colometry provide a way forward and the information needed to substantiate linguistic arguments that involve the rhythm and length of lines in 1:3–4. These arguments have previously depended on subjective notions of the delimitation, combination, and acceptable length of cola. Recent studies provide a firmer basis of knowledge about the colon as the fundamental compositional unit for ancient prose writings. They indicate that a colon should consist of an entire clause, include a complete thought or a complete part of one, and comprise seven to thirty syllables.

When the four hypotheses on the punctuation of 1:3–4 are analyzed from this perspective, it becomes clear that most of them depend on subjective impressions of how cola can be delimited. Structural features such as balanced cola and repetitions in parallel positions over several cola establish prose rhythm. A correct delimitation of the cola in 1:3–4 is therefore imperative for an accurate understanding of its rhythmical properties as well as for any linguistic argument based on rhythm. How the cola are defined has an even greater impact on the strongest rhetorical figure in the passage, the *gradatio*, or staircase parallelism, which covers 1:4–5. Since *gradatio* depends on repetition in different positions of consecutive cola (a word near the end of one colon is repeated near the beginning of the next), a faulty delimitation of the cola risks negating the figure.

Examined from the perspective of ancient colometry, an approximate rhythm and a successful beginning of the *gradatio* can be achieved only through Reading A, according to which the full stop is positioned after οὐδὲ ἕν (or οὐδέν) and ὃ γέγονεν belongs to the sentence in 1:4. In Readings B–D, the cola are not balanced, which weakens the rhythm, and the *gradatio* cannot start with the repetition of ζωή. Readings B–D place the phrase ζωὴ ἦν either in a fragmentary line (a phrase that is too brief comprises a *comma*, which cannot constitute an independent colon) or merge it with the following colon, which weakens the *gradatio*.

The analysis of the proposed readings thus confirms earlier scholars' impression that only Reading A maintains balanced lines in 1:3–4. More importantly, the insights from developments in ancient colometry provide a firm foundation upon which several linguistic arguments can be built. The stricter definition of a colon invalidates several readings of 1:3–4 and thus makes it impossible to use the same type of linguistic argument to confirm diametrically opposed readings.

The present state of research, which supports both Reading A (ὃ γέγονεν belongs to the sentence in 1:4) and Reading B (ὃ γέγονεν belongs to the sentence in 1:3), is based primarily on textual evidence. Linguistic arguments have proven inconclusive and regularly cancel one another out. This study shows that linguistic arguments can nevertheless be effective, if they are first firmly substantiated in ancient sources to the same degree that the textual arguments are. Rather than rely almost exclusively on manuscript evidence, the case for understanding ὃ γέγονεν as part of 1:4 is thus more conclusively based on both linguistic and textual evidence. The fact that Reading A also provides the *lectio difficilior* and can explain the origin of Reading B, which has firm support only in later manuscript witnesses and church fathers, makes it probable that it constitutes the original reading of John 1:3–4.

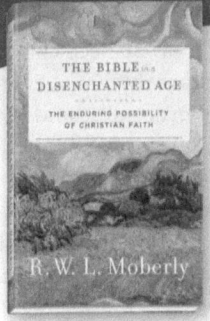

How Jewish Is God? Divine Ethnicity in Paul's Theology

PAULA FREDRIKSEN
augfred@bu.edu
The Hebrew University, Jerusalem 91905, Israel

*For E. P. Sanders,
in honor of the fortieth anniversary
of the publication of
Paul and Palestinian Judaism*

Land, language, family connection, gods: these were the prime markers of ancient ethnicity, both for pagans and for Jews. Ethnicity, like divinity, was a category that spanned heaven and earth: gods and their humans formed family groups, and gods often shared in the ethnicity of the peoples who worshiped them. In this regard, the Jewish god was no exception. What was exceptional was the Jewish god's claims to cross-ethnic supremacy: at the end of days, the gods of the nations as well as their peoples would acknowledge Israel's god alone. Paul's gospel to τὰ ἔθνη ("the nations") coheres completely with this Jewish eschatological paradigm, and the Jewish identity of Paul's god illumines essential aspects of Paul's language of gentile ἁγιασμός ("separateness, sanctification") and υἱοθεσία ("adoption as sons").

Divine ethnicity might seem like a strange idea, but in Greco-Roman antiquity, gods often shared the ethnicity of the peoples who worshiped them. In this regard, the Jewish god was no exception. What *was* odd, in the view of their

E. P. Sanders's *Paul and Palestinian Judaism: A Comparison of Patterns of Religion* (Philadelphia: Fortress; London: SCM, 1977) revolutionized New Testament studies. That great book began the serious academic retrieval of Second Temple Judaism as the defining context, in positive ways, of Paul's life and work. Thank you, Ed, for your moral summons, as well as for your enduring intellectual achievement.

Earlier versions of this essay were presented as a public lecture at Lund University and as a main paper at the 2016 meeting of the Studiorum Novi Testamenti Societas. The current article draws on material from my book *Paul: The Pagans' Apostle* (New Haven: Yale University Press, 2017). I thank Magnus Zetterholm for his kind invitation to speak at Lund, and my colleagues in the SNTS, especially Shelly Matthews and Laura Nasrallah, for their critical feedback and suggestions.

non-Jewish contemporaries, was the Jews' insistence that their particular god was *also* the universal god, the highest god, the supreme god. Even odder was the claim of some Jews of apocalyptic bent: the Jewish god, they said, would ultimately be worshiped by ethnic others, both human and divine.

This idea of linked ethnicity, human and divine, illumines essential aspects of Paul's gospel to the gentiles. Foreign gods, Paul says, will "bend knee" to the returning Davidic messiah and, thus, to his father, the god of Israel (Phil 2:10, presumably at or after the parousia; cf., e.g., Ps 97:7). Pagan peoples (τὰ ἔθνη), through holy πνεῦμα, will be both set apart ("sanctified") and provided with new lineage—thus, with a new family. Further, and ultimately, they will be "ruled" by the "root of Jesse," that is, by the eschatological Davidic messiah (Rom 15:12, Isa 11:10). Moreover, like their gods, all the nations will also worship the god of Israel. Before turning to Paul's vision of redemption in Christ, however, we must consider, first, ancient ideas of ethnicity; second, the Jewish ethnicity of Israel's god; and, third, the ways that the Greek translation of Jewish scriptures accommodated ancient Mediterranean ideas about divine multiplicity.

I. Divinity, Ethnicity, and Multiplicity

The simplest way to articulate the idea of ancient constructs of ethnicity is to list some of the relevant vocabulary: γένος ("people, family, race"); ἔθνος ("people group"); συγγένεια ("kinship"); συγγενεῖς ("kinfolk"); *gens* ("family"); *domus*/οἶκος ("household"); *mos maiorum, fides patrum,* παραδόσεις τῶν πατέρων, ἔθη, τὰ πάτρια ἔθη, τὰ πάτρια ("ancestral custom"); πατρίς ("fatherland"). These words, taken together, express a concept cluster connecting blood relations (family), shared customs, inherited protocols for showing respect to gods (what we might refer to—cautiously!—as "religion"), and ancestral land or locality.

Συγγένεια—"kinship"—also served as a term for citizenship: citizens of a city were imagined as members of the same γένος (e.g., Josephus, *Ant.* 12.3.2 §§125–126, also stressing the connection to gods). This family connection extended not only horizontally, between citizens of the Hellenistic polis; it also extended vertically, between heaven and earth. Greek and Roman gods were known to have taken human sexual partners, from whose progeny whole human populations might descend. Sometimes the fruit of these unions might be the founder of a city. (Venus, Aeneas, and Rome provide a familiar example.) Sometimes this divine descent might extend to other citizens.[1] Sometimes ancestor-gods glittered in the family

---

[1] For example, as evinced in the Roman claim to be "Aeneadae." For discussion, with sources, see Christopher P. Jones, *Kinship Diplomacy in the Ancient World*, Revealing Antiquity 12 (Cambridge: Harvard University Press, 1999), 12, 154 n. 16. He notes that this "belief that such [divine] heroes were also the ultimate ancestors of cities or nations was widespread in Greek thought, and was then taken up by the Romans" (12).

tree of important political figures and dynasties.² In war, the gods of the vanquished were bested by the gods of the victors—a natural extension of this idea that gods and humans formed family groups.³

These junctures between heaven and earth were conceived so concretely that they served as the basis for intercity diplomacy. Citizens of two different cities might trace their genealogies—or, in our view, generate them—back to common divine ancestors. This ancient family link then served to stabilize current intercity agreements. A Jewish refraction of this practice of kinship diplomacy remains in 1 and 2 Maccabees, repeated by Josephus. Thanks to Heracles's relationship with a granddaughter of Abraham, Judeans and Spartans established diplomatic συγγένεια (1 Macc 12:21; 2 Macc 5:9; cf. Josephus, *Ant.* 1.15 §§240–241). "After reading a certain document," announces a Spartan king to the Jewish high priest, "we have found that Judeans and Lacedaemonians are of one γένος, and share a connection [οἰκειότης] with Abraham" (Josephus, *Ant.* 12.4.10 §226).

Hellenistic and early Roman cities, in short, were not secular spaces. They were family-run religious institutions. Much of the city's activity that we might consider "cultural" or "athletic" or "political"—competitions in rhetoric or in foot racing, theatrical performances, spectacles, meetings of the city council (the βουλή or the curia)—were dedicated to the presiding god(s). Keeping gods happy went a long way toward protecting the common weal. Jews who were citizens of these cities were accordingly and occasionally placed in an awkward situation: because of the liturgical peculiarities of their own god, their showing respect to their "other gods," the gods of their cities, could present problems. Were they part of the urban γένος or not? If they were, then why did they not worship the same gods (Josephus, *C. Ap.* 2.6 §65; cf. *Ant.* 12.3.2 §§125–126)?

Jewish sources both Hebrew and Greek, as well as pagan sources, express ethnicity through this concept cluster aligning heaven and earth. A prime example occurs in Gen 10, supplemented by Deut 32:8–9.⁴ Right after the flood and the

---

²Alexander the Great descended from Heracles, as did the family of Ptolemy; Julius Caesar and the Julii, through Aeneas, famously enjoyed a connection to the goddess Venus; the Seleucids claimed descent from Apollo. In *Kinship Diplomacy,* Jones provides a fascinating discussion of the generation, and diplomatic manipulation, of these various human-divine household groups.

³That gods were defeated when their humans were was an extension of the normal identification of peoples and pantheons: we hear echoes of this idea in those Christian apologies that insist on the high status of Israel's god despite the Jews' defeat by Rome. Speaking in the voice of a skeptical pagan, Christian author Minucius Felix wrote, "The lonely and miserable nationality of the Jews worshiped one god, peculiar to itself; and he has so little force or power that he is enslaved, with his own special nation, to the Roman gods" (*Oct.* 10.4 [*ANF*]; cf. Tertullian, *Apol.* 26.3; cf. 25.14–16, on other defeated, ethnic gods; Origen, *Cels.* 4.32; Faustus apud Augustine, *Faust.* 15.1). Jews were themselves no less traumatized by the theological implications of military defeat; see Adiel Schremer, "The Lord Has Forsaken the Land: Radical Explanations of the Military and Political Defeat of the Jews in Tannaitic Literature," *JJS* 59 (2008): 183–200.

⁴This paragraph draws on the fundamental study by James M. Scott, *Paul and the Nations:*

survival of Noah and his family, Gen 10 speaks of the renewal of humanity through Noah's three sons. The Table of Nations in this chapter traces out the descent of seventy "nations" (גוים/ἔθνη) "according to their lands, their languages, their families, and in their nations" (vv. 5, 20, 31). It is noteworthy that "gods" are conspicuously missing from this bundle of ethnic identifiers. At this point in the biblical narrative, other gods (אלהים) have yet to appear. In Deut 32:8–9, however, when Moses reprises this episode, he speaks of God's dividing humanity "according to the number of the gods" (NRSV).[5]

The relation of these lower gods to Israel's god is managed variously in biblical and extrabiblical antipagan polemics. Jubilees characterizes these superhuman beings as evil spirits who lead the nations astray; Wisdom of Solomon repeats invective against human-made representations of these beings, "idols." These antipagan polemics will not detain us here.[6] The chief point to note, rather, is that, in biblical imagination, this clustering of gods, lands, languages, and human descent groups indicates ethnic distinctions between "the nations." Altogether, their global total—the πλήρωμα τῶν ἐθνῶν, as Paul says (Rom 11:25)—is seventy nations.

Herodotus (fifth century BCE) offers a similar concept cluster when defining τὸ Ἑλληνικόν, the ethnicity of "Greekness." He lists shared blood (ὅμαιμον), a "family" and descent connection. Like the book of Genesis, he singles out language (ὁμόγλωσσον). The vertical silo of heaven/earth lines up around shared sanctuaries and sacrifices (θεῶν ἱδρύματα τε κοινὰ καὶ θυσίαι) and, governing these, the heritage of shared customs (ἤθεα ὁμότροπα; *Hist.* 8.144.2–3). Peoples are "ethnic," and so are their gods.[7]

The Old Testament and Jewish Background of Paul's Mission to the Nations with Special Reference to the Destination of Galatians, WUNT 84 (Tübingen: Mohr Siebeck, 1995).

[5] This verse has an intriguing textual backstory. The LXX gives "angels" as the divine appointees, ἀγγέλων θεοῦ echoing the בני אלהים ("sons of God") of 4QDeut^j, where the MT has בני ישראל ("sons of Israel"). In Jub. 15:31, these "ruling spirits" deceive the nations: they are descended from the watchers; cf. Jub. 10:2–9. See Paul Sanders, *The Provenance of Deuteronomy 32*, OtSt 37 (Leiden: Brill, 1996), 154–60; on the plurality of divinities in Jewish scriptural traditions, see further William Horbury, "Jewish and Christian Monotheism in the Herodian Age," in *Early Jewish and Christian Monotheism*, ed. Loren T. Stuckenbruck and Wendy E. S. North, Early Christianity in Context (London: T&T Clark, 2004), 16–44 (see esp. 20–21 for many primary references in Jewish sources to "gods").

[6] For a full consideration of the vocabulary and polemical logic of Jewish texts coping with categorizing these superhuman powers while concerned "to assert the incomparable power of the high God" of Israel, see Emma Wasserman, "'An Idol Is Nothing in the World' (1 Cor 8.4): The Metaphysical Contradictions of 1 Corinthians 8.1–11.1 in the Context of Jewish Idolatry Polemics," in *Portraits of Jesus: Studies in Christology*, ed. Susan E. Myers, WUNT 2/321 (Tübingen: Mohr Siebeck, 2012), 201–27; quotation from 227. On the related issue of "monotheism" and "henotheism," see also n. 16 below.

[7] The cross-identification of gods seems to run in a cultural systole/diastole with these constructions of divine ethnicity (so similarly Jones, *Kinship Diplomacy*, 65): the Roman Jupiter took on characteristics of the Greek Zeus, images of Minerva replicated aspects of Athena, and

My third example of ancient constructs of ethnicity comes from the apostle Paul, Rom 9:3–5. In this passage Paul lists the identifiers of *his* kinship group, Israel, his συγγενεῖς. To members of this descent group belong the "adoption of sons," υἱοθεσία. (Note that, in contrast to the ἔθνη, Israel's "sonship" is not contingent upon Christ's πνεῦμα.) This sonship establishes the family connection between heaven and earth: the god of Israel is also Israel's "father." To them is the δόξα, translated "glory" in the RSV and in the NRSV. This vague-sounding attribute refers both to heaven and to earth, that is, both to the glorious presence of Israel's god and to the place of that presence, Jerusalem, or, more specifically, the temple, his earthly dwelling place. To them are the covenants (διαθῆκαι) and the giving of the law (νομοθεσία) and the "worship." This last item, λατρεία, "cult," again indicates place—the altar of Jerusalem's temple—as well as the inherited or ancestral practices and traditions for enacting that cult (what Paul elsewhere calls αἱ πατρικαί μου παραδόσεις, Gal 1:14).

These distinctive privileges echo the shared blood, sanctuaries, sacrifices, and customs listed by Herodotus: both sets of protocols, pagan and Jewish, bind the human ethnic groups to one another (transtemporally across generations as well as contemporary within the current group) and to their god(s). In addition, in contrast to Genesis and Herodotus, Paul cannot use ὁμόγλωσσον, shared language, as a specific identifier for his people, who were broadly divided in his lifetime between Semitic languages (Hebrew and/or Aramaic) and Greek. But, as we will see, Paul does lift up ethnic language—God's no less than Israel's—in a very important connection as a family/ethnicity identifier. Finally, among Paul's kinfolk by family descent (κατὰ σάρκα) is God's eschatological champion, the Davidic messiah (cf. Rom 1:3, 15:12). I will return to these last two ideas, Χριστός and γλῶσσα, further on.

Regarding Jewish constructs of divine ethnicity, our second preliminary concern, did Jews think that the Jewish god was "Jewish"? That is to say, did they "ethnically identify" him with themselves—or, rather, did they think that *he* ethnically identified himself with them?[8] With them specifically as "family"? With Jewish "place," that is, the land of Israel or, specifically, Jerusalem, the Jews' *metropolis*? With Jewish ancestral practices? With Jewish "identity-markers," such as Shabbat or circumcision?

---

so on. But this homogenizing Hellenistic overlay could mask difference, too. The Semitic god בעל שמין, "Lord of Heaven," resided beneath his Olympian name ("Zeus"), and while Romans and Carthaginians contested over title to the favor of the divine Heracles, the Carthaginian deity was a hellenized expression of the Tyrian Melkart. See further Glen W. Bowersock, *Hellenism in Late Antiquity*, Jerome Lectures 18 (Ann Arbor: University of Michigan Press, 1990), 18–25; see also, specifically on the theological dimension of the Punic wars, Richard Miles, *Carthage Must Be Destroyed: The Rise and Fall of an Ancient Mediterranean Civilization* (New York: Viking, 2011).

[8] I use the masculine pronoun because, in the first century (and long thereafter), the Jewish god is gendered male.

Of course, the answer we get depends on which Jew we ask: Philo would probably nuance these questions differently from the ways that Paul would and does. As our quick survey of Rom 9:3–5 already hints, however, I think that the answer is yes. First, the Bible foregrounds the language of love/חשק/ἀγάπη that characterizes Israel's relationship: God "chooses" Israel because he "falls in love" with them.[9] Second, God sets them apart from all the other peoples of the earth by giving them his instruction (e.g., Lev 20:22–24). He reveals himself to them alone at Sinai, when he gives them the law. He specifically refers to himself as the "father" of Israel and speaks of them as his "son" (e.g., Exod 4:22). With the (almost) synchronous founding of two Jerusalem-based "houses," that of the Davidic dynasty and that of God on the Temple Mount, this father-god becomes in a special way the "father" of the anointed rulers of David's line as well (Pss 2:7, 89:26–27, 2 Sam 7:14). God may be everywhere, but his earthly dwelling place is the temple itself (see Pss 76:2, 84:1; cf. 1 Cor 3:16, Matt 23:21).

Finally, God himself keeps a premier Jewish practice. This idea, expanded upon in Jubilees, is present already in Jewish Scripture. According to Gen 2:2–3, God rested on the Sabbath, a privilege and a responsibility that he will share uniquely with his own people, Israel.[10] In Jubilees, we find out that God kept not only the first Shabbat: he continues to keep Shabbat weekly. How? And how does the world continue to do what it does, if one day out of seven God is not "working"? The angel reveals to Moses:

> He [God] gave us a great sign, the Sabbath day, so that we might work six days and observe a Sabbath from all work on the seventh day. And he told us—all the angels of the presence and all the angels of sanctification, these two great kinds [who are also circumcised! 15:27]—that we might keep the Sabbath with him in heaven and on earth. And he said to us, "Behold, I will separate for myself a people from among all the nations. And they will also keep the Sabbath. And I will sanctify them for myself, and I will bless them.… And they will be my people and I will be their god. And I have chosen the seed of Jacob from among all that I have seen. And I have recorded them as my firstborn son, and have sanctified him for myself forever and ever. And I will make known to them the Sabbath day." (Jub. 2:17–20; O. S. Wintermute, *OTP*)[11]

---

[9] "It was not because you were more numerous than any other people that the Lord set his heart on you and chose you—for you were the fewest of all peoples. It was because the Lord loved you" (Deut 7:7–8 NRSV). "Although heaven and the heaven of heavens belong to the Lord your God, the earth with all that is in it, yet the Lord set his heart in love on your ancestors alone and chose you, their descendants after them, out of all the peoples, as it is today. Circumcise, then, the foreskin of your heart" (10:14–16 NRSV).

[10] This question was debated in Second Temple Jewish circles: see A. J. Droge, "Sabbath Work/Sabbath Rest: Genesis, Thomas, John," *HR* 47 (2007): 112–41, here 128–34.

[11] See further James Kugel, "4Q369 'Prayer of Enosh' and Ancient Biblical Interpretation," *DSD* 5 (1998): 119–48, esp. 123–26.

Thinking socially, not theologically, for the moment: the Sabbath was one of the most visible and, together with circumcision, one of the most commented upon of Jewish practices in the diaspora. It distinguished Jews from other populations in their cities of residence. If heaven itself holds circumcised angels—who keep God company on Shabbat while lower angelic orders keep the world running to time— and if God himself, not only in Genesis but also evermore thereafter "rests" one day out of seven (with these circumcised angels for company), then God is "Jewish." If God spoke Hebrew when he revealed his will to his people, then God is "Jewish." If he is the father of the people Israel and of Israel's rulers, referring to each as his "son," then God is "Jewish." If, of all the places on the earth, his glorious presence dwells most particularly in Judea, within Jerusalem's temple, then God is "Jewish." And if, ultimately, at the end of time, all other humans *and* their gods will acknowledge him by conforming to two fundamental protocols of Jewish worship—that is to say, with no other gods and without images (see Exod 20:3–4, Deut 5:7–8)— while they gather together with a reunified Israel in Judea, on הר בית יהוה ("the mountain of the Lord's house," Isa 2:2–4), then God is "Jewish."

I mean of course that the god of Israel is "Jewish" in antiquity, by antiquity's criteria of ethnicity: land, language, kinship, and custom. What confuses this idea, or makes it seem complicated or paradoxical to us, is the biblical god's no less insistent claim to universality and to absolute, indeed to unique, divinity. We will turn to those ideas momentarily, when we consider ancient "monotheism." Let me close this segment of our preliminary considerations by noting quickly that many *pagans* were likewise convinced that the highest god was "Jewish."

This pagan conviction arose out of two ancient idiosyncrasies of Jewish religious culture: its aniconism and its cultic focus on Jerusalem. Pagans knew that Jerusalem's temple held no statue of the god. Josephus had publicized this fact; Tacitus and Dio Cassius both comment on it (*J.W.* 5.5.5 §219; Tacitus, *Hist.* 5.5.4; Dio, *Hist.* 37.17.2). This aniconism was, for the rest of the world, an odd thing liturgically, but it was extremely interpretable theologically (see, e.g., Philo, *Leg.* 3.36; *Decal.* 66–76). Pagan philosophical παιδεία ("culture") held that the highest god was not capable of representation, being radically transcendent, beyond body of any sort, "visible" to the mind alone. By worshiping their god without recourse to images, both in their main sanctuary in Jerusalem and throughout their communal spaces in the diaspora, Jews, in paying homage to their own god, paid homage to the highest god (so Tacitus, *Hist.* 5.5.4). Origen observed similarly: "The supreme god is called 'the god of the Hebrews' even by people alien to our faith" (*Cels.* 5.50).[12]

---

[12] Trans. Henry Chadwick, *Origen: Contra Celsum* (Cambridge: Cambridge University Press, 1980). The emperor Julian, himself a convert from orthodox Christianity to "classical" paganism, made the same identification. Informing Jewish subjects that he wished to rebuild the temple in Jerusalem, Julian pledged to "invest all my enthusiasm in restoring the temple of the Highest God [ὑψίστου θεοῦ]" (*Ep. et leg.* No. 134 [Bidez and Cumont]).

The Jews' cultic focus on Jerusalem reinforced this association of their god with pagan παιδεία's highest god. The nations of the world not only worshiped images; they sacrificed before them. Jewish prayer houses or synagogues or "schools," however, not only held no images: Jews made no blood offerings (at least in principle) outside of Jerusalem. This means that, well before the year 70 CE, Jews were the only conspicuously nonsacrificing population in the diaspora. *Mente sola*—Tacitus, again (*Hist.* 5.5.4)—they worshiped through prayer and the study of the law. This *absence* of an all-but-universal practice—making offerings before images—behaviorally and socially reinforced the Jews' claim that theirs was the highest god.[13]

But what, then, about all the other gods, the gods of the nations? How did Israel—and Israel's god—relate to them?

This question leads us to our third preliminary consideration: the ways that the LXX facilitated the expression of divine multiplicity. Our attachment to the idea and to the rhetoric of "monotheism" can make our appreciation of antiquity's god-congested universe more difficult than it need be. Ancient monotheism did not mean a belief that "only one god" existed. In antiquity, by our measure, monotheism was a species of polytheism. That is, while one god might reign supreme, at the metaphysical summit of superhuman powers, ancient people (whether pagans, Jews, or, eventually, Christians) knew that other divine powers ranged below. Ancient monotheism expressed the *architecture* of heaven, not its absolute population. As long as one god stood on top—"megatheism," one historian has suggested; not "monotheism"[14]—as many as needed or wanted could operate in the lower cosmic realms.

Where and how did Jews encounter the gods of the nations? In their cities of residence, certainly, and in dreams (think of Moschos son of Moschion[15]), and

---

[13] In other words, pagan philosophical criteria, interpreting these idiosyncratic Jewish traditions, ended up affirming the Jews' claims of theological superiority. The idea that high gods neither want nor need sacrifices but that lower gods do was originally pagan, hence Porphyry's reference to Theophrastus, *On Abstinence* 2.27.1–3.

[14] Pagan monotheism, both that of educated elites and that of patriotic city dwellers ("Great is Artemis of the Ephesians!" Acts 19:28), has recently been explored in two excellent scholarly anthologies: *Pagan Monotheism in Late Antiquity*, ed. Polymnia Athanassiadi and Michael Frede (Oxford: Clarendon, 1999); and *One God: Pagan Monotheism in the Roman Empire*, ed. Stephen Mitchell and Peter van Nuffelen (Cambridge: Cambridge University Press, 2010). In this last book, see esp. the essays by Christoph Markschies ("The Price of Monotheism: Some New Observations on a Current Debate about Late Antiquity," 100–111, conceptualizing the issue vis-à-vis the study of ancient religions), Angelos Chaniotis ("Megatheism: The Search for the Almighty God and the Competition of Cults," 112–40, on the ways that the claim εἷς θεὸς ἐν οὐρανῷ, "one god in heaven," asserted superiority, not singularity), and Nicole Belayche ("*Deus deum ... summorum maximus* [Apuleius]: Ritual Expressions of Distinction in the Divine World in the Imperial Period," 141–66, on divine hierarchy and plurality). Belayche observes that the Jews' high god functioned as "an ethnic god, as indeed he also was" (145).

[15] For discussion and the text of this inscription, wherein Moschos Ioudaios commemorates

whenever they beheld the night sky. (Our planets still answer to the names of these gods.) But first of all, foreign gods presented themselves in Jewish scriptures. אלהים (*ĕlōhîm*) as a plural are there associated with other nations: as Israel confronts these peoples, so Israel's god confronts their gods (e.g., Exod 12:12). Who are these other gods, and where do they come from? Eventually Jews will generate myths accounting for other divinities as errant angels, or as their offspring or as failed members of the heavenly court. Often in biblical narrative, however, the gods/ אלהים are just there.[16]

Once the אלהים became θεοί, new interpretative possibilities opened up. Greek enabled ways to distinguish between degrees of divinity, speaking of multiple gods while making clear the supreme divinity of the Jewish god. This distinction was not native to Hebrew, where, as we have seen, the plural form אלהים could indicate either the Jewish god himself or a multitude of other deities. Indeed, the LXX translators of Exod 22:28 took advantage precisely of the Hebrew word's ambiguity when they rendered the older text's "Do not revile God [אלהים]" as "Do not revile the god*s* [τοὺς θεούς]."[17]

Extremely usefully, also, the LXX acquired δαιμόνια, "demons." These beings, like the structure of the Hellenistic cosmos itself, articulated divinity along a gradient, as a category spanning heaven and earth. Δαίμων in Greek originally had no negative connotation in the way that the English *demon* now does: the word simply indicated "a lower god." "Lower" within Greek philosophical-scientific discourse meant, literally, spatially "lower": below the divine intelligences embodied in stars and planets,[18] closer to earth, which stood in the center of antiquity's map of the universe.[19]

---

his obedience to the prompting of two pagan gods, see Emil Schürer, *A History of the Jewish People in the Age of Jesus Christ (175 B.C.–A.D. 135)*, rev. and ed. Geza Vermes and Fergus Millar, 3 vols. (Edinburgh: T&T Clark, 1973-1987), 3:65.

[16] See further Michael S. Heiser, "Monotheism, Polytheism, Monolatry, or Henotheism? Toward an Assessment of Divine Plurality in the Hebrew Bible," *BBR* 18 (2008): 1-30. Some biblical passages, for example, Isa 44:9-20 or Jer 10:1-16, can and eventually will be interpreted as "monotheist," but the burden of these polemics is to mock the powerlessness of idols. Idols are representations, not the superhuman powers themselves.

[17] On the LXX rendering of Exod 22:28(27) and its "liberal" interpretation by Philo and by Josephus, see Peter W. van der Horst, "Thou Shalt Not Revile the Gods," *SPhiloA* 5 (1993): 1-8.

[18] Philo deftly captures this nexus of ideas in his commentary on Genesis. The firmament, Philo said there, is "the most holy dwelling place of the manifest and visible gods [θεῶν ἐμφανῶν τε καὶ αἰσθητῶν]" (*Opif.* 7.27): manifest and visible gods are "lower" than, thus subordinate to, the highest god, who was invisible.

[19] Pagan δαίμονες could be either good or evil; see Henry Chadwick, "Oracles of the End in the Conflict of Paganism and Christianity in the 4th Century," in *Mémorial André-Jean Festugière: Antiquité païenne et chrétienne; Vingt-cinq études*, ed. Enzo Lucchesi and H. D. Saffrey, Cahiers d'orientalisme 10 (Geneva: Cramer, 1984), 125-29, on Plutarch and Porphyry; James Rives, "Human Sacrifice among Pagans and Christians," *JRS* 85 (1995): 65-85, esp. 80-83; Maijastina Kahlos, *Debate and Dialogue: Christian and Pagan Cultures, c. 360-430*, Ashgate New Critical

This Greek idea of a gradient of divine power cohered with and facilitated Hellenistic Jewish theologies. "The אלהים of the גוים are idols," the psalmist had sung in Hebrew (Ps 96:5). "The θεοί of the ἔθνη are δαιμόνια," however, is the way that his words were sounded in Greek: "the [lower] gods of the nations are demons" (Ps 95:5 LXX; cf. 1 Cor 10:20). This translation (or reinterpretation) of "idols" as "demons" held theological significance. Idols (as Jewish texts tirelessly taught) were human-made representations of powers: "they have eyes that cannot see; they have ears that cannot hear" (Pss 115:5–6, 135:16–17, and frequently elsewhere). A demon, however, is not an image of a supernatural power but the power itself, the (lower) divinity. *Any* human can destroy an idol; *no* human can destroy a god. This Jewish translation of Ps 95 (96), then, at once both elevated and demoted the Greek gods, granting that they were more than mere idols while placing them, qua δαιμόνια, in positions subordinate to the Jewish god on Hellenism's own cosmic map. To paraphrase Augustine, the difference between Jews and pagans was that Jews called gods "demons," while pagans called demons "gods" (*Civ.* 9.23).

To sum up, before turning specifically to Paul: (1) In antiquity, cult is an ethnic designation, and ethnicity is a cult designation. Put otherwise, gods and humans form family groups. Divine-human "family" by definition spans heaven and earth. In this way, gods share in the ethnicity of the peoples who worship them. (2) Just as other ancient people have a family relationship with their divinities, so do ancient Jews with theirs. They are his people, Israel; he, their god and father, shares many of their ethnic identifiers (land, language, locality, family connection, and custom, namely, the Sabbath, not to mention the circumcised angels). The Jews' god is "Jewish." (3) For all ancient people, all gods exist. Jewish "monotheists," however, also conceived of their own god as supreme, a point that some pagans willingly conceded. But Jews also and uniquely made the claim—especially in apocalyptic inflections of their tradition—that their god represented the religious destiny of all humankind. Not only would all other gods "bow down" to Israel's god (Ps 97:7); so too would all humanity. Or, as Paul says in Romans, "Is God the god of the Jews

---

Thinking in Religion, Theology, and Biblical Studies (Aldershot: Ashgate, 2007), 172–81. Origen, evidently annoyed by the pagan Celsus's conflation of lower gods, angels ("messengers"), and demons, enunciates clearly this difference between pagan and septuagintal, thus Christian, views: "Celsus fails to notice that the name of daemons is not morally neutral like that of men, among whom some are good and some are bad; nor is it good like the name of gods, which is not to be applied to evil daemons.... The name of daemons is always applied to *evil* powers ... they lead men astray and distract them, and drag them down" (*Cels.* 5.5).

Some Hellenistic Jews, such as the author of Wisdom and, eventually, the apostle Paul, took δαιμόνια as exclusively evil, bound up as they were with the cultic worship of images. We find this same view in later Christian writers, for example, Justin; see Annette Yoshiko Reed, "The Trickery of the Fallen Angels and the Demonic Mimesis of the Divine: Aetiology, Demonology, and Polemics in the Writings of Justin Martyr," *JECS* 12 (2004): 141–71. On the particular link between (malevolent) demons (qua pagan gods) and blood sacrifices, see Justin, *2 Apol.* 5; *Dial.* 19, 22, 43 (there aimed against Jewish sacrifice), and frequently.

only? Is he not also the god of the ἔθνη?" (3:29). In other words, even the universality of (eschatological) worship does not dilute this god's ethnic specificity.

In speaking in these ways, Paul thinks "ethnically." His world divides up between two human groups, Israel κατὰ σάρκα, his συγγενεῖς, and "everybody else," "the nations," or, as he calls them otherwise, "the foreskin" (ἀκροβυστία). He shares this sharp "us/them" dichotomizing with his great scriptural source, Isaiah, I think for the same reason: whether for Isaiah or for Paul, *the more intense the pitch of apocalyptic expectation, the greater the contrast between Israel and the nations*.[20] The *narrative* function of the nations in these traditions is precisely to represent *not*-Israel, all those other nations who have not known God and who do not know God. Eschatological redemption emphasizes and intensifies this high contrast between Israel (knowing God) and everyone else (not knowing God until the end-time). The sharp us/them distinction, to phrase this slightly differently, is drawn on *theological* lines, and, therefore, it articulates ethnic lines as well. Consider Isa 66:18–20, which echoes Gen 10:

> I am coming to gather all the nations and tongues, and they will come and see my glory.... From them I will send survivors to the nations ... to the distant islands that have neither heard my fame nor seen my glory. And they shall declare my glory among the nations. And they shall bring all your brothers from all the nations as an offering to the Lord ... to my holy mountain, Jerusalem, says YHWH.

God's Jewish ethnicity, even eschatologically, remains constant. This divine ethnicity, refracted through the lens of prophetic eschatology, reveals and highlights three interconnected ideas: first, that Israel alone has "known" God; second, that the other nations have not known God; and, third, that at the end-time, these nations, too, will know God, and they, too, will worship him in Jerusalem, on the Temple Mount. Despite its insistence on God's ethnicity, in other words, Jewish tradition presses this larger claim peculiar to its religious culture: Israel's god is *also* and ultimately the god of all other ethnic groups as well. He is the nations' god qua Jewish god who dwells in Jerusalem. But the nations (and their gods) by and large will know this only at the end-time. Seen in this light, the establishment of his kingdom is quite literally the Jewish god's ultimate act of cross-ethnic outreach.

The ethnic-theological difference between Israel and the nations, the nations' ignorance of the true god, is what binds all of these other ἔθνη together into one

---

[20] For an analysis of Paul's ethnic reasoning as a point in the development of the rabbinic concept of "the goy" as an individual non-Jew, see two recent articles by Ishay Rosen-Zvi and Adi Ophir, "Goy: Toward a Genealogy," *Diné Israel* 28 (2011): 69–112; and "Paul and the Invention of the Gentiles," *JQR* 105 (2015): 1–41. On ethnic reasoning as constitutive of later forms of gentile Christianity, see Denise Kimber Buell, *Why This New Race? Ethnic Reasoning in Early Christianity* (New York: Columbia University Press, 2005). On the way that Isaiah undergirds Paul's thought, especially in Romans, see J. Ross Wagner, *Heralds of the Good News: Isaiah and Paul "in Concert" in the Letter to the Romans*, NovTSup 101 (Leiden: Brill, 2002).

undifferentiated mass of lumpen idolators. In the end, for Isaiah as for Paul, this sharp dichotomy is resolved *theologically* but <u>not</u> *ethnically*: Israel remains Israel (ὁ λαός), the nations remain the nations (τὰ ἔθνη; cf. Deut 32:43 LXX, Rom 15:10). Paul, convinced that he was living in the very last days, and convinced no less of the importance of his own role in bringing the ἔθνη to the worship of the god of Israel, emphasizes and dichotomizes this ethnic difference even more than does Isaiah.

But Paul's circumstances are also different from those of his great scriptural source. His mission (and those of others, such as whoever first established the community at Rome) had generated "eschatological gentiles"—ἔθνη who *do* know God and who, *as* ἔθνη, worship him alone—in advance of the apocalyptic end-time. (Their existence, combined with his vision of the risen, thus soon-returning Christ, indeed supported Paul's conviction that he lived and worked at the very edge of the end-time: 1 Thess 4:15–18; Phil 4:5; 1 Cor 7:29; 10:11; 15:51–52; 2 Cor 6:2; Rom 13:11–12; 16:20, 25.) Paul's discourse of ethnic dichotomizing accordingly left him with a conundrum: he, like us, has no good term for the ἐκκλησία's non-Jewish ex-idol-worshipers. They are *not* "converts"/προσήλυτοι: the only thing for these pagans to "convert" to in the mid-first century was Judaism, an idea that Paul heatedly rejects. Yet they are not "godfearers"—at least, fumes Paul, they had better not be!—affiliated with Jewish communities and yet still involved with their own gods as well.[21] Nor are they "Christians"—a term, and arguably a concept, that had yet

---

[21] Confusion still characterizes scholarly references to "godfearers." These gentiles were not "halfway" converts, nor were they "monotheists" (especially not in the modern, anachronistic sense of that term), nor had they "renounced idolatry." They were voluntarily Judaizers, non-Jews who assumed some interest (in varying degrees) in Jewish practices, active pagans who added the god of Israel (to some extent or other) into their native pantheons. For a review of the inscriptional evidence, see Irina Levinskaya, *The Book of Acts in Its Diaspora Setting*, BAFCS 5 (Grand Rapids: Eerdmans, 1996), 51–82; for a discussion emphasizing such persons' continuing "paganism," see Paula Fredriksen, "If It *Looks* Like a Duck, and It *Quacks* Like a Duck…: On *Not* Giving Up the Godfearers," in *A Most Reliable Witness: Essays in Honor of Ross Shepard Kraemer*, ed. Susan Ashbrook Harvey et al., BJS 358 (Providence, RI: Brown Judaic Series, 2016), 25–34.

Did eating meat sacrificed to lower gods mean that Paul's ex-pagan pagans were somehow still involved in idol worship (1 Cor 8 and 10)? Paul evidently thought not, unless presence at public cultic events were involved. At private dinners, questions about the status of things served was subordinate to community concerns (i.e., not partaking if doing so risked scandalizing another member of the ἐκκλησία, 10:28–29). For all we know (and as E. P. Sanders long ago pointed out), such instruction might very well represent a diaspora *Jewish* standard of behavior: the status of foodstuffs in mixed company would have been an issue for those Jewish communities well before the creation of Christ-following ones. See Sanders, *Jewish Law from Jesus to the Mishnah: Five Studies* (Philadelphia: Trinity Press International, 1990), 281. For Paul on the issue (or, for him, the nonissue) of the imperial cult, see now John M. G. Barclay, "Why the Roman Empire Was Insignificant to Paul," in *Pauline Churches and Diaspora Jews* (Grand Rapids: Eerdmans, 2016), 363–87.

to be invented.²² So what word appropriately names these people? Paul stumbles around: they are ex-pagans/ex-gentiles ("When you were ἔθνη," 1 Cor 12:2; cf. 10:1), and yet they are still pagans/still gentiles ("Now I am speaking to you ἔθνη," Rom 11:13). Sometimes he calls them ἅγιοι, "holy" or "separated-out" ones; at other times, ἀδελφοί, brothers (we will soon look at both sets of associations closely). But if we take the last chapters of Romans as in some sense Paul's final word, ἔθνη remains his term of choice (15:8–12, 16–18, 27; 16:4 [the ἐκκλησίαι τῶν ἐθνῶν], 26).²³

II. Cosmic Redemption and Gentile Adoption

The normal and normative ethnic embeddedness of divinity in the ancient Mediterranean, where gods and peoples form family groups, meant that Paul

---

²² On the anachronism of the term "Christian" for this first generation of the movement, see esp. William Arnal, "The Collection and Synthesis of 'Tradition' and the Second-Century Invention of Christianity," *MTSR* 23 (2011): 193–215; Anders Runesson, "Inventing Christian Identity: Paul, Ignatius, and Theodosius I," in *Exploring Early Christian Identity*, ed. Bengt Holmberg, WUNT 226 (Tübingen: Mohr Siebeck, 2008), 59–92, further developed in "The Question of Terminology: The Architecture of Contemporary Discussions of Paul," in *Paul within Judaism: Restoring the First-Century Context to the Apostle*, ed. Mark D. Nanos and Magnus Zetterholm (Minneapolis: Fortress, 2015), 53–78; John Marshall, "Misunderstanding the New Paul: Marcion's Transformation of the *Sonderzeit* Paul," *JECS* 20 (2012): 1–29. Marshall notes, "Using a category of 'Christianity' is fundamentally erroneous when interpreting Paul. It exercises transformative influence on his writings in the same way the [later] pseudepigraphical Pastoral epistles do.... By reading Paul's writings as instances of 'Christianity,' the new, but later, religion is already retrojected onto the letters, the force of Paul's eschatological conviction is blunted, and the specificity of his address to Gentiles is effaced. These effects of the term 'Christianity' are largely distorting in the way it takes over and transforms, Christianizes, or simply eradicates Paul's conviction at Rom 11.26 that 'all Israel' would be saved" (6).

²³ Joshua Garroway proposes "Gentile-Jews" as Paul's term for these people: given their hybrid ethnoreligious status—gentiles whose πίστις ("trustfulness" or "faithfulness") toward the god of Israel's messiah has grafted them into Israel (cf. Rom 11:17–24)—the hyphenated term, he argues, is apt. But Paul's metaphor of the olive tree does not overcome, to my mind, the distinction between Israel and the ἔθνη that he insists on even as he hymns their common redemption at the letter's end, 15:9–12. Through Abraham/Christ, these gentiles do indeed become God's adopted children (Gal 4). But Jews are Jews "by nature" (φύσει, Gal 2:15), through being of the same γένος as the patriarchs, blood descendants of Abraham, Isaac, and Jacob (Rom 9:4–5). These two groups, Jews and "everybody else," are to be eschatologically conjoined, but they nevertheless remain distinct: Jews belong in the olive tree κατὰ φύσιν, "naturally"; non-Jews are grafted into the tree παρὰ φύσιν, "against nature" (Rom 11:24). See Garroway, *Paul's Gentile-Jews: Neither Jew nor Gentile, but Both* (New York: Palgrave Macmillan, 2012). On the eschatological preservation of ethnic distinction, the fundamental study is Caroline Johnson Hodge, *If Sons, Then Heirs: A Study of Kinship and Ethnicity in the Letters of Paul* (New York: Oxford University Press, 2007). On Gal 6:16 referring not to the ἐκκλησία but to ethnic Israel, see 208 n. 28 below.

affirmed a paradox. The nations who in Christ turn from their own gods are to worship Israel's god *in Jewish ways:* no other gods and no images. In this sense, his gentiles "Judaize"; that is, they as non-Jews assume some (singularly) Jewish practices. But nonetheless—and Paul is absolutely adamant on this point—these ex-pagan pagans are still *not*-Israel. What, then, is their relationship with Israel and, thus, with Israel's god? How, in Christ, is this relationship established? Paul's answer: by ἁγιασμός and by υἱοθεσία. Both are the accomplishment of holy *pneuma*.

Ἁγιασμός mobilizes the language of temple imagery and of the sacrificial protocols of Leviticus.[24] Paul's gentiles, he says, are ἅγιοι in the Levitical sense of separated-out (קודש). From what? From the "common" (חול), that is, from those gentiles who do *not* know God (1 Thess 4:4–5). Paul's gentiles, as ἅγιοι, are fit for intimate contact with the divine. They proleptically experience this new closeness both through the in-dwelling of divine spirit and through the "sacrifice" of the bread and wine (1 Cor 10:14–18, explicitly likening community participation in the Lord's table to sacrifices in the Jerusalem temple). In their support of Paul's mission, they metaphorically stand by Israel's altar, making "a fragrant offering, a sacrifice acceptable and pleasing to God" (Phil 4:18; cf. 2 Cor 2:15—the community is itself the "sweet smell" of the sacrifice of Christ). This temple imagery does not substitute for, supersede, or displace Jerusalem's temple, in my view; rather, it resonates with and reaffirms it. If Paul did not value the sanctity, dignity, and probity of the Jerusalem cult, he would not have named it in Rom 9, nor would he have used it as a touchstone for gentile community identity here.

Υἱοθεσία mobilizes the language of lineage, kinship, and inheritance: through reception of Christ's spirit, or of God's, gentiles become ἀδελφοί, "brothers." Eschatological fraternity—one of Paul's most brilliant improvisations—is a very rich, original, and complex concept. Paul's ideas on gentile "adoption" in (and into) Christ reveal his thought at one and the same time at its most *Roman*, at its most traditionally *Jewish*, and at its most *ancient*.

Roman legal culture had long availed itself of this form of fictive kinship—sons not begotten but made—as a way to settle and to stabilize the next generation of "family" both for issues of property/inheritance and for issues of ancestry/continuation of patrilineal cult.[25] The new son was thereafter responsible to and for his

---

[24] Paula Fredriksen, "Judaizing the Nations: The Ritual Demands of Paul's Gospel," *NTS* 56 (2010): 232–52, here 244–49.

[25] Michael Peppard (*The Son of God in the Roman World: Divine Sonship in Its Social and Political Context* [New York: Oxford University Press, 2011], 50–60) quotes Cicero (202 n. 7) that the laws of adoption concern "the inheritance of the name and of the property and of the sacred rites of the family" (*Dom.* 35). On the Roman legal and cultural context of adoption, see further Suzanne Dickson, *The Roman Family*, ASH (Baltimore: Johns Hopkins University Press, 1992); Jane F. Gardner, *Family and* Familia *in Roman Law and Life* (Oxford: Clarendon, 1998); Christiane Kunst, *Römische Adoption: Zur Strategie einer Familienorganisation*, Frankfurter althistorische Beiträge 10 (Hennef: Clauss, 2005). James M. Scott assembles a tremendous amount of material, both Greco-Roman and scriptural, around issues internal to Paul's letters (*Adoption as Sons of*

"new" paternal ancestors and to and for the *genius* of his new father and family (*gens*). In Paul's reuse of this idea of adoption, it is immersion and conferral of spirit (variously the spirit of God, or of Christ, or simply "holy spirit") that binds the Christ-following gentiles into a new family, so that they, too, can inherit.

Especially in Gal 3-4, arguing against apostolic competitors who want male Christ followers to be circumcised, Paul stresses that this sonship, υἱοθεσία, comes only through spirit (thus πίστις, faithfulness to or confidence in the good news, Gal 3:2-5), not through flesh (the site of circumcision; thus, through Jewish law). Spirit binds the believer in and to Abraham's seed (σπέρμα), Christ, bringing the gentile into a new family as a son and, thus, as an heir (4:7; cf. 3:26, 29). The ex-pagan gentile thereby becomes a "son of Abraham" apart from the law, apart from the flesh, so that he, too, can inherit the promised redemption (3:6-9). The spirit of Christ, God's son, indeed, binds the entire community of Christ followers together (4:6), so that there is "neither Jew nor Greek, neither slave nor free, neither male and female: you are all one in Christ Jesus" (3:28).

"All one," a single family, but exclusively according to "the spirit of his [God's] son" (Gal 4:6). Κατὰ σάρκα, "according to flesh," however, these people still retain their ethnic and social differences, which Paul elsewhere emphatically asserts and which the lack of circumcision, for gentile male Christ followers, evinces and even reinscribes. Redeemed gentiles rejoice *with* Israel but do not "join" Israel or "become" Israel (Rom 15:7-12). Runaway slaves return to their owners (Philemon).[26] Corinthian women submit to the authority of their husbands (1 Cor 11:3-16). United in and by spirit, Jewish and gentile Christ followers together await Christ's return and the cascade of final events (surveyed in 1 Thess 4, 1 Cor 15, Phil 2, and Rom 8-16). Κατὰ σάρκα, however, these siblings remain distinct, as indeed is the case with all human adoption.

Here Paul's allegiances to his συγγενεῖς, Israelites κατὰ σάρκα, are unambiguous and, therefore, transparent upon biblical paradigms (cf. Rom 9:4-5). Abraham in these final days may have become the father of "many nations" through the spirit of his σπέρμα, the Christ, but Israelites themselves have many "fathers"—Abraham, Isaac, Jacob, the twelve patriarchs of the eponymous tribes. To them God has made many promises (15:8; cf. 9:4, 11:29).[27] It was precisely to fulfill those promises that

---

God: An Exegetical Investigation into the Background of υἱοθεσία *in the Pauline Corpus*, WUNT 2/48 [Tübingen: Mohr Siebeck, 1992]), though he emphasizes biblical aspects of Paul's idea of adoption more than the Roman.

[26] On Philemon as a letter that "did not so much proclaim Messiah Jesus as discuss a private business transaction about a slave," see J. Albert Harrill, *Paul the Apostle: His Life and Legacy in Their Roman Context* (Cambridge: Cambridge University Press, 2012), 18.

[27] On this distinction between "the promise to Abraham" (in the singular) that benefits gentiles and the irrevocable "many promises" to Israel, Stanley K. Stowers notes, "For Israel, there were many promises, not one. Because Romans is about gentiles, the promises peculiar to Jews bear only a mention [i.e., in 9:4 and 15:8].... In 15.8, Paul speaks of the fathers (plural), who include Jacob, Joseph, Moses, and many others who are not fathers of the gentiles in the same way

Christ came as a servant to his own blood kinsmen ("the circumcision," 15:8; cf. 1:3, 9:6). The salvation of all Israel—ethnic, genealogical, fleshly Israel—is, indeed, the gospel's goal (Rom 11:25–26), "for the gifts and the promises of God are irrevocable" (11:29). Πᾶς Ἰσραήλ—*all* Israel, all twelve tribes (11:26; itself, of course, an eschatological concept)—are the "natural" heirs to their god's kingdom.

These distinctions bear emphasizing, because many readers often think that Paul speaks of an undifferentiated humankind united "in Christ." "Israel" in these interpretations changes from the real (or realistically imagined) historical kinship community that Paul describes in Rom 9:4–5 to a metaphor for the church, "spiritual" Israel, "the Israel of God" (Gal 6:16).[28] Paul's much-touted proclamation of oneness in Christ, Gal 3:28, trumps all those many other places where Paul speaks of communities striated by significant internal distinctions: apostles, prophets, interpreters, healers (1 Cor 12:7–26, Rom 12:4–8); male and female (1 Cor 11:5–16; cf. 14:34–36); Jew and Greek (Rom 2:9, 11); Israel and the nations (Rom 11:25–26, 15:9–12).

Paul's kinship language, however, does indeed put his different *gentiles* all on the same basis: they are siblings together with and through Christ, who is "the firstborn of many ἀδελφοί" (Rom 8:29). But within this family unity, Paul nonetheless asserts his own people's singular, enduring identity. Ethnic Israelites, quite apart from Christ, already have υἱοθεσία (Rom 9:4; cf. Exod 4:22, "Israel is my firstborn son"); they are already in a family relationship with Christ (Rom 9:5, Christ is from Israel κατὰ σάρκα); and the ἔθνη—the redeemed nations—rejoice *with* God's λαός, his people Israel (Rom 11:1; 15:10; Deut 32:43).

In his reconfiguring gentile lineage via Abraham through υἱοθεσία, adoption, Paul is at his most innovatively Roman: gentiles-in-Christ now count as sons, thus heirs. They are now responsible to the patrilineal cult of their new adoptive family, and they can, together with Israel, inherit God's kingdom. And, in his adherence to the biblical paradigm, wherein God through the giving of his law has separated Israel out for himself, wherein Israel remains Israel even (as in Isaiah) at the endtime, Paul is at his most traditionally, most recognizably Jewish.

But in its eschatologically inspired "cross-ethnic" outreach, whereby some gentiles before the parousia—and, at the very end, all seventy nations (their πλήρωμα,

---

as Abraham. Only Abraham received the promise that in his seed the gentiles would be blessed. This promise does not lessen the significance of the other fathers for the Jews (9.5)" (*A Rereading of Romans: Justice, Jews, and Gentiles* [New Haven: Yale University Press, 1994], 133).

[28] Galatians 6:16 ("Peace and mercy be upon all who walk by this rule, and on the Israel of God"/ καὶ ὅσοι τῷ κανόνι τούτῳ στοιχήσουσιν, εἰρήνη ἐπ' αὐτοὺς καὶ ἔλεος, καὶ ἐπὶ τὸν Ἰσραὴλ τοῦ θεοῦ) has long been read by many (though not by all) commentators as indicating the Christian church rather than ethnic Israel. Against such a construal, most recently, see Susan Grove Eastman, "Israel and the Mercy of God: A Re-reading of Galatians 6.16 and Romans 9–11," *NTS* 56 (2010): 367–95; see too Krister Stendahl, *Final Account: Paul's Letter to the Romans* (Minneapolis: Fortress, 1995), 5, 40.

"fullness" or "full number," Rom 11:25)—turn to worship Israel's god, Paul's adoption model ultimately coheres with the broader, ancient, pan-Mediterranean construction of divine–human relations: *gods and their humans form family groups*. Thus, despite their new Abrahamic lineage, the "father" who ultimately counts for these gentiles is *not* Abraham. It is God (cf. Gal 3:26). *God*, not Abraham, is whom these gentiles—like their older brother Jesus and like ethnic Israel—can now call "Father" (Gal 4:7, Rom 8:15).[29] Note, too, the significance of the divine appellative whereby gentiles-in-Christ address the Jewish god by his "Jewish" family name, in the "native" γλῶσσα of the Jewish family tongue. God's new sons call him Ἀββά (Gal 4:6, Rom 8:15).

III. Ethnicities, Divinities, and History

How does this argument about the ethnicity of ancient gods, and specifically about the Jewishness of Paul's god, interact with current scholarly conversations about ethnicity in antiquity, about ancient "monotheism," and about the post–New Perspective Paul?

"Ethnicity" in antiquity, as I hope I have demonstrated, is, like "divinity," a category that bridges heaven and earth. The language of divine–human parenting, of deities' special (sometimes "biological") connection to human groups, of their role in revealing what become "ancestral customs" tells us something important about ancient conceptualizations of divinity and of (steeply hierarchical) family. Ancient gods, local in two senses, attached both to places and, quite literally, to peoples.[30] Kinship diplomacy would have been impossible had these attachments been constructed and imagined in any way other than "realistically." When we

---

[29] For this reason, I am persuaded by Richard Hays on the question of how to translate Rom 4:1: Τί οὖν ἐροῦμεν εὑρηκέναι Ἀβραὰμ τὸν προπάτορα ἡμῶν κατὰ σάρκα; The RSV translates: "What then should we say about Abraham, our forefather according to the flesh?" But Paul addresses *gentiles* in the assembly at Rome (1:5–6), and the whole point of "adoption" through Abraham is that the gentiles do *not* have a connection κατὰ σάρκα: if they did, they would not be candidates for "adoption" (Rom 8:23, made sons through spirit; 8:14; cf. Gal 4:5–7). Hays proposes instead: "What then shall we say? Have we found Abraham [to be] our forefather according to the flesh?" (*The Conversion of the Imagination: Paul as Interpreter of Israel's Scripture* [Grand Rapids: Eerdmans, 2005], 61–84). For a counterargument, see John M. G. Barclay, *Paul and the Gift* (Grand Rapids: Eerdmans, 2015), 483 n. 88.

For Romans as addressed explicitly and solely to gentile Christ followers, see Stowers, *Rereading of Romans*; Runar M. Thorsteinsson, *Paul's Interlocutor in Romans 2: Function and Identity in the Context of Ancient Epistolography*, ConBNT 40 (Stockholm: Almqvist & Wiksell, 2003); and the essays recently assembled in *The So-Called Jew in Paul's Letter to the Romans*, ed. Rafael Rodríguez and Matthew Thiessen (Minneapolis: Fortress, 2016).

[30] On mapping and ethnicity in antiquity, see esp. Laura Salah Nasrallah, *Christian Responses to Roman Art and Architecture: The Second-Century Church amid the Spaces of Empire* (Cambridge:

think "ethnicity," we need to see how gods function as active members—indeed, as the supreme member(s)—of human kinship groups.

Why is this so hard for us to see? For two reasons, I think, and they are related. First, in our own historical context, "ethnicity" is a category of anthropology, not of theology. Thus, when we peer at our ancient people groups with their ethnicities in mind, we too often stand with our backs to their sky. We fail to see how *they* saw their gods: as active and involved social agents and as senior family members, easily angered by human failures to show *pietas*, correct deference.[31]

The second reason why divine ethnicity—specifically, the ethnicity of Paul's god—is hard for us to see has to do with our habitual ways of conceiving of "God." The formative development of Christian (thus, Western) theological thinking occurred in the second century, through appeal to the categories of Middle Platonism. It was during the second century that the Jewish god qua high god underwent a double identity crisis. Gentile Christian theologians—Valentinus, Marcion, Justin—all insisted (as had Paul) that the high god was the father of Christ. But they insisted with equal vehemence (and very *un*like Paul) that the high god was not to be identified with the active deity of Jewish scriptures. That Jewish god was demoted to a demiurgic status, whether as a middling deity poised between the high god and Satan (Ptolemy, *Letter to Flora* apud Epiphanius, *Pan.* 33.7.1–6) or as the moral opposite of the high god and, in some sense, his opponent (Tertullian, *Marc.* 1 passim), or as a ἕτερος θεός ("another god"), the pre-incarnate Son (Justin, *Dial.* 56). The high god formerly of Jewish tradition, meanwhile, assumed the radical transcendence and ethnic featurelessness of the high god of philosophical παιδεία.[32] In short, for gentile Christian theologians in the course of the second century, God the Father lost his Jewish identity. It is hard to think back through twenty centuries to the time—Paul's time—when for Jews the one god of all was the one god of all

---

Cambridge University Press, 2010), 51–84; also Scott, *Paul and the Nations*, correlating biblical lands and peoples.

[31] In so doing, we miss an obvious explanation for Paul's "persecutions," both giving and getting; see Martin Goodman, "The Persecution of Paul by Diaspora Jews," in *The Beginnings of Christianity: A Collection of Articles*, edited by Jack Pastor and Menachem Mor (Jerusalem: Yad Ben-Zvi, 2005), 179–87; Paula Fredriksen, "Why Should a 'Law-Free' Mission Mean a 'Law-Free' Apostle?," *JBL* 134 (2015): 637–50, here 644, 648–49, https://doi.org/10.15699/jbl.1343.2015.2974; Fredriksen, *Paul: The Pagans' Apostle*, 77–93.

[32] "The nature of the Ungenerated Father of All is incorruption and self-existent," explained Valentinus's disciple Ptolemy, "simple, and homogeneous light" (*Letter to Flora* apud Epiphanius, *Pan.* 33.7.7 [*ANF*]). This god, insisted Marcion, the *summum bonum et optimus* (Tertullian, *Marc.* 1.24.7; 1.27.2; 2.11.3), was pure benignity (1.2.3), absolutely good (1.26.2)—and, before the revelation of Christ, utterly unknown. God "abides eternally above the heavens, invisible, holding personal intercourse with none … the Father of All," taught Justin (*Dial.* 56). Unbegotten and without passion, this god was also without form, unchanging, unnamed (*1 Apol.* 9.1; 10.1; 13.4; 25.2).

quite specifically *because* he was the god of Deuteronomy, Numbers, Leviticus, Exodus, and Genesis.

But the "one" god was never the "only" god, not even in his own book. Paul knew this. Therefore, calling Paul—or any ancient person, pagan, Jew, or Christian—a "monotheist" only confuses this issue.[33] In none of these systems was the high god solitary. Within specifically Jewish thought, God's "oneness" did not prevent him from fathering other supernatural beings, his "sons" (בני אלהים), some of whom, according to various Second Temple traditions, went on to have careers as the gods of the nations.[34] For Paul, these other gods provided the cosmic forces that the returning Christ, at his parousia, would subdue (e.g., 1 Cor 15:24–28, Phil 2:9–11). How can the label "monotheism" help us to describe and to understand this god-filled universe? Rather than constantly qualifying the term ("ancient monotheism," "polytheistic monotheism," "messy monotheism"), we should just retire it.[35]

Finally, how does—or should—the Jewish ethnicity of Paul's god complicate current Pauline scholarship? New Perspective scholars used Sanders's *Paul and Palestinian Judaism* as a springboard into the argument that Paul did not repudiate Judaism per se, just its "ethnic identity markers": circumcision, Sabbath, kashrut, and so on.[36] Needless to say—but I will say it anyway—this is tantamount to the Old Perspective, which holds that Paul (the universalist Christian) had indeed renounced (ethnically particular) Judaism. Different versions of this last view have very recently been championed yet again.[37] But if Paul's god himself remained "Jewish," how does it make sense to conceptualize Paul's gospel as a principled renunciation of Jewishness?

Further to the point: thinking with this ancient idea of divine ethnicity—and specifically with the idea of Paul's god's ethnicity—entails recognizing how much of Paul's message to gentiles was ethnically specific as well. His gospel promoted Israel's god in Jewish ways: no more λατρεία to lower gods and no worshiping of images. Its origins lay in Paul's experience of the resurrection of the messiah:

---

[33] Pagan "monotheism," like its Jewish and Christian inflections, attests to heaven's hierarchical organization, not to its absolute population. In philosophical perspective, the highest god was solely self-existent, the lower gods contingent in some sense upon him (or "it"). Christian "monotheists," adopting septuagintal usage, called these other gods δαιμόνια: rebellious divine subordinates but subordinates nonetheless. Much after this period, later christological and Trinitarian orthodox theologies will complicate Christian ideas about the high god's "oneness" in different ways.

[34] See n. 5 above.

[35] For the full argument, see Paula Fredriksen, "Mandatory Retirement: Ideas in the Study of Christian Origins Whose Time Has Come to Go," *SR* 35 (2006): 231–46, here 241–43.

[36] Since 1977, this leitmotif has shaped the work particularly of James D. G. Dunn and of N. T. Wright.

[37] N. T. Wright, *Paul and the Faithfulness of God*, 2 vols., Christian Origins and the Question of God 4 (Minneapolis: Fortress, 2013); Barclay, *Paul and the Gift*.

"resurrection" and "messiah" are two other ideas specific, indeed peculiar, to Judaism. He expounded his message by appealing to Jewish texts, practices, and customs. By receiving divine spirit, Paul's gentiles would turn from their own gods to Paul's god, enabled thereby to fulfill that god's law.[38] Paul's gentiles were to assume, *as* gentiles, those behaviors and convictions otherwise associated solely with Jews. In a word—and in the contemporary meaning of that word—Paul urged his gentiles to "Judaize."[39]

The rhetoric especially of Galatians and the habitual discourse of New Testament scholarship obscure the ethnic specificity of this behavior that Paul enjoined on non-Jews. What is at stake if we acknowledge it? Nothing less, I think, than our conceptualization of "Christian origins." Paul's message neither articulated nor embodied a "parting of the ways," though by the second century, in some circles, he will be read that way (and is still read that way). His argument with Peter in Antioch notwithstanding (Gal 2:14), Paul himself urged his ex-pagan pagans to Judaize; and, especially in light of his vivid eschatological expectation and foreshortened time frame, he never contemplated a movement separated from—much less antagonistic toward—the traditions and (many of the) practices of Israel.

What we call "Christianity" is post-Pauline—indeed, arguably, it is even un-Pauline.[40] If we want to understand Paul's gospel, and Paul himself, in his own context, we will interpret it, and him, not over against Judaism but within it.[41]

---

[38] Paula Fredriksen, "Paul's Letter to the Romans, the Ten Commandments, and Pagan 'Justification by Faith,'" *JBL* 133 (2014): 801–8, https://doi.org/10.15699/jbibllite.133.4.801.

[39] On outsiders' adopting the customs of others and antiquity's "verbing" of ethnic nouns (to hellenize; to persianize; to Judaize), see the remarks of Brent Nongbri, *Before Religion: A History of a Modern Concept* (New Haven: Yale University Press, 2013), 46–50; earlier, and specifically on "Judaizing," see Shaye J. D. Cohen, *The Beginnings of Jewishness: Boundaries, Varieties, Uncertainties*, HCS 31 (Berkeley: University of California Press, 1999), 185–92; Steve Mason, "Jews, Judaeans, Judaizing, Judaism: Problems of Categorization in Ancient History," *JSJ* 38 (2007): 457–512. For the full argument about Paul's own Judaizing, see Fredriksen, "Why Should a 'Law-Free' Mission?," 637–50.

[40] John G. Gager, *The Jewish Lives of the Apostle Paul*, American Lectures on the History of Religions 18 (New York: Columbia University Press, 2016), 13. See, too, his *The Origins of Anti-Semitism: Attitudes toward Judaism in Pagan and Christian Antiquity* (New York: Oxford University Press, 1983), for a narrative history of Paul's gentile afterlives in the second and third centuries; more recently, see Fredriksen, *Paul: The Pagans' Apostle*, 167–74.

[41] Fredriksen (*Paul: The Pagans' Apostle*) places Paul's activity entirely within his native religious (thus, ethnic) context. For different and differing interpretations of various aspects of Paul's life and work along these same lines, see the essays collected in Nanos and Zetterholm, *Paul within Judaism*; in *Paul the Jew: Rereading the Apostle as a Figure of Second Temple Judaism*, ed. Gabriele Boccaccini and Carlos A. Segovia (Minneapolis: Fortress, 2016); and in Rodríguez and Thiessen, *So-Called Jew in Paul's Letter to the Romans*.

SBL PRESS

New and Recent Titles

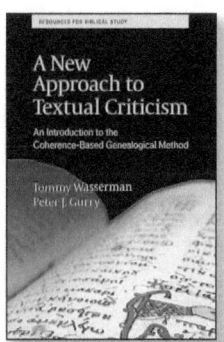

A NEW APPROACH TO TEXTUAL CRITICISM
An Introduction to the Coherence-Based Genealogical Method
Tommy Wasserman and Peter J. Gurry
Paperback $19.95, 978-1-62837-199-4   162 pages, 2017   Code: 060399
Hardcover $34.95, 978-0-88414-267-6 E-book $19.95, 978-0-88414-266-9
Resources for Biblical Study 80

TOWARD A LATINO/A BIBLICAL INTERPRETATION
Francisco Lozada Jr.
Paperback $36.95, 978-1-62837-200-7   148 pages, 2017   Code: 060385
Hardcover $51.95, 978-0-88414-270-6 E-book $36.95, 978-0-88414-269-0
Resources for Biblical Study 91

A SAMOAN READING OF DISCIPLESHIP IN MATTHEW
Vaitusi Nofoaiga
Paperback $29.95, 978-1-62837-197-0   156 pages, 2017   Code: 063808
Hardcover $44.95, 978-0-88414-263-8 E-book $29.95, 978-0-88414-262-1
International Voices in Biblical Studies 8

GOSPEL JESUSES AND OTHER NONHUMANS
Biblical Criticism Post-poststructuralism
Stephen D. Moore
Paperback $24.95, 978-1-62837-190-1   164 pages, 2017   Code 060691
Hardcover $39.95, 978-0-88414-252-2 E-book $24.95, 978-0-88414-251-5
Semeia Studies 89

MIXED FEELINGS AND VEXED PASSIONS
Exploring Emotions in Biblical Literature
F. Scott Spencer, editor
Paperback $49.95, 978-1-62837-194-9   418 pages, 2017   Code: 060396
Hardcover $64.95, 978-0-88414-257-7 E-book $49.95, 978-0-88414-256-0
Resources for Biblical Study 90

EARLY JEWISH WRITINGS
Eileen Schuller and Marie-Theres Wacker, editors
Paperback $44.95, 978-1-62837-183-3   316 pages, 2017   Code 066006
Hardcover $59.95, 978-0-88414-233-1 E-book $44.95, 978-0-88414-232-4
The Bible and Women 3.1

SBL Press • P.O. Box 2243 • Williston, VT 05495-2243
Phone: 877-725-3334 (toll-free) or 802-864-6185 • Fax: 802-864-7626
Order online at www.sbl-site.org/publications

EXPLORE THE THEME OF EXILE IN SCRIPTURE

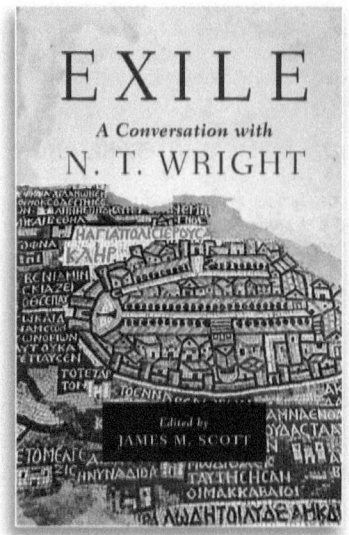

EXILE: A CONVERSATION WITH N. T. WRIGHT

Edited by James M. Scott, with contributions by N. T. Wright

N. T. Wright is well-known for his view that the majority of Second Temple Jews saw themselves as living within an ongoing exile. This book engages a lively conversation with this idea, beginning with a lengthy thesis from Wright, responses from eleven New Testament scholars, and a concluding essay from Wright responding to his interlocutors.

336 pages, hardcover,
978-0-8308-5183-6, $40.00

"This collection of perceptive essays engages Wright's thesis in a dialogical manner, generally affirming but also refining, developing, and challenging aspects of it. A book not to be missed by anyone interested in this important topic."

MICHAEL J. GORMAN,
Raymond E. Brown Professor of Biblical Studies and Theology,
St. Mary's Seminary and University, Baltimore

Visit IVPACADEMIC.COM to request an exam copy.

 Follow us on Twitter   Join us on Facebook   800.843.9487 | ivpacademic.com

Subsistence, Swapping, and Paul's Rhetoric of Generosity

RYAN S. SCHELLENBERG
rschellenberg@mtso.edu
Methodist Theological School in Ohio, Delaware, OH 43015

Although there is broad consensus that the majority of the early Christ followers were poor, descriptions of the economic practices of their assemblies have focused on the contributions of a surplus-possessing minority. This article employs ethnographic accounts of the economic activities of the poor to challenge the assumption that Paul's injunctions to generosity were targeted primarily at wealthier members. Since there is ample evidence from numerous societies of sharing among the poor, one cannot deduce from the fact that Paul commends generosity that he is addressing those with surplus resources. Moreover, the moral rhetoric employed by Paul addresses just such concerns as commonly arise when the poor participate in networks of reciprocal exchange. Paul envisions and seeks to nurture local networks of Christ followers who utilize their mostly subsistence-level resources for their mutual benefit.

In an important new study, David Downs identifies two distinct modes of almsgiving that are advocated in early Christian texts.[1] The first, which he calls philanthropic almsgiving, consists of the sort of charitable activity with which we usually associate the term—that is, giving that "funnels funds along a vertical axis from those with an abundance of assets to those with minimal resources."[2] The second, which Downs, following Justin Meggitt, terms mutualism, involves a rather different mode of economic practice, one that most moderns are not likely to designate almsgiving at all—namely, the "horizontal exchange of resources among those of lesser means."[3]

---

[1] David J. Downs, *Alms: Charity, Reward, and Atonement in Early Christianity* (Waco, TX: Baylor University Press, 2016), 15–17; see also Downs, "Redemptive Almsgiving and Economic Stratification in *2 Clement*," *JECS* 19 (2011): 493–517.

[2] Downs, *Alms*, 17.

[3] Ibid., citing Justin J. Meggitt, *Paul, Poverty and Survival*, SNTW (Edinburgh: T&T Clark, 1998); Denise Kimber Buell, "'Be Not One Who Stretches Out Hands to Receive but Shuts Them When It Comes to Giving': Envisioning Christian Charity When Both Donors and Recipients Are

For those familiar with the debate regarding the economic practices of the ἐκκλησίαι founded by Paul, this distinction will be a familiar one.[4] Characteristic of the scholarship associated with the so-called new consensus on the social composition of the early Christ groups was an interest in the role of relatively wealthy householders whose benevolence sustained poorer members.[5] These scholars were interested, in other words, in a particular species of what Downs would call philanthropic almsgiving: the provision of meals, meeting spaces, and occasional financial assistance by those with surplus resources.[6] The most prominent challenge to this model—that of Meggitt himself—found in Paul's letters a summons to "economic mutualism" among the poor: a shared commitment to interdependence and common well-being manifested in the horizontal exchange of economic resources.[7]

Although subsequent work has brought significant refinement and nuance,[8]

Poor," in *Wealth and Poverty in Early Church and Society*, ed. Susan R. Holman, Holy Cross Studies in Patristic Theology and History (Grand Rapids: Baker Academic, 2008), 37–47.

[4] For surveys of the relevant scholarship, see Abraham J. Malherbe, *Social Aspects of Early Christianity*, 2nd ed. (Philadelphia: Fortress, 1983), 4–11; Steven J. Friesen, "Poverty in Pauline Studies: Beyond the So-Called New Consensus," *JSNT* 26 (2004): 324–37; Annette Merz, "Gerd Theißens Beiträge zur Sozialgeschichte des hellenistischen Urchristentums in der neueren Diskussion," in *Neutestamentliche Grenzgänge: Symposium zur kritischen Rezeption der Arbeiten Gerd Theißens; Festschrift für Gerd Theißen zum 65. Geburtstag*, ed. Peter Lampe and Helmut Schwier, NTOA/SUNT 75 (Göttingen: Vandenhoeck & Ruprecht, 2010), 96–113.

[5] E. A. Judge, *The Social Pattern of the Christian Groups in the First Century: Some Prolegomena to the Study of New Testament Ideas of Social Obligation* (London: Tyndale, 1960), esp. 36, 49–61; Gerd Theissen, *The Social Setting of Pauline Christianity: Essays on Corinth*, trans. John H. Schütz (Philadelphia: Fortress, 1982); Malherbe, *Social Aspects*, 29–59; Wayne A. Meeks, *The First Urban Christians: The Social World of the Apostle Paul* (New Haven: Yale University Press, 1983), 51–73. See also, more recently, Alexander Weiß, *Soziale Elite und Christentum: Studien zu ordo-Angehörigen unter den frühen Christen*, Millennium-Studien 52 (Berlin: de Gruyter, 2015).

[6] Much debate has ensued regarding the moral foundation of such generosity. Does Paul advocate what Gerd Theissen called "love-patriarchalism," which "takes social differences for granted, but ameliorates them through an obligation of respect and love, an obligation imposed on those who are socially stronger" (*Social Setting*, 107)? Or does he seek to subvert such hierarchical moral logic, in particular by undermining the ideology of patronage? So, e.g., John K. Chow, *Patronage and Power: A Study of Social Networks in Corinth*, JSNTSup 75 (Sheffield: JSOT Press, 1992); Verlyn D. Verbrugge and Keith R. Krell, *Paul and Money: A Biblical and Theological Analysis of the Apostle's Teachings and Practices* (Grand Rapids: Zondervan, 2015), 83–103. See also David G. Horrell, *The Social Ethos of the Corinthian Correspondence: Interests and Ideology from 1 Corinthians to 1 Clement*, SNTW (Edinburgh: T&T Clark, 1996), 126–98; Steven J. Friesen, "Paul and Economics: The Jerusalem Collection as an Alternative to Patronage," in *Paul Unbound: Other Perspectives on the Apostle*, ed. Mark D. Given (Peabody, MA: Hendrickson, 2010), 27–54, here 45–49.

[7] Meggitt, *Paul, Poverty and Survival*, 155–78.

[8] Particularly noteworthy here is Steven Friesen's "poverty scale," subsequently revised by Bruce W. Longenecker and now widely employed. See Friesen, "Poverty in Pauline Studies,"

these two models—philanthropic almsgiving and mutualism—persist as rival descriptions of the economic practices of the earliest assemblies. Each continues to attract advocates.[9] Each has also been subjected to sharp criticism, not only for failing to account for the evidence but also for importing modern economic ideology into the ancient world. Those who emphasize the beneficence of the wealthy few have been accused of projecting onto the past "capitalist views of economy, society, personal agency, and religion,"[10] whereas Meggitt's vision of egalitarian mutualism has been pilloried as a naïve "romantic wish."[11] If both critiques be thought to hit the mark, we are left to choose between passive poor and romanticized poor. This is surely a false alternative.

My aim in this study is to avoid both the Scylla of neglect and the Charybdis of romanticization by pursuing what appears to be a point of agreement among all parties to the debate: that most people in the earliest assemblies were poor[12] and that, consequently, any responsible description of the assemblies' economic practices must provide a plausible account of the economically poor as active moral and economic agents.[13] This is easier said than done, for the fact is that real poor people—which is to say, poor people with human agency—are difficult to find, at least in our ancient sources, where the poor, in general, are either ignored or caricatured.[14] But we are not altogether at a loss. As predicted, the poor are with us still,

---

337–58; Walter Scheidel and Steven J. Friesen, "The Size of the Economy and the Distribution of Income in the Roman Empire," *JRS* 99 (2009): 61–91; Longenecker, "Exposing the Economic Middle: A Revised Economy Scale for the Study of Early Christianity," *JSNT* 31 (2009): 243–78.

[9] On philanthropic almsgiving, see Bruce W. Longenecker, *Remember the Poor: Paul, Poverty, and the Greco-Roman World* (Grand Rapids: Eerdmans, 2010); L. L. Welborn, "'That There May Be Equality': The Contexts and Consequences of a Pauline Ideal," *NTS* 59 (2013): 73–90. On mutualism, see Neil Elliott, "Strategies of Resistance and Hidden Transcripts in the Pauline Communities," in *Hidden Transcripts and the Arts of Resistance: Applying the Work of James C. Scott to Jesus and Paul*, ed. Richard A. Horsley, SemeiaSt 48 (Atlanta: Society of Biblical Literature, 2004), 97–122; Friesen, "Paul and Economics"; Gordon Mark Zerbe, *Citizenship: Paul on Peace and Politics* (Winnipeg: CMU Press, 2012), 75–92.

[10] Friesen, "Poverty in Pauline Studies," 358; see also Friesen, "Paul and Economics," 28–32.

[11] Dale B. Martin, "Review Essay: Justin J. Meggitt, *Paul, Poverty and Survival*," *JSNT* no. 84 (2001): 51–64, here 64.

[12] By "poor," here and throughout this study, I mean to designate those living at or near subsistence level—that is, ES5, 6, and 7 on Longenecker's scale. That these were the majority of early believers is all but universally acknowledged. See, e.g., Longenecker, *Remember the Poor*, 295; Friesen, "Poverty in Pauline Studies," 357–58.

[13] So Meggitt, *Paul, Poverty and Survival*, 14–15; Longenecker, *Remember the Poor*, 290; L. L. Welborn, "The Polis and the Poor: Reconstructing Social Relations from Different Genres of Evidence," in *Methodological Foundations*, vol. 1 of *The First Urban Churches*, ed. James R. Harrison and L. L. Welborn, WGRWSup 7 (Atlanta: SBL Press, 2015), 189–243.

[14] See esp. Welborn, "Polis and the Poor," 189–93. Neville Morley describes the Roman poor as those who "failed to leave any significant mark in the historical record" ("The Poor in the City of Rome," in *Poverty in the Roman World*, ed. Margaret Atkins and Robin Osborne [Cambridge:

and, what is more, ethnographic accounts of their economic practices are available. My purpose here, then, is to put such accounts into conversation with two representative descriptions of early ecclesial economy—that of Meggitt (mutualism) and that of Bruce Longenecker, who sees in Paul's letters evidence of what Downs would call philanthropic almsgiving. What the ethnographic literature will provide is ample evidence from numerous societies that the economically poor ameliorate their circumstances by participating in informal networks of reciprocal exchange and sustain such networks by utilizing just the sort of moral rhetoric that is employed by Paul. This is not best described, I will argue, as mutualism, for such networks are neither egalitarian, in the idealizing sense of the word, nor reliably harmonious—two characteristics that Meggitt's language has generally been taken to imply. Instead, they represent the fragile and often fractious but determined attempt of the economically constrained to share (in) the good life. What I will attempt to describe, then, is a practice of "swapping" among the early Christ followers that is considerably more pervasive than Longenecker allows and rather more fraught and fragile than Meggitt seems to imagine.

I. Mutualism or Charity?

It will be helpful to begin with a brief overview of the alternatives Meggitt and Longenecker provide. Meggitt depicts the economy of the ancient world in starkly binary terms: "Society was split into two distinct groups," he asserts, "with a wide gulf separating them."[15] A tiny elite controlled the vast majority of social and economic resources, while "those devoid of political power, the non-élite, over 99% of the Empire's population, could expect little more from life than abject poverty."[16] The early Christ followers, claims Meggitt, could be found exclusively in this latter group, struggling for subsistence alongside the rest of the empire's teeming non-elite.[17] In Paul's gospel, though, the early believers heard a call to "economic mutualism," and their cooperative care for one another helped to mitigate their experience of poverty.[18]

Meggitt's monograph must be credited with helping to initiate a resurgence of interest among Pauline scholars in the material conditions of the nonelite. His argument is hampered, however, by three key shortcomings: First, as has often been noted, Meggitt's undifferentiated treatment of 99 percent of the empire's inhabitants

---

Cambridge University Press, 2006], 31). See also Justin J. Meggitt, "Sources: Use, Abuse, Neglect; The Importance of Popular Culture," in *Christianity at Corinth: The Quest for the Pauline Church*, ed. Edward Adams and David G. Horrell (Louisville: Westminster John Knox, 2004), 241–53.

[15] Meggitt, *Paul, Poverty and Survival*, 50.
[16] Ibid.
[17] Ibid., 75.
[18] Ibid., 158.

as "the poor" is unsatisfactory, obscuring significant differences in access to resources among the nonelite.[19] Second, as Dale B. Martin has observed, Meggitt provides no "*ancient* examples of [mutualism as an] 'economic strategy' other than his own interpretation of early Christian groups."[20] This failure to provide meaningful analogues renders his account considerably less plausible. Third, and consequently, Meggitt's conception of mutualism is never really grounded in a description of concrete social interaction but remains a theoretical construction describing the dispositions of an aggregate and thus idealized "poor."

Longenecker, building on Friesen's "poverty scale," works admirably to tease out more subtle gradations of nonelite economic life.[21] Although he still identifies 65 percent of his "typical urban group of Jesus-followers" as poor—which is to say, struggling to subsist—and agrees with Meggitt that few or none came from the social and economic elite, Longenecker's focus is on what he calls "middling groups"—25 percent or so that possessed stable resources (ES5) and an additional 10 percent that had moderate economic surplus (ES4).[22]

These latter are the believers, claims Longenecker, to whom Paul's moral-economic discourse was primarily directed. Meggitt's notion of mutuality among the believers he dismisses out of hand as ineffectual—"very little plus very little still leaves very little."[23] Rather, he argues, the assemblies relied on "injections of resources from those who were more economically secure."[24] What Longenecker envisions, then, are those with (modest) surplus resources—those at levels ES4 or ES5 on his "economy scale"—contributing to the needs of those struggling to subsist (ES6 or ES7). The conventional name for such practice is, of course, charity, although Longenecker, in an attempt to preserve the agency of its beneficiaries, resists this label.[25]

Although *Remember the Poor* is valuable in many respects—above all, in my view, for its detailed exegesis of passages the economic implications of which have

---

[19] Martin, "Review Essay: Justin J. Meggitt," 54–56; Friesen, "Poverty in Pauline Studies," 339–40; Longenecker, "Exposing the Economic Middle," 247–49. Although once common, this binary conception of the ancient economy has, in the years since Meggitt wrote, largely been rejected by Roman economists. See, e.g., Walter Scheidel, "Stratification, Deprivation and Quality of Life," in Atkins and Osborne, *Poverty in the Roman World*, 43–54; William V. Harris, *Rome's Imperial Economy: Twelve Essays* (Oxford: Oxford University Press, 2011), 31–32.

[20] Martin, "Review Essay: Justin J. Meggitt," 62 (emphasis his). What Meggitt does provide is a footnote guiding readers to recent scholarship on "economic mutual aid in developing societies" (*Paul, Poverty and Survival*, 164 n. 42). Had Meggitt followed up this lead, the present study would perhaps not be necessary.

[21] Longenecker, *Remember the Poor*, 36–59, citing Friesen, "Poverty in Pauline Studies"; Scheidel and Friesen, "Size of the Economy."

[22] Longenecker, *Remember the Poor*, 295.

[23] Ibid., 261 n. 4.

[24] Ibid.

[25] Ibid., 287. Cf. Downs, *Alms*, 11–12.

long been obscured—Longenecker's portrait of the early Christ groups is, in the end, unconvincing. Despite his attempt to describe the poor as contributing members of the assemblies, he in fact offers no account of how the poor function as economic agents.[26] In other words, as in Meggitt's model, what is missing here is a plausible account of how poor people use what material resources they do have. This, I suggest, is where comparative ethnography can be of use.

II. Subsistence and Swapping

In our efforts to conceptualize the economic lives of the assemblies founded by Paul, we do well to consider the constraints on our own habits of thought. Few will be enlightened by the observation that the predominantly North Atlantic economic imagination of our guild differs profoundly from that of our ancient subjects. Let us be frank: Most of us have a hard time thinking like poor people, let alone ancient poor people. And so our common sense—a tool on which we inevitably rely even when our toolkit also includes social-scientific methods and models—may obscure more than it illuminates.

Consider, for example, the definition of poverty that both Meggitt and Longenecker borrow from classicists Peter Garnsey and Greg Woolf: "The poor," these scholars agree, "are those living at or near subsistence level, whose prime concern it is to obtain the minimum food, shelter, and clothing necessary to sustain life, whose lives are dominated by the struggle for physical survival."[27] That the struggle for physical survival looms especially large in the lives of the poor can hardly be disputed. But there is a subtle distortion of the experience of poverty in the notion that the poor are possessed of some common and singular "prime concern," as though their economic constraints somehow have robbed them of the complex of interests and motivations—social, emotional, religious, and so on—that the rest of us navigate.

Indeed, there is an echo here of the spent notion of humans as rational economic actors, an idea that, though generally discarded by economists, continues to haunt North Atlantic moral discourse, appearing whenever the poor express some inadequately pecuniary interest—the desire for fashionable sneakers, say, or for whatever comfort alcohol will provide. In other words, if we define poverty as having as one's primary concern the acquisition of food, shelter, and clothing, we will inevitably find ourselves scandalized, or at least mystified, by how bad a job poor people do at being poor. And so I venture that this way of describing poverty tells

---

[26] See esp. Longenecker, *Remember the Poor*, 289–90.

[27] Peter Garnsey and Greg Woolf, "Patronage of the Rural Poor in the Roman World," in *Patronage in Ancient Society*, ed. Andrew Wallace-Hadrill, Leicester-Nottingham Studies in Ancient Society 1 (London: Routledge, 1989), 153–70, here 153, cited by Meggitt (*Paul, Poverty and Survival*, 5), Longenecker (*Remember the Poor*, 54), and Welborn ("Polis and the Poor," 195–96).

us much more about the common sense of Garnsey and Woolf—what they imagine their prime concern would be were they struggling for subsistence—than it does about the experience of those who are actually poor.[28]

This is not merely quibbling about definitions. For in fact significant portions of Longenecker's argumentation are dependent on this conception of what constitutes poverty. The presence of a handful of participants in Paul's assemblies who possessed relative surplus (ES4) or at least economic stability (ES5) can, Longenecker and others assert, be deduced from prosopographic analysis.[29] But it is another sort of inference that carries the load of Longenecker's claim that not only a few but a substantial minority of assembly members belonged at these economic levels. The reasoning goes like this: If Paul invited believers to give to those in need, he must have been addressing people who were not poor, since, by definition, the poor—those living at or near subsistence—had nothing to give.[30]

This is perfectly logical. It is also wrong. Imagine a day in the life of Apelles— an early Christ follower (Rom 16:10a) about whom we know practically nothing.[31] But let us say, for the sake of argument, that he is an independent artisan, perhaps a cobbler, and that he belongs at Longenecker's level ES6—that is, "at subsistence level (and often below minimum level to sustain life)."[32] Apelles is not dead, which means that on average his caloric and at least his basic nutritional needs have been met. But of course that is no guarantee that he has had an adequate meal today or that he has sufficient resources to find a healthier place to sleep than his vermin-infested shop.[33] So what says Apelles when Mary, another member of his assembly, asks whether he might repair her son's worn-out shoes, though the only payment she can offer is a few leftovers smuggled out of her master's kitchen—not enough to cover the materials, let alone to compensate his labor? "I'm sorry, my dear sister, but I am living at subsistence level myself—just below subsistence today, in fact— and have no economic surplus to share"?

A fundamental difficulty with Longenecker's approach, then, is that as soon as we start thinking about real people we begin to see that the concept of subsistence, though useful as a tool for macro-analysis, has very little to do with the

---

[28] For a related critique of Garnsey and Woolf's definition, see Harris, *Rome's Imperial Economy*, 30.

[29] Longenecker, *Remember the Poor*, 235–53; Horrell, *Social Ethos*, 92–101; Friesen, "Poverty in Pauline Studies."

[30] Longenecker, *Remember the Poor*, 256, 258, 271, 280–81, 283–86, 288.

[31] Robert Jewett, *Romans: A Commentary*, Hermeneia (Minneapolis: Fortress, 2007), 965– 66; Peter Lampe, "The Roman Christians of Romans 16," in *The Romans Debate*, ed. Karl P. Donfried, rev. and exp. ed. (Peabody, MA: Hendrickson, 1991), 216–30, here 228. Readers will rightly notice here echoes of the imaginative reconstruction undertaken by Peter Oakes, *Reading Romans in Pompeii: Paul's Letter at Ground Level* (Minneapolis: Fortress, 2009).

[32] Longenecker, *Remember the Poor*, 45.

[33] Cf. Ronald F. Hock, *The Social Context of Paul's Ministry: Tentmaking and Apostleship* (Philadelphia: Fortress, 1980), 32; Meggitt, *Paul, Poverty and Survival*, 65.

experience of poverty. On the whole, poor people seek to avoid hunger, certainly, but that is not quite the same thing as working to ensure that one's average caloric and nutritional intake is sufficient. Harry W. Pearson's classic essay put the problem well:

> We know that large or small sections of the population of every society live at a level of subsistence which science has established as inadequate. As a consequence infant mortality will be high, and life expectancy low as disease takes its devastating toll, but does this mean that every member of these groups is therefore engaged in producing food during all his waking hours? There is no support for this assumption from contemporary primitive societies, even the poorest, for they too dance and sing, and fight wars, thus using their small resources in non-utilitarian ways.[34]

They also share with one another, as an ample ethnographic literature attests. Indeed, reciprocal modes of exchange among those living at or near subsistence have been documented not only in tribal societies but also among the urban poor in both the "developed" and "developing" worlds.[35] Economic anthropologists

---

[34] Harry W. Pearson, "The Economy Has No Surplus: Critique of a Theory of Development," in *Trade and Market in the Early Empires*, ed. Karl Polanyi, Conrad M. Arensberg, and Harry W. Pearson, Economies in History and Theory (Glencoe, IL: Free Press, 1957), 320–41, here 324. The objection, raised by a number of Pearson's critics, that a subsistence level can in fact be calculated is moot here. The point is simply that the poor are not in the habit of calculating it.

[35] For numerous examples and further bibliography, see Marshall Sahlins, *Stone Age Economics* (London: Tavistock, 1974), 185–275; Carol B. Stack, *All Our Kin: Strategies for Survival in a Black Community* (New York: Harper & Row, 1974), 32–44; Larissa Adler Lomnitz, *Networks and Marginality: Life in a Mexican Shantytown*, trans. Cinna Lomnitz, Studies in Anthropology (New York: Academic Press, 1977), 131–58, 189–213; Susan E. Brown, "Household Composition and Variation in a Rural Dominican Village," *Journal of Comparative Family Studies* 8 (1977): 257–67, here 262–66; Ellen Ross, "Survival Networks: Women's Neighbourhood Sharing in London before World War I," *History Workshop Journal* 15 (1983): 4–28; Nancy Scheper-Hughes, *Death without Weeping: The Violence of Everyday Life in Brazil* (Berkeley: University of California Press, 1992), 98–108; Peregrine Horden, "Household Care and Informal Networks: Comparisons and Continuities from Antiquity to the Present," in *The Locus of Care: Families, Communities, Institutions, and the Provision of Welfare since Antiquity*, ed. Peregrine Horden and Richard Smith, Studies in the Social History of Medicine 7 (London: Routledge, 1998), 21–67; Polly Wiessner, "Experimental Games and Games of Life among the Ju/'hoan Bushmen," *Current Anthropology* 50 (2009): 133–38; Amber Wutich, "Shifting Alliances: Reciprocal Relationships during Times of Economic Hardship in Urban Bolivia," *Chungara: Revista de Antropología Chilena* 43 (2011): 123–33. Ancient evidence is sparse but suggestive. See esp. Hesiod, *Op.* 342–351; Dio Chrysostom, *Ven. (Or. 7)* 68–69; m. Šeb. 5:9; m. Giṭ. 5:9. For further discussion, see Thomas W. Gallant, *Risk and Survival in Ancient Greece: Reconstructing the Rural Domestic Economy* (Stanford, CA: Stanford University Press, 1991), 156–57; Miriam Peskowitz, "'Family/ies' in Antiquity: Evidence from Tannaitic Literature and Roman Galilean Architecture," in *The Jewish Family in Antiquity*, ed. Shaye J. D. Cohen, BJS 289 (Atlanta: Scholars Press, 1993), 33–34; Horden, "Household Care and Informal Networks," 44–45, 54–58.

routinely refer to this mode of reciprocity[36] as a "survival strategy"—language that should be familiar to readers of Meggitt. But just how does sharing help the poor survive, if indeed "very little plus very little still leaves very little"?

Here it is important to remember that poverty usually entails not only having few resources but also acquiring them unpredictably.[37] Our Apelles, for example, knows neither when a profitable contract will turn up nor when illness will render him unable to work.[38] Sharing, then, is a way of managing economic uncertainty. As John Lombardi explains,

> It is clear that no amount of redistribution can possibly increase the average wealth available to members of the society. The necessity for reciprocity arises from the need to smooth out the fluctuations of acquisition and needs that occur often in a seemingly random pattern. Elaborate mechanisms of reciprocity are not so necessary in a more affluent society because relative abundance ... can serve as a cushion against sudden need.... However, for a group forced to subsist on marginal resources, some form of reciprocity may be the only mechanism to ensure survival.[39]

As E. E. Evans-Pritchard once quipped, "It is scarcity and not sufficiency that makes people generous."[40]

The poor understand this. As one informant told Carol Stack in her classic study of "swapping" in a poor African-American neighborhood, "Sometimes I don't have a damn dime in my pocket, not a crying penny to get a box of paper diapers, milk, a loaf of bread. But you have to have help from everybody and

---

[36] Following Karl Polanyi and most economic anthropologists, I use the term *reciprocity* here in a limited sense to denote a form of economic integration—specifically, "movements between correlative points of symmetrical groupings"—and thus distinguish reciprocity from, for example, patronage, despite the fact that the latter does indeed involve reciprocity in its more general sense. See Polanyi, "The Economy as Instituted Process," in Polanyi, Arensberg, and Pearson, *Trade and Market*, 243–70, here 250; Lomnitz, *Networks and Marginality*, 189–91, 202–3.

[37] Lomnitz, *Networks and Marginality*, 204; Morley, "Poor in the City of Rome," 33.

[38] On "structural underemployment" and thus the unpredictability of income among urban craftsmen, see John S. Kloppenborg, "Precedence at the Communal Meal in Corinth," *NovT* 58 (2016): 176–203, here 195–96.

[39] John R. Lombardi, "Reciprocity and Survival," *Anthropological Quarterly* 48 (1975): 245–54, here 246. See also Bram Tucker, "Giving, Scrounging, Hiding, and Selling: Minimal Food Sharing among Mikea of Madagascar," *Research in Economic Anthropology* 23 (2004): 43–66, here 64; Wutich, "Shifting Alliances," 123–24.

[40] E. E. Evans-Pritchard, *The Nuer: A Description of the Modes of Livelihood and Political Institutions of a Nilotic People* (Oxford: Clarendon, 1940; repr., New York: Oxford University Press, 1969), 85. Evans-Pritchard's statement is true at least up to a point. In situations of extreme scarcity—that is, when individuals face the prospect of immediate starvation—they tend to fend for themselves, sometimes abandoning even close kin. See Lomnitz, *Networks and Marginality*, 204; Scheper-Hughes, *Death without Weeping*, 132–35.

anybody, so don't turn no one down when they come round for help."[41] Notice here how want motivates not hoarding, as the affluent might expect, but instead a wider dispersal of what resources one does have, reluctant but determined investment in a network of mutual support that can be called on when one faces the more acute need that the future is sure to bring. Hence the proverbial wisdom among Stack's subjects: "The poorer you are, the more likely you are to pay back."[42]

Apelles's hypothetical situation brings to light another benefit of reciprocal exchange: it helps the poor to manage what economists would call the insufficient liquidity of their assets. Apelles is hungry and tired after a long day of work. He has scraps of leather; he does not have hot food, nor sufficient coin to purchase some. Yet, even if the exchange is, for the moment, to his net economic disadvantage, Apelles's sense of moral obligation, his genuine concern for Mary's well-being, and his knowledge—conscious or not—that more meals may yet be had from her master's kitchen have an ally in his growling stomach. In short, where cash is hard to come by, the sharing of resources provides an important mechanism for turning what one has into what one needs.

Larissa Lomnitz's description of a "network of reciprocal exchange" in Cerrada del Cóndor, a shantytown on the outskirts of Mexico City, provides a vivid glimpse into this reality:

> Among the outward signs of reciprocity relations within this network, one notices that any adult will ask any of the children to bring some water, to take care of the babies, or to go on small errands.... The women are forever borrowing money, food, pots, pans, and clothing from each other. The men as well as the women borrow and swap items of clothing. Whenever a member of the network is sick in bed, the others take care of him or her and, if necessary, take charge of the children.[43]

Particularly striking here is the inextricability of swapping and sociability, of economic cooperation and of care. All of this activity is economic; none of it is just economic. An ethnographer might observe that reciprocity, in addition to providing some measure of economic stability, generates and sustains social ties.[44] A local might simply note that friendship, too, is part of what constitutes the good life.

---

[41] Stack, *All Our Kin*, 32. Similarly, one of the poorest of Larissa Lomnitz's subjects explained that "she is nice to everybody so that someone may be nice to her in case of need" (*Networks and Marginality*, 147).

[42] Stack, *All Our Kin*, 43.

[43] Lomnitz, *Networks and Marginality*, 144. See, similarly, Brown, "Household Composition," 264–65; Isabel Nieves, "Household Arrangements and Multiple Jobs in San Salvador," *Signs* 5 (1979): 134–42, here 141–42; Scheper-Hughes, *Death without Weeping*, 99.

[44] So, e.g., Claude Lévi-Strauss, *The Elementary Structures of Kinship* (Boston: Beacon, 1969), 55. See also John M. G. Barclay, "Money and Meetings: Group Formation among Diaspora Jews and Early Christians," in *Pauline Churches and Diaspora Jews*, WUNT 275 (Tübingen: Mohr Siebeck, 2011), 110, 117; Downs, *Alms*, 23.

Clearly, then, Longenecker's insistence that the poor have nothing to share fundamentally misconstrues the nature of subsistence as well as the behavior of those who live "at or near subsistence level." There are no good grounds for concluding from Paul's injunctions to generosity that what he primarily envisages is charity given from the relatively wealthy to the poor. Thus, there are no good grounds for inferring from these injunctions the existence of a substantial minority of relatively wealthy (ES4 and ES5) assembly members. Such a conclusion does not rule out, of course, the possibility of some social stratification in the early assemblies, a phenomenon for which there is indeed good evidence.[45] But it does demand that we reflect on what Paul's rhetoric of generosity would have meant not only for the relatively secure few but also for the precariously situated majority.

III. The Rhetoric of Reciprocal Generosity

In a thoughtful essay that, unfortunately, has not been taken up by participants in the "Paul and poverty" debate, Denise Kimber Buell draws attention to a number of early Christian texts that appear to depict just such a scenario as we have been describing, that is, "almsgiving" that functioned "more like mutual assistance, insofar as a person might be a recipient at one time and an almsgiver at another."[46] Particularly striking is an exhortation to generosity in the Didache:

> Do not be one who reaches out your hands to receive but draws them back from giving. If you acquire something with your hands [διὰ τῶν χειρῶν], give it as a ransom for your sins. Do not doubt whether to give, nor grumble while giving. For you should recognize the good paymaster of the reward. Do not shun a person in need, but share [συγκοινωνήσεις] all things with your brother and do not say that anything is your own. For if you are partners [κοινωνοί] in what is immortal, how much more in what is mortal? (Did. 4.5–8 [trans. Ehrman, LCL])

Here the reference to what one acquires by one's hands (διὰ τῶν χειρῶν) suggests that, like Paul in 1 Thess 4:11, the author has manual laborers in mind (cf. Did.

---

[45] For a judicious survey, see Steven J. Friesen, "Prospects for a Demography of the Pauline Mission: Corinth among the Churches," in *Urban Religion in Roman Corinth: Interdisciplinary Approaches*, ed. Daniel N. Schowalter and Steven J. Friesen, HTS 53 (Cambridge: Harvard University Press, 2005), 352–70.

[46] Buell, "Be Not One," 47. Buell also cites 1 Clem. 55.2 and Herm. Sim. 5.3.5–9 (56.5–9). See also Did. apost. 19; Aristides, *Apol.* 15.7; Sent. Sextus 267; Athenagoras, *Leg.* 11.4. David Downs, noting esp. 2 Clem. 4.3, comes to a similar conclusion regarding the admonition to almsgiving in 2 Clement, which he sees as "an invitation for *all* believers, perhaps even those living at or near subsistence level, to practice mutual assistance" ("Redemptive Almsgiving," 495). Such a reading fits well the interpretation of the language of early Christian almsgiving advocated by Peter Brown, *The Ransom of the Soul: Afterlife and Wealth in Early Western Christianity* (Cambridge: Harvard University Press, 2015), esp. 34–35, 102–4.

12.3–5).⁴⁷ The recurring κοινων- language, appearing alongside the document's only reference to a fellow believer as "brother" (ἀδελφός), indicates that what our text advocates is sharing of possessions modeled on the "generalized reciprocity" that obtains among kin.⁴⁸ Hence all members, even those who are also receivers of aid, are urged to make what contribution they can to the needs of the fictive household—to stretch out their hands not only to receive but also to give, even when their own concern for the future might cause them to doubt the adequacy of divine repayment.⁴⁹ As Buell puts it, "In a context where resources are scarce … many in the community could reasonably view themselves as in need; the onus is placed on the individual to strive to be a giver rather than a receiver—reinforcing the likelihood that the same person could potentially occupy both positions."⁵⁰

Analogous scenarios, and thus analogous moral discourses, are widespread among those poor who participate in networks of reciprocal exchange. Observe, for example, the denunciation of a one-way hand-stretcher reported by Stack: "Some people like my cousin don't mind borrowing from anybody, but she don't loan you no money, her clothes, nothing. Well she ain't shit. She don't believe in helping nobody."⁵¹ The folk idiom differs from that of the Didache, but the point is the same: Those struggling to subsist are tempted to receive more willingly than they give, and thus it takes a large investment of what we might call the community's moral capital to keep the redistributive wheels turning. Stinginess is thus loudly condemned, and the obligation to share keenly felt.⁵² Often, as the statement of one Ghanaian woman attests, the threat of supernatural sanction helps to encourage generosity even among those with few resources: "If you don't have it, even God knows you don't have it [cf. 2 Cor 8:12]. But if you have even a little, you must help with that bit.… Otherwise, you'll have difficulty the next day, it's not good … it's a sin."⁵³

---

⁴⁷ Aaron Milavec, *The Didache: Faith, Hope, and Life of the Earliest Christian Communities, 50–70 C.E.* (New York: Newman, 2003), 204; Richard S. Ascough, "The Thessalonian Christian Community as a Professional Voluntary Association," *JBL* 119 (2000): 314–15, https://doi.org/10.2307/3268489.

⁴⁸ The phrase is that of Sahlins, *Stone Age Economics*, 193–94. For analogous use of fictive kinship to reinforce networks of reciprocal exchange, see Lomnitz, *Networks and Marginality*, 145–46, 159–74; Stack, *All Our Kin*, 29–30; Scheper-Hughes, *Death without Weeping*, 104.

⁴⁹ See Kurt Niederwimmer, *The Didache: A Commentary*, trans. Linda M. Maloney, Hermeneia (Minneapolis: Fortress, 1998), 108.

⁵⁰ Buell, "Be Not One," 45; and see Downs, *Alms*, 235–36; Meggitt, *Paul, Poverty and Survival*, 163. Cf. Did. apost. 17.

⁵¹ Stack, *All Our Kin*, 35.

⁵² See, e.g., Wutich, "Shifting Alliances," 126–27; Scheper-Hughes, *Death without Weeping*, 100; James C. Scott, *The Moral Economy of the Peasant: Rebellion and Subsistence in Southeast Asia* (New Haven: Yale University Press, 1976), 168. On the importance of social sanction in networks of exchange, see esp. Wiessner, "Experimental Games and Games of Life."

⁵³ Lauren MacLean, "Exhaustion and Exclusion in the African Village: The Non-state Social

This is just the sort of moral work, I submit, that Paul's rhetoric of generosity aims to accomplish—namely, to foster giving among the economically insecure by appealing to shared norms and promising divine recompense. Let us begin with the most unusual and therefore most visible act of sharing commended by Paul, the collection for "the poor among the saints in Jerusalem" (Rom 15:26).

Whatever Paul's personal motivation,[54] he insisted to the Corinthians that the purpose of the collection was to facilitate economic "equality" among the assemblies:

> I do not mean that there should be relief for others and pressure on you, but it is a question of a fair balance [ἐξ ἰσότητος] between your present abundance and their need, so that their abundance may be for your need, in order that there may be a fair balance [ἰσότης]. (2 Cor 8:13–14 NRSV)

The ideal of ἰσότης to which Paul appeals here is, in ancient moral discourse, closely linked with reciprocity (e.g., Aristotle, *Eth. nic.* 8.5.5 [1157b]; Philo, *Leg.* 84–85) and contrasted with avarice: "Honor equality; do not act greedily toward anyone," says Menander.[55] Thus, Paul does not describe the Corinthians' potential contribution as charity or euergetism; rather, it constitutes one moment in a relationship of mutual exchange—what he elsewhere calls κοινωνία (Rom 15:26, 2 Cor 8:4, 9:13)[56]—on the expectation that it will be of mutual benefit.[57] Indeed, as Downs

---

Welfare of Informal Reciprocity in Rural Ghana and Cote d'Ivoire," *Studies in Comparative International Development* 46 (2011): 118–36, here 125. Such beliefs are not restricted to monotheists: "It's obligatory that I give to him. If I don't give to him, that will go badly and witchcraft will intervene" (125). See, similarly, Marcel Mauss, *The Gift: Forms and Functions of Exchange in Archaic Societies*, trans. Ian Cunnison (London: Cohen & West, 1966), 8–9.

[54] For a useful survey, see David J. Downs, *The Offering of the Gentiles: Paul's Collection for Jerusalem in Its Chronological, Cultural, and Cultic Contexts*, WUNT 2/248 (Tübingen: Mohr Siebeck, 2008), 3–26.

[55] Menander, *Mon.* 259: Ἰσότητα τίμα, μὴ πλεονέκτει μηδένα. Trans. from Hans Dieter Betz, *2 Corinthians 8 and 9: A Commentary on Two Administrative Letters of the Apostle Paul*, Hermeneia (Philadelphia: Fortress, 1985), 68 n. 233. See also Philo, *Conf.* 48; Pseudo-Ecphantus, *De regn.* (apud Stobaeus, *Flor.* 4.7.66). In my view, the term is altogether too common in ordinary speech to deduce from Paul's use of it allusion to a more specific ideological domain.

[56] On κοινωνία here, see Julien M. Ogereau, "The Jerusalem Collection as Κοινωνία: Paul's Global Politics of Socio-economic Equality and Solidarity," *NTS* 58 (2012): 360–78. It further strengthens Ogereau's case that Paul in 2 Cor 8:4 closely associates κοινωνία with χάρις, which often refers to grateful reciprocation of a gift. So David Konstan, "Reciprocity and Friendship," in *Reciprocity in Ancient Greece*, ed. Christopher Gill, Norman Postlethwaite, and Richard Seaford (Oxford: Oxford University Press, 1998), 279–301, here 285; Michael P. Knowles, "Reciprocity and 'Favour' in the Parable of the Undeserving Servant (Luke 17.7–10)," *NTS* 49 (2003): 256–60, here 257–58. But to conclude, as Ogereau does, that Paul therefore aimed at "reforming the structural inequalities of Graeco-Roman society … by fostering socioeconomic ἰσότης between Jews and Gentiles" (377) is, I think, misleading, since it foists on Paul a concept of "society"—to say nothing of "structural"—for which there is no evidence in his letters.

[57] See esp. Friesen, "Paul and Economics," 45–51. See also John M. G. Barclay, "Manna and

observes, Paul's argument here assumes that the Corinthians, too, are economically vulnerable: Why else should he depict them as potential recipients of the Jerusalem assembly's abundance?[58] And why, if they are not themselves economically constrained, should he emphasize that the acceptability of their gift depends not on its absolute size but only upon their giving what they are able: "If the eagerness is there, the gift is acceptable according to what one has—not according to what one does not have" (2 Cor 8:12)?[59] Indeed, it is telling that in 2 Cor 9 Paul finds it necessary to assure the Corinthians that, if they do contribute, God will ensure that they nevertheless have enough:

> Each of you must give as you have made up your mind, not reluctantly or under compulsion, for God loves a cheerful giver. And God is able to provide you with every blessing in abundance, so that by always having enough of everything [ἐν παντὶ πάντοτε πᾶσαν αὐτάρκειαν ἔχοντες], you may share abundantly in every good work. (2 Cor 9:7–8)

As in Did. 4.5–8, assurance of divine reciprocation is intended to embolden the hesitant giver for whom "having enough of everything" cannot be taken for

---

the Circulation of Grace: A Study of 2 Corinthians 8:1–15," in *The Word Leaps the Gap: Essays on Scripture and Theology in Honor of Richard B. Hays*, ed. J. Ross Wagner, C. Kavin Rowe, and A. Katherine Grieb (Grand Rapids: Eerdmans, 2008), 409–26, here 422–23.

[58] Downs, "Redemptive Almsgiving," 499; Downs, *Alms*, 168–70. Downs follows Meggitt—rightly, I think—in rejecting interpretations of the passage that see only spiritual benefits coming from Jerusalem (cf. Rom 15:26–27). See Andreas Lindemann, "Hilfe für die Armen: Zur ethischen Argumentation des Paulus in den Kollektenbriefen II Kor 8 und II Kor 9," in *Exegese vor Ort: Festschrift für Peter Welten zum 65. Geburtstag*, ed. Christl Maier, Rüdiger Liwak, and Klaus-Peter Jörns (Leipzig: Evangelische Verlagsanstalt, 2001), 199–216, here 204–5; Meggitt, *Paul, Poverty and Survival*, 160–61; Alfred Plummer, *A Critical and Exegetical Commentary on the Second Epistle of St. Paul to the Corinthians*, ICC (Edinburgh: T&T Clark, 1915), 245. Welborn's reading, which sees the logic of Rom 15:26–27 implicit also in 2 Cor 8:1–15 and views the Corinthian contribution as restoring equality to an "unequal friendship," unaccountably reverses the sequence of gifts Paul envisions here—that is, it falters on the ἵνα of verse 14b ("That There May Be Equality," 80–81).

[59] Friesen, "Paul and Economics," 50. Such a reading may appear to stand in tension with Paul's description of the Corinthians' present "abundance" (περίσσευμα) in verse 14 (so Welborn, "That There May Be Equality," 90). But the function of the term and its cognate verb in the rhetoric of the chapter complicates the assumption that he is in fact describing the Corinthians, in contrast with the "poor" Macedonians (v. 2), as materially well off. Paul has established a close (potential) parallel between the Macedonians and the Achaians according to which both possess "abundant" eagerness that results—or at least should result—in an "abundant" gift (vv. 2, 7). That he is patently not attributing wealth to the Macedonians when he speaks of their "abounding" generosity should cause us to hesitate before taking the "abundance" of the Corinthians as a description of economic plenty. Certainly the Corinthians are better off than the Jerusalemites, but Paul speaks of "abundance" here not because the Corinthians are rich but because of the rhetorical weight with which he has endowed the term.

granted.⁶⁰ Indeed, as in the story of the Israelites in the desert (Exod 16:18), to which Paul had alluded in 2 Cor 8:15, the promise of God's generous abundance mitigates the temptation to hoard by alleviating the fear of scarcity.⁶¹

Still, if Paul's rhetoric in 2 Cor 8 and 9 depicts the collection as "multidirectional, occasional, need-based redistribution" among the poor, as Friesen has it,⁶² one might nevertheless object that such a singular project can hardly provide the basis for a more general reconstruction of the economic practice of the assemblies. It would be naïve to treat Paul's description of the collection as though it unproblematically described what the collection meant as social practice.⁶³ Moreover, there is a very substantial difference between sharing with one's immediate neighbors and pooling resources with one's neighbors in order to share with distant coreligionists. In my view, it looks very much like what we have here is Paul seeking to utilize the rhetoric of mutual exchange in a situation to which its applicability was rather in doubt. Still, the point is that Paul could hardly have expected such rhetoric to be effective if it did not already have currency in the Corinthian assembly.⁶⁴ In other words, Paul's strained attempt to mobilize interassembly generosity provides a glimpse into the moral (theo)logic of the more pedestrian and therefore more sparsely attested reality of intraassembly sharing.

Sparsely attested, yes, but by no means unattested. "Share [κοινωνοῦντες] in the needs of the saints," Paul instructs the Romans, with no further elaboration (Rom 12:13; cf. Gal 6:6, 9–10; 1 Thess 5:14–15; 2 Cor 9:13).⁶⁵ Perhaps he felt that they, like the Thessalonians, hardly needed specific instruction:

> Now concerning love of the brothers and sisters [φιλαδελφία], you do not need to have anyone write to you, for you yourselves have been taught by God to love one another; and indeed you do love all the brothers and sisters throughout Macedonia. But we urge you, beloved, to do so more and more, to aspire to live quietly, to mind your own affairs, and to work with your hands, as we directed you, so that you may behave properly toward outsiders and be dependent on no one. (1 Thess 4:9–12 NRSV)

Commentators have long puzzled over the connections in this passage, clear in the grammar but not quite so clear topically, between φιλαδελφία, manual labor, and outsiders.⁶⁶ The suggestion that some Thessalonian idlers were sponging off other

---

⁶⁰ Margaret E. Thrall, *A Critical and Exegetical Commentary on the Second Epistle to the Corinthians*, 2 vols., ICC (Edinburgh: T&T Clark, 1994), 2:580.

⁶¹ See here Friesen, "Paul and Economics," 51 n. 65.

⁶² Ibid., 51.

⁶³ So, rightly, Martin, "Review Essay: Justin J. Meggitt," 63.

⁶⁴ Cf. Lindemann, "Hilfe für die Armen," 207, 215–16.

⁶⁵ On the economic connotations of these texts, see the valuable exegesis of Longenecker, *Remember the Poor*, 140–55.

⁶⁶ See Trevor J. Burke, *Family Matters: A Socio-historical Study of Fictive Kinship Metaphors in 1 Thessalonians*, JSNTSup 247 (London: T&T Clark, 2003), 204–5.

members—either due to laziness or eschatological fervor⁶⁷—fails adequately to explain Paul's concern for the assembly's reputation with outsiders. And the notion that some Thessalonians were giving up work for evangelism and thus incurring disapproval from outsiders fails meaningfully to engage with the theme of φιλαδελφία that structures Paul's paraenesis.⁶⁸ As Philip Esler has shown, however, these apparently disparate topics in fact hold together well if one imagines Paul to be thinking in terms of household economics⁶⁹—a redundant phrase, of course, in the Greek, which fact serves as a helpful reminder that the οἶκος, not the individual, was the fundamental economic unit in the ancient world.⁷⁰ Thus, it was households, not individuals, that strove to be economically self-sufficient, and they did so by incorporating the diverse labors of their members. If this is the analogy operating here, it is not at all surprising that Paul would advocate hard work as a demonstration of shared commitment to the honorable well-being of the household⁷¹ or that he would employ the term φιλαδελφία—which, before Paul, always denoted love and its manifestations between actual kin⁷²—to describe this commitment to

---

⁶⁷ For the former view, see Colin R. Nicholl, *From Hope to Despair in Thessalonica: Situating 1 and 2 Thessalonians*, SNTSMS 126 (Cambridge: Cambridge University Press, 2004), 104. For the latter, see Ernst von Dobschütz, *Die Thessalonicher-Briefe*, 7th ed., KEK 10 (Göttingen: Vandenhoeck & Ruprecht, 1909), 180–83; Ernest Best, *The First and Second Epistles to the Thessalonians*, BNTC (London: Black, 1972), 175–76.

⁶⁸ The suggestion is that of John M. G. Barclay, "Conflict in Thessalonica," *CBQ* 55 (1993): 512–30. The same objection pertains to the theory that Paul is counseling against political engagement, as proposed by Hock, *Social Context*, 46–47; see also Callia Rulmu, "Between Ambition and Quietism: The Socio-political Background of 1 Thessalonians 4,9–12," *Bib* 91 (2010): 393–417.

⁶⁹ Philip F. Esler, "'Keeping It in the Family': Culture, Kinship and Identity in 1 Thessalonians and Galatians," in *Families and Family Relations as Represented in Early Judaisms and Christianities: Texts and Fictions; Papers Read at a NOSTER Colloquium in Amsterdam, June 9–11, 1998*, ed. Jan Willem van Henten and Athalya Brenner, STAR 2 (Leiden: Deo, 2000), 145–84, esp. 172: "1 Thess. 4:10b–12 draws upon the image of a respectable non-elite family in a world of limited good, which lives quietly, engages in hard manual labour, presents a united and harmonious front to the outside world and looks after its own." Cf. Burke, *Family Matters*, 203–24.

⁷⁰ See esp. Richard Saller, "The Roman Family as a Productive Unit," in *A Companion to Families in the Greek and Roman Worlds*, ed. Beryl Rawson, Blackwell Companions to the Ancient World (Malden, MA: Wiley-Blackwell, 2011), 116–28. The reliance of Pauline scholars on prosopography can be distorting in this regard, giving the false impression that individuals have economic profiles that can meaningfully be understood apart from their embeddedness within households.

⁷¹ Cf. Ascough, "Professional Voluntary Association," 321–22. One need not, then, posit as an occasion for Paul's injunction any problem with laziness beyond that which afflicts any household. Cf. Did. 12.3–5 as well as Rom 12:11 with Oakes, *Reading Romans in Pompeii*, 112–13.

⁷² Peter Pilhofer, "Περὶ δὲ τῆς φιλαδελφίας … (1 Thess 4,9): Ekklesiologische Überlegungen zu einem Proprium früher christlicher Gemeinden," in *Die frühen Christen und ihre Welt: Greifswalder Aufsätze, 1996–2001*, WUNT 145 (Tübingen: Mohr Siebeck, 2002), 140–42; John S.

mutual well-being. As Musonius Rufus has it, "What better disposed sharer of common goods [κοινωνὸν ἀγαθῶν] could one find than a good brother?" (frag. 15.100.9–10).[73]

Paul's paraenesis assumes, then, that laziness is detrimental to the honor of the assembly because it threatens the sufficiency of its economic resources—resources that must therefore have been considered, morally if not factually, the shared resources of the assembly. Notably, this is just the scenario presupposed also by 2 Thess 3:6–13, which, in my view, is the earliest evidence for the reception history of 1 Thess 4:9–12 (plus 2:9–12; 5:14). "If anyone will not work, let him not eat" (3:10b; cf. Did. 12.3–5), writes our would-be Paul—a regulation that, as Robert Jewett has seen, is meaningful only in a setting in which, as in a household, the labor of each member contributes to a shared store of food.[74] When one is dining off the largesse of a wealthy patron, idleness is a peccadillo; when one's fellow diners have sweat and sacrificed to put food on the table—which is to say, when everyone eating is poor—it is a serious affront.

IV. Conclusion

Since there is ample evidence from numerous societies of sharing among the poor, one cannot deduce from the fact that Paul commends generosity that he is addressing those with surplus resources. On the contrary, the rhetoric of generosity employed by Paul addresses precisely those concerns that commonly arise when the poor participate in networks of reciprocal exchange. Paul's rhetoric, then, does moral work that is in many respects rather ordinary. It emphasizes that honor requires one to contribute to the economic well-being of one's (fictive) kin, and it promises divine recompense. (What is perhaps most distinctive here is that Paul, like Jesus [Mark 10:21, Matt 6:4, 10:41–42, Luke 14:14], emphasizes divine reward for generosity rather than threatens divine punishment for stinginess—though the latter theme is not altogether absent [1 Cor 11:30, Luke 16:19–31].)[75] In sum, then, what Paul envisions and seeks to nurture are, in John Dominic Crossan and Marcus

---

Kloppenborg, "ΦΙΛΑΔΕΛΦΙΑ, ΘΕΟΔΙΔΑΚΤΟΣ and the Dioscuri: Rhetorical Engagement in 1 Thessalonians 4.9–12," *NTS* 39 (1993): 265–89, here 272–73.

[73] Text and translation from Cora E. Lutz, "Musonius Rufus, 'the Roman Socrates,'" *Yale Classical Studies* 10 (1947): 3–147, here 100–101.

[74] Jewett, *Romans*, 66–69; and see already Meggitt, *Paul, Poverty and Survival*, 162–63. This need not mean that members had renounced private ownership. Cf. Did. 4.5–8 (quoted above), where believers are urged to consider nothing their own but where what that means, in practice, is giving from their (retained) possessions to those in need.

[75] For a thoughtful treatment of this theme in Paul, see Downs, *Alms*, 143–73.

Borg's phrase, "share communities";[76] local—and, with limited success, translocal—networks of Christ followers who utilize their mostly subsistence-level resources for their mutual benefit.

In the wake of recent work by Andrew Wallace-Hadrill, who has stressed the importance of social networks within ancient neighborhoods (*vici*) for conceptualizing urban life, a number of studies have now sought to describe the early Christ groups as neighborhood-based networks rather than "house churches" centered on a single domestic unit.[77] If correct, this would provide an eminently plausible social/architectural context for such local networks of exchange as I am positing, for indeed such a scenario is frequently described in the ethnographic studies I have cited: a cluster of residences occupied by multiple households, members of which are sometimes but not invariably related by kinship or occupation, sharing courtyards and, often, sanitation and cooking facilities.[78]

To focus as I have on informal networks of exchange is not to deny the significance of other redistributive practices within the early assemblies.[79] In particular, the reader should not infer that I am denying the significance of patronage or suggesting that exchange networks constituted an intentional or systematic alternative thereto.[80] The poor are apparently quite willing simultaneously to engage in networks of reciprocal exchange and patronage relationships as opportunity permits. What merits our interest is precisely how such different economic relationships—and the moral convictions that underlie them—interact.[81]

---

[76] Marcus J. Borg and John Dominic Crossan, *The First Paul: Reclaiming the Radical Visionary behind the Church's Conservative Icon* (New York: HarperOne, 2009), 188–90.

[77] Andrew Wallace-Hadrill, "*Domus* and *Insulae* in Rome: Families and Housefuls," in *Early Christian Families in Context: An Interdisciplinary Dialogue*, ed. David L. Balch and Carolyn Osiek, Religion, Marriage and Family (Grand Rapids: Eerdmans, 2003), 3–18; Bradly S. Billings, "From House Church to Tenement Church: Domestic Space and the Development of Early Urban Christianity—The Example of Ephesus," *JTS* 62 (2011): 541–69; Richard Last, "The Neighborhood (*vicus*) of the Corinthian *ekklēsia*: Beyond Family-Based Descriptions of the First Urban Christ-Believers," *JSNT* 38 (2016): 399–425.

[78] See esp. Brown, "Household Composition," 262–66; Wutich, "Shifting Alliances," 126; Lomnitz, *Networks and Marginality*, 31, 142–43.

[79] I remain skeptical, however, of recent suggestions that, by analogy with other ancient voluntary associations, the early assemblies were sustained by membership fees. So, tentatively, Kloppenborg, "Precedence at the Communal Meal," 184–93; and, more confidently, Richard Last, *The Pauline Church and the Corinthian* Ekklēsia: *Greco-Roman Associations in Comparative Context*, SNTSMS 164 (Cambridge: Cambridge University Press, 2016), 109, 114–48. Were this the ordinary practice among first-century Christ groups, one would expect to find some vestige of it in the second century, where, on the contrary, one finds Christian writers differentiating themselves from other associations precisely by highlighting the voluntary nature of contributions to the church treasury. See Tertullian, *Apol.* 39.5–6; Justin, *1 Apol.* 67.6–7.

[80] The suggestion of Elliott ("Strategies of Resistance") and Friesen ("Paul and Economics").

[81] See Lomnitz, *Networks and Marginality*, 202–3; Scheper-Hughes, *Death without Weeping*, 98–127; Horden, "Household Care and Informal Networks," 58.

It should by now be clear that, in describing the early assemblies as "share communities," I have no intention of attributing to them a uniquely Christian mode of economic practice.[82] As I have emphasized, reciprocal exchange is a common practice whereby the poor manage economic uncertainty. The early Christians, like (other) Jews before them, may have endowed such sharing with unusually weighty theological significance[83] and may have become notorious for the eagerness with which they pursued it (Lucian, *Peregr.* 12-13; Julian, *Ep.* 22 [430d]), but they did not invent it.[84] Neighbors borrowed bread from each other, in Galilean villages and elsewhere, long before Jesus told a story about it.

Nor is it my intent to romanticize the economic practices of the early Christ followers—or, for that matter, of the poor in general. Wistful visions of selfless and egalitarian sharing among the poor may provide a useful moral foil for the hoarding of the modern rich, but they do not make very good historiography. Nor do they survive a reading of the ethnographic literature, wherein one finds, unsurprisingly, no shortage of envy, greed, boastfulness, and resentment[85]—in other words, precisely those threats to social harmony that Paul's moral discourse seeks to restrain (e.g., Gal 6:2-4; Rom 12:16; 1 Thess 5:13b-14; Phil 2:4, 14) and to which we can thus safely assume the early Christians were not immune. Indeed, this is one reason to prefer the language of the ethnographers, who speak of "sharing," "swapping," or "reciprocal exchange," to Meggitt's "mutualism."[86] In any case, the antidote to romanticizing poverty is not to ignore it but to study it.

This necessarily will involve comparative ethnography. The ancient poor are, with very few exceptions, visible in our sources only through the eyes of the elite. It is therefore not surprising that it is much easier to locate ancient evidence of charity or patronage—in other words, evidence of how the rich treated the

---

[82] Cf. Martin, "Review Essay: Justin J. Meggitt," 63; Richard Last, "The Myth of Free Membership in Pauline Christ Groups," in *Scribal Practices and Social Structures among Jesus Adherents: Essays in Honour of John S. Kloppenborg*, ed. William E. Arnal et al., BETL 285 (Leuven: Peeters, 2016): 495-516, here 497-99. Pace Elliott, "Strategies of Resistance," 103.

[83] See esp. Downs, *Alms*; Brown, *Ransom of the Soul*. See also Pieter W. van der Horst, "Organized Charity in the Ancient World: Pagan, Jewish, Christian," in *Jewish and Christian Communal Identities in the Roman World*, ed. Yair Furstenburg, AGJU 94 (Leiden: Brill, 2016), 116-33.

[84] On "mutual financial assistance" within other ancient associations, see Philip A. Harland, "Associations and the Economics of Group Life: A Preliminary Study of Asia Minor and the Aegean Islands," *SEÅ* 80 (2015): 26-31; and, more generally, Peter Brown, *Through the Eye of a Needle: Wealth, the Fall of Rome, and the Making of Christianity in the West, 350-500 AD* (Princeton: Princeton University Press, 2012), 58-62.

[85] Lomnitz, *Networks and Marginality*, 31, 142; Stack, *All Our Kin*, 38-39; Wiessner, "Experimental Games and Games of Life," 136-37; Wutich, "Shifting Alliances," 126.

[86] Jewett has proposed the phrase "agapaic communalism" (*Romans*, 66), which seems to me perfectly apt as a description of Paul's ideal and/or the assemblies' aspiration but untenable as a description of social practice.

poor—than it is to determine how the poor treated each other. If we depend only on our ancient sources, it will be difficult to avoid reproducing this perspective, generating, as Susan Holman has seen, studies in which "the poor are referents, not subjects."[87]

That such an approach is rarely questioned is perhaps not surprising. After all, this perspective dovetails very well with the ethical concern that typically animates such studies—studies that tend, of course, to be written by and for those with economic power. The moral problem posed to the world's wealthy by unequal distribution of wealth in the era of globalized capital is pressing indeed. Still, if we can set aside for a moment our own preoccupations, we may notice that Paul's rhetoric of generosity provides a moral resource for the hungry, too.

---

[87] Susan R. Holman, *The Hungry Are Dying: Beggars and Bishops in Roman Cappadocia*, OSHT (Oxford: Oxford University Press, 2001), 12; cited in Buell, "Be Not One," 38.

JBL 137, no. 1 (2018): 235–254
doi: http://dx.doi.org/10.15699/jbl.1371.2018.196908

Is There a Kenosis in This Text? Rereading Philippians 3:2–11 in the Light of the Christ Hymn

DOROTHEA BERTSCHMANN
d.h.bertschmann@dur.ac.uk
Durham University, Durham DH1, UK

Does Paul recount his own kenosis in Phil 3:2–11? This proposal has been affirmed and refined by quite a few scholarly voices in recent decades. Paul, it is argued, willingly and humbly gives up his Jewish privileges and embraces suffering and death in conformity to Christ; in the same way, Christ willingly "emptied himself" of his divine privileges and obediently embraced suffering and death. Paul puts himself forward as a model to be emulated by the Philippians, embodying the prototype of an ethos that is pleasing to God and that was revealed and established in Christ. This reading offers an alternative to the traditional Protestant reading that sees Phil 3:2–11 as Paul's rejection of Jewish work-righteousness. In this article I will first briefly sketch out the proposed parallels between the Christ hymn in Phil 2 and Paul's autobiographical account in chapter 3. I will then argue that, despite its attractive aspects, the kenosis reading of chapter 3 is resisted by the flow of the text itself. I will then suggest that there is both a gesture of violent renunciation and a gesture of willing conformity in the passage. These aspects are closely connected but must not be read along a seamless trajectory. Together they describe the destructive and constructive moment of Christian identity in the perspective of soteriology. I argue for a reading that leads beyond equally problematic notions of Jewish work-righteousness and kenotic notions of Jewish national pride.

I. Is There a Kenosis in This Text?

Philippians 3:2–11 has created headaches for its exegetes. Without any prior announcement Paul starts to warn his readers about certain people who are characterized in very bitter but imprecise invectives as dogs (κύνες, v. 2), as evil workers (κακοὶ ἐργάται, v. 2; cf. the ἐργάται δόλιοι in 2 Cor 11:13), and as the mutilation (κατατομή, v. 2). The abrupt change of topic and tone in 3:2 led to speculation that

235

the chapter was a separate letter written by Paul on a different occasion.¹ The shadowy figures of the people thus attacked, on the other hand, have fueled elaborate theories about their precise identity.² Though Paul here mentions περιτομή ("circumcision") in a positive way, contrasting it with κατατομή ("mutilation," vv. 2b, 3a), it is probably safe to say that these people are believers in Christ who advertise and advocate a fuller adaptation of Jewish identity markers by the gentile converts to the Christian faith, most prominently circumcision.³ These attempts are summed up by Paul as "trust in the flesh" (πεποίθησις ἐν σαρκί). Paul counters the rival propaganda with a unique enumeration of his own Jewish credentials: What the Judaizing missionaries advocate was fully owned by Paul, either by birth or by performance: circumcision, an unblemished Jewish genealogy, Pharisaic zeal for the law to the point of persecuting the church, and blamelessness on the law's own terms. While this gave Paul very solid grounds for "trust in the flesh," he states that he has come to see all this, his former gains (κέρδη), as loss (ζημία). This pair of κέρδη/ζημία is detailed in varying statements in verses 7–8 before Paul states in verse 9 that he wants to be found in Christ, a desire further unfolded in verse 10: Paul wants to know the power of Christ's resurrection and the fellowship of his sufferings (κοινωνία τῶν παθημάτων αὐτοῦ); more strikingly, he wants to be co-conformed (συμμορφιζόμενος) to Christ's death in order (εἴ πως) to attain the "standing up" (ἐξανάστασις) from the dead (v. 11).

Two scholarly trends have encouraged exegetes to read this account in close connection with the Christ hymn in Phil 2:5–11. There is widespread agreement on the Pauline integrity of the letter; consequently, exegetes have given weight to repeated vocabulary or to perceived echoes of and allusions to key vocabulary.⁴ In addition, the Philippian hymn has been interpreted afresh in its present literary context after decades in which exegesis focused on its possible tradition-historical

---

¹ For a survey, see Pheme Perkins, "Theology for the Heavenly Politeuma," in *Thessalonians, Philippians, Galatians, Philemon*, vol. 1 of *Pauline Theology*, ed. Jouette M. Bassler (Minneapolis: Fortress, 1991), 89–104, esp. 89–90, "The Integrity of Philippians."

² A good summary of the discussion can be found in K. Grayston, "The Opponents in Philippians 3," *ExpTim* 97 (1986): 170–72.

³ Paul never refers to himself with the term ἐργάτης ("worker"); the term is used in the Synoptic tradition in the sense of missionary, e.g., Matt 9:37–38; 10:10; Luke 10:2, 7. This is an important clue "dass Paulus mit dem Ausdruck Kontrahenten christlicher Herkunft bezeichnet" (Ulrich B. Müller, *Der Brief des Paulus an die Philipper*, THKNT [Leipzig: Evangelische Verlagsanstalt, 1993], 143).

⁴ According to Peter S. Oakes, "Many elements of NT texts that were once seen as indicating redactional seams are now seen as features of rhetorical, epistolary and narrative technique" (*Philippians: From People to Letter*, SNTSMS 110 [Cambridge: Cambridge University Press, 2001], 78). See also Duane F. Watson, "A Rhetorical Analysis of Philippians and Its Implications for the Unity Question," *NovT* 30 (1988): 57–88; and Robert Jewett, "The Epistolary Thanksgiving and the Integrity of Philippians," *NovT* 12 (1970): 40–53.

backgrounds.[5] Scholars have rightly affirmed that Paul is prompted by ethical concerns to introduce the hymn in the first place (2:5). A series of thoughtful proposals have at last put the traditional Protestant dread of *imitatio* to rest.[6] They have shown convincingly that an ethical reading of the Christ hymn is not confined to the language of mechanical or meritorious imitation.[7] This development has invited further explorations of how the hymn might generate ethical patterns throughout the letter.

The turn to synchronic and literary methods has encouraged the recognition of repetitions, echoes, and allusions in Paul's choice of vocabulary. With regard to Phil 3:2–10, συμμορφίζω and θάνατος in verse 10 bear the greatest significance, repeating key vocabulary of the first part of the Christ hymn (the nouns μορφή and θάνατος occur in 2:5–8), which Paul has quoted or composed earlier in the letter.[8] Morna D. Hooker famously pioneered a synthetic reading of μορφή language in

---

[5] Gordon D. Fee gives an overview of the vastly different proposals together with some biting criticism (*Paul's Letter to the Philippians*, NICNT [Grand Rapids: Eerdmans, 1995], 43–44).

[6] The term "traditional Protestant" in this article refers not to a denomination and its members but to a particular reading strategy, which sees Paul pointing to the problem of "work-righteousness" in Phil 3. This distinctive traditional Protestant reading is contrasted not with a "Catholic reading" but rather with attempts (often conducted by Protestant exegetes) to overcome the former's shortcomings by offering an alternative "kenotic" reading. I comment on these historically influential reading strategies solely from an exegete's point of view, without wishing to support or disparage any denominational agenda.

[7] For a vocal protest against language of *imitatio*, see Ernst Käsemann, "Kritische Analyse von Phil. 2, 5–11," in *Exegetische Versuche und Besinnungen*, 2 vols. (Göttingen: Vandenhoeck & Ruprecht, 1967), 1:51–95. On the unique role of Christ as Lord, see Larry W. Hurtado, "Jesus as Lordly Example in Philippians 2:5–11," in *From Jesus to Paul: Studies in Honour of Francis Wright Beare*, ed. Peter Richardson and John C. Hurd (Waterloo, ON: Wilfrid Laurier University Press, 1984), 113–26. Stephen E. Fowl has highlighted notions of reasoning as part of Christian conformity (*The Story of Christ in the Ethics of Paul: An Analysis of the Function of the Hymnic Material in the Pauline Corpus*, JSNTSup 36 [Sheffield: Sheffield Academic, 1990]). Some older commentaries note similarities between Christ and Paul; see, e.g., J. L. Houlden, *Paul's Letters from Prison: Philippians, Colossians, Philemon, and Ephesians*, PNTC (Harmondsworth: Penguin, 1970), 106. Among newer commentaries, see, e.g., Charles B. Cousar, *Philippians and Philemon: A Commentary*, NTL (Louisville: Westminster John Knox, 2009); and, in a cautious and qualified way, Stephen E. Fowl, *Philippians*, Two Horizons New Testament Commentary (Grand Rapids: Eerdmans, 2005). N. T. Wright's forthcoming commentary on Philippians was not available at the time this article was finished.

[8] Other repeated words are εὑρίσκω (2:7, 3:9) and κύριος (2:11, 3:8). The important term ἡγέομαι will be discussed below. For a critical evaluation of the shared vocabulary between Phil 2 and 3, see Brian J. Dodd, "The Story of Christ and the Imitation of Paul in Philippians 2–3," in *Where Christology Began: Essays on Philippians 2*, ed. Ralph P. Martin and Brian J. Dodd (Louisville: Westminster John Knox, 1998), 154–61, here 156. Fee, while thinking that the "parallels are inexact" (*Paul's Letter to the Philippians*, 304), still thinks that "the linguistic echoes and the general 'form' of the narrative seem intentionally designed to recall the Christ narrative in 2:6–11" (315).

Philippians by suggesting that Christ's taking up of the form of a slave (μορφή δούλου, 2:7) invites conformity with Christ on the part of the believers: in the present they are to be conformed to Christ's suffering and death (3:10), and ultimately they will be co-conformed (σύμμορφον, 3:21) to Christ's own body of glory. Hooker called this dynamic of mutual conforming "interchange."[9]

Kenotic readers of Phil 3:2–11 take this imagery one step further: if Paul conforms to Christ's obedient death and in the future to his glorified body, is there also a moment of divesting himself of privilege, just as Christ is said to have done by "emptying himself" (2:7)?[10] In other words, is there not only conformity to Christ's suffering and death but, equally and crucially, conformity to Christ's kenosis, or self-emptying? For kenotic readers, this divesting moment is indeed described in 3:2–11, especially verses 7–11. According to Pheme Perkins, "Conversion implies an 'emptying' analogous to that of Christ."[11] She goes on to say, "The hymn suggests that renouncing at risk to one's life even the legitimate appearances of status and exaltation in order to identify with the lowly reflects God's saving activity."[12] Earlier on, William S. Kurz pioneered the understanding of a pattern of double imitation as the key to unlock the difficult chapter 3 of Philippians, drawing attention to the συμμιμηταί in verse 17.[13]

According to Craig Steven de Vos, "Paul ... presents himself as a model for the renunciation of status for the sake of the gospel in his rejection of his Jewish status in 3:2–11. Indeed, in this passage Paul parallels Christ's renunciation of his status in the 'hymn.'"[14] De Vos sees this ethical posture in polemical contrast to the proud status seeking of Greco-Roman elites. On the loss of status Wendy Cotter comments, "Paul shows that he too left the life of prestige and honour as a scrupulous observer of the Law."[15] This process of letting go of status and honor is described

---

[9] Morna D. Hooker, "Interchange and Suffering," in *From Adam to Christ: Essays on Paul* (Cambridge: Cambridge University Press, 1990), 42–55. Other supposed "echoes" such as εὑρεθείς (2:7)/εὑρεθῶ (3:9) might support the idea of interchange: Paul wants to be found in Christ, just as Christ willed to be found in human nature (*pace* Dodd, who discards the parallel ["Story of Christ," 156]).

[10] The category "kenotic reading/reader" is a loose one and merely points to a shared approach among exegetes of this passage who might disagree on many other counts.

[11] Perkins, "Theology for the Heavenly Politeuma," 94.

[12] Ibid., 96.

[13] William S. Kurz, "Kenotic Imitation of Paul and of Christ in Philippians 2 and 3," in *Discipleship in the New Testament*, ed. Fernando F. Segovia (Philadelphia: Fortress, 1985), 103–26, here 105. This scheme is picked up strongly by Cousar, *Philippians and Philemon*, 75.

[14] Craig Steven de Vos, *Church and Community Conflicts: The Relationship of the Thessalonian, Corinthian, and Philippian Churches with Their Wider Civic Communities*, SBLDS 168 (Atlanta: Scholars Press, 1999), 284.

[15] Wendy Cotter, "Our Politeuma Is in Heaven: The Meaning of Philippians 3.17–21," in *Origins and Method: Towards a New Understanding of Judaism and Christianity; Essays in Honour of John C. Hurd*, ed. Bradley H. McLean, JSNTSup 86 (Sheffield: Sheffield Academic, 1993), 92–104, here 97.

as painful, for example, by L. Gregory Bloomquist: "In giving up his ascribed honor, the honor of being born as a Jew of the royal pre-Davidic line of Israel (that of Saul), and the acquired honor consequent upon having become a zealous Pharisee, Paul had suffered immensely."[16] Peter Oakes, too, is sympathetic to notions of a shared kenotic ethos in the hymn and Phil 3:2–11: "As Kurz, Fowl and others have noted, Paul's path broadly mirrors that of Christ. Paul begins in a privileged position, he renounces his privileges, then faces suffering, then finally gains higher privileges than he began with."[17]

Paul S. Minear argues most clearly for a distinctive two-stage descent of Paul, giving up his privileges first and, second, embracing suffering and death.[18] The latter proposal can draw support from recognition of the two clear steps in Christ's own downward career (Phil 2:6–8), indicated by the two verbs "he emptied himself" (ἑαυτὸν ἐκένωσεν, 2:7) and "he humbled himself" (ἐταπείνωσεν ἑαυτόν, 2:8). The action of emptying, or rather self-emptying (ἑαυτόν), in verse 7 is further characterized by three participles: λαβών ("taking"), γενόμενος ("being"), and εὑρεθείς ("being found"). Christ's emptying somehow took place by his taking on the form of a slave, by being in the likeness of a human being (ἄνθρωπος), and by being found in the shape (σχῆμα) of a human being. Almost every single word is debated in this rich and dense text, which has become one of the most important New Testament texts for later christological reflections. For our purpose, it suffices to see that κενόω is somehow characterized by "becoming human," which is simultaneously described as having the form of a slave, in a clear contrast to having the form of God (2:6).[19]

Furthermore, the Christ hymn presents the activity or self-emptying as the contrasting alternative to either grabbing or clutching Godlikeness: οὐχ ἁρπαγμὸν ἡγήσατο. The meaning of this phrase is debated, though Roy W. Hoover's solution of proposing an idiomatic reading along the lines of "not using selfishly" has gained

---

[16] L. Gregory Bloomquist, "Subverted by Joy: Suffering and Joy in Paul's Letter to the Philippians," *Int* 7 (2007): 270–82, here 278.

[17] Oakes, *Philippians: From People to Letter*, 116. Oakes is alert and sensitive toward differences in Christ's and Paul's examples, but he holds that "each model calls the Philippians to the same actions: willingness to lose privileges (which, in the context of Philippi, probably centers on status) and to suffer" (116).

[18] Paul S. Minear, "Singing and Suffering in Philippi," in *The Conversation Continues: Studies in Paul and John in Honor of J. Louis Martyn*, ed. Robert T. Fortna and Beverly R. Gaventa (Nashville: Abingdon, 1990), 202–19, esp. 205–7, "The Hymn and the Autobiography."

[19] While patristic conceptions of incarnation would rather envision incarnation as "taking on the human nature," Phil 2:7 pictures it as the loss of something, of Christ's or even God's self-emptying. For a discussion of the historical roots of contemporary kenotic christologies, see T. R. Thompson, "Nineteenth-Century Kenotic Christology: The Waxing, Waning, and Weighing of a Quest for a Coherent Orthodoxy," in *Exploring Kenotic Christology: The Self-Emptying of God*, ed. C. Stephen Evans (Oxford: Oxford University Press, 2006), 74–111; Sarah Coakley, "Kenōsis and Subversion: On the Repression of 'Vulnerability' in Christian Feminist Writing," in *Powers and Submissions: Spirituality, Philosophy, and Gender*, CCTh (Oxford: Blackwell, 2002), 3–39.

wide popularity.[20] For this article and for the purposes of the kenotic readers of chapter 3, it does not matter whether the attitude rejected by Christ is grabbing, clutching, or selfishly using Godlikeness. The attitude sketched out is somehow about Christ rejecting the wrong acquisition or use of something good, which was possibly already in his reach or fully his, namely, Godlikeness or closeness to the divine sphere, and which is clearly given to him in an intensified form in the second part of the hymn ("the name above all names" in v. 9 with its striking echoes of Isa 45). There seems to be a clear structure of Jesus embodying a "not this—but that" attitude, which leads to the divine response of "because of that—therefore."[21]

Paul's own life, then, mirrors very closely and deliberately Christ's career. Like Christ, Paul is in a superior position to start, at least from the perspective of the Judaizers and from Paul's old Pharisaic "I," that is, owning privileges, honorific attributes, and achievements—in a word, status. Like Christ, Paul voluntarily and radically divests himself of all this in a kind of self-emptying or kenosis. In a second stage, both Christ and Paul willingly and humbly embrace suffering and death (though suffering is implied rather than explicitly stated in the Christ hymn). In Paul's case as in Christ's, this is not the end but becomes the basis for unprecedented glory and honor in God's counterintuitive and countercultural economy.

In a thoughtful twist of the kenotic reading of Phil 2 and 3, some commentators point out that Paul's self-emptying might be expressed not so much as a real loss but first and foremost as a different *attitude*, which reevaluates privilege and status in the light of the Christ event.[22] Fowl argues that Paul calls for the cultivating of a Christlike mind-set that enables a new pattern of practical reasoning rather than a literal imitation in the life of the believers, as the numerous verbs of thinking and reasoning in Philippians suggest.[23] As in Christ's case, this dramatic change

---

[20] Roy W. Hoover, "The Harpagmos Enigma: A Philological Solution," *HTR* 64 (1971): 95–119. For a critique, see Samuel Vollenweider, "Er 'Raub' der Gottgleichheit: Ein religionsgeschichtlicher Vorschlag zu Phil 2,6(–11)," in *Horizonte neutestamentlicher Christologie: Studien zu Paulus und zur frühchristlichen Theologie*, WUNT 144 (Tübingen: Mohr Siebeck, 2002), 263–84.

[21] Various exegetes rightly emphasize that the conjunction signaling the transition from humiliation to exaltation in Phil 2:9 is not ἀλλὰ but διό (see, e.g., Minear, "Singing and Suffering," 205).

[22] This is very strongly emphasized by N. T. Wright, who states that the attitude asked from the Philippian believers in response to Paul's Christlike model is not the renunciation of their Roman citizenship but a renewal of uncompromising loyalty to Jesus ("Paul's Gospel and Caesar's Empire," in *Paul and Politics: Ekklesia, Israel, Imperium, Interpretation; Essays in Honor of Krister Stendahl*, ed. Richard A. Horsley [Harrisburg, PA: Trinity Press International, 2000], 160–83, here 179).

[23] See Fowl, *Story of Christ*. See also Fowl, "Christology and Ethics," in Martin and Dodd, *Where Christology Began*, 140–53. Fowl calls his approach "phronetic," alluding to the frequent lexeme φρονεῖν in Philippians. He suggests that a "phronetic application of 2:6–11 can be extended more broadly throughout the epistle" (141). Φρονεῖν and related terms can be found in Phil 1:7; 2:2 (2x), 3, 5; 3:15 (2x), 19; 4:2, 10 (2x); for ἡγέομαι, see Phil 2:3, 6; 3:7 (2x), 8. Other phrases such

can be expressed by reference to a certain attitude, of (not) *considering* (ἡγέομαι) something to be the case (2:6, 3:7/8): Christ did not consider Godlikeness to be something to be grabbed or clutched; Paul considered his erstwhile privileges to be loss rather than gain.[24] Paul models and advocates both the voluntary loss of privilege and the voluntary surrender to death, which have already been authoritatively modeled for him by Christ and need to be embodied by the Christian believers in Philippi.

It is easy to see the appeal of the kenotic reading of Phil 2 and 3. This reading builds on and further develops the notion that Paul uses the Christ hymn in 2:5–11 in a context of ethical admonitions to make a strong ethical point. Instead of speculating about the two natures of Christ and how the interplay of those natures might have brought about salvation, there is a more direct and straightforward message: Christ reveals a human being after God's own heart, motivated by self-sacrificial, humble, suffering love. In some more elaborate proposals, Christ also reveals a God, whose divine nature is kenotic, risking the divine self for the sake of love. This authoritative revelation about what it means to be human in conformity to the ultimate revelation of the divine is meant to be taken up by the Christ believers, as modeled by Paul.[25]

According to the kenotic reading, the point of Phil 3:2–7 is not to vilify Jewish law. This reading offers an attractive alternative to the more familiar, traditional Protestant view, which post-Sanders Pauline scholarship widely and rightly suspects as promoting inadequate if not dangerous caricatures of Jewish law obedience. What Paul takes issue with is not law obedience as such but an *attitude* of selfish pride.[26] A voluntarily chosen posture of self-effacing and self-sacrificial lowliness is at the heart of this new vision, which has considerable prophetic force in any culture that hails competing for honor and status. But does the text lend itself to such a reading?

---

as τὰ ἑαυτῶν ἕκαστος σκοποῦντος ("let each of you look," 2:4) and τὰ ἑαυτῶν ζητοῦσιν ("are seeking their own interests," 2:21) are also meaningful.

[24] R. W. L. Moberly also highlights the attitudinal correspondence, as "Paul's functional equivalent, or non-identical imitations, with regard to Jesus' *kenosis*: the surprising relinquishing of what he might have been expected to hold on to" (*Prophecy and Discernment*, Cambridge Studies in Christian Doctrine [Cambridge: Cambridge University Press, 2006], 176).

[25] On the kenotic or "cruciform" character of the divine revelation and Christian ethics, see John Howard Yoder, "The Disciple of Christ and the Way of Jesus," in *The Politics of Jesus: Vicit Agnus noster*, 2nd ed. (Grand Rapids: Eerdmans, 1994), 112–33; Michael J. Gorman, *Inhabiting the Cruciform God: Kenosis, Justification, and Theosis in Paul's Narrative Soteriology* (Grand Rapids: Eerdmans, 2009).

[26] De Vos comments, "The real issue in Phil. 3:2–11 does not appear to be circumcision and the Law" (*Church and Community Conflicts*, 269). Wright stresses that Paul did not "regard covenant membership itself as unimportant or to be jettisoned" (Wright, "Paul's Gospel," 177). Similarly, Perkins, "Theology for the Heavenly Politeuma," 92.

II. Elements That Resist a Kenotic Reading

Some terms from the hymn are not repeated in Phil 3:2–11: Paul does not describe his activities or attitudes as self-humbling or self-emptying at any stage in this passage.[27] While Paul can make an appeal to embody the virtue of ταπεινοφροσύνη ("humility") in 2:3, this striking expression is not found in chapter 3.[28] Later Paul will mention the transformation of τὸ σῶμα τῆς ταπεινώσεως ἡμῶν ("the body of our humiliation") in 3:21, a term that can indicate a state of general lowliness and neediness without any ethical connotations.[29] In the passage under scrutiny, Paul does not mention the cross, though it will appear again in 3:18 when Paul attacks the "enemies of the cross."[30] Paul does not at this point bring in δοῦλος language, though he started his letter with the introduction as Παῦλος καὶ Τιμόθεος δοῦλοι Χριστοῦ Ἰησοῦ (1:1). Absent, too, is the language of obedience, which is central to the depiction of Christ's attitude in the hymn (ὑπήκοος, 2:8). The key term to link Paul's and Christ's suffering is simply κοινωνία ("communion," 3:10), a term used a few times in the letter to denote Paul or the Philippians as "partners" or "shareholders" in the gospel mission (see Phil 1:5, 7; 2:1; 4:14, 15).[31]

---

[27] Paul does worry, however, that he might have run and labored εἰς κενόν ("in vain") in 2:16. He mentions κενοδοξία ("conceit") as a negative concept in 2:3. In explicit vocabulary at least, Paul makes no appeal to a virtue of self-emptying in the way he appeals to the virtue of humility (ταπεινοφροσύνη) in 2:3.

[28] Philippians 2:3 may offer the first occurrence of ταπεινοφροσύνη in the Pauline corpus; even if Paul did not coin the term (cf. the only slightly later occurrences in Josephus, *J.W.* 4.9.2 §494 and Epictetus, *Diatr.* 3.24.56), he likely used it the first time in a positive way (see Reinhard Feldmeier, *Power, Service, Humility: A New Testament Ethic*, trans. Brian McNeil [Waco, TX: Baylor University Press, 2014], 61).

[29] The term ταπείνωσις can express a range of meaning from a modest position in life to a reversal in fortune and even active self-abasing (for the latter, see Ps. Sol. 3:8; T. Jos. 10:2; Jos. Asen. 11:1; see BDAG, s.v. "ταπείνωσις"). The lack of the lexeme φρονεῖν seems to indicate a state rather than an active (ethical) deliberation or virtue. Cf. also 4:12, where Paul juxtaposes ταπεινοῦσθαι with περισσεύειν in the sense of material poverty or wealth.

[30] The degree to which the first and last parts of chapter 3 can be integrated depends on the identity of these "enemies." Are they the Judaizers, and do the expressions "their god is their belly" and "their glory is in their shame" refer to Jewish food laws and circumcision (Karl Barth, *The Epistle to the Philippians* [London: SCM, 1962], 113)? Or do these enigmatic descriptions refer to more general vices of gluttony and licentiousness or even to a strategy of avoiding suffering? (see Minear, "Singing and Suffering," 208–9; Fowl, *Philippians*, 149). These questions have not been resolved conclusively.

[31] There is a legal-commercial element connected with the terminology, especially in chapter 4; the Philippians form a partnership (*societas*) with Paul for the gospel cause (see Julien M. Ogereau, *Paul's Koinonia with the Philippians: A Socio-historical Investigation of a Pauline Economic Partnership*, WUNT 2/377 [Tübingen: Mohr Siebeck, 2014]). Michael Wolter has pointed out the centrality of the term κοινωνία in Hellenistic friendship discourse ("Der Apostel und seine

Although I do not discount possible verbal links and echoes with the Christ hymn, the expressions mentioned above are weighty omissions that counsel caution. Still, the mere counting or discounting of words is not a sufficient criterion to decide on parallels or echoes between Phil 2 and 3. The account of the dramatic loss of privilege and status and the subsequent suffering to the point of death can still evoke the Christ hymn, if not in shared expressions then in a shared spirit. I do, however, think there are at least two strong reasons why the passage should not be read this way.

Privilege, Loss, and Gain: Not Grading Goods but Juxtaposing Incommensurable Patterns

It is certainly true that Paul gives up a lot. Even if some of the things in his list, such as being a "Hebrew of Hebrews," his knowledge of the law, and also his circumcision, which he never attempts to undo, are still his, it is not hard to imagine that Paul's conversion would have cost him quite a lot of his former prestige, honor, and friendships. We can imagine that losing all this was painful, and the passive aorist in 3:8 can indeed be translated as the NRSV does: "I *suffered* the loss of all things." In the greater scheme of things, however, neither does Paul dwell on this *loss* nor does he rationalize it. Stanley K. Stowers, for example, observes, "Paul truly had great benefits in his life as a faithful Jew but surrendered that life in order to be faithful to his call to be an apostle to the Gentiles."[32] Paul did not humbly and voluntarily give up his erstwhile privileges in order to serve God's mission, but he violently discards them in order to "know Christ." The first strong indicator that Paul does not narrate his own kenosis lies in the way he radically juxtaposes ἐμὴν δικαιοσύνην (further characterized as ἐκ νόμου, "a righteousness of my own that comes from the law," v. 9) with the δικαιοσύνη ἐπὶ τῇ πίστει (further characterized as ἐκ θεοῦ and with the qualification διὰ πίστεως Χριστοῦ, "one [righteousness] that comes through faith in Christ, the righteousness from God based on faith," v. 9 NRSV).[33] Paul does not contrast pride with humility but contrasts two kinds of

---

Gemeinden als Teilhaber am Leidensgeschick Jesu Christi: Beobachtungen zur paulinischen Leidenstheologie," *NTS* 36 [1990]: 535–57), though the term φιλία is actually absent (see the critique by Ulrich Heckel, *Kraft in Schwachheit: Untersuchungen zu 2. Kor 10–13*, WUNT 2/56 [Tübingen: Mohr Siebeck, 1993], 240 n. 166). While there is certainly a strong element of partaking, of sharing, and even of practical solidarity implied by the term, the partaking is not just in a friend's well-being but in the cause of the gospel. Connotations of intimate communion are implied by phrases such as "my Lord" (3:8) and probably less by the term κοινωνία as such.

[32] Stanley K. Stowers, "Friends and Enemies in the Politics of Heaven," in Bassler, *Thessalonians, Philippians, Galatians, Philemon*, 105–21, here 120.

[33] This verse is an especially popular candidate in the πίστις Χριστοῦ debate, since πίστις is mentioned twice and could therefore be seen as the faithfulness of Christ (first occurrence, subjective genitive), to which human faith responds (see Peter T. O'Brien, *The Epistle to the Philippians: A Commentary on the Greek Text*, NIGTC [Grand Rapids: Eerdmans, 1991], 398; and

δικαιοσύνη, which are incommensurable in his estimate. He only hints at this in this very brief and dense text, which has been rightly called a "little meteorite from Romans."[34] While central concepts such as δικαιοσύνη are not expanded and are open to a certain range of meanings, it seems clear that Paul subsumes all his achievements and status markers as a faithful Jew under the problematic term "my righteousness" (cf. the parallel in Rom 10:3, ἰδία δικαιοσύνη), which is contrasted with the righteousness ἐκ θεοῦ.[35]

The central aspect of this passage is not that Paul lets go—perhaps with considerable heartache—what is dear and valuable to him in order obediently to fulfill God's mission or to approach his fellow human beings in a spirit of humility. Instead, the sole stated goal is "to gain Christ," which is specified with the parallel construction (ἵνα plus aorist subjunctive) to "be found in him," further specified in verses 10–11 with an infinitive construction that is also final and gives "to know him" as the third reason.[36] Knowing Christ, however, is not just the *goal* but also equally the *cause* for Paul's reevaluation. He builds a crescendo of διά in verses 7 and 8: Gain has become loss διὰ τὸν Χριστόν (v. 7). Indeed, Paul considers it all to be loss διὰ τὸ ὑπερέχον τῆς γνώσεως Χριστοῦ Ἰησοῦ ["because of the surpassing value of knowing Christ Jesus" NRSV] ... δι' ὅν ["for his sake" NRSV] he has lost it all (v. 8).[37] In the light of Christ, Paul cannot help discarding what was precious to him. At the same time, he *must* discard it all, in order to win Christ (ἵνα Χριστὸν κερδήσω, v. 8). There is a tightly constructed circular movement: Christ is the reason for the upheaval in discarding prior values but also the goal of that upheaval.

Paul's reevaluation is completely dependent on the reality of Christ and is in

---

Ralph P. Martin, *Philippians*, NCB [London: Oliphants, 1976], 132–33, but cf. Fee, who reads both instances as objective, most naturally taken as repetition [*Paul's Letter to the Philippians*, 325]). While it is possible to read the first occurrence as a subjective genitive, the matter must not be pressed too far. The wider context makes it quite clear that Paul is not speaking of "having faith/believing" as a human activity (1:29), just as he is not speaking about "knowing" as a human activity (3:10). Both the πίστις Χριστοῦ and the γνῶσις Χριστοῦ imply a human component, the proper direction of human trusting and knowing, which is nevertheless wholly dependent and enfolded by the reality of Christ, the object of knowledge and trust, established prior to human activities.

[34] Fee, *Paul's Letter to the Philippians*, 320.

[35] The striking ἐκ indicates the source of righteousness, which can easily be conceptualized as something granted to the human partner and less easily as a divine attribute, such as "covenant faithfulness." On the latter suggestion, brought to prominence by the work of N. T. Wright, see Stephen Westerholm, *Justification Reconsidered: Rethinking a Pauline Theme* (Grand Rapids: Eerdmans, 2013), 51–74.

[36] For the final meaning of infinitives, see BDF §400.5.

[37] The preposition διά with the accusative primarily expresses causality ("the reason why something happens, results, exists"; BDAG, s.v. "διά," B.1.). Although διά can have a prospective final meaning ("for the sake of"), the more natural meaning is causal. Since Paul will later use an unmistakably final conjunction (ἵνα), it makes the best sense to take the threefold διά in verses 7 and 8 as "because of."

no sense freestanding. There even is a strong element of a surplus, the ὑπερέχον τῆς γνώσεως Χριστοῦ Ἰησοῦ (v. 8), which might be seen in parallel to the ὑπερύψωσεν of the hymn in 2:9: Christ and Paul let go something good in order to gain something far better. Yet seeing Christ as the "better" that makes the "less good" merely pale in comparison would be to misunderstand the circularity: only by dramatically degrading the one can the other be gained.[38] Paul, unlike Christ, does not (temporarily) lose or give up his privileges in order to win back something far better. In Paul's case there is a simultaneous and interdependent counting gain as loss, so that loss can be counted as all-surpassing gain.[39]

This brings us to the second point: The two occurrences of the verb ἡγέομαι in Phil 3:8 cannot refer to an imitation of Christ's attitude in 2:6.

The Phrase ἡγοῦμαι σκύβαλα ("I Regard [Them] as Rubbish" NRSV) Is Not "Using without Selfishness"

In view of Paul's change of *attitude*, modeled on Christ's attitude of not grasping, could not Paul's stance of *considering* gain as loss (cf. the threefold ἡγοῦμαι in vv. 7–8) echo and imitate Christ's posture of not *considering* (ἡγήσατο, 2:6) something to be a "robbery" or to be used for his own advantage? In this case, Paul's Jewish identity markers and his blameless observance of the law are not bad in themselves; the only problematic aspect would be Paul's wrong attitude, which is generally characterized as false pride. As Wright puts it, Paul, in close parallel to Christ, "did not regard his covenant membership in Israel as something to be exploited. It did not entitle him to adopt a position of effortless superiority over the lesser breeds without the law."[40] One could argue that the only difference is that for

---

[38] *Pace* Stowers, who argues that "Paul's narrative no more regards his past Jewish life as worthless than the exalted prerogatives that Christ gave up should be regarded as worthless. Rather, the first pales in comparison with the second" ("Friends and Enemies," 120).

[39] It is not wrong to state, as Richard S. Ascough does, that "Paul was able to have a net gain far surpassing the value of his former achievements" or that "Paul's former achievements are not 'refuse' in and of themselves, they are 'refuse' in comparison with what Paul now has" (*Paul's Macedonian Associations: The Social Context of Philippians and 1 Thessalonians*, WUNT 2/161 [Tübingen: Mohr Siebeck, 2003], 120). Ascough still misses the point that "because of Christ" and "in order to gain Christ" these achievements are *bound* to be refuse. Gerald F. Hawthorne, on the other hand, says, "One might have expected him to say, in the light of what he said before, that his previous personal advantages, although still good, are being left behind because he has found something better. But no! In Paul's thinking, the decision he made was not the decision to go from good to better, nor was it the surrender of a valued possession; it was an abandoning to ζημία, 'loss'" (*Philippians*, rev. and expanded by Ralph P. Martin, WBC 43 [Nashville: Nelson, 2004], 189). Similarly Joachim Gnilka, who speaks of the "Umwertung der Werte: Es war kein Übergang vom Guten zum Bessern, auch nicht Preisgabe eines Besitzes. Ζημίαν kann man nicht preisgeben" (*Der Philipperbrief: Auslegung*, HThKNT [Freiburg im Breisgau: Herder, 1976], 191).

[40] Wright, "Paul's Gospel," 177.

Christ this sort of "using a good thing badly" was always purely hypothetical, whereas for Paul it was a sad reality of which he had to repent, which might account for the strong language.

Paul's change of attitude is clearly triggered by his encounter with Christ, and in that sense it was a christologically powered renewal of *phronēsis*, to use Fowl's term. But Paul does not advocate modesty or generosity by repenting of self-reliant or nationalistic pride.[41] The expression ἡγοῦμαι σκύβαλα most strongly resists a kenotic reading, whether σκύβαλον is translated as "rubbish," stressing the uselessness, or as "filth," stressing the revulsiveness.[42]

Paul does not dwell on how he became an outcast to his former peers—or, in fact, to everybody—as he freely does in 1 Cor 4:9–13 (ὡς περικαθάρματα τοῦ κόσμου, v. 13). He does not describe *himself* as having become the scum or "refuse" of the world through his loss of Jewish status, but his former *treasures* are now "rubbish" in his eyes. Even what Paul still owns he reevaluates "not just [as] worthless but [as] positively detrimental and repulsive," as Markus Bockmuehl aptly puts it.[43] The verb ἡγοῦμαι might indeed recall Phil 2:6 and the new mind-set Paul advocates, but Paul's mind-set of considering what was gain as loss fundamentally differs from Christ's, who did not consider equality with God something to be grasped or clutched or selfishly used. The powerful kenotic gesture of Christ does not discard or discount divine privileges but, at most, gives them up for a while, though this attitude surely has value beyond the period of kenotic self-humbling. It is, however, inconceivable for Christ to call the privileges "dirt" that were in some sense his before his kenosis. Here the parallel seriously breaks down.[44] Paul's case, on the

---

[41] Contra Wright (ibid.) and Markus Bockmuehl, who titles his commentary section 3:4b–6 "Paul's Nationalistic Past" (*The Epistle to the Philippians*, BNTC [Peabody, MA: Hendrickson, 1998], 194–203) and states that Paul "seems to link his pre-Christian life to hard-line concerns for the national purity of Israel and its faithfulness to the Torah" (200). The Paul of Phil 3:2–11 is not an enlightened Peter who confesses upon entering the house of the gentile centurion: "I truly understand that God shows no partiality, but in every nation anyone who fears him and does what is right is acceptable to him" (Acts 10:34–35 NRSV).

[42] BDAG has "refuse, rubbish, leavings, dirt, dung"; Friedrich Lang differentiates between (1) "dung," "muck," even "excrement"; (2) "scraps," "leavings," "leftovers of a meal," "sweepings"; and (3) "refuse" ("σκύβαλον," *TDNT* 7:445–47, here 445). On a silver cup from Boscoreale, σκύβαλα points to a buried man's remains as refuse (F. Winter, "Der Silberschatz von Boscoreale," *Jahrbuch des Kaiserlich-Deutschen Archäologischen Instituts* 11 [1896]: 82; A. Michaelis, "Der Silberschatz von Boscoreale," *Preussische Jahrbücher* 85 [1896]: 17–56, here 43). Sirach 27:4 compares σκύβαλα to lumps of manure; Philo speaks of the parts of an offering that are to be given as "leftover" or "refuse" to the mortal race (*Sacr.* 109); Josephus mentions how the hungry inhabitants of Jerusalem searched the sewers and dunghills for "refuse" they could eat (*J.W.* 5.13.6 §571).

[43] Bockmuehl, *Epistle to the Philippians*, 207. Similarly O'Brien, *Epistle to the Philippians*, 385.

[44] Fowl comments, "There is nothing in Christ's preexistence which could be classified as 'garbage' in the light of the cross" (Fowl, "Christology and Ethics," 152 n. 44).

other hand, presents a dramatic, if not disturbing, reevaluation of things once held precious. What was previously showcased in a glass vitrine has now been labeled "trash." It is important to Paul that his converts not adopt and embrace that which, for those who are "in Christ," has become either anachronistic and meaningless, like a heap of scrap paper, or even revulsive, like the search for food in a rubbish bin. Paul warns the Philippians, metaphorically speaking, not to pay a meager first installment into an account that he personally had closed down though it contained a fortune.

Neither the violence of the discarding gesture nor the concrete and passionate warning to gentile believers not to be circumcised can be adequately captured by kenotic readers, who see Paul modeling an attitude of humble and voluntary letting go of privilege in order to serve others.[45] Regardless of what Paul says elsewhere about his Jewish inheritance,[46] we have no indication in Phil 3 that Paul repented of petty nationalism or pride in ethnic or religious status. Paul calls his privileges loss, and, in case we should mistake this as a nostalgic sentiment for some favorite things now given up for something better, he further describes "loss" as "crap."

III. Reading Philippians 3:2–11 Again: Beyond Work-Righteousness and Self-Emptying

There are two crucial moments in Phil 3:2–11: (1) the radical reevaluation of privileges and (2) the conformity to Christ's career in verse 10. Instead of seeing these as two steps in one organic process, I suggest that they are closely connected but also clearly distinguished. The grammar of the text indicates that verse 10 can be seen as an elaborating parallel that describes further the goal of "gaining Christ" (v. 8b) and "being found in him" (v. 9a) by adding the goal as τοῦ γνῶναι αὐτόν ("to know him," v. 10).

According to this reading, the reevaluation of former treasures and the knowledge of Christ are two sides of the same coin. They are closely related but also mutually exclusive. If the coin shows "Christ," meaning "knowing Christ" and "gaining Christ," then it cannot show "law," seen as shorthand for the Jewish identity markers, the privileges and achievements that Paul formerly valued so deeply. And in showing "Christ," the coin in fact shows "knowing Christ, both the power of his resurrection and the fellowship of his sufferings" (v. 10). The aspect of

---

[45] According to Dodd, "Paul's self-exemplification is not of humility ... but very literally is designed to reject the need for circumcision" ("Story of Christ," 155). The rejection of circumcision does not exclude the call to humility, but the call to humility cannot make Paul's harsh tone intelligible.

[46] At this point Paul does not attempt to show the abiding continuity between God's promises fulfilled in Christ and Israel as he does elsewhere, for example, in Rom 3:1–5 or 9:1–5 (see Bockmuehl, *Epistle to the Philippians*, 184).

conformity to Christ (v. 10) thus is the fuller picture of what it means to be "found in Christ." Verses 7–8 describe the *precondition* to "being found in Christ," not an *aspect* thereof.[47] They negatively prepare the field for the positive statement of being in communion with Christ. I call the first moment, the aspect of dramatic reevaluation of values, "foundational" and the second moment, the aspect of conformity, "formative." There is a destructive element in Paul's discarding as rubbish his former treasures, which corresponds negatively to the gaining of Christ, further elaborated as conformity. The encounter with Christ is the foundational datum for Paul, which sets his entire life on different premises, on a different fundament. What is built upon this fundament is conformity with Christ, expressed as fellowship with Christ's sufferings and conformity to his death, which is nevertheless surrounded by resurrection power and resurrection hope and is ultimately headed for glory (3:20).

The destructive and, in a sense, foundational moment must not be confused with a voluntary first step of following the humble Christ humbly. Instead, Paul describes a radical and quite disturbing religious reorientation. Paul claims that nothing less than Christ has brought to naught what was good in him, that he has been attacked and deconstructed at the strongest point of his human existence, not caught out at his weakest.[48] It seems to me that the traditional Protestant, especially Reformed, readings of our passage show a greater readiness to accommodate and acknowledge the radicalism of Paul's theology at this point.[49] John Calvin is representative at this point, summing up Paul's reasoning in Phil 3:2–10 as "Fides offert nudum hominem deo" ("Faith offers a person naked to God").[50]

We thus have this moment of nullification, of cancelling out, of bringing to

---

[47] Precondition must not be understood in a chronological way but rather as strictly causal: without A, there can be no B.

[48] Müller comments, "Der Blick in die Vergangenheit enthält keinerlei pessimistische Züge" (*Der Brief des Paulus an die Philipper*, 148). Paul does not look back on the law with disgust because of his "own frustrated efforts to live by it" (contra William Barclay, *The Letters to the Philippians, Colossians, and Thessalonians*, rev. ed., Daily Study Bible [Edinburgh: St Andrew Press, 1975], 63). Only κατὰ ζῆλος διώκων τὴν ἐκκλησίαν ("as to zeal, a persecutor of the church," 3:6 NRSV) will be read as a negative, even from the perspective of the (Christian!) Judaizers. It comes as the penultimate element in Paul's enumeration, just before the summary κατὰ δικαιοσύνην τὴν ἐν νόμῳ γενόμενος ἄμεμπτος ("as to righteousness under the law, blameless," 3:7 NRSV). Its rhetorical effect might be to bind together in a shocking way Paul's existence as a law-abiding Jew and his persecuting activities.

[49] This does not mean that traditional Protestant readings are without their own danger. They correctly state that there *is* such an earth-shattering encounter between Paul and Christ, nullifying his prior identity and all confidence attached to it, but they go wrong in their diagnosis of *why* this identity needs to be erased.

[50] John Calvin, *Comentarii in Pauli Epistolas ad Galatas, ad Ephesios, ad Philippenses, ad Colossenses*, vol. 16 of *Ioannis Calvini Opera Exegetica*, ed. Helmut Field (Geneva: Droz, 1992), 356. (Calvin continues: ut Christi iustitia induatur—that he [the believer] might be clothed with the righteousness of Christ).

naught, which is the shadow side of Paul's being found in Christ. Unlike in Romans, where Paul takes care to integrate a vision of a moral/ethical life into his narrative of grace, Paul gives here no ethical rationale for this, much to the dismay and puzzlement of exegetes on both sides of the Old and New Perspective divide.[51] All we can say from this text is that being reconstituted in Christ somehow presupposes being *deconstituted*—stripped naked, in Calvin's imagery.

We might like to call this the apocalyptic Paul, who perceives of God's final deed as something radically new and discontinuous.[52] At this point Paul looks strangely amoral, construing his encounter with Christ over a moral abyss, in Friedrich Nietzsche's terminology "jenseits von Gut und Böse." In short, Phil 3, the "little meteorite from Romans" with its brief allusions to δικαιοσύνη language, might just as appropriately be called a "little meteorite from 1 Cor 1:19," which has God saying, "I will destroy the wisdom of the wise" (ἀπολῶ τὴν σοφίαν τῶν σοφῶν, quoting Isa 29:14), not merely surpass it.

This foundational moment, with its destructive moment, aims intrinsically at "knowing Christ" and "being found in Christ." This "being" has indeed strong connotations of conformity, and the language of conformity to Christ's death echoes the hymn verbatim. Moreover, the chronological sequence in the second part of the verse recalls the sequence of going down–moving up in the Christ hymn (though with different vocabulary).[53] The expression κοινωνία τῶν παθημάτων αὐτοῦ ("sharing of his sufferings") takes up the middle ground of the chiastic

---

[51] For worries about nationalistic pride or looking down on gentile Christians, see n. 39 above. Among newer commentaries Carolyn Osiek is representative of this view, stating that "those who pride themselves on their ritual purity are as unclean as are the Gentiles in their own estimation!" (*Philippians, Philemon*, ANTC [Nashville: Abingdon, 2000], 82). On the other end of the spectrum, Calvin worries about mere outward "perfection" (*Comentarii in Pauli Epistolas*, 351) and about *arrogantia* as major problems (353). For "pride, not privilege as such," see Hawthorne, *Philippians*, 189; for "self-righteousness, not zeal for law as such," see O'Brien, *Epistle to the Philippians*, 396; for "self-reliance, confidence in his own capacity to please God," see F. W. Beare, *A Commentary on the Epistle to the Philippians*, HNTC (New York: Harper, 1959), 106. It is fascinating to see how a number of attempts to diagnose Paul's problem prior to his conversion settle on pride, whether conceived vertically as human hubris before a holy God or horizontally as religious chauvinism, dividing people.

[52] E. P. Sanders's dictum that Paul finds fault with the old righteousness only because it is not the new one (*Paul, the Law and the Jewish People* [London: SCM, 1985], 140) has its limited application, provided it is not taken as abstract and mechanical. There is a new age, putting an end to the old—not in the way one turns over a page and finds a new chapter but rather in the way that music modulates to an altogether new key, rhythm, and pace. In the age of the Spirit, being "blameless according to the law" is discarded as "trust in the flesh," though not apart from it. *Why* this should be so is not explained in Phil 3:2–11, and we should be wary to jump to self-righteous pride or nationalistic pride too quickly. Cousar rightly states that Paul does not repent of his past but reassesses it (*Philippians and Philemon*, 72).

[53] Dodd's claim that "Paul's desire to be conformed to Christ's death and resurrection indicates Paul's understanding of the gospel rather than reflecting any intentional patterning of

construction together with συμμορφιζόμενος τῷ θανάτῳ αὐτοῦ ("becoming like him in his death"), the latter further explaining the former with a participial construction. The suffering and prospect of death are, however, framed by strong notions of resurrection: Paul wants to know τὴν δύναμιν τῆς ἀναστάσεως αὐτοῦ ("the power of his resurrection"), and he hopes for τὴν ἐξανάστασιν τὴν ἐκ νεκρῶν ("the resurrection from the dead").[54] Paul has not only a notion of a sequential conformity to Christ, where resurrection follows death, but a strong sense of Christ's resurrection power as being present. How this power might be manifested in Paul's life is not further explained.[55] The resurrection power is often seen as little more than a motivational or instrumental force to embrace suffering.[56] While the correlation between the two καίs (*both* the resurrection power *and* the fellowship of suffering) does not suggest that one aspect is subordinated to the other, some older manuscripts have δύναμις and κοινωνία share the same article, which binds them together more closely.[57] Somehow the resurrection power and fellowship of his sufferings simultaneously make an imprint on the Christian's existence. Fee is certainly right to remark critically that "Paul knows nothing of the rather gloomy stoicism that is so often exhibited in historic Christianity, where the lot of the believer is basically that of 'slugging it out in the trenches,' with little or no sense of Christ's presence and power."[58]

The prominent position of the "power of his resurrection" further resists the reading of verse 10 as merely the second stage in a downward movement. Strictly speaking, there can be no suffering without resurrection power *post-Christum* for those in Christ and, in that sense, no precise emulation of Christ's career.

While theories of Paul fighting gnostic enthusiasts who deny the "earthiness" and suffering of the Christian life have been rightly put to rest, they have been replaced by new ones that see the avoidance of suffering as the most pressing problem in Philippians.[59] It is more natural, however, to see Paul's tone as one of

---

himself after Christ's story" is too weak ("Story of Christ," 156). There is an element of concrete and costly conformity.

[54] The somewhat hesitant character of εἴ πως together with the unique expression of ἐξανάστασις (v. 11) is theologically difficult. It might express Paul's modesty or his ignorance as to *how* and when the final resurrection happens or simply express the "not yet" of the resurrection reality (see the discussion in Fee, *Paul's Letter to the Philippians*, 335–36).

[55] Gnilka suggests forgiveness, life in the spirit, and the experience of rescue from death (*Der Philipperbrief*, 196).

[56] Cousar comments, "Christ's resurrection is known in the sharing of his sufferings" (*Philippians and Philemon*, 74). Barth is most extreme by stating that "the way in which the power of Christ's resurrection works powerfully in the apostle is, that he is clothed with the *shame of the Cross*" (*Philippians*, 103).

[57] Cf. Gnilka, *Der Philipperbrief*, 196 n. 65.

[58] Fee, *Paul's Letter to the Philippians*, 331.

[59] Minear, "Singing and Suffering," 208–9; Bloomquist even thinks that Paul has to counter Christian Epicureans and that he advocates "meaningful suffering *sub specie resurrectionis*" (*The

encouragement and assurance, while he speaks to people who already suffer in some way as a consequence of being believers in Christ.[60] These sufferings have intensified for Paul at this stage: he is in prison (1:13) and seems torn by his hope for release (1:26) and his willingness in sacrificial language to pour out his life as a libation (2:17). Paul no doubt viewed his situation as more than simply an accidental similarity of fate; he interpreted it as communion with Christ, which carries in itself the hope of glory. Paul assures the believers that this suffering is communion with rather than separation from Christ, a point he similarly makes in Rom 8:17 and 35.[61]

It is in this sense that Paul, alongside his trusted fellow workers Timothy and Epaphroditus, indeed puts himself forward as exemplary in his commitment to the gospel mission μέχρι θανάτου ("[because he came close] to death," 2:30) and in his confident and courageous hope.[62] In short, the "fellowship of his sufferings" should not be read as a continuation and intensification of the reevaluation of values and status. It is an integral part of the new *locus* one finds oneself in after having been uprooted from all formerly trustworthy identities and values. It should not be read as an ongoing spiritual appropriation of the foundational experience of destruction. If read in parallel with Rom 6, especially verse 5, Phil 3:10 might suggest daily mortification or abnegation. Romans 6, however, speaks about the participation in Christ's death, not the fellowship in his sufferings. The overlap and distinction of these concepts need further careful exploration.[63]

Philippians 3:10, however, neither continues the movement of a self-denying, self-emptying, downward spiral that was initiated by Paul's willing renunciation of status[64] nor perpetuates an initial conversion experience in the form of daily

---

Function of Suffering in Philippians, JSNTSup 78 [Sheffield: JSOT Press, 1993], 181); Fowl, "Story of Christ," 100.

[60] For a concrete and sensitive picture of what this suffering might have consisted in *prior to* waves of persecution orchestrated by the state authorities, see Oakes, *Philippians: From People to Letter*, 89–90.

[61] Cf. Phil 1:29, where Paul calls both faith and suffering a gracious gift.

[62] *Pace* Osiek, *Philippians, Philemon*, 86; there is a thread of good examples from Christ through Timothy/Epaphroditus and to Paul but not necessarily for "how to renounce one's own will rather than impose it on others" (86).

[63] This reading strategy is nevertheless quite popular: Barnabas M. Ahern, while allowing for aspects of persecution for the sake of Christ, emphasizes the daily dying, the "lifelong *state of death* through the power of the Spirit, to the world, to the flesh, and to sin" ("The Fellowship of His Sufferings," *CBQ* 22 [1960]: 1–32, here 31). Moisés Silva, while acknowledging the concrete suffering, wants to explain it as transforming and sanctifying suffering along the lines of Rom 6 (*Philippians*, 2nd ed., BECNT [Grand Rapids: Baker Academic, 2005], 164–65); but see Fee, *Paul's Letter to the Philippians*, 328.

[64] Humble, kenotic suffering for others is not emphasized at all in this passage (*pace* Oakes, who cautions that "Paul … models loss for the sake of gaining Christ, rather than loss for the sake of others," but Oakes still thinks that "the practical consequences of following this model in Philippi are likely to be loss for the sake of others" [*Philippians: From People to Letter*, 119]). Fowl,

spiritual mortification.⁶⁵ The knowledge of Christ is the axis that negatively causes Paul to discard everything that held value for him and that positively states conformity with Christ as its central content ("knowing him"). By "being found in Christ," Paul is placed in the realm of both resurrection power and suffering. He walks toward death, which is nevertheless connected with the "standing up" from the dead. "Paul is narrating himself into the story of salvation that begins, climaxes and will end with Christ, particularly as related in 2:6–11."⁶⁶ In that sense we have a strong echo of the Christ hymn.

IV. Conclusions

"History does not repeat itself, but it rhymes," as Mark Twain is famously alleged to have said. In the following conclusions I sum up both what I acknowledge as "rhyming" between Paul's and Christ's fate and what I question as evidence of a "repeat." I also indicate where further exploration is desirable.

1. There is an overall "rhyming" between Christ's fate and the apostle's fate, which is well known from other letters and is unfolded as well in Phil 3: To be in Christ means to participate in Christ's death and life. Both are aspects of being shareholders in the gospel. The overall movement of "going down and going up" of the Christ hymn resonates in many ways with Paul's life and, in a more limited sense, with every believer's life. If the first half of Christ's career puts Christian life under the signature of suffering and death, which seem unavoidable and even desirable for Paul, the second half puts those who are "in Christ" under the signature of life and glory. These attributes are given in a unique way to Christ, who is granted "the name above all names," but they are also shared in a representative way with all believers, who will have their bodies of humility "changed around" and brought into conformity with Christ's body of glory (Phil 3:21).

2. This rhyming can be called "conformity" and is expressed densely in Phil 3:10, which describes what "knowing Christ" entails. Kenotic readers have, on the

---

too, seeks to show how Paul models his practical reasoning in conformity with Christ's death around the characteristics of "seeking others' benefit," "resulting from willed self-emptying," and "obeying God" (Fowl, *Philippians*, 156), of which the last one makes the most sense.

⁶⁵ O'Brien offers an emphatic case for a mortification/sanctification reading on the basis that συμμορφιζόμενος τῷ θανάτῳ αὐτοῦ explicates both the resurrection power and the sufferings as daily transformation into the image of Christ (O'Brien, *Epistle to the Philippians*, 405–11). O'Brien offers some good grammatical observations as an alternative to the chiastic structure, but it is unclear why "conforming to his death" should be seen as transformation into the image of Christ. It seems more natural to take "the conformity to the death" as the last horizon of suffering, the willingness to die in the service of the gospel, obedient to the end, like Christ (2:8).

⁶⁶ Fowl, *Philippians*, 153.

whole, a good eye for this sort of rhyming, with all its concrete connotations of suffering for the sake of Christ in the service of the gospel, which involves the ultimate willingness to pay obediently with one's life. These connotations cohere more naturally with the context of Philippians than do spiritualizing proposals of mortification along the lines of Rom 6. Further work needs to be done on Paul's distinction between "dying with Christ" and "suffering with/for Christ."

3. Against kenotic proposals, I hold that there is no full repetition of Christ's career in Paul's own story. In particular, I reject the reading of Phil 3:7–8 as Paul's kenotic gesture of voluntary renunciation of erstwhile privileges. The moment of renunciation expresses a fierce gesture of discarding prior values, triggered by the "knowledge of Christ." This knowledge is the all-surpassing gain that effects the nullification of past achievements and values. This has no parallel in Christ's own humble self-emptying. The force of this passage and the sharp discontinuity it posits between Paul's blameless life as a law-abiding Jew and his present identity "in Christ" are better captured by traditional Protestant readings.[67]

4. The moment of renunciation and the moment of conformity must not be seen as two stages in one seamless process, whether in a kenotic sense in which suffering follows voluntary self-abasement or in a traditional Protestant sense in which mortification/sanctification follows an initial spiritual crisis/conversion moment. The issue is not obedient kenosis but the earth-shattering encounter with Christ, who deconstructs and reconstructs Paul's identity. There is a sense of sharp discontinuity, which is not properly grasped by readers who want to suggest a model of straightforward ethical appropriation and enactment of the Christ event, no matter how thoughtfully this is put forward. The moment of conformity defines and spells out the reconstructed identity in Christ, which is dependent on and therefore closely connected to the deconstruction. The formative moment spells out the goal of the foundational moment but is distinct from it.

5. Paul does not give a freestanding moral rationale why his blameless walk in the law has become "refuse" in the light of Christ. From the text itself it becomes abundantly clear that it was not Paul's failure to keep the law that drove him to Christ. But Paul is still more radical: while traditional Protestant readers readily diagnose "self-righteousness" as the root sin, kenotic readers see pride, possibly seen as nationalistic pride, as the problem that needs a solution. Paul does neither. He proposes a radical change of paradigm by which God in Christ uproots people from their prior identities and relocates them in the precarious eschatological identity of the Christ event.

6. The reading offered in this article proposes that Paul first and foremost unfolds a soteriological story line in Phil 3:2–11, in which ethics, especially

---

[67] This does not imply that all the "readers" have to be members of Protestant denominations.

interpersonal ethics, are not emphasized at all. It is certainly the *lectio difficilior* in a time and age that frequently sees the generating of interpersonal ethics as the only valid function of religions. This story line juxtaposes "trust in the flesh" (3:4) with "worship in the spirit" (3:2), in both a salvation-historical and an existential-biographical sense. This reading does not prematurely release one from the task of wrestling with issues of continuity and discontinuity in Paul's theology. Further, it poses the question afresh in what ways Paul proposes his soteriology as divine salvation "beyond good and evil" and in what ways he wants it to be understood as closely connected with a moral life. This reading resists the attractive shortcut from Christology to ethics and instead reminds us that, before there is "acting" in Christian ethics, there is always "being acted upon." Before the self-exemplification of the gospel, a profound relocation is taking place. It reminds us that Paul has a way to speak of salvation as a reality that is constructed outside what is known and owned, rendering the trustworthy shaky and turning assets into liabilities. In exchange for old gains and securities, a far more dynamic and, indeed, precarious identity is offered for those who have not yet grasped it but have been "taken hold of" (3:12). They run toward the goal with all their might but rely on being met and transformed from the "other side" (3:20). This new reality no doubt forms a distinctive Christlike ethos and has consequences, not least for interpersonal ethics, as Paul's introduction to the hymn in 2:1–5 shows. This is *not*, however, the topic of Phil 3:2–11. To investigate how the Christlike ethos in 2:1–5 connects with the soteriological story line laid out in 3:2–11, not least with the suffering implied by it, is a fruitful task for another day.

SBL PRESS

New and Recent Titles

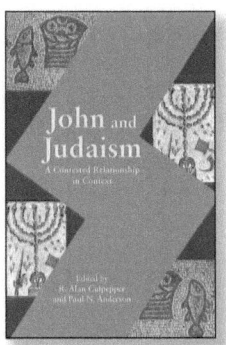

JOHN AND JUDAISM
A Contested Relationship in Context
R. Alan Culpepper and Paul N. Anderson, editors
Paperback $60.95, 978-1-62837-186-4   464 pages, 2017   Code 060398
Hardcover $80.95, 978-0-88414-242-3 E-book $60.95, 978-0-88414-241-6
Resources for Biblical Study 87

AMBROSIASTER'S COMMENTARY ON THE PAULINE EPISTLES
Romans
Translated with Notes by Theodore S. de Bruyn, with an Introduction to the Commentary by Stephen A. Cooper, Theodore S. de Bruyn, and David G. Hunter
Paperback $57.95, 978-1-62837-195-6   450 pages, 2017   Code: 061645
Hardcover $77.95, 978-0-88414-259-1 E-book $57.95, 978-0-88414-258-4
Writings from the Greco-Roman World 41

THE BOOK OF THE TWELVE AND BEYOND
Collected Essays of James D. Nogalski
James D. Nogalski
Paperback $49.95, 978-1-62837-164-2   380 pages, 2017   Code: 062631
Hardcover $64.95, 978-0-88414-206-5 E-book $49.95, 978-0-88414-205-8
Ancient Israel and Its Literature 29

DIDYMUS THE BLIND AND THE ALEXANDRIAN CHRISTIAN RECEPTION OF PHILO
Justin M. Rogers
Paperback $36.95, 978-1-62837-198-7   272 pages, 2017   Code: 062308
Hardcover $51.95, 978-0-88414-265-2 E-book $$36.95, 978-0-88414-264-5
Studia Philonica Monographs 8

HOW AMERICA MET THE JEWS
Hasia R. Diner
Paperback $31.95, 978-1-946527-02-8   152 pages, 2017   Code: 140360
Hardcover $46.95, 978-1-946527-04-2 E-book $31.95, 978-1-946527-03-5
Brown Judaic Studies 360

SBL Press • P.O. Box 2243 • Williston, VT 05495-2243
Phone: 877-725-3334 (toll-free) or 802-864-6185 • Fax: 802-864-7626
Order online at www.sbl-site.org/publications

CORE BIBLICAL STUDIES
New this Spring!

The Holy Spirit in the New Testament

John T. Carroll | ISBN: 9781426766374

Explore the diverse ways that the New Testament presents the meaning, activity, and significance of the Holy Spirit.

Ecclesiology in the New Testament

E. Elizabeth Johnson | ISBN: 9781426771934

How the New Testament writers talk about the Church. This book investigates New Testament texts about the church from a comparative standpoint.

Wisdom Literature

Samuel E. Balentine | ISBN: 9781426765025

Wisdom literature is foundational to our life and learning and its end is the shaping of a moral self and community attunded to the character of God.

See all current and forthcoming volumes at
AbingdonAcademic.com/Core

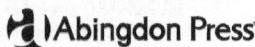